GREGG TYPING *1*

General Course/
Series Eight

KEYBOARDING AND PROCESSING DOCUMENTS

ALAN C. LLOYD, Ph.D.
Director, Employment Testing,
The Olsten Corporation,
Westbury, New York

FRED E. WINGER, Ed.D.
Former Professor, Office Administration and
Business Education, Oregon State University,
Corvallis, Oregon

JACK E. JOHNSON, Ph.D.
Coordinator of Business Education,
Department of Vocational and Career Development,
Georgia State University,
Atlanta, Georgia

PHYLLIS C. MORRISON, Ph.D.
Professor of Administrative Management and
Business Education, Robert Morris College,
Coraopolis, Pennsylvania

REBECCA A. HALL, Ph.D.
Department Chairperson, Business and Office
Education, Centerville High School,
Centerville, Ohio

GREGG DIVISION/McGRAW-HILL BOOK COMPANY

New York   Atlanta   Dallas   St. Louis   San Francisco   Auckland   Bogotá   Guatemala   Hamburg
Lisbon   London   Madrid   Mexico   Montreal   New Delhi   Panama   Paris
San Juan   São Paulo   Singapore   Sydney   Tokyo   Toronto

Sponsoring Editors/Barbara N. Oakley, Gina M. Ferrara
Editing Supervisors/Julie A. Bokser, Matthew Fung, Elizabeth Huffman, Frances Koblin
Cover, Level Openings, and Interior Designer/Art and Design Supervisor/Patricia F. Lowy
Production Supervisors/Frank Bellantoni, Mirabel Flores

Technical Studio/Burmar Technical Corp.
Cover, Level Openings, and Text Photographer/Ken Karp

This edition of *Gregg Typing* is dedicated to Phyllis
C. Morrison, who contributed much time, creativity,
and hard work to the development of the manuscript
and who passed away shortly before its publication.

Library of Congress Cataloging-in-Publication Data

Main entry under title:

Gregg typing 1: general course, series eight.

  Includes index.
  Summary: A textbook for a two-semester general course in typewriting for
the secondary school. Includes formatting of correspondence, reports, tables,
and other forms.
  1. Typewriting. [1. Typewriting] I. Lloyd, Alan C.
Z49.G818   1987   652.3   85-23802
ISBN 0-07-038342-1

**Gregg Typing 1, General Course, Series Eight
Keyboarding and Processing Documents**

  3 4 5 6 7 8 9 0 DOCDOC 8 9 3 2 1 0 9 8 7

ISBN 0-07-038342-1

PREFACE

Series Eight is an all-new edition of the famous *Gregg Typing* programs. Developed with the needs of students and teachers in mind, *Series Eight* offers all the text and workbook materials needed for a comprehensive, modern typewriting program. It also offers many exciting features that make it an effective instructional system.

PARTS OF THE PROGRAM

Designed to meet the needs of one-semester, one-year, or two-year courses of instruction, *Series Eight* offers a variety of student's textbooks and workbooks, as well as a special Teacher's Edition for each student's text:

Gregg Typing 1. The first-year text offers 150 lessons of instruction. The first 75 lessons (one semester) are devoted to learning the keyboard and typing for personal use.

Gregg Typing 2. The second-year text includes a comprehensive Reference Section for students. It also includes, of course, Lessons 151 through 300 of the *Gregg Typing* program.

Gregg Typing, Complete Course. Specially designed for the two-year program of instruction, the *Complete Course* text offers all 300 lessons from *Typing 1* and *Typing 2* in one binding.

Teacher's Editions. The three separate Teacher's Editions—one for each of the student's texts—include all the pages in the corresponding student's texts plus annotations intended only for the teacher. Each Teacher's Edition also includes a separate section of teaching methodology, as well as lesson-by-lesson teaching notes for all the lessons in that text.

Learning Guides and Working Papers. Four workbooks—one for each 75 lessons of instruction—provide the stationery and forms needed for all text jobs and in-baskets and a variety of reinforcement and enrichment exercises correlated to the text copy and to the LABs (Language Arts for Business).

Instructional Recordings. The *Keyboard Presentation Tapes for Gregg Typing* are cassettes correlated to the textbook keyboard lessons in *Gregg Typing 1* and in *Gregg Typing, Complete Course.*

Transparency Masters. These teaching tools will enhance the classroom presentation. They contain the masters for the transparencies. In addition, there are teaching suggestions and annotated illustrations.

Test Book. A *Test Book* provides masters for production, LAB, and objective tests for all 12 levels of the program. They parallel the production tests in the textbook and may be reproduced for classroom use as formal tests.

Test Bank. A *Computer Test Bank* contains all the questions covered in the 12 objective tests. Teachers may use these questions to develop their own objective tests for the program.

Keys. Complete keys to all text jobs and projects (both in pica and elite) are in the *Resource Manual and Key for Typing 1* and the *Resource Manual and Key for Typing 2.*

Computer Teaching Suggestions Manual. If you are using microcomputers instead of typewriters in your classroom, this manual will provide instruction for adapting the lessons and the formatting directions.

FEATURES OF GREGG TYPING, SERIES EIGHT

The *Series Eight* program incorporates many time-tested features from past editions of *Gregg Typing;* at the same time, it introduces some new features. For example:

Diagnostic Exercises. Many timings utilize the Pretest/Practice/Posttest routine, which allows each student to diagnose areas in which additional skill development is needed. After taking a Pretest, students practice according to their specific needs (as diagnosed from the Pretest). After the Practice session, students take a Posttest, which enables them to see how the Practice session improved their skill.

Skill-Building Routines. In addition to the Pretest/Practice/Posttest routine, a variety of other skill-building routines are provided in the program. These routines help maintain student interest while developing the basic keyboarding skill.

Clinics. Clinics (every sixth lesson) are designed to strengthen skill development. Most Clinics use diagnostic routines.

Language Arts for Business (LABs). Concise, easy-to-understand LABs help students to review the basic uses of punctuation, capitalization, and abbreviations and to avoid the most common errors in using plurals, contractions, possessives, and so on. Students reinforce and apply the LAB rules as they type sentences and production assignments.

Cyclical Approach. In *Series Eight,* concepts are taught once and recycled several times, with each cycle building on the previous one and becoming progressively more complex. Each cycle is a "level," lasting five weeks. Thus the full two-year program includes 12 levels—6 per year.

Five-Week Tests. At the conclusion of each level of work, a test provides both the student and the teacher with an opportunity to check the student's level of performance. These tests may be used as informal or formal evaluations. Parallel tests are provided in the *Test Book.*

Information Processing. Word processing and data processing terminology and applications are integrated into the text. Students, for example, format (and later fill in) form letters, type from "dictated" copy, and prepare a word processing procedures manual. Technology notes throughout the text point out how electronic equipment simplifies formatting procedures.

Decision-Making Exercises. To simulate real-life business experience, the *Series Eight* program includes many exercises that require students to make realistic "on-the-job" decisions. The complexity of the decisions to be made increases as students progress through the program.

Various Input Modes. Students will format letters, memos, and so on, from various input modes—for example, from unarranged copy, from handwritten copy, from rough drafts, and from incomplete information.

The *Series Eight* program greatly reflects the comments, suggestions, and recommendations we received from many teachers who used *Series Seven* and participated in the extensive review process. We sincerely appreciate their contributions to the effectiveness of this publication.

The Authors

CONTENTS

LEVEL 4
GOAL: 36/5'/5e

LEVEL 5
GOAL: 38/5'/5e

LEVEL 6
GOAL: 40/5'/5e

TOPICAL INDEX

INTRODUCTION

The *Series Eight* program has been specially designed to help you develop your typewriting skills through a carefully planned, step-by-step process. To be sure that you understand the terms, the procedures, and the directions used throughout this book, as well as the operation of the machine you are using, be sure to read this introduction and refer to it whenever you have any question or problem.

GLOSSARY OF TERMS

The special terms and symbols used throughout this text are very easy to understand. Read the following glossary to be sure you know the meaning of the terms and symbols, and refer to the glossary whenever necessary.

GOAL STATEMENTS

Skill Goal. At the beginning of every unit, a skill goal is given—the goal you are aiming to achieve by the end of that unit. For example, the skill goal *To type 35/5'/5e* means "to type 35 words a minute for 5 minutes with 5 or fewer errors."

Production Goal. At the beginning of every lesson, one or more production goals are given for that lesson; for example, "To format a report from handwritten copy." Production goals alert you to the kinds of activities that you will type in each lesson.

FORMATTING INSTRUCTIONS

Formatting means arranging a document according to a specific set of rules.

A number of formatting terms and symbols are used to help you understand the directions for completing each activity in *Series Eight*. The most commonly used terms and symbols and their meanings are given below.

Single spacing (or *double* or *triple spacing*) tells you how to set your typewriter for that particular lesson.

40-, 50-, 60-, or 70-space line tells you the specific line length to use.

6-inch line or **60P/70E** indicates a 60-space line for typewriters with pica (P) type, a 70-space line for typewriters with elite (E) type.

5-space tab tells you precisely where to set your tab stops for a particular lesson—in this case, 5 spaces from the left margin.

Arrows in production work are used as follows:

→ This arrow is used in some tables to show you the vertical center of your work.

↓₃ Arrows with numbers tell you how many lines down the next line should be typed—in this case, 3 lines.

Standard format will be stated in the directions for letters, tables, and so on, once you have learned the standard format for these kinds of jobs. To refresh your memory of the standard format, page numbers are often provided; for example, "Standard format (see page 209)."

Body 120 words tells you there are 120 words in the body of a letter. Knowing the approximate length of a letter will help you to adapt the standard format to position the letter on the page. Thus the number of words in the body of the letter is given to help guide you.

Workbook 86 indicates that a form or a letterhead for that specific job is provided in the *Learning Guides and Working Papers* workbook. If no workbook page is cited, then you are to use plain paper.

TECHNOLOGY NOTES

This symbol is used to point out a special feature on electronic equipment (electronic typewriters, word processors, computers) that makes formatting and keyboarding easier. For example, when you learn how to return the carriage or carrier, the technology note will describe *wordwrap,* which is an automatic return feature on electronic equipment.

SKILL-BUILDING ROUTINES

Typewriting is a skill, and a skill is best developed through directed practice. *Series Eight* provides a variety of effective skill-building routines to improve the speed and the accuracy of your typing, including the following:

A variety of **Pretest/Practice/Posttest** routines is offered—all designed to improve either speed or accuracy through a proven, step-by-step procedure. First the *Pretest* (a 2-, 3-, or 5-minute timing) helps you identify your speed or accuracy needs. Having identified your needs, you then do the *Practice* exercises—a variety of intensive improvement drills. After you have completed the *Practice* exercises, you take a *Posttest*. Because the Posttest is identical to the Pretest, the Posttest measures your improvement.

12-Second timings are routines in which you take a series of short timings to boost speed.

30-Second speed timings are slightly longer routines in which you take a series of short timings to boost speed.

30-Second "OK" timings help you build accuracy on alphabetic copy (that is, copy that includes all 26 letters of the alphabet). You take three 30-second timings on the copy to see how many error-free copies you can type.

SCALES AND INDEXES

Series Eight uses a variety of scales and indexes designed to help you (1) measure quickly—with little counting—how many words you have typed, (2) analyze whether you should practice speed drills or accuracy drills, and (3) identify the relative difficulty of the copy you are typing.

Word Count Scales. You get credit for typing a "word" whenever you advance 5 spaces. Thus when you have typed a 60-space line, you have typed 12 words. To save you time, word counts that appear at the right of a timing tell you the cumulative number of words you have typed at the end of each completed line.

The scale shown at the right, for example, is used with timings that have 12 words a line. In production work the scale at the right also gives you stroking credit for using the tabulator, for centering, and for other nonstroking movements.

| |
| 12 |
| 24 |
| 36 |
| 48 |
| 60 |
| 72 |
| 84 |

To quickly determine the words typed for *in*complete lines, use the scale that appears below each timing:

| 1 | 2 | 3 | 4 | 5 | 6 | 7 | 8 | 9 | 10 | 11 | 12 |

This scale quickly indicates the number of words typed. Just align the last word typed with the number on the scale.

When you take a 3- or 5-minute timing, use the speed markers (the small numbers above the copy) to quickly find your words-a-minute speed.

This special scale appears with 12-second timings:

| 5 | 10 | 15 | 20 | 25 | 30 | 35 | 40 | 45 | 50 | 55 | 60 |

It converts your typing speed during a 12-second timing into words a minute.

Practice Guide. In certain skill-building routines, you will use the following chart to find the drill lines you should type:

Pretest errors	0–1	2–3	4–5	6+
Drill lines	9–13	8–12	7–11	6–10

For example, if you made only 1 error in the Pretest, then the guide directs you to complete "Drill lines 9–13"; if you made 3 errors, you should complete "Drill lines 8–12"; and so on.

Syllabic Intensity (SI) Index. To indicate the relative difficulty of copy, syllabic intensity (SI) is often listed. The SI number is computed by dividing the number of actual words in the copy into the total number of syllables of all words. Thus 1.00 indicates copy that has one syllable per word; 1.50 indicates copy that has an average of one and a half syllables per word; and so on. The higher the number, the more difficult the copy.

LABs

Effective typewriting requires a knowledge of at least the basics of grammar, punctuation, and style. The *Series Eight* program provides Language Arts for Business (LABs) that offer concise, practical reviews and application exercises on punctuation, capitalization, and number use, for example. Thus you may review the most common language arts principles *as you type* sentences and production activities.

Before you start to type, take a few minutes to get to know the names, locations, and uses of the main parts of your typewriter. First, note whether you are using an electric element machine or an electronic typewriter similar to the ones illustrated below or an electric typebar machine or a microcomputer similar to the ones illustrated on the next page. Then refer to the proper illustration as you take these steps for learning each machine part listed and described below and on the next page.

1. Read the description of the machine part.

2. Look at the drawing and note the location of the part.

3. Find the part on your machine—but do not operate it until instructed to do so. (The location of some parts varies from one make of machine to another.) If you cannot find a part quickly, ask your teacher or a classmate to help you find it.

MAIN PARTS OF AN ELEMENT MACHINE

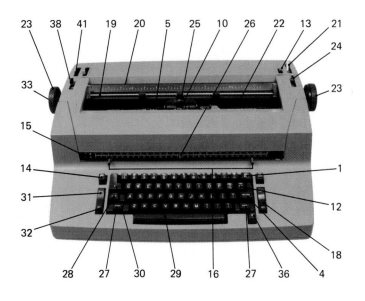

MAIN PARTS OF AN ELECTRONIC TYPEWRITER

1 BACKSPACE KEY. Moves the carriage or carrier backward one space at a time.

2 CARRIAGE (typebar only). Movable part of the machine that allows the typewriter to print across the page.

3 CARRIAGE RELEASE (typebar only). Frees the carriage so you can move it by hand.

4 CARRIER/CARRIAGE RETURN KEY. Used for returning carrier/carriage to left margin and advancing the paper for start of next line.

5 CARRIER (element and electronic only). Movable part of the machine that allows the typewriter to print across the page.

6 CPU (computer only). The *central processing unit*—the main part of a computer.

7 CURSOR (computer only). Functions as the printing point indicator of a typewriter.

8 CURSOR KEYS (computer only). Move the cursor up, down, left, right.

9 DISK DRIVE (computer only). The device that records information from and reads information on a disk.

10 ELEMENT (element and electronic only). Ball-like device or daisy wheel that contains all the letters and symbols.

11 ENTER/RETURN KEY (computer only). May be used to return cursor to left margin and advance one line, to enter data in memory, or to execute a command.

12 EXPRESS KEY (element and electronic only). Moves the carrier rapidly to the left without line spacing.

13 LINE SPACE SELECTOR. Controls space between lines of typing.

14 MARGIN RELEASE. Temporarily unlocks the margin.

15 MARGIN SCALE. Guides setting the margins (sometimes called *carriage-position scale*).

16 MARGIN STOPS. Key or lever used to block off side margins.

17 MONITOR (computer only). A television-like screen on which you can see what is being keyboarded prior to printing it out. Also called *video display*.

18 ON-OFF SWITCH. Controls motor power.

19 PAPER BAIL. Holds paper against the platen.

20 PAPER GUIDE. Blade against which paper is placed when paper is inserted.

21 PAPER RELEASE. Loosens paper for straightening or removing.

22 PLATEN. Large roller around which paper is rolled.

23 PLATEN KNOBS. Used to turn paper into the machine.

24 PLATEN RELEASE LEVER. Allows a temporary change in the line of writing.

25 PRINTING POINT. The place where the typebar or the element strikes the paper.

26 PRINTING POINT INDICATOR. Shows the position on the margin scale where the machine is ready to print.

27 SHIFT KEY. Positions the typebar or the element so that a capital letter can be typed.

28 SHIFT LOCK KEY. Permits typing a series of all-capital letters.

29 SPACE BAR. Used for spacing between characters or words.

30 TAB/TABULATOR. Moves the carriage or carrier freely to preset points.

31 TAB CLEAR. Used to remove tab stops one at a time.

32 TAB SET. Positions tab stops.

33 VARIABLE LINE SPACER. Permanently changes the line of writing.

34 VIDEO DISPLAY. A screen on which you can see what is being keyboarded. On a computer it is a full-sized screen; on an electronic typewriter it may only show 10 to 40 characters.

OPTIONAL FEATURES

35 ANTI-GLARE SHIELD. Used in connection with sound hood; eliminates glare on sound hood from lights.

36 CORRECTION KEY (element and electronic only). Used to lift errors off paper or delete from memory.

37 FUNCTION KEYS (electronic and computer only). Eliminate the need to use codes or commands to access special functions, such as boldface.

38 HALF SPACER (typewriters only). Allows carriage/carrier to move only a half space; aids in spreading and squeezing corrections.

39 MODE SELECTOR (electronic only). Used to select method of operation—keying into memory with delayed print, simultaneous print, justified margins, etc.

40 PAPER SUPPORT (typewriters only). Paper rests on support; may be marked with end-of-page scale.

41 PITCH SELECTOR (element and electronic only). Used to select the size and spacing of type.

42 SOUND HOOD (element, electronic, and computer). Covers the opening over the print head; suppresses the noise of print head striking the paper.

MAIN PARTS OF A TYPEBAR MACHINE

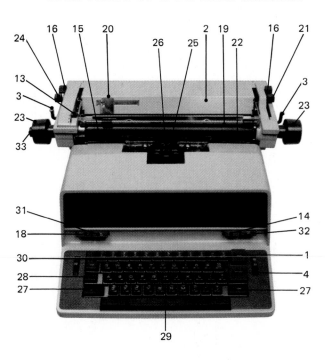

MAIN PARTS OF A MICROCOMPUTER

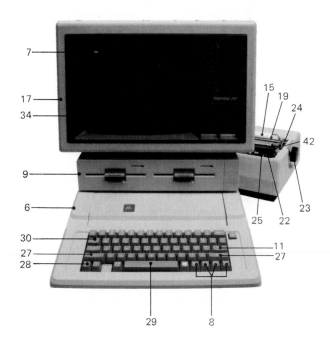

GETTING READY TO TYPE

TYPE SIZES

There are two commonly used type sizes—pica and elite. Pica type (also called *10 pitch*) is larger than elite. Pica prints 10 letters to an inch. Elite type (called *12 pitch*) prints 12 letters to an inch.

Some typewriters and many computer printers have a third type size called *micron,* which prints 15 characters per inch.

```
This is pica type--10 pitch.
```
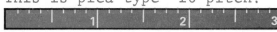
```
This is elite type--12 pitch.
```

The width of standard paper is 8½ inches, which is equal to 85 spaces of pica type, 102 spaces of elite type, or 127 spaces of micron type.

CENTERING POINT

Three common methods for selecting a centering point are explained below. Each requires you to set the paper guide differently.

1. Set the paper guide at 0 and insert a sheet of paper. If you are using pica type, your centering point will be 42 ($85 \div 2 = 42\frac{1}{2}$). If you are using elite type, your centering point will be 51 ($102 \div 2 = 51$). If you use 42P/51E as the centering point, be sure to set your paper guide at 0 before you insert your paper.

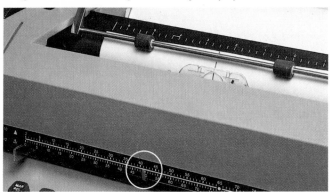

2. The second method is to use 50 (or some other common centering point) as the centering point for any size of type. Follow these steps to determine where the paper guide belongs:
   a. Pull the paper bail forward or up.
   b. Move the paper guide all the way to the left.
   c. Set the carriage or carrier at 50 (or the centering point of your choice).
   d. Mark the center of a sheet of paper by creasing it.
   e. Insert the creased sheet: hold it in your left hand, place it behind the platen, and draw the paper into the machine by turning the platen knob with your right hand.
   f. Engage the paper release to loosen the paper; then slide the paper left or right until the center crease is at the printing point—the point where the printing occurs. Then return the paper release to its original position.
   g. Slide the paper guide to the right until its blade edge is snugly against the sheet of paper.

Note on the margin scale exactly where you have set the paper guide. Now you will be able to confirm or correct the position of the paper guide very easily and quickly. Do so each time you begin typing.

3. Another method is to use the center of the platen as the centering point. (The center is usually marked by a small dot on the margin scale.) Follow the same steps given in method 2 to determine where the paper guide belongs.

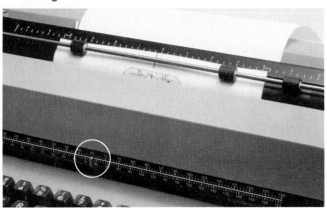

PAPER HANDLING

Practice this routine several times:

1. Confirm the paper guide setting.
2. Pull the paper bail forward or up.
3. With your left hand, place the paper behind the platen and against the paper guide; use your right hand to turn the right platen knob to draw in the paper. Advance the paper until about a third of the front is visible.
4. Check that the paper is straight by aligning the left edges of the front and the back against the paper guide. If they do not align, loosen the paper (by engaging the paper release) and straighten it.

PAPER HANDLING (CONTINUED)

5. Place the paper bail back against the paper. Adjust the rollers on the bail so that they are spread evenly across the paper.

6. Turn the right-hand platen knob until about ¼ inch of the paper shows above the bail. Now the paper is in the correct position for the opening drill of each lesson.

7. To remove the paper, draw the bail forward or up. Then engage the paper release (right hand) as you silently draw out the sheet of paper (left hand). Finally, return the paper release to its normal position.

FORMATTING

Formatting a document means arranging it according to a specific set of rules (or, sometimes, according to your own preference). Deciding on margins and line spacings is part of formatting.

MARGIN PLANNING

Margins at the left and right sides of a typed page are controlled by margin stops that limit the line of typing. To plan the left and right margin settings:

Left Margin. Subtract half the desired line from the center. For example, for a 40-space line, subtract 20 from the centering point you are using.

Right Margin. Add half the desired line length to the center. Then add 5 extra spaces (an allowance for line-ending adjustments).

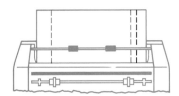

Some sample margin settings appear below.

Margin settings using 50 as the center:

Line Length	Pica	Elite
40-space line	30–75	30–75
50-space line	25–80	25–80
60-space line	20–85	20–85

Margin settings using 42P/51E as the center:

Line Length	Pica	Elite
40-space line	22–67	31–76
50-space line	17–72	26–81
60-space line	12–77	21–86

MARGIN SETTING

Hand-Set Machines. Many typewriters (including most element machines and most portables) have hand-set levers or hand-set buttons. Each lever is moved separately by hand: (1) press down, or push in, the lever, (2) slide the stop left or right to the desired scale point, and (3) release the lever.

Hook-On Machines. Some typewriters have margin set keys on the keyboard. For the *left margin:* (1) move the carriage to the left margin, (2) hook onto the left margin stop by holding down the margin set key, (3) move the carriage to the desired scale point, and (4) release the set key. For the *right margin:* (1) move the carriage to the right margin, (2) hook onto the right margin stop by holding down the set key, (3) move the carriage to the desired scale point, and (4) release the set key.

Spring-Set Machines. Some typewriters have a margin set key at each end of the carriage. For the *left margin:* (1) press the left margin set key, (2) move the carriage to the desired scale point, and (3) release the set key. For the *right margin:* (1) press the right margin set key, (2) move the carriage to the desired scale point, and (3) release the set key.

LINE SPACING

The blank space between lines is controlled by the line space selector. Set it at *1* for single spacing, which provides no blank space between typed lines, and at *2* for double spacing, which provides 1 blank line between lines. Many machines also have 1½ spacing, 2½ spacing, and/or triple spacing.

Line Space Selector

Set at 1	Set at 1½	Set at 2	Set at 3
single	one and a half	double	triple
single	one and a half		
single		double	
single	one and a half		triple
single	one and a half	double	
single			
single	one and a half	double	triple

WORKSTATION ARRANGEMENT

Organizing the workstation around the typewriter helps you complete your assignments more efficiently. For most typewriters and desk styles, the most efficient way to organize a typewriting workstation is to:

1. Place the typewriter near the center of the desk, even with the front of the desk.
2. Place supplies to one side of the typewriter (usually the left side).
3. Place materials to be typed on the opposite side of the typewriter (usually the right).
4. Store away all other items that are not being used.

TYPEWRITING POSTURE

Your accuracy and speed in operating the typewriter will be affected by your posture. Use appropriate posture from the first day so that you can learn to type well. Sit like the typist in the illustrations.

Head erect and facing the book, which is tilted to reduce reflected light on the paper.

Back straight with body leaning forward slightly; shoulders level.

Body a handspan from the machine, centered opposite the J key.

Feet apart, firmly braced on the floor, one foot ahead of the other.

Fingers curved so that only the tips touch the keys.

Wrists up slightly, off the front of the machine so that the fingers are free to move as you type.

Arms hanging loosely at sides, forearm at the same angle as the keyboard.

Elbows close to the body.

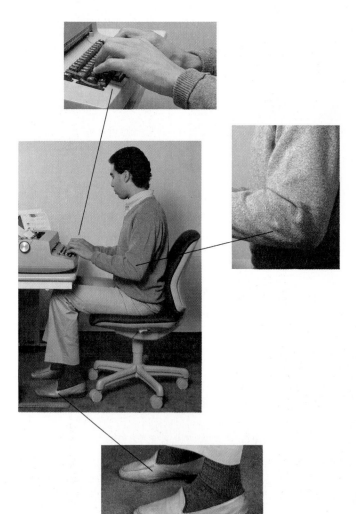

LEVEL 1

GOALS

1. Demonstrate which fingers control each key on the keyboard and each part of the typewriter.

2. Use home key anchors to assist in developing location security.

3. Control the keyboard at a useful level of operation with a goal of 25 words a minute for 2 minutes with 4 or fewer errors.

4. Demonstrate an ability to center vertically and horizontally.

SPECIAL REPORT FORMAT

Minutes of a Meeting. The minutes of a meeting usually consist of three parts—*ATTENDANCE, UNFINISHED BUSINESS,* and *NEW BUSINESS*—which are typed as side headings in all caps at the left margin. Minutes are usually saved in a three-ring binder, so the margins for a bound report should be used. Three space-saving rules for typing minutes of a meeting are:

1. Type the title on line 7.

2. Use single spacing in the body.

3. Leave 1 blank line before and after each side heading.

MECHANICS OF TYPING FORMS

ALIGNMENT

Forms have printed guide words to show where to type names, dates, and so on. Align typed insertions with the bottom of the printed guide words, 2 spaces after the longest printed word (or the colon that follows that word). When one guide word is below another, begin the insertions at the same point.

To align properly, you must know how close your typewriter prints to its aligning scale. Type the alphabet and study the space between the typing and the scale. You will then know how much to adjust the paper (using the variable line spacer) whenever you are aligning the typed words with the guide words of a form.

When you are typing on ruled lines, the ruled line should be in the position of the underscore.

MEMOS

1. Set your left margin at the point where you begin the fill-ins in the heading.

2. Set your right margin so that it is the same width as your left margin.

3. Begin the body a triple space below the last line of the heading.

4. Type the writer's initials at the same tab used for the second column in the heading.

BILLING FORMS

1. Align number columns on the right; center visually within the column.

2. Align word columns on the left; begin 2 spaces after the vertical rule.

3. Double-space; single-space turnover lines and indent them 3 spaces.

4. Align total lines with the *D* in *Description.*

5. Do not type the symbol $ in money columns.

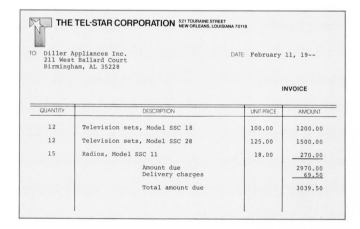

■ **GOAL**
To strike the home keys, holding anchors; operate the space bar; and return to a new line with eyes on copy.

■ **FORMAT**
Single spacing   40-space line

HOME KEY POSITION

In touch typing, each finger is used to control a limited number of keys. In order to make sure that the correct fingers are used, all reaches will be made from the middle row of alphabet keys. The dark keys shown with white letters in the keyboard chart below are the **home keys.**
Left Hand. Place your fingertips on the **A S D** and **F** keys.
Right Hand. Place your fingertips on the **J K L** and **;** keys.

Curve your fingers so that only their tips lightly touch the keys. (Drop your arms to your sides and shake your hands to relax. Without moving your fingers, raise your hands up and place them over the keyboard. Your fingers will be in the correctly curved position.)

Your fingers are named for the home keys on which they rest: A finger, S finger, D finger, and so on, ending with Sem finger for the little finger on the ; key.

SPACE BAR

USING ANCHORS

An anchor is a home key position that will help you bring a typing finger back to its home key position. When you learn new keys, the fingers to be anchored will be shown next to the keyboard along with the message "Hold Those Anchors." If more than one anchor is given for a key, the first one shown is the most important. Try to hold all the anchors listed, but be sure to hold the number one anchor.

SPACE BAR

Strike the space bar with the thumb of your writing hand—the right thumb if you are right-handed, the left thumb if you are left-handed. Whichever thumb you use should be poised above the middle of the space bar. The other thumb is not used; hold it close to its adjacent forefinger.

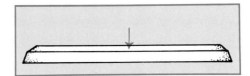

Strike center of space bar with thumb.

Now practice using the space bar with the right or left thumb.

Space once [*tap the space bar once*] . . . twice [*tap the space bar twice*] . . . once . . . once . . . twice . . . once . . . twice . . . once . . . twice . . . twice . . . once . . . once. . . .

Repeat.

Reports are very commonly used communications—both in school and in business. The parts listed below typically appear in most reports.

Parts of a Report

1. *Title*—Centered in all capitals on line 13.

2. *Subtitle*—Centered in capital and lowercase letters on line 15.

3. *Byline*—Centered in capital and lowercase letters on line 17.

4. *Side Headings*—At left margin in all capitals, preceded by 2 blank lines and followed by 1 blank line.

5. *Short Quotation* (not longer than three typed lines)—Typed in quotation marks as part of the text of the report.

6. *Paragraph Heading*—Indented, in capital and lowercase letters, underscored, and followed by a period.

7. *Page Number*—Backspaced from the right margin on line 7. Triple-space to the text of the report. (**Note:** Do not number the first page.)

8. *Long Quotation* (longer than three typed lines)—Single-spaced, preceded and followed by a blank line, and indented 5 spaces from each margin.

9. *Separation Line*—To separate footnotes from the text of the report, type a rule 20P/24E spaces long, beginning at the left margin. Use a minimum of a single space before the separation line, and always use a double space after it.

10. *Footnote*—Type footnotes at the bottom of the page from margin to margin; single-space, with a double space between footnotes. Indent the first line of the footnote 5 spaces. **Note:** Footnotes may also be placed in their entirety on a separate page at the end of the report. See "Endnotes" on page 121.

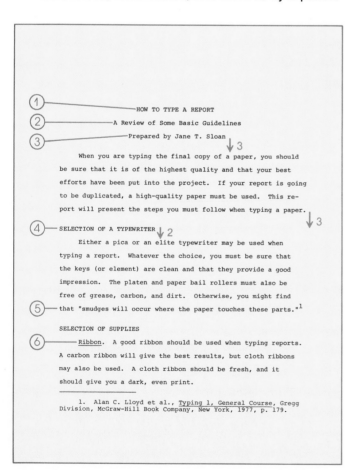

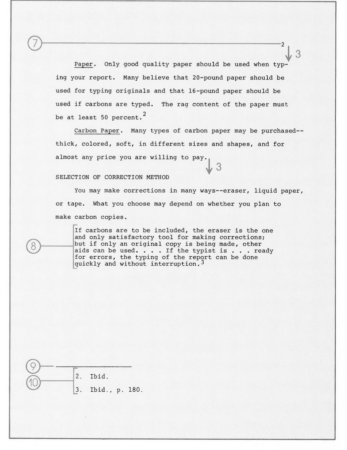

RETURN

 On a computer, word processor, or electronic typewriter, the cursor will automatically return to the left margin when it reaches the right margin stop. This is called word wrap.

As you type, the carriage on a typebar typewriter, the carrier on an element or daisy wheel typewriter, or the cursor on a computer moves from left to right. Operating the return mechanism will move the carriage/carrier/cursor back to the left margin.

Electric Typewriter, Electronic Typewriter, or Computer. Extend the Sem finger to the adjacent return key. Lightly press the return key causing the carriage, carrier, or cursor to return automatically, and return the finger to home key position.

Now practice using the return.

Space once . . . twice . . . once . . . twice. . . . Ready to return [*move finger to return key*]. Return! [*Return the carriage, carrier, or cursor.*] . . . Home! [*Place fingers on home keys.*] . . .   *Repeat.*

Hold Those Anchors

For **A** anchor F
For **S** anchor F or A
For **D** anchor A S
For **F** anchor A S D

SPACE BAR

Hold Those Anchors

For **;** anchor J
For **L** anchor ; or J
For **K** anchor ; L
For **J** anchor ; L K

STROKING PRACTICE

Practice the F and J and space strokes shown in the drill below. Type each line once. After completing a set of lines, return twice.

Left forefinger, spacing thumb. fff fff ff ff f f ff ff f f   *Return.*

Right forefinger, spacing thumb. jjj jjj jj jj j j jj jj j j   *Return twice.*

 **KEYS**

Use forefingers.

Type each line once.

1 fff jjj fff jjj fff jjj ff jj ff jj f j   *Return.*

2 fff jjj fff jjj fff jjj ff jj ff jj f j   *Return twice.*

 **KEYS**

Use second fingers.

Type each line once.

3 ddd kkk ddd kkk ddd kkk dd kk dd kk d k

4 ddd kkk ddd kkk ddd kkk dd kk dd kk d k

OPEN TABLES (CONTINUED)
Format

1. Use 6 spaces between columns (unless there is a special reason for using more or fewer spaces).
2. Underscore all words in the column headings.
3. Sequence the items, when appropriate, by putting them in alphabetic order, putting them in numeric order, arranging them by dollar amount, and so on.
4. Use a 10P/12E line to separate a footnote from the body of the table. Block one-line footnotes; indent two-line footnotes 5 spaces.

```
          INTERNATIONAL TREATIES AND AGREEMENTS*
                                                  ↓3
                          Year          Number of
            Name         Adopted        Countries
Common Market             1957              9
Commonwealth of Nations   1931             43
NATO                      1949             15
OAS                       1948             28
_____

*Warsaw Pact and Yalta not included.
```

RULED TABLES

Ruled tables are often used for formal reports and research papers. The ruled lines (solid lines of underscores) are typed before and after the column headings and also at the end of the table. Do not underscore the words in the column headings.

Format

1. Type the ruled lines the exact width of the table.
2. Single-space before each ruled line, and double-space after each ruled line.
3. If the table ends with a Total line, type a ruled line before and after the Total line.

```
                    SALES ANALYSIS
          Borden Manufacturing Company
 ss                                       ↓1
 ds _____
                                           ↓2
     Salesperson     Units        Sales
 ss
 ds _____
     Robert Brazinski   10       $ 427.70
     Carol Dawkins       18        769.86
     Janice Greene       20        855.40
     Jose Herrera        17        727.09
 ss
 ds _____
     TOTAL              65       $2780.05
 ss
```

LEADERED TABLES

Leadered tables have typed rows of periods between the columns. The periods "lead" the reader's eyes from column to column within the table.

Format

1. Type rows of solid periods (no space between periods).
2. Leave 1 blank space before the first and after the last period in each row.
3. Use at least three periods in a row of leaders.
4. **Note:** You must look at your work as you type leadered tables to be certain you type the exact number of periods for each row.

```
                 SUMMER SEMINAR SCHEDULE


     "Time Management" ............. June 7-8

     "Financial Planning" ......... June 11-13

     "Budgeting Techniques" ........ July 6-9

     "Advertising Principles" ...... July 16-18
```

Hold Those Anchors

For **A** anchor F
For **S** anchor F or A
For **D** anchor A S
For **F** anchor A S D

SPACE BAR

Hold Those Anchors

For **;** anchor J
For **L** anchor ; or J
For **K** anchor ; L
For **J** anchor ; L K

 **KEYS**

Use third fingers.

Type each line once.

5 sss lll sss lll sss lll ss ll ss ll s l
6 sss lll sss lll sss lll ss ll ss ll s l

 **KEYS**

Use fourth fingers.

Type each line once.

7 aaa ;;; aaa ;;; aaa ;;; aa ;; aa ;; a ;
8 aaa ;;; aaa ;;; aaa ;;; aa ;; aa ;; a ;

TECHNIQUE CHECKPOINT

Workbook 1–2.

Type each character and space with a quick, sharp stroke. Hold your anchor key positions as you reach for each key you type.

A Technique Checkpoint is a drill designed to give you a chance to practice the keys you just learned. It is an opportunity for your teacher to check your development of proper technique in using the correct fingering and anchoring; using the return without looking; maintaining correct posture and correct arm, hand, and elbow positions; and keeping eyes on copy. Marginal notes will accompany the checkpoints to assist you in improving as you type.

Type lines 9–10 once. Then repeat lines 1 and 3 (page 3), 5, and 7.

9   ff jj dd kk ss ll aa ;; f j d k s l a ;
10 ff jj dd kk ss ll aa ;; f j d k s l a ;

PRETEST

Type lines 11–12 at least once, keeping your eyes on the copy.

11 fad fad ask ask lad lad dad dad sad sad   *Return.*
12 as; as; fall fall alas alas flask flask   *Return twice.*

PRACTICE

Leave a blank line after each set of drills (13–14, 15–16, and so on) by returning twice.

Type lines 13–24 once.

13 fff aaa ddd fad fad aaa sss kkk ask ask
14 fff aaa ddd fad fad aaa sss kkk ask ask
15 aaa lll lll all all sss aaa ddd sad sad
16 aaa lll lll all all sss aaa ddd sad sad
17 lll aaa ddd lad lad aaa ddd ddd add add
18 lll aaa ddd lad lad aaa ddd ddd add add
19 ddd aaa ddd dad dad aaa sss ;;; as; as;
20 ddd aaa ddd dad dad aaa sss ;;; as; as;

(Continued on next page)

MECHANICS OF CENTERING

HORIZONTAL CENTERING

Horizontal centering is used to position copy horizontally in the center of the paper—that is, so that there are equal margins on both sides of the copy. Remember that the width of standard-size paper is 85P/102E. The width of metric (A4) paper is approximately 83P/100E.

To center copy horizontally on standard-size paper:

1. Center the carriage or carrier.

2. As you say each pair of strokes to yourself (including spaces), depress the backspace key once for each *pair* of strokes. Do not backspace for an extra letter left over at the end.

3. Type the material. It should appear centered horizontally on the page.

VERTICAL CENTERING

Vertical centering is used to position copy between the top and the bottom margins—that is, so that there are equal margins above and below the copy. Remember that standard typewriting paper is 66 lines long from top to bottom. Metric (A4) paper is 70 lines long.

To center copy vertically on a sheet of standard-size paper:

1. Count the number of lines (including blank ones) that will be used to type the copy.

2. Subtract that number from 66.

3. Divide the difference by 2 to find the line on which you should begin typing. (Drop any fraction you get when dividing by 2.)

4. Type the copy. It should appear centered vertically on the page.

MECHANICS OF TYPING TABLES

OPEN TABLES

Of all the different table styles, the *open* style is the easiest to set up and type. Open tables are commonly used in business offices.

Table Parts

1. Title—Centered in all capitals.

2. Subtitle—Centered with first and main words in capital and lowercase letters.

3. Column Headings—Centered over the column (may be blocked at the start of the column in drafts).

4. Body—The contents of the table.
   *Key Line—The longest item in each column (the longest item will sometimes be the column heading), plus the number of spaces between columns.

```
21  a al ala alas alas; f fa fal fall falls
22  a al ala alas alas; f fa fal fall falls
23  l la las lass lass; f fl fla flas flask
24  l la las lass lass; f fl fla flas flask
```

POSTTEST

Type lines 25–26 at least once, keeping your eyes on the copy. Note your improvement as compared with your Pretest on lines 11–12 (page 4).

```
25  fad fad ask ask lad lad dad dad sad sad
26  as; as; fall fall alas alas flask flask
```

AT THE END OF CLASS

If you are using a typewriter:

1. Remove the paper using the paper release.
2. Center the carriage.
3. Turn the machine off.
4. Cover the machine at the end of the last period.

If you are using a computer:

1. Save the document on a disk.
2. Exit the system.
3. Remove the disks from the computer and store them in sleeves.
4. Turn off the computer system.
5. Cover the computer at the end of the last period.

Note: Steps 2 and 3 may be reversed on some computers.

LESSON 2

■ **GOAL**
To control H, E, and O keys by touch, holding home key anchors.

■ **FORMAT**
Single spacing   40-space line

KEYBOARDING REVIEW

Type each line twice; repeat if time allows.

```
1  ff jj dd kk ss ll aa ;; f j d k s l a ;
2  asks asks fall fall lads lads lass lass
```

Hold Those Anchors

For **H** anchor ; L K
For **E** anchor A
For **O** anchor J or ;

SPACE BAR

 KEY

Use J finger.

Type each line twice.

```
3  jjj jhj jhj hjh jhj jjj jhj jhj hjh jhj
4  jhj ash ash jhj had had jhj has has jhj
5  jhj; a lad has; a lass has; add a half;
```

Personal-Business Letter Parts

A personal-business letter also has a heading, an opening, a body, and a closing, but the personal-business letter usually differs from the business letter in the following respects:

1. The heading is typewritten, not printed, and consists of the writer's full address (street, city, state, and ZIP Code) and the current date.

2. The closing includes the complimentary closing and the writer's name. Reference initials are omitted.

Personal-business letters may also include carbon copy notations, enclosure notations, and so on.

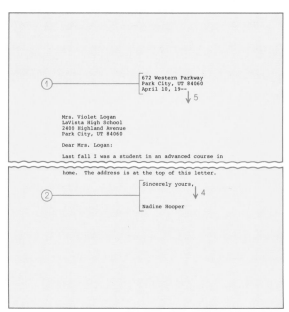

PERSONAL-BUSINESS LETTER

Letter Formats

Standard Format. The most popular format for business letters is the modified-block style—the *standard format* used in business. As illustrated below, in the standard format the date line and the closing lines (complimentary closing and writer's name and/or title) begin at the center. All other lines begin at the left margin.

Other Letter Formats. Two other letter formats are illustrated below: (1) A *variation of the standard format* is to indent paragraphs 5 spaces rather than type them at the left margin. (2) The *block* format shows all lines beginning at the left margin.

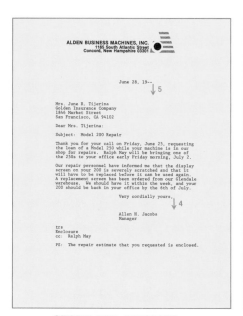

**STANDARD FORMAT—
MODIFIED-BLOCK STYLE**

BLOCK FORMAT

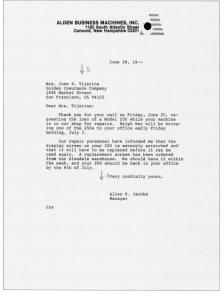

**STANDARD FORMAT WITH
INDENTED PARAGRAPHS**

Hold Those Anchors

For **H** anchor ; L K
For **E** anchor A
For **O** anchor J or ;

SPACE BAR

 KEY

Use D finger.

Type each line twice.

6 ddd ded ded ede ded ddd ded ded ede ded
7 ded she she ded led led ded he; he; ded
8 ded; he led; she led; he sees; she sees

 KEY

Use L finger.

Type each line twice.

9 lll lol lol olo lol lll lol lol olo lol
10 lol hoe hoe lol odd odd lol foe foe lol
11 lol old ode; oak hoe; sod fed; old foe;

TECHNIQUE CHECKPOINT

Keep eyes on copy. Hold home key anchors.

Type lines 12–13 once. Then repeat lines 3 (page 5), 6, and 9.

12 she sells jade flakes; he sells old oak
13 he has a salad; she has half; old jokes

PRETEST

Type lines 14–15 at least once, keeping your eyes on the copy.

14 half dead hold sash jell look lake seed
15 half dead hold sash jell look lake seed

PRACTICE

When You Repeat a Line:

Speed up on the second typing.

Make second typing smoother too.

Leave a blank line after second typing (return twice).

Type each line twice.

16 half half hall hall hale hale hole hole
17 dead dead deal deal heal heal head head
18 hold hold sold sold fold fold folk folk
19 sash sash dash dash lash lash hash hash
20 jell jell sell sell self self elf; elf;
21 look look hook hook hood hood hoof hoof
22 lake lake fake fake fade fade jade jade
23 seed seed deed deed feed feed heed heed

POSTTEST

Workbook 3–4.

Type lines 14–15 at least once, keeping your eyes on the copy. Note your improvement.

MECHANICS OF TYPING LETTERS

LETTERS

Business Letter Parts

A business letter contains a *heading,* an *opening,* a *body,* and a *closing.*

The *heading* consists of (1) the printed letterhead and (2) the date the letter is typed.

The *opening* includes (3) the inside address (the name and address of the party to whom the letter is being sent), (4) the attention line (if used, it directs the letter to a specific person or department), and (5) the salutation. If (6) a subject line is used, it is typed a double space below the salutation.

The *body* is (7) the message of the letter. Single-space lines, but use double spacing between paragraphs.

The *closing* includes the following parts: (8) the complimentary closing (such as *Yours truly, Sincerely yours,* or *Cordially yours,*), which is typed a double space below the last line of the body, (9) the handwritten signature of the person who composed the letter, (10) the signer's identification (name and title), and (11) the reference initials of the signer and/or typist.

The closing may also include the following optional parts: (12) an enclosure notation (specifying that something is enclosed with the letter), (13) a carbon copy (*cc*) notation (specifying that copies of the letter have been sent to other parties), and (14) a postscript (an added message that, when used, is always typed as the final item in a letter). In addition, some companies include (15) the firm name, which, if used, is typed a double space below the complimentary closing in all-capital letters.

Two additional letter parts are the continuation-page heading and the blind carbon copy (*bcc*) notation. The continuation-page heading, used on continuation pages for long letters, indicates the addressee's name, the page number, and the date. The *bcc* notation is a copy notation that appears only on the copies—so that the addressee does not see who has received copies.

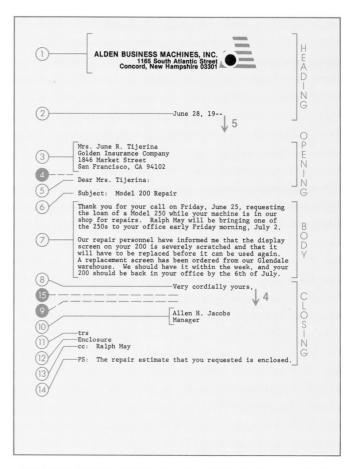

THE STANDARD FORMAT FOR BUSINESS LETTERS: MODIFIED-BLOCK STYLE

LESSON 3

■ **GOAL**
To control M, R, and I keys by touch, holding home key anchors.

■ **FORMAT**
Single spacing   40-space line

KEYBOARDING REVIEW

Type each line twice; repeat if time allows.

```
1  asdf jkl; heo; asdf jkl; heo; asdf jkl;
2  fake fake lose lose jade jade held held
```

Hold Those Anchors

For **M** anchor ; L K
For **R** anchor A S D
For **I** anchor ;

SPACE BAR

 KEY

Use J finger.

Type each line twice.

```
3  jjj jmj jmj mjm jmj jjj jmj jmj mjm jmj
4  jmj me; me; jmj mom mom jmj ham ham jmj
5  jmj; fold a hem; make a jam; less fame;
```

 KEY

Use F finger.

Type each line twice.

```
6  fff frf frf rfr frf fff frf frf rfr frf
7  frf for for frf far far frf err err frf
8  frf; from me; for her marks; more jars;
```

 KEY

Use K finger.

Type each line twice.

```
9  kkk kik kik iki kik kkk kik kik iki kik
10 kik lid lid kik dim dim kik rim rim kik
11 kik; dear sir; for his risk; if she is;
```

TECHNIQUE CHECKPOINT

Eyes on copy.
Hold home key anchors.

Type lines 12–13 once. Then repeat lines 3, 6, and 9.

```
12 her dark oak desk lid is a joke; he has
13 added a rare look from some old red oak
```

LETTER 8

Business letter with second-page heading, attention line, indented enumeration, and enclosure and postscript notations. Body 345 words.

(Today's date) / Division of Business / Wayne State ~~University~~ College / Wayne, NE 68778 / Attention: Business Faculty / Ladies and Gentlemen:

Dr. E. P. Howard, a member faculty in the Division of Business, informed me the other day that some of you might be interested in purchasing an household goods insurance policy ~~from our company~~. May I take a few moments of your time to explain some of the terms of the (basic) household goods policy ~~available~~ from mid-States Insurancy of St. Paul.

Our household goods insurance covers all personal belongings, to including (1) yours, (2) your spouses, (3) your dependents', and (4) others' goods when they are in your custody. We do have special limits on some property such as guns, watches, and furs, ~~etc.~~ Some items such as airline tickets, ~~food~~ stamps, trailers, and mobile homes are not covered by our policy. We will provide a more detailed list of these items if you would like to study our policy in greater detail.

First of all, you will find that our premiums are lower than those ~~suggested by~~ of our competitors. Mid-States can offer these lower premiums because we do not employ field agents to service our customers. All our ~~policies and~~ claims are handled

through a toll-free number in St. Paul, and the savings that result ~~because of~~ from this service are passed on each year to our policy holders.

We will pay for the direct loss of or damage to your property from the following causes: fire, lightning, smoke, water, flood, hail, earthquake, explosion, theft, vandalism, aircraft, and collapse of building. There are some exclusions to these causes; most of them pertain to losses or damages caused by the insured or by others covered by the policy.

To file a claim after a loss has occurred, you simply:

1. Notify the police, if necessary.
2. Write or call us as soon as possible, giving all pertinent information about your loss or damage.
3. File your claim within 100 days after the loss is discovered.

(Indent 5 spaces from margin)

We have enclosed a folder that will give you further information on our household insurance goods. If you have any other questions or would like additional details, please call me at 1-800-555-1000.

Sincerely Yours, / Paul R. Eldridge, President / (Your initials) / Enclosure / PS: We also carry life and health insurance policies and will send you information on these coverages if you would like.

Type lines 14–15 at least once, keeping your eyes on the copy.

14 mare hire elms foal lame dark aide jars

15 mare hire elms foal lame dark aide jars

Type each line twice.

Eyes on Copy
It will be easier to keep your eyes on the copy if you:

Review the charts for key positions and anchors.

Maintain an even pace.

Resist looking up from your copy.

16 mare mare mere mere mire mire more more

17 hire hire fire fire dire dire sire sire

18 elms elms alms alms arms arms aims aims

19 foal foal loam loam foam foam roam roam

20 lame lame dame dame fame fame same same

21 dark dark dare dare dale dale sale sale

22 aide aide side side hide hide ride ride

23 jars jars jams jams jade jade joke joke

Type lines 14–15 at least once, keeping your eyes on the copy. Note your improvement.

LESSON 4

■ **GOALS**
To control T, N, and C keys by touch, holding home key anchors.
To figure speed (typing rate) by using the speed scales.

■ **FORMAT**
Single spacing   40-space line

KEYBOARDING REVIEW

Type each line twice; repeat if time allows.

1 asdf jkl; heo; mri; asdf jkl; heo; mri;

2 safe safe herd herd joke joke mild mild

Hold Those Anchors

For **T** anchor A S D
For **N** anchor ; L K
For **C** anchor A

SPACE BAR

T KEY

Use F finger.

Type each line twice.

3 fff ftf ftf tft ftf fff ftf ftf tft ftf

4 ftf kit kit ftf ate ate ftf toe toe ftf

5 ftf; it is the; to the; for the; at it;

LETTER 6
Business letter with a display. Body 102 words.

[Today's date] / Mr. Jerry Lydell / Ads Department / Blue Hill News / Blue Hill, ME 04614 / Dear Mr. Lydell:

We wish to place in your paper the following ad for a bank programmer. Please arrange the ad in two columns, 3 inches deep, in the same format that you used for our records clerk ad two weeks ago.

BANK PROGRAMMER OPENING
We have a position for a senior programmer and bank analyst for our Blue Hill office. The salary is open. At least five years' experience in banking or programming is required. You may choose your own hardware. If you are interested, please write to

DATA SOFTWARE CO.
124 BLAINE DRIVE
AUGUSTA, ME 04330

Please run the ad for one week. / Sincerely, / Grace T. West / Director of Personnel / [Your initials]

LETTER 7
Business letter with a table. Body 127 words.

[Today's date] / Ms. Sharon T. Santos, Office Manager / Drake Publishing Company / 3579 Harvard Avenue South / Tulsa, OK 74135 / Dear Ms. Santos:

Thank you for requesting information on our line of executive desks. Naturally, we believe our product is the top of the line; and we hope you'll stop by our showroom to look at all the fine furniture we have for your new building.

As you requested, we are providing you with the following price list for our executive desks:

EXECUTIVE DESK PRICE LIST
June 30, 19--

Desk	Size	Price
Model F775	72" x 36"	$550.95
Model F675	60" x 30"	485.55
Model G330	72" x 36"	450.95
Model G230	60" x 30"	365.95

Yours truly, / Jeremy L. Sloan / Sales Manager / [Your initials]

Hold Those Anchors

For **T** anchor A S D
For **N** anchor ; L K
For **C** anchor A

SPACE BAR

 KEY

Use J finger.

Type each line twice.

6 jjj jnj jnj njn jnj jjj jnj jnj njn jnj

7 jnj ten ten jnj and and jnj not not jnj

8 jnj; for the; in an effort; of an honor

 KEY

Use D finger.

Type each line twice.

9 ddd dcd dcd cdc dcd ddd dcd dcd cdc dcd

10 dcd can can dcd ace ace dcd arc arc dcd

11 dcd; on a deck; in each car; cannot act

TECHNIQUE CHECKPOINT

Eyes on copy. Hold home key anchors.

Type lines 12–13 once. Then repeat lines 3 (page 8), 6, and 9.

12 there is a carton of jade on this dock;

13 mail a file card to the nearest stores;

FIGURING SPEED

Workbook 5.

1. **If you type for 1 minute:** Find out how many "average" words you type in the time allowed. Every 5 strokes (letters and spaces) counts as 1 average word. Thus a 40-stroke line is 8 words long; two such lines, 16 words; and so on.

2. For an incomplete line, use the scale (below line 15 on this page); the number above which you stop is your word count for that incomplete line. **Example:** If you type lines 14 and 15 (see below) and start over, getting as far as the word *sink* in line 14, you have typed 16 + 1 = 17 words.

3. **If you type for more than 1 minute:** To find out your 1-minute rate, you will

need to *divide* the word total by the number of minutes you typed. **Example:** 37 words in 2 minutes would be 37 ÷ 2 = 18½ = 19 wam (words a minute). Count a fraction as a whole word.

4. **If you type for less than 1 minute:** To find out your 1-minute rate, you will have to *multiply* the total number of words typed because you typed for less than 1 minute. If you type for 30 seconds, you will have to multiply by 2 (2 × 30 = 60, or 1 minute). If you type for 12 seconds, you will have to multiply by 5 (5 × 12 = 60, or 1 minute). **Example:** 9 words in 30 seconds would be 9 × 2 = 18 wam.

PRETEST

Take a 1-minute timing on lines 14–15, keeping your eyes on the copy.

14 sink cane tone then tick jots hand rain   8

15 sink cane tone then tick jots hand rain   16

| 1 | 2 | 3 | 4 | 5 | 6 | 7 | 8

LETTER 3

Business letter. Special parts: attention line and enclosure notation. Body 102 words.

[*Today's date*] / Firestone Fireplace Accessories / 11805 Glen Mill Road / Rockville, MD 20854 / Attention: Sales Department / Ladies and Gentlemen:

Reynolds Homes has just recently purchased a large tract of land in the prestigious Paradise Hills development area. We are going to build at least 100 three- and four-bedroom homes in this area in the next five years and wish to install fireplaces in each of our homes.

Would you please send us an estimate for purchasing 100 Model Z-58 fireplace screens to install in these homes. The screens we would like are illustrated in the enclosed brochure.

Since we must make our decision within the next four weeks, we would appreciate hearing from you by the 16th.

Sincerely yours, / Robert P. Arnold / General Contractor / [*Your initials*] / Enclosure

LETTER 4

Business letter with enclosure and *cc* notations. Body 119 words.

[*Today's date*] / Ms. Annette Rudd / Business Teacher / Tulsa Technical High School / 2370 Yale Avenue, S / Tulsa, OK 74114 / Dear Ms. Rudd:

Thank you for writing us and asking whether we might have a person from our office come to speak to the students in your office procedures class.

Mr. Jeffrey Scott, a member of our personnel staff, will plan to join you at 9 a.m. on Tuesday, December 13. He will speak to your students on "What a Temporary Position Can Do for You," and his presentation will last about 45 minutes. A copy of his handout is enclosed for you to review.

Mr. Scott has had considerable office experience, and he has worked for Tulsa Temporaries for the past five years. I am sure you will enjoy his enthusiastic and professional presentation on temporary employment in the Tulsa area. / Very truly yours, / John R. Blake / Personnel Manager / [*Your initials*] / Enclosure / cc: Karen Turner

LETTER 5

Personal-business letter with enclosure, postscript, and *bcc* notations. Body 111 words.

1726 Lee Street / Flint, MI 48560 / (Today's date) / R. B. Wards Inc. / 1100 Griswold Avenue / Detroit, MI 48226 / Gentlemen:

On September 12 I purchased an electric iron, Model gT-246A, from your Griswold store. the price of the iron was $43.50. When I found out that the iron did not work, I sent it back immediately to you asking that my account be credited for $34.50. ¶On my October 15 statement, I noticed that my account had not been credited and that I had been charged for that iron. The same was true in my Nov. 15 statement.

Please take care of this matter & see that the correction is reflected in my Dec. statement. I have enclosed all correspondence on this transaction, including a copy of my receipt of purchase. / Cordially, / Edgar Mills / Enclosures / PS: My account number is 88-345-909. / bcc: R. A. Hendley

Type each line twice.

16 sink sink rink rink link link ink; ink;
17 cane cane came came cake cake care care
18 tone tone done done lone lone none none
19 then then than than thin thin this this
20 tick tick lick lick sick sick kick kick
21 jots jots lots lots lets lets jets jets
22 hand hand hard hard harm harm farm farm
23 rain rain raid raid said said sail sail

POSTTEST

Take another 1-minute timing on lines 14–15 (page 9), keeping your eyes on the copy. Note your improvement.

LESSON 5

■ GOALS
To control the V, right shift, and period keys by touch, holding home key anchors.
To identify typographical errors in copy and count them.
To use the paper bail as an aid for locating copy errors.

■ FORMAT
Single spacing   40-space line

KEYBOARDING REVIEW

Type each line twice.

1 asdf jkl; jh de lo jm fr ki ft jn dc ;;
2 cash free dine jolt milk iron trim star

Hold Those Anchors

For **V** anchor A S D
For **Right Shift Key** anchor J
For **.** anchor ; or J

V KEY

Use F finger.

Type each line twice.

3 fff fvf fvf vfv fvf fff fvf fvf vfv fvf
4 fvf vie vie fvf via via fvf eve eve fvf
5 fvf; via a van; move over; vie for love

LETTER 1

Personal-business letter with an enumeration. Body 138 words.

304 West Geneva Road / Wheaton, IL 60187 / [Today's date] / Mr. R. C. Hargrove, Manager / The Stardust Manor Hotel / 46 Franklin Street / Baltimore, MD 21225 / Dear Mr. Hargrove:

Last week I had the privilege of staying at the Stardust Manor. I was somewhat in a hurry when I left because I had a plane to catch the morning of my departure. In my haste, I did not look closely at my bill. Upon arriving home, however, I found an error in the charges to my room.

The bill includes three long-distance phone calls to New York City, for a total of $13.25. The calls were listed as follows:

1. 212-555-1870, for 2 minutes.
2. 212-555-1255, for 10 minutes.
3. 212-555-5261, for 3 minutes.

I did not make these calls and do not know the names of the parties called. Would you please look into this matter and refund me the $13.25.

My apologies for not finding the error in my bill until this late date.

Yours truly, / Stacy Maxton

LETTER 2

Business letter. Special part: subject line. Body 55 words.

(Today's date) / Ms. Inez T. Williams / Business Department / Central High School / Grand Forks, ND 58210 / Dear Ms. Williams: / Subject: Co-op Students

We were delighted to hear that 5 of your part-time cooperative education students will be working on a basis for our company starting March 10. Please have your students report to the personnel office, Building A, on the 3d floor at our University Ave. location. Their work assignments will be made at that time. / Sincerely, / J. D. Hill / Personnel Director / (Your initials)

Hold Those Anchors

For **V** anchor A S D
For **Right Shift Key**
  anchor J
For **.** anchor ; or J

SPACE BAR

RIGHT SHIFT KEY

Use Sem finger.

Use the right shift key to capitalize letters typed with the left hand. To make the reach easier, curl the second and third fingers of your right hand as you complete the following three-step sequence:

1. Cap! Keeping J finger in home position, extend Sem finger to press the right shift key and hold it down firmly.

2. Strike! (or the name of the letter to be capitalized). While the shift is still depressed, use the left hand to strike the letter that is to be capitalized.

3. Home! Release the shift key, and return all fingers to home position.

For a capital A, for example, you would think "Cap!" as you press the right shift, "A!" as you strike the letter, and "Home!" as all fingers snap back to home position.

Type each line twice.

```
 6   ;;; C;; C;; ;;; S;; S;; ;;; T;; T;; ;;;
 7   ;;; Cal Cal ;;; Sam Sam ;;; Ted Ted ;;;
 8   ;;; Ada Ada ;;; Rae Rae ;;; Dee Dee ;;;
```

. KEY

Use L finger.

Type each line twice.

```
 9   lll l.l l.l .l. l.l lll l.l l.l .l. lll
10   l.l Sr. Sr. l.l Fr. Fr. l.l Dr. Dr. l.l
11   vs. ea. Co. St. Rd. Ave. div. ctn. std.
```

PUNCTUATION

Space twice after a period at the end of a sentence. Do not space after the end of a line.

Type each line twice.

```
12   Roll the dimes.  There are five stacks.
13   See Ann at the door.  She has the food.
```

Space once after a period that follows an abbreviation and after a semicolon.

Type each line twice.

```
14   Dr. S. Romer called; he read the lines.
15   Elm St. is ahead; East Ave. veers left.
```

TECHNIQUE CHECKPOINT

Eyes on copy.
Hold home key anchors.

Type lines 16–17 once. Then repeat lines 3 (page 10), 6, and 9.

```
16   Dr. Sara is on call; she asked Anne for    8
17   five half liters of cold milk in a jar.   16
       |  1  |  2  |  3  |  4  |  5  |  6  |  7  |  8
```

The number of people capable of using this system at one time is limited only by the number of telephone extensions in use in the office.

SELECTING EQUIPMENT

When choosing input equipment for your word processing center, you should weigh several factors. The cost factor, of course, is very important. Prices will vary greatly, depending on the options and special features you wish to have and the number of units you want. You must decide whether you want a service contract. You must be sure that service can be obtained on short notice and that the people who service your equipment are well trained.

You must set up a training session for all the people who are going to operate the equipment. Find out if the manufacturer will train operators free of charge or if you will have to provide your own training. The equipment you buy must be easy to operate by both the dictators and the transcribers.

And lastly, be sure that the equipment you buy is flexible and will be able to meet the changes that will take place in your business in the years to come.

CENTER SURROUNDINGS

Once you know what kind of equipment you are going to buy, you must also decide just where that equipment is going to be placed. Whatever space you choose, you must control the air in the office both for the protection of the equipment and for the comfort of the operator. Is the air too cold or too warm? Is it clean? And does it have the right humidity level?[2]

Because of all the typing, reading, handwriting, and editing that are done in a word processing center, it is important to have the right lighting.

Sound must also be controlled so that excessive noise does not affect people's health and performance on the job.[3]

FOOTNOTES

1. Marilyn K. Popyk, Word Processing and Information Systems, 2d ed., McGraw-Hill Book Company, New York, 1986, p. 4.
2. Ibid., pp. 256, 257.
3. Ibid., p. 256.

COUNTING ERRORS

Workbook 6.

Dr. ②Saar① is on call③, she asked Anne② for
five half liters of cold m lk④ in a jar.
Dr.⑤ Sara is on dall⑥ ;she astde⑥ Anne for
five⑦ half liters⑧ cold milk in in⑨ a jar.

1. Circle any word in which there is an error.
2. Count a word as an error if the spacing after it is incorrect.
3. Count a word as an error if the punctuation after it is incorrect.
4. Count a word as an error if it contains a letter so light that you can't read it.
5. Count a word as an error if it contains an incomplete capital letter.

6. Count only 1 error against 1 word, no matter how many errors the word may contain.
7. Count each failure to follow directions in spacing, indenting, and so on, as an error.
8. Count each word that is omitted as an error.
9. Count each word that is repeated incorrectly as an error.

PROOFREAD USING THE PAPER BAIL

When you proofread copy, you are looking mainly for typographical errors (incorrect characters or spaces). Proofreading your typewritten copy accurately is as important as typing accurately in the first place. Using your paper bail like a ruler to guide your eyes line by line across the page will help you proofread accurately.

LESSON 6

CLINIC

■ **GOALS**
To complete special drills to strengthen key control.
To type 16 words a minute for 1 minute.

■ **FORMAT**
Single spacing   40-space line

SPACE BAR

PRETEST Take two 1-minute timings on lines 1–3 to determine your typing rate. Figure your speed and count your errors.

```
1   keel dose fell seat fool sale veer tone   8
2   fall dear mail reed coil jest dead race   16
3   tee; heal amt. Todd keel dose fell seat   24
    |  1  |  2  |  3  |  4  |  5  |  6  |  7  |  8
```

THE ADVENT OF WORD PROCESSING
By Don Martin

HISTORY

The concept of word processing has been with us for quite a few years, back to the late 1800s when C.L. Sholes from Wisconsin invented the first typewriter for commercial production (1873).[1] The touch system (1889) used on the typewriter was responsible for changing the outlook of the modern office in terms of the amount of work that could be done by a typist who used all the fingers working at the task instead of just two or four fingers. Dictating machines were also responsible for causing rapid changes in the office.

Thus, like their predecessors, word processing systems have had great influence on the amount of work produced in the office of today. The completion of more work is made possible through the use of such equipment as the automatic typewriter and the cathode ray tube. Magnetic tape and magnetic card typewriters are able to capture on tape or card all that is placed into the machine and change or delete those words or sections that must be revised before the final copy is typed. The cathode ray tube shows on a screen above the keyboard what is being placed into the storage unit of the typewriter. The keyboard of this machine allows for changes to be made very easily in the text, and these changes are displayed on the screen.

DICTATION EQUIPMENT

Many different kinds of input dictation equipment for word processing are available. You can buy portable units that can be carried away from your desk, and these units are small enough to fit into your coat pocket. A desktop unit can be purchased from many different suppliers. Many of these units operate with cartridges or cassette tapes; you can dictate, transcribe, or perform both functions on these machines.

Some offices have centralized systems that use private wire connections to all dictators. Sometimes a telephone system can be used for a word processing dictation system.

(Continued on next page)

If You Omit a Space Between Words, Then:

Check that your palms do not touch the machine.

Think "space" for each space bar stroke.

Type calmly, evenly—not hurriedly.

Check that thumb is slightly above space bar.

Workbook 7–8.

Type lines 4–11 twice each. Then proofread and circle errors. Repeat lines in which you made errors.

4 keel keel feel feel heel heel reel reel
5 dose dose nose nose rose rose lose lose
6 fell fell tell tell sell sell jell jell
7 seat seat feat feat heat heat meat meat
8 fool fool food food mood mood hood hood
9 sale sale male male tale tale dale dale
10 veer veer jeer jeer seer seer deer deer
11 tone tone done done lone lone cone cone

Type lines 12–23 twice each. Then proofread and circle errors. Repeat lines in which you made errors.

12 fall fall mall mall tall tall hall hall
13 dear dear hear hear fear fear near near
14 mail mail sail sail jail jail rail rail
15 reed reed need need deed deed heed heed
16 coil coil soil soil toil toil foil foil
17 jest jest vest vest nest nest rest rest
18 dead dead head head lead lead read read
19 race race lace lace face face mace mace
20 tee; tee; teen teen seen seen see; see;
21 heal heal veal veal meal meal real real
22 amt. amt. dis. dis. std. std. ins. ins.
23 Todd Todd Sara Sara Vera Vera Cass Cass

POSTTEST

Take two 1-minute timings on lines 1–3 (page 12). Figure your speed and count your errors. Note your improvement.

LESSON 7

UNIT 2 Keyboarding—The Alphabet
UNIT GOAL 20 WORDS A MINUTE

■ GOAL
To control W, comma, and G keys by touch, holding home key anchors.

■ FORMAT
Single spacing   40-space line

KEYBOARDING REVIEW

Type each line twice.

1 jest fail sake not; mist card Rev. chin
2 Rick loves that fame; Val did not join.

REPORT 2
One-page report.

FEASIBILITY OF A FOUR-DAY CLASS WEEK

By (Your name)

There is a trend in the business community toward a 4-day work week. The idea of a shorter work week is filtering in to the educational community. There is definitely a need for alternatives to the present system of 5 days, which is becoming costly for all involved.

SELECTION OF THE PARTICIPANTS

The researcher decided to limit the sample to two separate categories: (1) faculty, staff, and students who live on campus; and (2) commuting students who live off campus.

PURPOSE OF THE STUDY

It was the purpose of the study to identify university opinions of a 4-day class week.

FINDINGS OF THE STUDY

One of the major findings of the study was that 55% of those surveyed wished to keep the 5-day class week. The majority of those with this opinion were students. Commuter students, however, wanted to try the 4-day class week; and faculty and staff were also of this opinion.

The most popular option for a four-day class week is for classes to be conducted on Monday through Thursday.

REPORT 3
Minutes of a Meeting.

Office Technology Inc.

MINUTES OF THE OCTOBER MEETING

October 20, 19—

ATTENDANCE

The October meeting of Office Technology Inc. was held on October 15, 19—, in the Executive Conference Room. The meeting began at 9 a.m. and was adjourned at 12 noon. Mr. Timothy R. O'Malley, Vice President for Sales, presided at the meeting. Harland Sanders and Rebecca Moreland were not in attendance.

UNFINISHED BUSINESS

The secretary read the minutes of the September meeting, and they were approved as read.

Ms. Toni Deaton responded to questions that were raised at the September meeting concerning Office Technology's involvement in the development of the new laser printers by the Southwest Division. Production on these printers will begin in late December.

NEW BUSINESS

Mr. Frank Anders gave a status report on the voice activation equipment. This project is in the early developmental stages this year, and final contracts will not be drawn until late next year.

Ms. Cathy Yaeger and Mr. Roberto Diaz shared several ideas that they gained at the Future Office Technologies meeting in Los Angeles, October 7–11.

Crandel T. Evans, Secretary

Hold Those Anchors

For **W** anchor F
For **,** anchor ;
For **G** anchor A S D

SPACE BAR

 KEY

Use S finger.

3 sss sws sws wsw sws sss sws sws wsw sws
4 sws saw saw sws own own sws was was sws
5 sws; white swans swim; sow winter wheat

 KEY

Use K finger.
Space once after a comma.

6 kkk k,k k,k ,k, k,k kkk k,k k,k ,k, k,k
7 k,k it, it, k,k an, an, k,k or, or, k,k
8 k,k; if it is, as soon as, two or three

 KEY

Use F finger.

9 fff fgf fgf gfg fgf fff fgf fgf gfg fgf
10 fgf egg egg fgf leg leg fgf get get fgf
11 fgf; give a dog, saw a log, sing a song

TECHNIQUE CHECKPOINT

Hold home key anchors.
Elbows in.

Type lines 12–14 once. Then repeat lines 3, 6, and 9.

12 While we watched, the first team jogged   8
13 to the front of the field. The win was   16
14 two in a row; the team likes victories.   24
   | 1 | 2 | 3 | 4 | 5 | 6 | 7 | 8

PRETEST

Take two 1-minute timings on line 15, and determine your speed; use the faster rate.

15 king scow well gown elk, crew mow, sag,
   | 1 | 2 | 3 | 4 | 5 | 6 | 7 | 8

PRACTICE

Type each line twice.

16 king king sing sing wing wing ring ring
17 scow scow stow stow show show snow snow
18 well well welt welt went went west west
19 gown gown town town tows tows toes toes

(Continued on next page)

TABLE 6

Multicolumn, with rules, a total line, and a footnote.

EMPLOYEE VACATION AND SPENDING HABITS

(Summer, 19--)

Vacation Site	Number Of Employees	Percent of Employees	Average Daily Expenses
Metropolitan City	24	27	$55.00
Sea side resort	25	23	70.00
Mountain resort	35	26	42.00
MotorTrip	22	14	88.30
Lake Resort	10	6	48.50
Misc.	21	14*	41.00
Total	155	100	$57.64

*A total of 18 percent of the employees colectively had other kinds of vacations.

REPORTS

REPORT 1

One-page report, with footnotes.

THE ART OF LISTENING
By [*Your name*]

Good listening requires certain responsibilities from all of us, as we shall see in the following paragraphs.

RESPONSIBILITIES OF THE LISTENER

To become an effective listener, we have to prepare for the task. "Choose whenever possible a position that allows you to see his or her gestures and clearly hear the tone of voice . . . ."[1] You should sit up straight and look directly at the speaker.

Leonard suggests an excellent idea for improving listening. He believes that

one good way of eliminating this obstacle to effective listening is to occupy your excess thinking time usefully. Think about the presentation itself. Every now and then, summarize what the speaker has said.[2]

RESULTS OF GOOD LISTENING

If you improve your listening techniques, you will develop a positive attitude, you will improve your interest level, and you will improve your decision-making abilities.

1. Herta A. Murphy and Charles E. Peck, <u>Effective Business Communications</u>, 3d ed., McGraw-Hill Book Company, New York, 1980, p. 679.

2. Donald J. Leonard, <u>Shurter's Communication in Business</u>, 4th ed., McGraw-Hill Book Company, New York, 1979, p. 415.

Type each line twice.

20 elk, elk, ilk, ilk, irk, irk, ink, ink,
21 crew crew grew grew grow grow glow glow
22 mow, mow, how, how, hot, hot, not, not,
23 sag, sag, wag, wag, rag, rag, gag, gag,

POSTTEST

Take two 1-minute timings on line 15 (page 14) and determine your speed; use the faster rate. Note your improvement.

LESSON 8

■ GOAL
To control B, U, and left shift keys by touch, holding home key anchors.

■ FORMAT
Single spacing   40-space line

KEYBOARDING REVIEW

Type each line twice.

1 wick foal corn them jive logo dim, wags
2 Coco gave me jewels; Frank mailed them.

Hold Those Anchors

For **B** anchor A S
For **U** anchor ; L K
For **Left Shift Key** anchor F

SPACE BAR

 KEY

Use F finger.

Type each line twice.

3 fff fbf fbf bfb fbf fff fbf fbf bfb fbf
4 fbf bag bag fbf rob rob fbf ebb ebb fbf
5 fbf, a bent bin, a big bag, a back bend

 KEY

Use J finger.

Type each line twice.

6 jjj juj juj uju juj jjj juj juj uju juj
7 juj jug jug juj flu flu juj urn urn juj
8 juj; jumbo jet, jungle bugs, just a job

TABLE 4
Multicolumn, with leaders and a footnote.

POPULATION OF AMERICAN COLONIES*

1760 to 1780

Colony	1780	1770	1760
Connecticut	206,701	183,881	142,470
Maryland	245,474	202,599	162,267
Massachusetts	268,627	235,308	222,600
New York	210,541	162,920	117,138
North Carolina	270,133	197,200	110,442
Pennsylvania	327,305	240,057	183,703
Virginia	538,004	447,016	339,726

Source: U.S. Bureau of the Census.
*Seven largest, according to the 1780 census.

TABLE 5
Multicolumn, with decimal tabs, a total line, and a footnote.

PRECIPITATION AMOUNTS*

(Selected U.S. Cities)

City	Rain	Sleet or Snow
Albuquerque	9.83	16.8
Birmingham	56.00	0.4
Boston	40.24	42.5
Buffalo	36.31	108.3
Fairbanks	7.72	85.1
Rochester	36.60	102.9
Total	186.70	356.0

*In inches.

Hold Those Anchors

For **B** anchor A S
For **U** anchor ; L K
For **Left Shift Key**
  anchor F

SPACE BAR

LEFT SHIFT KEY

Use A finger.

Use the left shift key to capitalize letters typed with the right hand. To make the reach easier, curl the second and third fingers of your left hand as you complete the following three-step sequence:

1. Cap! Keep F finger in home position

and extend A finger to press the left shift key and hold it down firmly.

2. Strike! While the shift key is still depressed, use the right hand to strike the letter that is to be capitalized.

3. Home! Release the shift key, and return all fingers to home position.

Type each line twice.

9 aaa Jaa Jaa aaa Kaa Kaa aaa Laa Laa aaa
10 aaa Joe Joe aaa Kim Kim aaa Lee Lee aaa
11 Otis Iris Nita Mark Uris Hans Jose Kebo

TECHNIQUE CHECKPOINT

Eyes on copy.

Hold home key anchors.

Wrists and arms quiet as you type.

Type lines 12–14 once. Then repeat lines 3 and 6 (page 15) and 9.

12 Sharing a new car with friends is great   8
13 fun. Just look at that engine; hear it   16
14 hum. Drive with a flair, but use care.   24
   | 1 | 2 | 3 | 4 | 5 | 6 | 7 | 8

PRETEST

Take two 1-minute timings on line 15, and determine your speed; use the faster rate.

15 beef just bout sun, blot vast gist bran
   | 1 | 2 | 3 | 4 | 5 | 6 | 7 | 8

PRACTICE

Check Your Feet. They Should Be:

In front of the chair.

Firmly on the floor, square, flat.

Apart, with 6 or 7 inches between the ankles.

So placed that one foot is a little ahead of the other.

Type each line twice.

16 beef been bean bead beak beam beat bear
17 just dust dusk dunk bunk bulk hulk hunk
18 bout boat boot bolt bold boll doll dole
19 sun, nun, run, bun, gun, gum, hum, sum,
20 blot blob blow blew bled bred brad bran
21 vast vest jest lest best west nest rest
22 gist list mist must gust dust rust just
23 bran brad bred brew brow crow crew craw

POSTTEST

Take two 1-minute timings on line 15, and determine your speed; use the faster rate. Note your improvement.

TABLE 1
Two-column, with subtitle and column headings.

EXECUTIVE OFFICERS
Crane Company

Officer	Title
Adrian L. Martinez	Chief Executive Officer
Nancy T. Pemberton	Executive Vice President
Harold E. Johnson	Vice President for Sales
Colleen L. LaBarge	Vice President for Personnel
Sharon W. Woodard	Vice President for Research

TABLE 2
Multicolumn, with rules and long column headings.

MOST APPEALING SPORTS

Gallup Poll ~~in U.S.~~

Name of ~~for~~ Sport	Participation	No.
Bicycling	27%	40.5 million
Bowling	23%	34.5 million
Camping	19%	28.5 million
Fishing	24%	36.0 million
Hiking	21%	31.5 million
Swimming	37%	55.5 million

TABLE 3
Multicolumn, with rules and two-line column headings.

JUNIOR ROOM ASSIGNMENTS

(First Semester)

Rooms and teacher names are correct—alphabetize order of surnames in first column. Double-space body.

Surname Grouping Identification	Room Number	Name of Teacher
Jackson Through Lorenz	141A	Ms. Franklin
Thomas Through Young	141B	Mr. Qually
Eastman Through Harms	142A	Ms. Yeung
Adams Through Desitaul	142B	Ms. Carlisle
Preston Through Song	143A	Mr. Kenton
Miller Through Olsen	143B	Mr. Baruch

LESSON 9

■ **GOAL**
To control P, Q, and colon keys by touch, holding home key anchors.

■ **FORMAT**
Single spacing   40-space line

KEYBOARDING REVIEW

Type each line twice.

1 blue java brag mold silk when face club
2 Cora waved flags, but Jama went hiking.

Hold Those Anchors

For **P** anchor J K
For **Q** anchor F
For **:** anchor J

 KEY

Use Sem finger.

Type each line twice.

3 ;;; ;p; ;p; p;p ;p; ;;; ;p; ;p; p;p ;p;
4 ;p; pen pen ;p; nap nap ;p; ape ape ;p;
5 ;p; a pen pal, a pale page, a proud pup

Q KEY

Use A finger.

Type each line twice.

6 aaa aqa aqa qaq aqa aaa aqa aqa qaq aqa
7 aqa quo quo aqa que que aqa qui qui aqa
8 aqa quiet quip, quick quote, aqua quilt

: KEY

Shift of **;**.
Use Sem finger and left shift key.
Space twice after a colon.

Type each line twice.

9 ;;; ;:; ;:; :;: ;:; ;;; ;:; ;:; :;: ;:;
10 Ms. Lia: Mr. Kwi: Dr. Que: Mrs. Doe:
11 Dear Ms. Jo: Dear Mr. Mai: Dear Jeri:

TECHNIQUE CHECKPOINT

Elbows in.
Hold home key anchors.

Type lines 12–14 once. Then repeat lines 3, 6, and 9.

12 TV lets us view the top news as it pops   8
13 up around the globe; an item takes life   16
14 with the clever quip of the journalist.   24

| 1 | 2 | 3 | 4 | 5 | 6 | 7 | 8 |

COMPOSITION EXERCISES

In this course you learned how to format typewritten letters, reports, and tables. But you also need to acquire the skill of composing copy at the typewriter. Then when you have developed your composition skills, you will be able to create projects in your own words and display each project in one of the various formats you learned in this course.

The following section is designed to strengthen your composition skills. The activities in this section are arranged from simple to complex, starting with a phrase response and concluding with an entire-paragraph response.

Follow the directions and examples given for each stage of composition as you compose your answers to each of the questions. Single-space each response, but double-space between responses.

PHRASE COMPOSITION

Use a phrase of two or three words to respond to each of the following questions. Use a clean sheet of paper, start on line 10 from the top, and type on a 50-space line. *Keep your eyes on your copy, and concentrate on each answer as you type.*

Example Question:
   Where would you like to live?

Example Response:
   In Colorado

1. What are your school colors?

2. Who is your best friend?

3. What is the name of your school newspaper or local newspaper?

4. What is your favorite television program?

5. What is your favorite record?

6. Name a book that you enjoyed reading.

7. What city and country would you like to visit?

8. Who is your favorite sports personality?

9. Name two large cities in the United States.

10. Name two large states in the United States.

11. Name a past president of the United States.

12. Name two jobs you would enjoy doing.

SENTENCE COMPOSITION

Answer each of the following questions by typing a complete sentence of six or more words. (Each sentence must have a subject and a predicate.) Use a clean sheet of paper, start on line 10 from the top, and type on a 50-space line. *Keep your eyes on your copy, and concentrate on each sentence as you type.*

Example Question:
   When do the leaves start to fall?

Example Response:
   In my state the leaves start to fall in September.

1. Why do we have taxes?

2. Why do we have insurance?

3. How is typewriting going to help you?

4. What have you learned from any one of your courses in school this year?

5. Why did you enroll in typewriting?

6. What kind of person would you like to have as a friend?

7. What are some of your assets?

8. What are you going to do when you finish high school?

9. What were some of the hardships faced by the pioneers?

10. What is significant about July 4, 1776?

PARAGRAPH COMPOSITION

Use a paragraph of at least three complete sentences to answer each of the questions below. Use a clean sheet of paper, start on line 10 from the top, and type on a 50-space line. *Keep your eyes on your copy, and concentrate on the words as you type.*

1. Where would you like to spend your next vacation and why?

2. Name your favorite season of the year, and tell why you prefer that time of year.

3. Describe what the world will be like in the year 2050.

4. What career do you want to pursue and why?

5. In what state would you like to live the rest of your life and why?

Take two 1-minute timings on line 15, and determine your speed; use the faster rate.

15 pace quit prep quad ping shop que; quod
    | 1 | 2 | 3 | 4 | 5 | 6 | 7 | 8

PRACTICE

Type each line twice.

16 pace pack park part pare page pane pale
17 quit quip quiet quill quick quirk quire
18 prep peep jeep weep beep seep step stop
19 quad aqua quack quail quake quart qualm
20 ping pint pins pink pine pike pile pipe
21 shop chop crop prop plop flop slop slow
22 que; ques quest queen quell queue queer
23 quod quot quota quoth quoit quote quori

POSTTEST

Take two 1-minute timings on line 15, and determine your speed; use the faster rate. Note your improvement.

LESSON 10

■ **GOAL**
To control Z, Y, and X keys by touch, holding home key anchors.

■ **FORMAT**
Single spacing   40-space line

KEYBOARDING REVIEW

Type each line twice.

1 left best dome quip wave jogs chin bake
2 Meg saved her worn black quilt for Pam.

Hold Those Anchors

For **Z** anchor F
For **Y** anchor ; L K
For **X** anchor A or F

 KEY

Use A finger.

Type each line twice.

3 aaa aza aza zaz aza aaa aza aza zaz aza
4 aza zip zip aza zap zap aza zed zed aza
5 aza, to zig, to zag, to zing, to seize,

TRANSPOSI-TION ERRORS
(we for ew)

1 few hew new anew blew crew drew grew renews reviews viewing
2 owe wed weak weed week weld went west weary wedding western
3 Few in the weary crew knew that the weed grew in wet grass.
4 A crew grew weak and weary viewing wet weather in the west.

TRANSPOSI-TION ERRORS
(er for re)

1 real rent reason regard regress relate relish remain remedy
2 ever leer alter fever lever lover sheer steer desert sorter
3 A store merchant had reasons for renting the camera to her.
4 He regretfully returned the sheer dress to the store clerk.

TRANSPOSI-TION ERRORS
(rt for tr)

1 try trot true trade tribe trust truth travel truant trouble
2 art cart dart mart part tart alert heart shirt start cohort
3 The tattered tramps toiled to tow the trailer to the truck.
4 The new report revealed that the river had started to rise.

TRANSPOSI-TION ERRORS
(po for op)

1 drop flop hoop hope loop opal open rope opera optic operate
2 poem poet pork port pose post porous porter portion posture
3 Those poems the poor poet composed were popular with Polly.
4 A job of the sponsor is to appoint the proper, polite poet.

TRANSPOSI-TION ERRORS
*(u for i;
i for u)*

1 fire hire inch milk mine pile size light limit waist finish
2 blue glue hulk much plug rust true lunch plump plush unhook
3 Jim Hunter had a delicious dinner with Muriel Mire at noon.
4 Hugh and Ivy Lute will visit their cousin in Biloxi in May.

TRANSPOSI-TION ERRORS
*(o for i;
i for o)*

1 light might quick nights simple identify quantity imaginary
2 hold home move once only crows occurs oppose people follows
3 A diary is a precise daily record of your personal actions.
4 A highlight at the spring fashion fair is an Oriental suit.

TRANSPOSI-TION ERRORS
*(a for s;
s for a)*

1 his lose loss lost miss mist pose rose snip snow stop knows
2 all ate way bake cake fake lake make rank take wait trained
3 Adam ate all the cake Barbara baked, but James had no cake.
4 Ms. Sarah Sands must stop at the Custer Museum some Sunday.

TRANSPOSI-TION ERRORS
*(e for d;
d for e)*

1 did lid duds duly duty card lard doubt drool ballad discard
2 elk east easy eves ebony empty emblem empire enchant energy
3 A dedicated editor decided to edit an address on education.
4 Ed Dodds read the report that Ted Edward prepared on weeds.

TRANSPOSI-TION ERRORS
*(m for n;
n for m)*

1 not now news note plan known night noble noise notch nickel
2 mad maid mail main male malt meal more maize magnet magnify
3 Ned nominated his nephew to navigate a nice, new steamship.
4 My magnificent machine managed to mangle the massive metal.

TRANSPOSI-TION ERRORS
*(l for o;
o for l)*

1 oak out coke cope home only open took cooked copper objects
2 lap let lip nil dell lace land lard lash large rifle ladder
3 I opened the cupboard doors and saw oranges and other food.
4 A large lumberjack loaded the last of the long, light logs.

Hold Those Anchors

For **Z** anchor F
For **Y** anchor ; L K
For **X** anchor A or F

SPACE BAR

Y KEY

Use J finger.

Type each line twice.

6 jjj jyj jyj yjy jyj jjj jyj jyj yjy jyj
7 jyj yes yes jyj aye aye jyj joy joy jyj
8 jyj; yard of yarn, yield a yawn, a Yule

X KEY

Use S finger.

Type each line twice.

9 sss sxs sxs xsx sxs sss sxs sxs xsx sxs
10 sxs mix mix sxs axe axe sxs tax tax sxs
11 sxs; next taxi, sixty Texans, lax taxes

TECHNIQUE CHECKPOINT

Feet on floor.
Hold home key anchors.

Type lines 12–14 once. Then repeat lines 3 (page 18), 6, and 9.

12 Our teams would not quit because of the   8
13 size and voice of their pep club crowd.   16
14 Their jumps and tricks brought the win.   24
    | 1 | 2 | 3 | 4 | 5 | 6 | 7 | 8

PRETEST

Take two 1-minute timings on line 15, and determine your speed; use the faster rate.

15 play zany yoke pays zest yews taxi jazz
    | 1 | 2 | 3 | 4 | 5 | 6 | 7 | 8

PRACTICE

To Type Faster:
Read copy before typing it.
Aim for smoothness in stroking.

Type each line twice.

16 play flay clay slay shay stay sway away
17 zany lazy hazy haze maze daze doze cozy
18 yoke yolk your you, year yea, yet, yes,
19 pays nays mays jays hays days cays bays
20 zest rest best pest test text next flex
21 yews yaws yams yaps yaks yard yarn yawn
22 taxi tax, lax, axe, axle exam exit mix;
23 jazz nuzzle muzzle puzzle dazzle razzle

POSTTEST

Take two 1-minute timings on line 15, and determine your speed; use the faster rate.
Note your improvement.

5-LETTER WORDS

1 abide affix alarm bakes blade blend cakes charm civic dealt
2 desks dough eight ended equal fancy fifth flags gleam grant
3 guess happy heirs helps issue items ivory labor lapse lathe
4 magic maple mayor occur ought owned parks photo plane range
5 rocks royal sense shade shape taken thank title visit vital
6 voted waist wants whale yacht yield youth acute blank chest

SPACE BAR DRILLS

1 a b c d e f g h i j k l m n o p q r s t u v w x y z a b c d
2 aa bb cc dd ee ff gg hh ii jj kk ll mm nn oo pp qq rr ss tt
3 aaa bbb ccc ddd eee fff ggg hhh iii jjj kkk lll mmm nnn ooo
4 1 2 3 4 5 6 7 8 9 0 1 2 3 4 5 6 7 8 9 0 1 2 3 4 5 6 7 8 9 0
5 11 22 33 44 55 66 77 88 99 00 11 22 33 44 55 66 77 88 99 00
6 111 222 333 444 555 666 777 888 999 000 111 222 333 444 555

TABULATOR KEY DRILLS

Set tab every 8 spaces.

1 aid   air   and   ant   apt   bid   big   bit
2 bow   bud   bus   but   cod   cow   cut   did
3 dig   dog   due   dug   dye   end   eye   fir
4 fit   fix   foe   for   fur   jam   key   lay
5 man   map   may   oak   own   pay   rid   rob
6 rod   row   rub   she   sit   six   sod   the

CAPITALIZATION DRILLS

1 A Alex B Barb C Carl D Dawn E Earl F Faye G Glen H Hope Hal
2 I Inez J Jeff K Kate L Lory M Mike N Nell O Opel P Phil Pam
3 R Rona S Suzy T Troy A Alan B Beth C Chad D Drew E Eric Eva
4 A Alvin B Betty C Carol D David E Edwin F Frank G Garth Gus
5 H Helen J Joann K Kevin L Lloyd M Mavis N Nancy O Olive Ora
6 P Patsy R Randy S Sarah T Twila V Viola R Ronny S Steve Sam

ACCELERATION SENTENCES

1 She is busy with the work but is to go to town for the pen.
2 Jan got the forms for the firm and may also work with them.
3 He may wish to pay them if and when they go to work for us.
4 Both the men may go to town if he pays them for their work.
5 The name of the firm they own is to the right of the forms.
6 The coal firm also pays them when they load down rock jams.

NUMBER DRILLS

1 101 191 181 171 161 151 141 131 121 202 292 282 272 262 252
2 242 232 212 303 393 383 373 363 353 343 323 313 404 494 484
3 474 464 454 434 424 414 505 595 585 575 565 545 535 525 515
4 606 696 686 676 656 646 636 626 616 707 797 787 767 757 747
5 737 727 717 808 898 878 868 858 848 838 828 818 909 989 979
6 969 959 949 939 929 919 090 080 070 060 050 040 030 020 010

SYMBOL DRILLS

1 a!a s@s d#d f$f f%f j&j k*k l(l ;); ;'; ;"; ;-; ;_; ;=; ;+;
2 aq!a sw@s de#d fr$f ft%f ju&j ki*k lo(l ;p); ;p-; ;p_; ;=+;
3 a!!a s@@s d##d f$$f f%%f j&&j k**k l((l ;)); ;--; ;__; ;++;
4 $56 $47 $38 $29 $10 56# 47# 38# 29# 10# 1/2 1/3 1/4 1/5 1/8
5 56% 47% 38% 29% 100% 1 & 2 & 3 & 4 & 5 & 6 & 7 & 8 & 9 & 10
6 (1)* (2)* (3)* (4)* (5)* 1-2 3-4 5-6 7-8 9-10 1 + 2 + 3 = 6

LESSON 11

■ **GOALS**
To control hyphen, diagonal, and question mark keys by touch, holding home key anchors.
To use correct spacing before and after punctuation within the context of sentences.

■ **FORMAT**
Single spacing   40-space line

KEYBOARDING REVIEW

Type each line twice.

1   deft lack vase more haze wing quip jibe
2   Zipp made quick jet flights over Nawbi.

Hold Those Anchors

For - anchor J
For / anchor J
For ? anchor J

 KEY

Use Sem finger.
Do not space before or after hyphens.

Type each line twice.

3   ;;; ;p- ;-; -;- ;-; ;;; ;p- ;-; -;- ;-;
4   ;p- ;-; self-made ;p- ;-; one-third ;-;
5   ;p- ;-; part-time ;p- ;-; one-fifth ;-;

 KEY

Use Sem finger.
Do not space before or after a diagonal.

Type each line twice.

6   ;;; ;/; ;/; /;/ ;/; ;;; ;/; ;/; /;/ ;/;
7   ;/; his/her ;/; her/him ;/; us/them ;/;
8   to/from slow/fast fall/winter April/May

 KEY

Shift of /.
Use Sem finger and left shift key.
Space twice after a question mark.

Type each line twice.

9   ;;; ;/; ;/? ;?; ;?; ;;; ;/; ;/? ;?; ;?;
10 ;/; ;?; now? now? ;?; how? how? ;?;
11 Who? When? Where? What? Why? Next?

PUNCTUATION SPACING

Space once after a semicolon or comma.

Type lines 12–21 once. Note the spacing before and after each punctuation mark.

12 The dance looks nice; it shows balance.
13 The skit was tops; it was so organized.

(Continued on next page)

RIGHT-HAND WORDS

1 mum pun lip yolk lion look loom lump oily holly jolly nippy
2 hip hop him join kink moll poll pink hook hilly lymph puppy
3 mom mop nip loll milk mill noon noun hull milky mummy poppy
4 kin joy oil honk holy hymn hook hunk loop lumpy union onion
5 pin you nun hoop link jump limp lily loin hooky nylon pupil
6 ink ill inn only pool pull pump upon pill knoll jumpy imply

LEFT-HAND WORDS

1 act bad car acre babe beat cage data ears gates safes taste
2 ads bag cat acts beet beds card date ease great seats taxed
3 are bar ear adds bags beef care draw east grade serve tests
4 ate bat eat ages bare bees cars dear edge grace staff texts
5 art bed far area bats best case debt eggs greet state tract
6 ade bet fed arts bear beer cast deed ever grate sweet trade

ALTERNATE-HAND SENTENCES

1 The lane to the lake may make the auto turn and go to town.
2 The man and the dog did go to the lake to dig for the dock.
3 The duck, the fox, and the fish make problems for the girl.
4 They may wish to blame me for the fight to end the problem.
5 She is busy with the work but is to go to town for the pen.
6 I am to go to work for the audit firm by the eighth of May.

DOUBLE-LETTER WORDS

1 burr ebbs eggs been less need fill look keep soon well tool
2 book will seem toss sees feel pool good pass mill miss ball
3 goods green skill added seeks proof small radii guess dizzy
4 fluff abbey sunny ditto apple gummy petty upper sleep shall
5 succeeds quitters withhold slowness grammar vacuums shopper
6 possible followed carriage occasion shipper accused cabbage

2-LETTER WORDS

1 ad am an as at ax be by do el go ha he hi ho id if in is it
2 la ma me my no of oh or ow ox oz pa re so to up us we ye yo

3-LETTER WORDS

1 aid air and ant apt bid big bit bow bud bus but cod cow cut
2 did die dig dog due dug dye end eye fir fit fix foe fur got
3 jam key lay man map may men oak own pay pep rid rob rod row
4 rub she sir sit six sod sue the tie tow via wit woe ago jet
5 bay can cad ink lab max van age boy fly had one par put sky
6 act add ads are art egg eve fee few sad sat saw see set sew

4-LETTER WORDS

1 able acid also bake bale band cake came chat days dial diet
2 else eyes fair fame felt firm game gift girl hair half halt
3 idle jury kept keys lake lame land mail make maps nail name
4 owns paid pair push rich ride rise self send sick tame than
5 vote wait want ants arms auto bird bite boat cite clay coal
6 does down dust fish flat fuel glad goal grow hand help horn

Space twice after a colon.	14	Two courses are open: science and art.
	15	Three members left: Ann, Lee, and Joe.
Space twice after a period at the end of a sentence.	16	Send it to me. I can print it so fast.
	17	The skirt is plaid. It matches a suit.
Space once after a period used with personal initials and titles.	18	Ms. Kebo asked Dr. T. S. Laos to speak.
	19	Mr. and Mrs. Lark were honored at noon.
Do not space after a period used with degrees or with geographic abbreviations.	20	She earned her Ph.D. from Oregon State.
	21	The U.S.A. and the U.S.S.R. were there.

Type lines 22–31 once. Again, note the spacing before and after each punctuation mark.

Space once after a comma.	22	When Jean called me, I was not at home.
	23	Send them red, white, and green copies.
Do not space before or after a hyphen.	24	The up-to-date calendar was so helpful.
	25	His mother-in-law is the new president.
Do not space before or after a dash (two hyphens).	26	That machine--the black one--is broken.
	27	The office gives good service--on time.
Do not space before or after a diagonal.	28	The fall/winter catalog has new colors.
	29	The on/off button is on the right side.
Space twice after a question mark.	30	Do you want to go to the movies? When?
	31	Are you getting a computer? What kind?

LESSON 12

CLINIC

■ **GOALS**
To strengthen reaches on third, home, and bottom rows.
To type 20 words a minute for 2 minutes with 4 or fewer errors.

■ **FORMAT**
Single spacing   40-space line

KEYBOARDING REVIEW

Type each line twice.

1 buzz lynx jury quip wave oxen game fern
2 Did they know if the current was ac/dc?

ALPHABETIC WORDS (CONTINUED)

P
31 page pale pail perk peat pert pile pike pine plea plop plot
32 paint pants paste pearl peach peace place plate pound pride

Q
33 quid quit quack quake queen quest quill quote quiet quavers
34 quip quiz quail quart quell quick quilt quirt quash quintet

R
35 rage raid read rest rink ripe roam roar rule rung rate ream
36 ranch raise reign reach rough round rainy recap rigid royal

S
37 sail said scar scan seal serf shin show skim soft span star
38 saint sauce scare scold serve share since slang smart solve

T
39 tale tart test teak them thus tilt time tone toil trap turn
40 taste taunt tempt tease there theme torch touch trade twist

U
41 urge used ugly undo uses unless unload unkind unfair unfold
42 undue upset union urban unite usher uncle until using under

V
43 vane vase veal veer vice view volt vote vast verb vine vise
44 vague verse value valve voice vault vocal verge vouch vowel

W
45 wade walk west were when whip word work wrap wise weld wing
46 waist waved weigh wedge wheat while worst would wreck wrist

X
47 flex hoax jinx apex text exam axle taxi axis exit waxy foxy
48 fixed mixed sixth exact extra relax sixty exile latex toxic

Y
49 yarn yawn yard year yell yelp yoke yolk your yule yowl yoga
50 yeast yield young yours yacht yearn youth yummy yucca yards

Z
51 zig zest zeal zinc zing zone zoom zero zany zips zoos zebra
52 zigzag zinnia zipper zodiac zircon zoology zealous zucchini

ALPHABETIC SENTENCES

1 Quietly, six zebras jumped back over the eight brown rafts.
2 Park my gray, bronze jet and quickly wax it for five hours.
3 Five more wax jugs have been glazed quickly for two people.
4 Jo quoted two dozen passages from Val's chemistry textbook.
5 The disc jockey won six bronze plaques for helping Mr. Van.
6 Ben auctioned off the pink gems and my quartz jewelry next.

SPEED SENTENCES

1 The book is new and will not be sold at the fair next year.
2 It is not the right time for us to talk about all the work.
3 The juice in that glass was cold, clear, and good to drink.
4 The light is dim, but it will give us all the light I need.
5 The bird flew way up in the sky to get away from the smoke.
6 We would like to know if you are going to the play at five.

Take a 1-minute timing on each line. Then proofread and circle errors.

Third row   3   They will type quiet quips from a page.   8

Home row   4   Jed had asked for the glass in a flash.   8

Bottom row   5   Zach, move that ax back into that cave.   8

| 1 | 2 | 3 | 4 | 5 | 6 | 7 | 8

PRACTICE

Check Your Hands

Palms low.

Hands flat.

All fingers curved.

Hold home key anchors.

Type lines 6–10 twice each.

6   rook work lurk dirk kirk keep kelp kilt

7   full foul fowl file fire four fort fore

8   jolt jets joke just jerk jugs jowl jaws

9   tort were quit quip tour prep pour were

10   your type true pert pipe wipe ripe prop

Type lines 11–15 twice each.

11   wade jade fade fads gads dads lads lass

12   hash mash cash wash rash gash lash dash

13   gall fall hall hale kale sale dale gale

14   skid slid sled fled flag slag shag shad

15   drag lark lake khan fast load glad clad

Type lines 16–20 twice each.

16   pan, tan, man, fan, ran, van, ban, can,

17   bend bind mine mice mace calm acme came

18   move cove cave nave vain vein vine vane

19   nabs cabs cubs cobs cons conk cone cane

20   mix, fix, nix, ace, size daze maze viz.

POSTTEST

Take a 1-minute timing on each of lines 3–5. Then proofread and circle errors. Note your improvement.

30-SECOND SPEED TIMINGS

Take two 30-second speed timings on lines 21 and 22. Then take two 30-second speed timings on lines 23 and 24. Or type each sentence twice.

21   I wanted to go down to the shore today,   8

22   but I think it will be much too chilly.   16

23   When I can go down to the shore, I will   8

24   find out if any friends can go as well.   16

| 1 | 2 | 3 | 4 | 5 | 6 | 7 | 8

SUPPLEMENTARY MATERIAL

DRILLS

ALPHABETIC WORDS

A
1 ache aged aide arch aunt able acid acre afar ajar alas apex
2 aisle abide about above abuse acorn actor acute adapt agent

B
3 baby bias body busy bare bark bike bell belt bend beak brag
4 batch beach birch black board boast braid burst brave bride

C
5 calm cent chap clam coat crew curb czar cane cede cord cuff
6 caulk cease chant clang coast crane curve catch chief cling

D
7 damp deal dine done drag dust deck dent disk down drip dime
8 dance depth ditch dodge draft drove doubt dread drawl drone

E
9 each earn ease east edge else etch easy echo ever evil emit
10 earth eaves eight elect erase evoke event excel every entry

F
11 fact feat file flaw folk from fuse fang fend film flip form
12 false fence first flare force frame frost fault field flour

G
13 gain germ gift glib goat grim gulf gait gear girl glad gown
14 gauge ghost gland glare gouge grand grind guest grain grape

H
15 hail hear hike hold hulk hark helm hide honk huge hire howl
16 harsh heist hoist hutch haste hence horse hunch hotel husky

I
17 inch itch idle into iron item idea imps ills irks ibex iris
18 icing ideal igloo image imply index inept inert infer inlet

J
19 jest jilt jinx join joke jump jugs just jury jade jail jabs
20 jaunt jeans joist judge juice jelly jewel joker jolly juror

K
21 keel knot keep kelp kemp kick kiss kite knew knee knit knob
22 knack knead knife knock kayak kitty knows kinks khaki karat

L
23 lace left lick loft lump lynx lack lash lend lens life loud
24 lapse large ledge leave lodge lymph lapel legal logic lower

M
25 made mast mesh melt mild mint mole mold mule must mask mere
26 month midst march match merge mound mouth movie music motor

N
27 name nail near news none nose numb next nice noun note neck
28 nerve niece night ninth noise north notch nurse nudge noble

O
29 once oath ouch oboe odor oily obey open only omit oval odds
30 ought ounce ocean offer often orbit olive order onion other

GOALS
To use the shift lock to type all capitals.
To use three tabular keys to set a tab, to clear a tab, and to indent a new paragraph.

*24 words a minute for 2 minutes with 4 or fewer errors.

FORMAT
Single spacing   50-space line

KEYBOARDING SKILLS

Type each line twice.

Words   1 aqua wish face join milk cozy play sobs over text
Speed   2 The girls may make a profit if they sing for Dot.
Accuracy 3 Just pack my box with five dozen quilts and rugs.

1-MINUTE TIMINGS

Take two 1-minute timings on lines 4–5, or type lines 4–5 twice.

4 When you go for a ride in a car, take a look from   10
5 the window and view the sights as you move along.   20

| 1 | 2 | 3 | 4 | 5 | 6 | 7 | 8 | 9 | 10

ACCURACY

Accuracy lines should be typed as a paragraph.

Type lines 6–10 twice.

6 aaa aye aaa air aaa ail aaa aim aaa aria aaa alma
7 eee elf eee ewe eee eye eee end eee even eee earn
8 iii six iii did iii win iii fin iii city iii give
9 ooo oak ooo sod ooo own ooo ore ooo oboe ooo oleo
10 uuu sub uuu cub uuu rub uuu cup uuu sure uuu much

SPEED

Speed lines should be repeated individually.

11 isle fuel flay gown keys then she for and the own
12 fish sign form wish duck they eye icy dig sow bug
13 pale idle gush slay torn roam sue hay sob man oak
14 goal bush firm chap lake city pay wit fur irk urn
15 lead coal pane risk half kept has lot yam cut fix

Type each line twice.

TYPING ALL-CAPITAL LETTERS

A formatting technique.

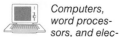 *Computers, word processors, and electronic typewriters have a special display feature called **boldface**.*

1. Press the shift lock. It is above one or both of the shift keys.
2. Type the words that are to be in all capitals.

3. Release the shift lock by touching a shift key. (**Caution:** Release the lock before typing a stroke that, like a hyphen, cannot be typed as a capital.)

16 I need ONE MORE letter to FINISH the word puzzle.
17 Our team is FIRST-RATE. We WON the CHAMPIONSHIP.
18 MARILEE and KIPP and BO were selected as LEADERS.

JOB 149/150 C. (CONTINUED)

month we will offer one to improve your writing skills. You may attend both sessions this month, but you must get approval from your shift supervisor. This new, exciting seminar will start on Monday, May 2. You may, if you wish, bring a recorder to the session. GF

JOB 149/150 D. BUSINESS INVOICE 38644

Standard format. Workbook 251.

[*To*] Davidson Office Furniture, 385 King Avenue, Dayton, OH 45420

10	Filing cabinets, #F780		
	[*Unit price*] 62.50	[*Amount*]	625.00
2	Filing cabinets, #F880		
	[*Unit price*] 72.50	[*Amount*]	145.00
6	Boxes of file folders		
	[*Unit price*] 7.75	[*Amount*]	46.50
4	Boxes of file guides		
	[*Unit price*] 2.50	[*Amount*]	10.00
	Total amount due		826.50

JOB 149/150 E. TWO-PAGE REPORT WITH TABLE AND FOOTNOTE

Double spacing. 5-space tab.

METHODS OF TRANSPORTATION
By James Rhoades

INTRODUCTION

The rising fuel costs in this country have had a profound effect on the driving habits and the means of transportation used by both young and old. The May issue of Car Report states that "student driving habits will change because of the rapidly rising fuel costs this nation is experiencing."[1] It appears that fuel costs will affect the methods by which students commute to their schools.

STATEMENT OF THE PROBLEM

The problem of this study is to reveal how students at Valley High School have changed their methods of transportation to and from school.

BACKGROUND OF THE PROBLEM

Valley High School is located between Greenville, Loan Oak, and Sulphur Springs on a 20-acre tract of land. Because of this central location, many students commute to and from school. In the past, students have commuted by driving alone in their own cars, by driving with other students, or by riding the bus.

FINDINGS

A total of 96 seniors were surveyed in the study—25 of them drove alone, 15 carpooled with other students, and 56 rode the school bus. Of the 40 students who drove cars (either alone or in a car pool), 35 percent drove midsize cars, 46 percent drove small cars, and 19 percent drove large cars.

An additional finding of this study revealed the miles-per-gallon averages for all students' cars. Table 1 below reveals that 55 percent of the cars obtained an average of 21 to 30 miles per gallon. Only one-half that number (27.5 percent) were able to obtain from 10 to 20 miles per gallon. Five of the students indicated that their cars were getting over 30 miles per gallon.

TABLE 1
MILES-PER-GALLON ESTIMATES

Miles per Gallon	Number of Drivers	Percentage
Less than 10	2	5.0
10 to 20	11	27.5
21 to 30	22	55.0
31 or more	5	12.5
Total	40	100.0

1. Sheila Torrance, "Driving in the '80s," Car Report, May 1986, p. 27.

TAB STOPS

A formatting technique.

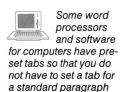

Some word processors and software for computers have pre-set tabs so that you do not have to set a tab for a standard paragraph indention.

To make the carriage, carrier, or cursor skip to a selected point, set a tab stop at that point and use the tab key.

1. Eliminate any stop that may be in the way: Press the all-clear key if your machine has one; or move the carriage or carrier to the right margin, and then hold down the tab clear key as you return the carriage or carrier.

2. Set the tab stop by moving the carriage or carrier to the point where you want it and pressing the tab set key.

3. Test the setting: Bring the carriage or carrier back to the left margin, and then press the tabulator key or bar—hold it down firmly until the carriage or carrier stops moving. It should stop where you set the tab stop.

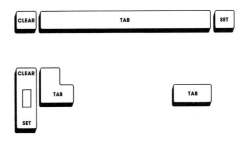

Practice: Set a tab stop 5 spaces in from the left margin, and type *The* indented on three lines.

→ 5

     The
     The
     The

INDENTING FOR PARAGRAPHS

A formatting technique.

When a paragraph is indented, as it is below, the indention is 5 spaces. Each indention counts as 5 strokes (1 word), the same as 5 space bar strokes would count. Use the tab to indent line 19 in the paragraph below.

1-MINUTE TIMINGS

Take two 1-minute timings on lines 19–21. Use the paper bail to proofread your copy. Circle your errors and figure your speed on each timing. Format: Double spacing. Begin with the carriage or carrier positioned at the left margin.

19   To watch the squirrel is a good lesson, some 10

20   say. It just takes time to zip from limb to limb 20

21   and fix a place to put the food it hopes to save. 30

| 1 | 2 | 3 | 4 | 5 | 6 | 7 | 8 | 9 | 10

LESSON 14

■ **GOALS**
To use the backspace key to center items horizontally.
To center items horizontally (across) on a page.

■ **FORMAT**
Single spacing   50-space line

KEYBOARDING SKILLS

Type each line twice.

Words 1 know deck file pogo jobs quay mare vote oxen hazy

Speed 2 This girl is to go to the field to work for them.

Accuracy 3 Packy quietly boxed these frozen jams with vigor.

JOB 149/150 A. LETTER

Block format. Workbook 247–248. Body 180 words.

Ms. Helene R. Casselberry, 238 Atlantic Avenue, Wakefield, RI 02879, Dear Ms. Casselberry: Subject: Freshman Days

Congratulations on your admission to Middlestate College! It is a pleasure to welcome you as one of our incoming freshmen for this academic year. To make your first few days at Middlestate more enjoyable, I'll briefly preview a few of the activities we have planned for all incoming freshmen. ¶ On Monday, September 11, you will be with your campus sponsor to take a tour of the campus. You will also view a short movie about our campus entitled The YOUniversity. ¶ On Tuesday, September 12, you will meet with your adviser so that your first-semester class schedule can be arranged. After lunch you will have free time to visit with your friends. ¶ On Wednesday, September 13, you will be spending both your morning and afternoon hours in the dorm to which you have been assigned. Several activities have been planned by the Dorm Council. ¶ We look forward to your year at Middlestate. If we can help you in any way, please feel free to contact us. We have enclosed a copy of the fall calendar for scheduled sports and social activities. Sincerely, Sheila Beach, Freshman Committee Chairperson, cc: Brad Calvin, Anne Weston, PS: Your dormitory assignment and the name and address of your roommate will be sent to you around the middle of August.

JOB 149/150 B. NEWSLETTER ARTICLE

Standard format.

```
         THE YEAR AT A GLANCE                12

      By Andrea McBain, President            31

        (23 Lines of 50 Spaces)             47

                past
      This year was one of the most          57

succ essful we have had ever in the pub-     64

lishing business.  The leading titles        72

for the year (and this should come as        79
```

no surprise) to anyone were all in the computer-related area. Our last quarterly earnings report revealed that computer texts outsold the noncomputer texts by more than two-to-one. ¶ Our research has shown us that there is an overwhelming need for quality computer-aided instruction (CAI) courseware. In the planning stages of this effort, we need to be aware of the individual problems teachers may have in using CAI courseware. We need to increase our efforts this year to expand the number of software support programs for the high-sales textbooks. Nothing will impact our sales more significantly in the coming year than the quality of our software programs.

¶ A special taskforce has been organized to expand our work in this area. Representatives from the high technology division will be working with us in the next 6 months to accelerate software development for all major titles. We look forward to an exciting, innovative year in product expansion.

JOB 149/150 C. MEMO

Standard format. Workbook 249.

[To:] Tony Adams, Nancy Chang, Alice Corbett, Juan Lopez, Stanley Posnick, [From:] Training Director, [Subject:] Writing Seminar

Last month we offered a seminar on planning meetings, and this

(Continued on next page)

Take two 1-minute timings on lines 4–5, or type lines 4–5 twice.

4 Can you think of all the things that you would do 10
5 if you could do just as you wanted to for a week? 20
| 1 | 2 | 3 | 4 | 5 | 6 | 7 | 8 | 9 | 10

ACCURACY

Type lines 6–10 twice.

6 see butt happy errors flivver carriage occasional
7 off poll dizzy middle blabber possible bookkeeper
8 zoo buff radii sizzle powwows followed additional
9 inn ebbs gummy bottle accused slowness beginnings
10 Hannah took a dotted Swiss dress to the Mall Inn.

SPEED

Type each line twice.

11 formal prisms blend panel busy chap cut ham is it
12 social glands visit field torn sign rid air to do
13 eighty blames audit forms half fuel apt owl of an
14 profit island slept right tidy cork fix hem am so
15 The theme for the eighth panel is When to Fix It.

**FORMATTING:
HORIZONTAL
CENTERING**

Workbook 15–16.

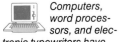

Computers, word processors, and electronic typewriters have an automatic centering feature. You can center a line without backspacing it.

To center horizontally:

1. Set the carriage or carrier at the center. (See "Getting Ready to Type.")
2. Find the backspace key (upper left or right corner of the keyboard).
3. Backspace once for every two letters or spaces.
4. Say the strokes (including spaces) in pairs to yourself, depressing the backspace key once after you say each pair. If you have an odd letter left over after calling off all pairs, do *not* backspace for it.

   Example: Center these
                  to center

5. Type the material. It should appear in the middle of the paper.

Note: When centering several lines, set a tab stop at the center point.

Practice: Type each of the two drills shown below. Use half sheets of paper. Format: Begin on line 14; double-space.

Check: Fold your paper in half. Compare your fold with the arrows in the illustration.

↓   ↓
Center these   It is easy
lines by using   to center
the backspace key.   by backspacing.

JOB 14 A. CENTERING
Format the terms shown below by centering them on a full sheet of paper. Double-space. Begin on line 14. Leave 5 blank lines between each group of terms.

mainframe   BASIC   input
minicomputer   PASCAL   memory
microcomputer   FORTRAN   CPU
terminal   COBOL   output
network   LOGO   program

Example: My determination to become a valuable asset to your firm is greater than ever. I look forward to a favorable decision on my employment with your company.

Practice. Compose and type the final paragraph for a follow-up letter. Use any one or more of the ideas suggested on page 247.

JOB G. FOLLOW-UP LETTER

Compose and type a complete follow-up letter using the three paragraphs you composed as Practice exercises. Add the following parts to complete the letter: (1) return address, (2) date line, (3) inside address, (4) salutation, (5) complimentary closing, and (6) signature line.

LESSONS 149/150

TEST

■ **GOALS**
To type 40/5'/5e.
To type a letter, a newsletter article, a memo, an invoice, and
   a report with a table and a footnote.

■ **FORMAT**
Double spacing   60-space line   5-space tab

PREVIEW PRACTICE

Accuracy

Speed

Type each line twice as a preview to the 5-minute timings below.

1 only quite explore equipment recognize enjoyable physically
2 entire mental socks make work also that both for and fit of

5-MINUTE TIMINGS

Take two 5-minute timings on lines 3–19.

3   Hiking is one of the best ways to keep in top physical   12
4 condition. Not only does it help your vital organs to keep   24
5 working well, it might also help improve your entire mental   36
6 attitude. It is important that a beginning hiker recognize   48
7 the rules that make hiking more enjoyable. First, one must   60
8 be comfortable while on the hike. All the clothing and the   72
9 shoes must fit quite well. A hiker should always wear good   84
10 shoes that are sturdy and well-fitting socks. The clothing   96
11 should be very protective for use in rugged country. Every   108
12 person should practice keeping both arms free while hiking.   120
13 This means that each hiker must carry all that equipment in   132
14 a backpack. Carrying a backpack requires that every person   144
15 use very good posture; otherwise, many aches might develop.   156
16 The beginning hiker should start with short distances. The   168
17 longer hike should be postponed until the person is in good   180
18 physical condition. Hiking truly provides a way to explore   192
19 the country and become physically fit.   200

| 1 | 2 | 3 | 4 | 5 | 6 | 7 | 8 | 9 | 10 | 11 | 12 | SI 1.50

GOAL
To center items horizontally on a page.

FORMAT
Single spacing   50-space line   5-space tab

KEYBOARDING SKILLS

Type each line twice.

Words   1 both cram dyed life give junk quip owes axle size
Speed   2 Six or eight pens go to the man with the oak cot.
Accuracy 3 Quickly box five dozen afghans for W. M. Jeptham.

ACCURACY

Type lines 4–8 twice.

4 on ear kin vat yip acre pill race upon face phony
5 we imp vex hip tag pink case limp zest lion cedar
6 in arc pin age you date jump were honk ease hilly
7 be joy tax oil fad noun tact yolk gear mink verse
8 After Kip agreed, John gave my dad a faster kiln.

SPEED

Type each line twice.

9 find this that who his and why him my be if do no
10 when wish like but out may for she me or am in to
11 them look they our the her got how by us it so up
12 what mine type now can fun put set of at on as go
13 She is to be there at a time when we can see her.

2-MINUTE TIMINGS

To figure speed for 1 minute, divide by 2 the total number of words typed for 2 minutes.

Errors, however, are not divided but recorded as a total for the entire timing.

Take two 2-minute timings on lines 14–18. Use your paper bail to proofread your copy. Circle your errors and figure your speed on each timing. Format: Double spacing.

14   Watch the river move across the plain and on   10
15 to the bluff beyond. It has a tale to tell about   20
16 the ones who have gone this way. The men and the   30
17 women were not unique. They just had the zeal to   40
18 take the extra risk.   44

   | 1 | 2 | 3 | 4 | 5 | 6 | 7 | 8 | 9 | 10

COMPOSING FOLLOW-UP LETTERS

The final step in the job application process is writing a follow-up letter. After you have had your interview, you should immediately send the interviewer a written thank-you for interviewing you. Note how each numbered paragraph of the letter shown below achieves the goals of a follow-up letter.

① In the **opening paragraph,** you should express appreciation for the interview and reaffirm your interest in the job.

② In the **second paragraph,** you may:
   a. Add new information that might be helpful in revealing your qualifications.
   b. Express pleasure at being considered a candidate for the job.
   c. Tell how you feel about the job now that the interview has been completed.

③ In the **final paragraph,** you may do one of the following:
   a. Express even greater interest in the job.
   b. Mention that you are looking forward to a favorable decision.
   c. Make yourself available for a second interview.

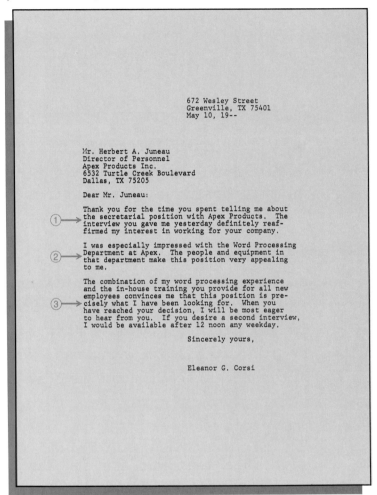

672 Wesley Street
Greenville, TX 75401
May 10, 19--

Mr. Herbert A. Juneau
Director of Personnel
Apex Products Inc.
6532 Turtle Creek Boulevard
Dallas, TX 75205

Dear Mr. Juneau:

① Thank you for the time you spent telling me about the secretarial position with Apex Products. The interview you gave me yesterday definitely reaffirmed my interest in working for your company.

② I was especially impressed with the Word Processing Department at Apex. The people and equipment in that department make this position very appealing to me.

③ The combination of my word processing experience and the in-house training you provide for all new employees convinces me that this position is precisely what I have been looking for. When you have reached your decision, I will be most eager to hear from you. If you desire a second interview, I would be available after 12 noon any weekday.

Sincerely yours,

Eleanor G. Corsi

Before you compose and type your own follow-up letter, you will have the opportunity to work on each of the separate paragraphs necessary in a follow-up letter. Study the examples provided here and on the next page, and then compose your own paragraphs for a follow-up letter.

Paragraph 1

Objectives. Say thank-you. Reaffirm interest.

Example: Thank you for the interesting time you spent with me this past Wednesday. My visit with you and the other members of your staff made me realize how very enjoyable it would be to work for your company.

Practice. Assume that the letter of application you wrote for Job E resulted in an interview. Compose and type the first paragraph of a follow-up letter concerning the job for which you applied.

Paragraph 2

Objectives. Strengthen your qualifications. Express pleasure to be a candidate.

Example: You mentioned that three people were being considered seriously for this secretarial position. I'm very glad to be one of those people. My extensive secretarial training would prove very beneficial for your company and would provide you with the administrative expertise you requested in the newspaper advertisement.

Practice. Compose and type the second paragraph for a follow-up letter. Use any one or more of the ideas suggested on this page.

Paragraph 3

Objectives. Express greater interest in the job. Appear optimistic about the decision.

JOB 15 A. CENTERING

Format the 5 lines below by centering on a half sheet of paper. Double-space. Begin on line 12.

OFFICE FURNITURE
Desk
Chair
Credenza
Bookcase

JOB 15 C. CENTERING

Format the 6 lines below by centering on a half sheet of paper. Double-space. Begin on line 11.

TEAM SPORTS
baseball
soccer
basketball
hockey
football

JOB 15 B. CENTERING

Format the 5 lines below by centering on a half sheet of paper. Double-space. Begin on line 12.

KINDS OF DOCUMENTS
letters
reports
tables
forms

JOB 15 D. CENTERING

Format the 7 lines below by centering on a half sheet of paper. Double-space. Begin on line 10.

PROGRAMMING LANGUAGES
BASIC
PASCAL
FORTRAN
COBOL
LOGO
RPG

LESSON 16

■ **GOALS**
To count vertical lines on a page.
To center items vertically (up and down) on a page.

■ **FORMAT**
Single spacing   50-space line   5-space tab and center tab

KEYBOARDING SKILLS

Type each line twice.

Words   1 away vice jeep high kiln form ribs exit zero quid

Speed   2 Jan works for us but may wish to work for Pamela.

Accuracy   3 Six jet-black vans quietly zip through wet farms.

Application forms vary from one company to another, but all ask for basically the same information. The illustrations at the right show two sides of an application form. This form, like most others, asks the applicant to provide information as follows (note that the numbers correspond to those included with the illustrations):

① **Date.** Include the month, day, and year.

② **Personal Data.** Be sure to provide your complete permanent address (and temporary address, if applicable)—your street address, city, state, and ZIP Code.

③ **Social Security Number.** Be prepared to fill in your social security number, because every person must have one when applying for a job.

④ **Type of Work.** A company will often inquire as to the type of position you are seeking. You may also be asked the salary you expect and the date you would be available for work. If you have special machine skills, you might be asked to identify your competencies on these machines.

⑤ **Education.** Many application forms ask for the name of your high school as well as any colleges or business schools, the dates you attended, and the courses you completed.

⑥ **Health.** Answer honestly all questions on health. The questions are essential for insurance purposes, as well as to find out who should be notified in case of a medical emergency.

⑦ **Employment History.** Employers want to know about previous work experience. Past work experience may help you obtain a better entry-level position, so be as honest and as thorough as you can in completing this section.

⑧ **References.** To complete this section, use the list of references that you included in your résumé. References should be people such as past employers and former teachers, who can attest to your character, work habits, and work potential.

⑨ **Signature.** DO NOT FORGET TO SIGN THE APPLICATION FORM in ink—and date it, too, if necessary.

JOB F. APPLICATION FORM
Apply for a job for which you are qualified. Workbook 243–246.

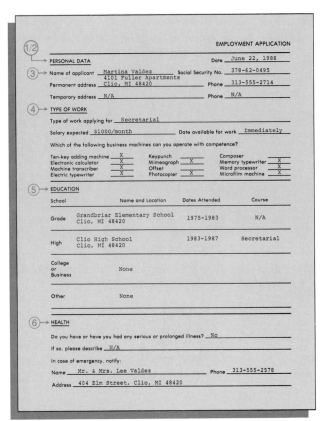

Application Form, Page 1

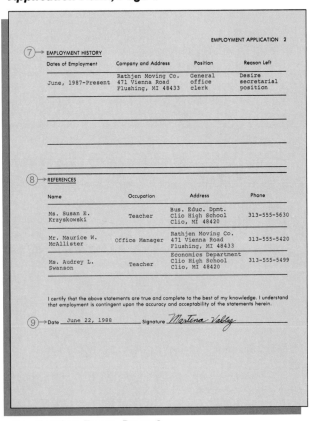

Application Form, Page 2

ACCURACY

Type lines 4–8 twice.

4 tr tram true trek tray trip trim trap trust tribe

5 as last cast fast wasp mast ease vast tease aspen

6 re care real tore pore sore wore lore flare chore

7 op drop stop flop crop open rope hope scope slope

8 ew brew flew crew stew drew chew grew strew shrew

SPEED

Type each line twice.

9 ful grateful faithful careful fateful tactful ful

10 est greatest interest nearest biggest longest est

11 ing thinking swimming sailing sending writing ing

12 ble portable probable taxable capable visible ble

13 ure fixtures features mixture futures torture ure

2-MINUTE TIMINGS

SI means "syllabic intensity"—the average number of syllables per word. A paragraph with all one-syllable words would have an SI of 1.00. The higher the SI, the more difficult the copy.

Take two 2-minute timings on lines 14–18. Use your paper bail to proofread your copy. Circle your errors and figure your speed on each timing. Format: Double spacing.

14   There is no equal to the flavor of ice cream   10

15 on hot, humid days. Choices of all types are out   20

16 to engage the eye, and the snappy clerks will fix   30

17 just the mix and size to suit you best. A cup or   40

18 a cone will be fine.   44

| 1 | 2 | 3 | 4 | 5 | 6 | 7 | 8 | 9 | 10 | SI 1.13

MEASURING FOR VERTICAL SPACING

Most typewriters space 6 lines to an inch. Standard typing paper is 11 inches long, so there are 11 × 6 = 66 lines on a full page or 33 lines on a half page. Some special and imported typewriters space 5¼ lines to an inch, giving 57 lines on a full page and 28 lines on a half page. A4 metric paper is slightly longer—70 lines to the page.

Practice: (1) Insert a sheet of paper, and count the single-spaced lines.

(2) Type the word *single* on six consecutive lines; then measure the lines with a ruler to see how much space they occupy.

```
 ┌──┬─┐ 1  single double
 │  │ │ 2  single ------
 │  │ │ 3  single double
 │  │ │ 4  single ------
 │  │ │ 5  single double
 └─1│ │ 6  single ------
```

JOB E. LETTER OF APPLICATION COMPOSED FROM A CLASSIFIED AD

Compose a letter of application from the information provided in one of the two classified ads below. Select the ad that most closely resembles the type of position for which you would like to apply and for which you are better qualified.

SECRETARY

The Dallas Morning News has an opening in the Data Processing Department for a secretary.

All interested applicants must type 50 wam, take shorthand at 80 wam, use transcribing equipment, and have at least two years of secretarial training and/or experience. You must be a self-motivator and work with little or no supervision.

We offer excellent working conditions and company benefits.

Send a letter of application and résumé to:

**PERSONNEL OFFICE
THE DALLAS MORNING NEWS
2400 ABRAMS ROAD
DALLAS, TX 75214**

An Equal Opportunity Employer

DATA ENTRY CLERK

Southwest Oil & Gas Company has an opening for a data entry clerk.

This is an entry-level position within our accounting department. Qualifications include dependability and willingness to learn. Applicant must have had some training in using data entry and/or word processing equipment.

Excellent benefits include a comprehensive medical and dental program, disability income protection, and free parking.

If interested, send a letter of application and résumé to:

**PERSONNEL DEPARTMENT
SOUTHWEST OIL & GAS COMPANY
504 STANLEY PLACE
TEMPE, AZ 85281**

SOGCO is an Equal Opportunity Employer

FILLING OUT APPLICATION FORMS

The third step in the job application process is the completion of an application form. Most business firms have the applicant fill out an application form either before or after the interview.

Before viewing a sample application form, you might find the following suggestions helpful when you are asked to complete such a form:

1. *Be neat and accurate.* Above all else, fill in the application form neatly, and be sure to check for spelling and/or grammatical errors. Make corrections carefully.

2. *Follow instructions.* Print neatly. If you are asked to type, then be sure to align all the typewritten responses on the lines provided for that purpose. Try to fill in all the blanks; but if certain items do not apply to you, print or type "Not Applicable" or "N/A" in the space provided for your answer.

3. *Do not omit continuous dates.* If you are asked to supply the dates you attended high school, be sure to enter all dates—from the beginning school year to the ending school year. If you enter your years of employment, do not omit any years that you worked.

Note: There will be many differences on application forms from different companies. Many companies are in the process of revising their application blanks to comply with existing or pending regulations regarding nondiscriminatory questions. Employers are no longer permitted to ask for the specific age of a person (age ranges are permitted because employers need to know whether an applicant is under age and needs a work permit or is eligible for social security benefits). Other questions that may not be asked are those regarding marital status, race, religion, and nationality.

FORMATTING: VERTICAL CENTERING

Workbook 17–18.

To place copy in the vertical center of a page, follow these steps:

1. Count the lines (including blanks) that the copy will occupy when typed.
2. Subtract that number from the available number of lines on your paper.
3. Divide the difference by 2 to find the number of the line on which you should begin typing (drop any fraction).

Example: To center 5 double-spaced lines on a half page, you need 9 lines for copy (5 typed, 4 blank); 33 − 9 = 24, and 24 ÷ 2 = 12. Begin typing on line 12.

Practice: Center these lines vertically and horizontally on a half sheet of paper. Use double spacing.

```
To center double-spaced
      lines vertically,
→you must count every
     typed line and all
      the blank lines.
```

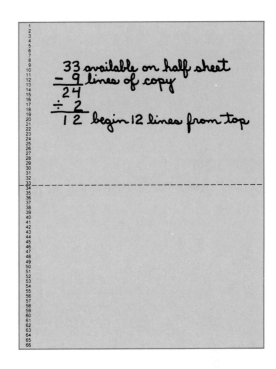

33 available on half sheet
− 9 lines of copy
24
÷ 2
12 begin 12 lines from top

Check: When finished typing, fold paper from top to bottom. The crease should be in the center, close to the point indicated by the arrow.

JOB 16 A. CENTERING
Format: Center vertically and horizontally. Half sheet of paper. Double spacing.

FREQUENTLY MISSPELLED WORDS
accommodate
questionnaire
judgment
counseling
edition
→ personnel
immediately
pertinent
correspondence
categories

JOB 16 B. CENTERING
Format: Center vertically and horizontally. Full sheet of paper. Double spacing.

```
PARTS OF THE TYPEWRITER
Backspace Key
Carriage or Carrier
Margin Stops
Paper Bail
Paper Guide
→Paper Release
Platen
Return Key
Shift Lock Key
Space Bar
Tab/Tabulator
```

The circled numbers refer to explanations on page 243.

2110 Ellen Lane
Memphis, TN 38109
May 22, 19--

Mr. Samuel Davis
A to Z Contractors, Inc.
4701 Hanna Drive
Memphis, TN 38128

Dear Mr. Davis:

① One of your employees, Chris Corsi, mentioned that you have a secretarial position available at A to Z Contractors, Inc. I would like to be considered as an applicant for this position.

② My typing rate of 65 words a minute and my shorthand speed of 120 words a minute will enable me to serve your company as a competent office worker. In addition, I possess a knowledge of filing procedures and have received special training on telephone usage, as you will see in the enclosed résumé.

③ In addition to these specific office skills, I have also been an active participant at several regional competitions for parliamentary procedure. These activities have provided me with valuable human relations and oral presentation skills.

④ I am definitely interested in working for A to Z Contractors. I will telephone your office on June 4 to arrange for an interview with you at your convenience. If you wish to speak with me before that date, please telephone me at 901-555-1212.

Sincerely,

Janice L. Dale

Janice L. Dale

Enclosure

LETTER OF APPLICATION

■ GOALS
To spread-center data.
To center announcements horizontally and vertically on a
   page.
■ FORMAT
Single spacing   50-space line   5-space tab

KEYBOARDING SKILLS

Type each line twice.

Words   1 fact bits girl with joke moon pulp quiz void exit
Speed   2 The eighty bushels of corn may be profit for Len.
Accuracy 3 Juarez vowed maximum support to buoy his legions.

1-MINUTE TIMINGS

Take two 1-minute timings on lines 4–5, or type lines 4–5 twice.

4 Just how much more time do you think it took them   10
5 to write all these drills that fill up this book?   20
   | 1 | 2 | 3 | 4 | 5 | 6 | 7 | 8 | 9 | 10

ACCURACY

Type lines 6–10 twice.

6 er mere error infer steer power finer tower newer
7 sa said sacks sails safes sakes sandy saves sages
8 ui suit ruins fruit guide fluid juice suite squid
9 io ions lions trios adios scion idiom idiot axiom
10 we were weeps wears welds weans weeds swept weave

SPEED

Type each line twice.

11 ity activity priority charity ability quality ity
12 ial official material cordial special initial ial
13 ify simplify identify specify clarify qualify ify
14 ion deletion relation section mention lesions ion
15 age coverage mortgage average postage package age

2-MINUTE TIMINGS

Take two 2-minute timings on lines 16–20. Use your paper bail to proofread your copy. Circle your errors and figure your speed on each timing. Format: Double spacing.

16   The old man who walks in the park always has   10
17 a big smile on his face. He talks to each person   20
18 who comes his way. He gives aid in his quiet way   30
19 and is excited when he makes a new friend. He is   40
20 amazed at those who join him there.   47
   | 1 | 2 | 3 | 4 | 5 | 6 | 7 | 8 | 9 | 10   SI 1.12

FORMATTING LETTERS OF APPLICATION

The résumé is a summary of your skills and experiences. When you send your résumé to a prospective employer, you must, of course, send a covering letter—the *letter of application*. Together, the résumé and the letter of application are your introduction to the company.

Limit your letter of application to one page—about four paragraphs, as shown in the letter on page 244. Note the exact purpose of each paragraph:

① **Introduction.** Tell the reader the purpose of the letter, which job you are applying for, and how you learned of the job.

② **Second paragraph.** Give special consideration to the qualifications you have that make you especially valuable in this position and the skills you have that can help the employer and the company. Refer to the résumé you are enclosing.

③ **Third paragraph.** Mention special skills that set you apart from other applicants. (Are you exceptionally well organized?)

④ **Final paragraph.** Restate your interest in the job. Ask for an interview; give the date on which you will call to set up that interview. Include your home phone number so that the employer can reach you easily.

JOB C. LETTER OF APPLICATION

Type the letter of application shown on page 244. Standard format (see page 99 for typing a personal-business letter). Use plain paper. 5-inch line (50P/60E). Center tab.

COMPOSING A LETTER OF APPLICATION

Before you compose and type your own complete letter of application, you will have the opportunity to work on each of the separate paragraphs necessary in a letter of application. Read and study the examples provided in the following paragraphs, and then compose individual paragraphs for your own letter of application.

Paragraph 1

Objectives. Specify the job applied for and mention how you found out about it.

> **Example:** I would like to apply for the position of clerk-typist for your company. My high school English teacher, Ms. Kathleen Hutchinson, informed me of this opening.

Practice. Compose and type the first paragraph for a letter of application in which you are applying for a position as clerk-typist. Add any information that you think is necessary.

Paragraph 2

Objective. List relevant skills.

> **Example:** The experience I gained as a typist for my father's insurance agency qualifies me for the clerk-typist position in your company, as most of my duties involved daily use of typing, filing, and communications skills. These skills would be especially beneficial to your company.

Practice. Compose and type the second paragraph for a letter of application. Include specific clerk-typist skills you possess that would be beneficial to the company.

Paragraph 3

Objective. Convince the reader that you have special skills. Sell yourself!

> **Example:** My secretarial skills and my English skills are well above average, and I feel that I could perform any of the jobs I would be called upon to do with a minimum of error and with a high degree of competence.

Practice. Compose and type the third paragraph for a letter of application. Identify in this paragraph any special skills that you have.

Paragraph 4

Objectives. Restate your interest. Arrange an interview. Give your telephone number.

> **Example:** It would be a pleasure to work for your company as a clerk-typist. If you wish to interview me for this position, please telephone me at 301-555-4774 any weekday after 3 p.m.

Practice. Compose and type the fourth paragraph for a letter of application. Review the illustration on page 244 to find out what information you should include in this paragraph.

JOB D. LETTER OF APPLICATION

Compose and type a complete letter of application using the four paragraphs you just composed. Standard format. Add the following parts to complete the letter: (1) return address, (2) date line, (3) inside address, (4) salutation, (5) complimentary closing, (6) signature line, and (7) enclosure notation.

SPREAD CENTERING

A formatting technique.

To give added emphasis to a display line, spread it by leaving 1 space between let-ters and 3 spaces between words, like this:

T H I S   I S   S P R E A D I N G

To center a spread line, be sure to include all the spaces as you say the pairs for backspacing, like "T-space, H-space, I-space, S-space, space-space, I-space," and so on. Do not backspace for a final single letter. **Practice:** Center the spread line above. Then center and spread this line:

SPREAD WORDS FOR EMPHASIS

FORMATTING DISPLAYS

A variety of display techniques is used to make items like announcements of meetings, invitations, and advertisements look attractive.

To format a display:

1. Center the material vertically.
2. Center each line horizontally.
3. Use a combination of display techniques—some lines typed in capital and lowercase letters, some lines typed in all-capital letters, some lines typed in lowercase letters, and some lines spread-centered.
4. Use single or double spacing.

JOB 17 A. ANNOUNCEMENT

Display format. Full sheet of paper. Double spacing. Spread line 5.

ANNOUNCEMENT
of the
COMPUTER PROGRAMMING TRIP
to
D A T A   C E N T R A L
during the
First Week of October

JOB 17 B. ANNOUNCEMENT

Display format. Full sheet of paper. Double spacing. Spread line 4.

The
Centerville Chapter
of the
NATIONAL MERIT SOCIETY
will meet with
Dotti Falkenstein
Room F
Wednesday after school

LESSON 18

CLINIC

■ **GOAL**
To refine techniques for spacing, shifting, returning, tabulating, and keeping eyes on copy while typing.

■ **FORMAT**
Single spacing   50-space line

SPACE BAR

Type each line twice.

1 ask met paw fix vie yam fog dim aye con bake even
2 jet war hot kin vet zip quo bat ace eke long oxen
3 As you know, a doe hides low before the big snow.
4 As they sat on a mat, a pup and a cat had a spat.

ALTERNATE FORMATS FOR RÉSUMÉS

The illustration below shows some alternate formats for the sections of a résumé. The basic format may be changed by using one or more of the alternate features.

(A) The name, address, and telephone number are blocked at the left to start in the same printing position as each of the entries in the major sections of the résumé.

(B) Section headings are typed in all capitals.

(C) Pertinent business courses are identified in the education section.

Note: No references are given; instead, a statement is made that references will be sent upon request.

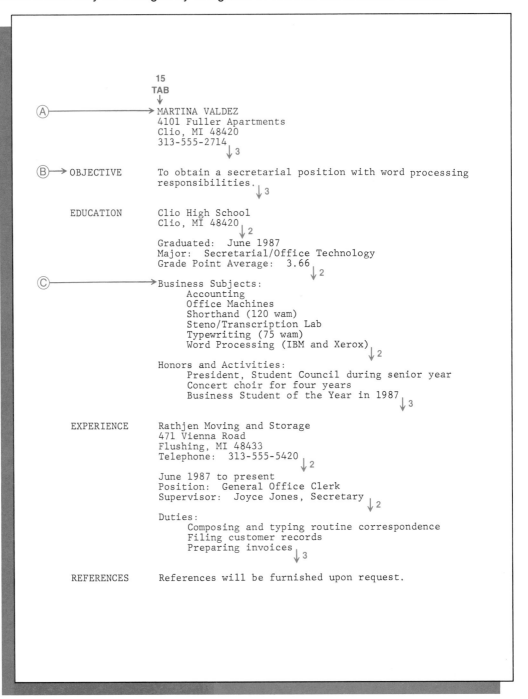

```
                              15
                              TAB
                               ↓
(A) ─────────────────────→ MARTINA VALDEZ
                           4101 Fuller Apartments
                           Clio, MI 48420
                           313-555-2714 ↓3

(B) ─→ OBJECTIVE           To obtain a secretarial position with word processing
                           responsibilities. ↓3

       EDUCATION           Clio High School
                           Clio, MI 48420 ↓2

                           Graduated:  June 1987
                           Major:  Secretarial/Office Technology
                           Grade Point Average:  3.66 ↓2

(C) ─────────────────────→ Business Subjects:
                               Accounting
                               Office Machines
                               Shorthand (120 wam)
                               Steno/Transcription Lab
                               Typewriting (75 wam)
                               Word Processing (IBM and Xerox) ↓2

                           Honors and Activities:
                               President, Student Council during senior year
                               Concert choir for four years
                               Business Student of the Year in 1987 ↓3

       EXPERIENCE          Rathjen Moving and Storage
                           471 Vienna Road
                           Flushing, MI 48433
                           Telephone:  313-555-5420 ↓2

                           June 1987 to present
                           Position:  General Office Clerk
                           Supervisor:  Joyce Jones, Secretary ↓2

                           Duties:
                               Composing and typing routine correspondence
                               Filing customer records
                               Preparing invoices ↓3

       REFERENCES          References will be furnished upon request.
```

JOB A. RÉSUMÉ

Type the résumé shown above.

JOB B. YOUR RÉSUMÉ

Prepare a résumé for yourself, using the guidelines introduced on pages 241 and 242. Include all sections that are pertinent and applicable to your background and experience. Do not include a section if you have no entries to place in that section. Use your typing teacher's name as one of your three references.

SHIFT LOCK

Type each line twice.

5 The SOPHOMORES were glad about having a SNOW DAY.
6 It was a DIESEL, and it was BLUE-GREEN, not GRAY.
7 She will be in the ELEVENTH grade, not the TENTH.
8 We may choose either a TOY POODLE or a CHIHUAHUA.
9 They typed TURF instead of SURF on my manuscript.

RETURN

Type each line once. Return after each name.

10 Helen Julie Kathy Laura Paula Hans Olga Uris Jill
11 Nancy Henry Mella Helga Porgy Jack Lisa Joni Myra
12 Perry Yetta Jenny Price Kevin Noel Lynn Jeff Kara

TABULATOR

Set four tabs—one every 10 spaces. Type each line once; tab between words.

13 Please	tab	across	the	page.
14 It	is	so	much	faster.
15 The	spaces	go	this	way.
16 Do	you	like	typing	this?
17 Can	you	tab	better	now?

**CONCEN-
TRATION**

Eyes on copy.

Fill in the missing vowels as you type each line once.

18 Wh-n y-- try t- f-ll -n th- bl-nks -s y-- typ- -n
19 th- l-n-s, y-- w-ll n--d t- st-dy th- p-tt-rns -f
20 --ch -f th- w-rds. D-d y-- s-- th-t -ll -f th--r
21 v-w-ls -r- m-ss-ng? Y-- c-n f-g-r- --t --ch -n-.
22 J-st k--p y--r -y-s -n th- c-py -s y-- typ- th-s.

LESSON 19

UNIT 4 Keyboarding—The Numbers

UNIT GOAL 25/2'/4e

■ **GOALS**
To control 1, 2, and 3 keys by touch, holding home key anchors.
To use typewriter formatting variations to change the appearance of displays.

■ **FORMAT**
Single spacing   50-space line

KEYBOARDING SKILLS

Words

Speed

Accuracy

Type each line twice.

1 maze elks corn idea flex give shot jobs quip whey
2 If the men do the audit work by six, they may go.
3 The clown from Quebec completely dazzled the man.

FORMATTING RÉSUMÉS

Once you have identified a job you want to apply for, your first step is to prepare a *résumé*—a summary of your training, background, and qualifications for the job.

A résumé contains different sections, depending on what information you want to include about your education, experience, personal background, and so on. The résumés illustrated at the right and on page 242 show the basic information to include. Read directions A through G for formatting résumés. Follow the margin settings, spacing directions, and tab setting shown below the illustration at the right.

Ⓐ **Heading.** For easy identification, begin the résumé with your name, address, and telephone number. Include your area code. (Center each line.)

Ⓑ **Objective.** This is a statement of your job preference. It indicates to a prospective employer the type of job you are seeking.

Ⓒ **Education.** If you have little business experience, list your education after your objective. The education section should begin with the highest level of education you have completed—that is, all items should be listed in *reverse* chronological order (the most recent first). For each entry you should include the name and address of the school, any diplomas earned and the years in which you earned them, the year you graduated, and your major area of study.

Ⓓ **Experience.** If your experience is stronger than your education, include it after your objective. If not, place the experience section after the education section. For each job you include, give the name, address, and telephone number of the company, the dates of employment, your job title(s), the name and title of your supervisor, and a brief description of the duties you performed.

Ⓔ **Personal Data.** By law, employers cannot ask certain questions—for example, an applicant's age. Thus many applicants choose *not* to include a personal data section. If you do choose to include a personal data section, you might wish to list such items as your height, weight, social security number, health, birth date, and marital status. If used, this section should be placed after the education and experience sections.

Ⓕ **Honors, Awards, and Activities.** Achievements mentioned in this section may give you an "edge" over other applicants. You should include your participation in clubs and organizations, any honors and awards you have received, and any special recognitions you have earned. You may also want to include your scholastic placement in your graduating class (such as "top 10 percent").

Ⓖ **References.** The final section of a résumé lists the names, job titles, addresses, and telephone numbers of at least three persons who can tell a prospective employer what kind of worker you are. For this reason most people use teachers, former supervisors, and former employers as references. Before you use anyone as a reference, you *must* get permission from each individual to use his or her name. Another option for the references section is to simply include this statement: "References will be furnished upon request."

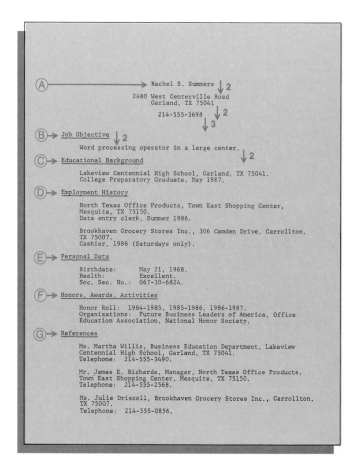

Top Margin: *On page 1, 9 lines; on continuation pages, 6 lines.*
Left/Right Margins: *1-inch (10P/12E).*
Bottom Margin: *6 to 9 lines.*

Single-space within each entry; double-space as indicated. Use 5-space tab.

Hold Those Anchors

For **1** anchor F
For **2** anchor F
For **3** anchor A or F

SPACE BAR

To Practice Top Row Reaches:

Type each reach slowly to feel the distance and direction of the reach.

Then type it again more smoothly.

 KEY

Use A finger on 1 if you have a 1 key.

Use small letter l for 1 if you do not have a 1 key.

Type each line twice.

4 aqa aqla ala lll ala l/ll ala ll.l ala ll,lll ala
5 ll arms, ll areas, ll adages, ll animals, or l.ll
6 My ll aides can type lll pages within ll minutes.

2 KEY

Use S finger.

Type each line twice.

7 sws sw2s s2s 222 s2s 2/22 s2s 22.2 s2s 22,222 s2s
8 22 sips, 22 sites, 22 swings, 22 signals, or 2.22
9 I saw 21 ads in Column 2 of 212 papers on July 1.

3 KEY

Use D finger.

Type each line twice.

10 ded de3d d3d 333 d3d 3/33 d3d 33.3 d3d 33,333 d3d
11 33 dots, 33 dimes, 33 dishes, 33 daisies, or 3.33
12 She asked 231 persons 132 questions in 123 hours.

TECHNIQUE CHECKPOINT

Keep eyes on copy while typing numbers.

Type lines 13–15 once. Then repeat lines 4, 7, and 10 or take two 1-minute timings on the Technique Checkpoint.

13 At least 23 of the 32 sketches were made by 12 of   10
14 the artists for the show on March 11, 12, and 13.   20
15 We need 2 or 3 more sketches for the 3 p.m. show.   30

| 1 | 2 | 3 | 4 | 5 | 6 | 7 | 8 | 9 | 10 |

2-MINUTE TIMINGS

Take two 2-minute timings on lines 16–20. Format: Double spacing, 5-space tab.

16   To see the artists paint is a joy. The zeal   10
17 with which they work to have the exact tints show   20
18 up on the pad is fun to watch. As they glide the   30
19 new brush quickly across the pad, the bright hues   40
20 take form and bring smiles to our faces.   48

| 1 | 2 | 3 | 4 | 5 | 6 | 7 | 8 | 9 | 10 | SI 1.10

JOB 19 A. ANNOUNCEMENT

Display format (see page 31). Half sheet of paper. Double spacing.

PROGRAMMING CONTEST
First week of November
Business Department
→ Jefferson High School
Prizes will be awarded

3. To form the possessive of a singular noun *ending* in an *s* sound, add an *apostrophe* plus *s* to the noun. However, if the addition of an extra syllable would make an *s*-ending word hard to pronounce, add the apostrophe only.

The glass's bottom was cracked.   The Burroughs' plane was late.

Type lines 23–29 once. Then repeat lines 23–29 or take a series of 1-minute timings.

```
23  The typists placed their papers on the two desks yesterday.     12
24  The businesses received their taxes in the mailboxes today.     12
25  Three stories were read to the children the past four days.     12
26  My brothers-in-law all reside in the city of San Francisco.     12
27  The managers' desks and the secretaries' chairs were moved.     12
28  The owner's gift and the employee's gift were brought here.     12
29  Dr. Roberts' class was canceled because he was out of town.     12
    |  1  |  2  |  3  |  4  |  5  |  6  |  7  |  8  |  9  |  10  |  11  |  12
```

JOB 143 A. LETTER

Block format. Form the possessive of the words in **boldface;** form the plural of the words in *italics*. Workbook 241–242.

Mr. Roger Brown, 348 Boyce Road, New Orleans, LA 70121, Dear Mr. Brown: Subject: Luncheon Speaker

How delighted I am that you have accepted our invitation to speak at our closing luncheon for the Advertising **Club** annual meeting in Nashville on June 14. Ever since hearing your speech in Knoxville last year, I have waited for the chance to invite you to Tennessee.

As one of the **country** foremost *authority* on consumerism, you will certainly be able to provide us with important, relevant information. All of us look forward to hearing you speak at our **Club** June meeting.

Your plane *ticket* and hotel confirmation will be sent to you shortly. The honorarium of $300 will be sent to you by June 30. Yours truly, Mary T. Collins

LESSONS
144–
148

UNIT 24 Applying for a Job
UNIT GOAL 40/5'/5e

■ GOAL
To format and type papers needed when applying for a job.

■ FORMAT
Margins and tabs as needed

Now that you are near the end of your first typing course, you may soon be looking for a part-time or full-time job. In applying for a job, you will need to use your typewriting skill (1) to prepare a résumé, (2) to compose a letter of application, (3) to complete an application form, and (4) to prepare a follow-up letter. Each of these tasks is discussed on the following pages.

JOB 19 B. ANNOUNCEMENT
Display format. Half sheet of paper. Single spacing.

M U S E U M   T O U R
Leaving Monday Morning
11 a.m.
Main Entrance
→ CENTRAL
VOCATIONAL SCHOOL

JOB 19 C. ADVERTISEMENT
Display format. Half sheet of paper. Double spacing.

WANTED
Someone to share a ride
to Campaign Headquarters
→ *on Mondays and Wednesdays*
from Roanoke Court
Leave name at main desk

LESSON 20

■ **GOALS**
To control 4, 5, and 6 keys by touch, holding home key anchors.
To use typewriter formatting variations to change the appearance of displays.

■ **FORMAT**
Single spacing   50-space line

KEYBOARDING SKILLS

Type each line twice.

Speed
1 The goal of the firm is to fix the antique autos.

Accuracy
2 Lazy Jacques picked two boxes of oranges with me.

Numbers
3 The answer is 33 when you add 12 and 21 together.

Hold Those Anchors

For **4** anchor A
For **5** anchor A
For **6** anchor ;

SPACE BAR

Reach Guide

Because 5 and 6 are long reaches, they are the hardest to control. Concentrate on them and master them, so that all the number keys will soon be easy for you.

 KEY

Use F finger.

Type each line twice.

4 frf fr4f f4f 444 f4f 4/44 f4f 44.4 f4f 44,444 f4f
5 44 foes, 44 films, 44 flukes, 44 folders, or 4.44
6 Show No. 4 is for May 1, 2, 3, 4, 12, 14, and 23.

 KEY

Use F finger.

Type each line twice.

7 ftf ft5f f5f 555 f5f 5/55 f5f 55.5 f5f 55,555 f5f
8 55 fins, 55 facts, 55 fields, 55 futures, or 5.55
9 There are 125 errors on 1545 of the 25,535 tests.

Take two 5-minute timings on lines 6–22.

```
              1                                    2
6        Commas might be used for more than a dozen purposes in    12
         3                          4
7   our language.  We use them to separate introductory clauses    24
      5                       6                         7
8   from main clauses, we use them to separate items in series,    36
                   8                      9
9   we also use them between clauses joined by conjunctions, we    48
            10                     11                      12
10  use them to illustrate a particular emphasis, and so forth.    60
               13                    14
11       The cousin of the comma is the semicolon.  A semicolon    72
          15                      16
12  can be used between two clauses that have no conjunction to    84
      17                    18                       19
13  connect them.  For example:  "Eva departed for Spain today;    96
                    20                   21
14  Rafael might depart Saturday."  A semicolon is also used if    108
                  22                 23                  24
15  one of the two clauses joined by a conjunction contains one    120
                 25                     26
16  or more commas and could be misread.  For example:  "George    132
             27                     28
17  plans to attend the session on Monday, Thursday, or Friday;    144
       29                    30                  31
18  and Wednesday all of us will attend."  In addition, a semi-    156
                 32                   33
19  colon can be used just to show a stronger break between two    168
            34                 35                        36
20  clauses, even though a conjunction is used, as follows:  "I    180
                     37                   38
21  insist that we must change this schedule; but you must give    192
              39                 40
22  us newer costs when we meet next time."                        200
    |  1  |  2  |  3  |  4  |  5  |  6  |  7  |  8  |  9  |  10  |  11  |  12   SI 1.50
```

PLURALS REVIEW

1. Plurals are formed by adding *s* to the singular form. However, when the singular ends in *s, x, ch, sh,* or *z,* the plural is formed by adding *es.*

shop, shops	executive, executives	help, helps
buzz, buzzes	trespass, trespasses	guess, guesses

2. To form a plural of a singular noun ending in *y* and preceded by a consonant, change the *y* to *i* and add *es.*

impurity, impurities	loyalty, loyalties	fifty, fifties

3. To form a plural of a singular noun ending in *y* and preceded by a vowel, add an *s.*

day, days	ashtray, ashtrays	deploy, deploys

4. To form a plural of a compound noun spelled with a hyphen or as two words, make the chief element of the compound plural.

sister-in-law, sisters-in-law
account payable, accounts payable

NOUN POSSESSIVES REVIEW

1. To form the possessive of a singular or plural noun *not ending* in an *s* sound, add an *apostrophe* plus *s* to the noun.

a person's good health	a car's engine	the children's books

2. Plural nouns that end in *s* show ownership by adding an apostrophe.

the sisters' clothes	the cars' motors

Hold Those Anchors

For **4** anchor A
For **5** anchor A
For **6** anchor ;

SPACE BAR

 KEY

Use J finger.

Type each line twice.

10 jyj jy6j j6j 666 j6j 6/66 j6j 66.6 j6j 66,666 j6j
11 66 jaws, 66 jokes, 66 judges, 66 jackets, or 6.66
12 Items 46, 56, and 66 are due by October 16 or 26.

TECHNIQUE CHECKPOINT

Keep eyes on copy while typing numbers.

Type lines 13–15 once. Then repeat lines 4 and 7 (page 34) and 10 or take two 1-minute timings on the Technique Checkpoint.

13 As you edit page 26, check line 14 to see that it   10
14 has exactly 35 spaces in it. Lines 12 and 14 are   20
15 both to be 35 spaces——space 36 is for the return.   30

| 1 | 2 | 3 | 4 | 5 | 6 | 7 | 8 | 9 | 10

2-MINUTE TIMINGS

Take two 2-minute timings on lines 16–20. Format: Double spacing, 5-space tab.

16   When you check your typed words, you need to   10
17 examine them for thoughts as well as for how they   20
18 look. The paper bail will help you to check. It   30
19 quickly guides your eyes across the maze of lines   40
20 and helps you pick out errors with ease.   48

| 1 | 2 | 3 | 4 | 5 | 6 | 7 | 8 | 9 | 10   SI 1.13

JOB 20 A. ADVERTISEMENT
Display format. Full sheet of paper. Double spacing.

SOFTWARE SALE
Monday, October 24
Main Lobby
11 a.m. until 1 p.m.
Sponsored by
Future Business Leaders of America

JOB 20 B. INVITATION
Display format. Half sheet of paper. Double spacing.

You are cordially invited
to attend the
COMPUTER SOFTWARE DISPLAY
Sponsored by
The Office Education Association
Wednesday through Friday
West Lobby

JOB 20 C. ADVERTISEMENT
Retype Job 20 A. Spread-center line 1 in all caps. Change *Main Lobby* to *Cafeteria*. Type last line in all-capital letters. Half sheet of paper.

JOB 142 A. BOUND REPORT
Standard format. Apply the semicolon and colon rules.

TYPING I LANGUAGE ARTS SKILLS
By [Your name]

Perhaps you have asked yourself why it is important for you to learn all the language arts rules covered in this book. The answer to that question is that the punctuation and style rules that you are learning in this book will help you to communicate more clearly.

No, you do not have to become an "expert" in grammar and punctuation you will have references that you can use to check rules. But you do have to master the basics -- those rules that you will use regularly as you type the following letters, memos, and reports. Let's review some of these rules.

PUNCTUATION RULES

We have studied the comma, the semicolon, and the colon. In total, approximately seven rules were introduced for comma usage three rules for semicolons and colons.

ADDITIONAL RULES

In addition to punctuation rules, the following rules were studied capitalization, number usage, plurals, and noun possessives. These rules will help you to write more clearly.

LESSON 143

■ **GOALS**
To type 40/5'/5e.
To review rules for plurals and noun possessives.
To type a letter applying rules for plurals and possessives.

■ **FORMAT**
Drills: Single spacing   60-space line
5-Minute Timings: Double spacing   5-space tab

SEMICOLON/ COLON REVIEW

Type lines 1–3 once, providing the missing semicolons and colons. Edit your copy as your teacher reads the answers. Then retype lines 1–3 from your edited copy.

1 The trial is over we must now proceed with our other plan.
2 We used red, blue, and green but it didn't look very good.
3 The following pages are gone from my book 13, 14, and 52.

PREVIEW PRACTICE

Type each line twice as a preview to the 5-minute timings on page 239.

Accuracy   4 next dozen between example emphasis particular conjunctions
Speed   5 language clause change today also them than for of by or to

LESSON 21

■ **GOALS**
To control 7, 8, and 9 keys by touch, holding home key anchors.
To determine the best format for displays.

■ **FORMAT**
Single spacing   50-space line

KEYBOARDING SKILLS

Type each line twice.

Speed   1 By the time the dial turns, it may be time to go.
Accuracy   2 Six bright families quickly plowed the vineyards.
Numbers   3 Lines 13, 24, and 56 were right; line 65 was not.

Hold Those Anchors

For **7** anchor ;
For **8** anchor ;
For **9** anchor J

SPACE BAR

7 KEY

Use J finger.

Type each line twice.

4 juj ju7j j7j 777 j7j 7/77 j7j 77.7 j7j 77,777 j7j
5 77 jets, 77 jumps, 77 jokers, 77 joggers, or 7.77
6 We sang 37 songs for 7657 students at 17 schools.

8 KEY

Use K finger.

Type each line twice.

7 kik ki8k k8k 888 k8k 8/88 k8k 88.8 k8k 88,888 k8k
8 88 kegs, 88 kilns, 88 knocks, 88 kickers, or 8.88
9 At 28 she has 18 titles in 38 of the 48 contests.

9 KEY

Use L finger.

Type each line twice.

10 lol lo9l l9l 999 l9l 9/99 l9l 99.9 l9l 99,999 l9l
11 99 laps, 99 loops, 99 lilies, 99 lifters, or 9.99
12 Do pages 19, 29, 39, 49, 59, 69, 79, 89, and 119.

TECHNIQUE CHECKPOINT

Keep eyes on copy while typing numbers.

Type lines 13–15 once. Then repeat lines 4, 7, and 10 or take two 1-minute timings on the Technique Checkpoint.

13 Plant the red bulbs in beds 2, 4, 6, and 8.   Then   10
14 plant the yellow bulbs in beds 1, 3, 5, 7, and 9.   20
15 Plant the white bulbs in 3, 5, and 7 for balance.   30

     | 1 | 2 | 3 | 4 | 5 | 6 | 7 | 8 | 9 | 10

LESSON 142

■ **GOALS**
To review semicolon and colon rules.
To type a one-page report applying semicolon and colon rules.

■ **FORMAT**
Single spacing   60-space line

COMMA USAGE REVIEW

Type lines 1–5 once, providing the missing commas. Edit your copy as your teacher reads the answers. Then retype lines 1–5 from your edited copy.

1   Yes that typist Joseph Nelson is very accurate and fast.
2   Call Kroft Plumbing and Heating for fast reliable service.
3   Joyce as you know proofread all the statistics carefully.
4   This lacquer is highly flammable but that one is harmless.
5   The captain was a strong dependable person to have around.

30-SECOND "OK" TIMINGS

Type as many 30-second "OK" (errorless) timings as possible out of three attempts on lines 6–8.

6   The four women in the jury box quickly spotted Dave dozing,   12
7   and they knew they had to awaken him as soon as they could.   24
8   Before any of them could make a move, though, Dave woke up.   36
    | 1 | 2 | 3 | 4 | 5 | 6 | 7 | 8 | 9 | 10 | 11 | 12

SEMICOLON/ COLON REVIEW

1. Two independent clauses can be joined by a comma plus *and, but, or,* or *nor.* When no conjunction is used, a semicolon is needed to join the clauses.

Cora explained it very clearly, but Ann did not understand.
Cora explained it very clearly; Ann did not understand.

2. If one of the clauses contains commas and a misreading is possible, use a semicolon even if a conjunction is used.

On our way to San Francisco, we will visit our office in Chicago, Illinois; and Tucson, Arizona, may be added to our itinerary.

3. When a main clause introduces a series of words, phrases, or clauses, use a colon between the main clause and the series.

Please use these pages: 12, 34, 45, and 67.

Type lines 9–14 once. Then repeat lines 9–14 or take a series of 1-minute timings.

9   Abe set the list price; Agnes Loo established the discount.   12
10   Summer is the zenith of your sales season; winter is quiet.   12
11   Ask Vera for a copy of the agenda; if you prefer, call Tex.   12
12   Teresa, James, Kenneth, and Ruth will go; Cynthia will not.   12
13   Please order the following: crayons, pencils, and erasers.   12
14   Purchase these items: plugs, tires, and unleaded gasoline.   12
     | 1 | 2 | 3 | 4 | 5 | 6 | 7 | 8 | 9 | 10 | 11 | 12

2-MINUTE TIMINGS

Take two 2-minute timings on lines 16–20. Format: Double spacing, 5-space tab.

16   The green tree in the corner of our yard has   10
17   grown just a little bit every year. It gives the   20
18   squirrel next door a place to make a home, and it   30
19   offers shade for our big, old, lazy dog. The big   40
20   tree has something to share with us all.   48

| 1 | 2 | 3 | 4 | 5 | 6 | 7 | 8 | 9 | 10   SI 1.14

SELECTING AN APPROPRIATE FORMAT FOR A DOCUMENT

Selecting a format is partly a matter of learning formatting guidelines and partly a matter of using your own good judgment. You have just practiced typing a series of jobs in which you used several formatting guidelines:

1. Typing in all capitals (page 23).

2. Indenting for paragraphs (page 24).

3. Centering horizontally (page 25).

4. Centering vertically (page 29).

5. Spread centering (page 31).

You may also vary the spacing—single, double, or a combination.

JOB 21 A. ADVERTISEMENT
Display format. Half sheet of paper. Double spacing.

FOR SALE
One Video Camera
One VCR
Five Blank Tapes
See Connie Emmitt
Room Central A

JOB 21 B. ADVERTISEMENT
Format: You decide.

WORD PROCESSING
One-Hour Lessons
Mondays and Wednesdays
See Roy Grimes
Computer Room

JOB 21 C. ANNOUNCEMENT
Format: You decide.

CAREER NIGHT
Sinclair Community College
Sixty Career Booths
Door Prizes
Tuesday, 8 p.m.

4. A compound sentence is a sentence that has two independent clauses joined by the conjunction *and, but, or,* or *nor.* Place a comma before the conjunction in a compound sentence.

Pamela recommended delaying delivery, *but* Angela objected.

5. Place a comma between adjectives that modify the same noun.

Ms. Franco wrote a *clear, concise* summary.

6. Use commas to set off nonessential elements and nonessential appositives.

Their offer is an excellent one, *in my opinion.*
We asked our manager, *Sarah Wells,* for approval.

Type lines 31–36 once. Then repeat lines 31–36 or take a series of 1-minute timings.

```
31  Cora explained it very clearly, but Ann did not understand.   12
32  The tall, modern building on Fifth is now our headquarters.   12
33  Jan prefers, as you know, working for a magazine publisher.   12
34  I'm going to mow the lawn, and my sister can edge the lawn.   12
35  The warm, windy day was just right for sailing on the lake.   12
36  Our supervisor, Debra Kovacs, handles this account herself.   12
    |  1  |  2  |  3  |  4  |  5  |  6  |  7  |  8  |  9  |  10  |  11  |  12
```

JOB 140/141 C. SPEECH
Standard format. Apply the comma rules.

OFFICE LAYOUT
By Meredith Ervin

Thank you Mr. Maher for the invitation to speak to your group on the topic of office layout. As I indicated to you the timing for this speech is very good because of your recent decision to relocate the sales department.

SLIDE 1

To begin with I would like to show you a slide of how the sales department looks today and how the office layout appears on the third floor of the Fifth Avenue building. We will discuss how the inadequate confined space has limited your operation in the last nine years. Your sales manager Ms. Brent has asked that I also spend some time presenting a brief look at what prompted the new changes you will see next year when the relocation will take place and how each employee will be affected by the move.

SLIDE 2

Here is a slide of what the sales department will look like after the relocation. Please note that square footage has been added to each office and every employee will have easier access to the word processing and filing operations. Also a new telecommunications network system has been installed so that each of you will have direct access to all regional offices. New furniture acoustic carpeting and micrographic storage facilities are also going to be added to the new sales department.

We hope that you will truly enjoy your new remodeled surroundings. Please feel free to call on me if you have any questions about your relocation.

■ **GOALS**
To control 0, ½, and ¼ keys by touch, holding home key anchors.
To block-center data horizontally.

■ **FORMAT**
Single spacing   50-space line.

KEYBOARDING SKILLS

Speed
Accuracy
Numbers

Type each line twice.

1 The ducks may be the first to go to the big lake.
2 Twelve zebras quickly jumped high over ten foxes.
3 Type 1 or 2 or 3 and 4 or 5 or 6 and 7 or 8 or 9.

Hold Those Anchors

For **0** anchor J
For **½** anchor J
For **¼** anchor J

SPACE BAR

 0 KEY

Use Sem finger.

Type each line twice.

4 ;p; ;p0; ;0; 000 ;0; 2.00 ;0; 30.0 ;0; 40,000 ;0;
5 600 parts, 700 planks, 800 parades, 900 particles
6 Our classes are set for 2:00 and 7:00 on Mondays.

 ½ KEY

Use Sem finger.

Type each line twice.

7 ;;; ;½; ;½; ½½½ ;½; 1½ ;½; 2½ ;½; 30½ ;½; 40½ ;½;
8 Is my size 7½, or did he say 6½? Maybe it is 8½?
9 Mark the boxes: 10½ or 29½ or 38½ or 47½ or 56½.

 ¼ KEY

Shift of ½. Use Sem finger.

Type each line twice.

10 ;½; ;½¼; ;¼; ¼¼¼ ;¼; 5¼ ;¼; 6¼ ;¼; 7¼ ;¼; 10¼ ;¼;
11 I think it is 3¼, or is it 4¼? I guess it is 5¼.
12 Label each box: 10¼ or 29¼ or 38¼ or 47¼ or 56¼.

TECHNIQUE CHECKPOINT

Keep eyes on copy while typing numbers.

Type lines 13–15 once. Then repeat lines 4, 7, and 10 or take two 1-minute timings on the Technique Checkpoint.

13 If you like to work with fractions, try adding up   10
14 these: 10½, 29¼, 38½, 47¼, and 56½. If you find   20
15 the answer to be 182, you are absolutely correct.   30

| 1 | 2 | 3 | 4 | 5 | 6 | 7 | 8 | 9 | 10

COMMA USAGE REVIEW

1. In a series of three or more words, numbers, phrases, or clauses, use a comma after each item in the series except the last item. In the following sentences, italics identify the items in a series:

> Our West Coast trip will take us to *Seattle, Eugene,* and *San Francisco.*
> She *quoted prices, checked bids,* and *prepared estimates.*

2. Use a comma after an introductory clause that begins with *if, as, when, although, since, because,* or a similar conjunction.

> *Before Leroy and Carolyn arrive,* let's review our agenda.
> *Whenever you have time,* please come to my office.

3. Place a comma after most introductory words and phrases.

> *No,* she has not yet approved the contract. (Word.)
> *Speaking distinctly,* Marvin answered each question thoughtfully. (Phrase.)
> *For the benefit of the audience,* Lisa explained her reasons. (Phrase.)

Type lines 25–30 once. Then repeat lines 25–30 or take a series of 1-minute timings.

```
25   When Mrs. Ulster arrives, we will discuss her tax problems.    12
26   Amy Zak, Paul Remy, and Bart Owens are the best applicants.    12
27   At the end of the month-long trial, our attorneys appealed.    12
28   If the quality is poor, then you should retype these memos.    12
29   George drafted it, Jerry typed it, and Sharon proofread it.    12
30   Therefore, Jack should mail the packages before next month.    12
     |  1  |  2  |  3  |  4  |  5  |  6  |  7  |  8  |  9  | 10  | 11  | 12
```

JOB 140/141 A. INTEROFFICE MEMO

Standard format. Apply the comma rules. Workbook 239 top.

[*To:*] All Department Heads, [*From:*] Lisa L. Montgomery, Office Manager, [*Subject:*] New Office Layout

As you now know we will be moving into our new building next year. When the actual move is made office space will be assigned in accordance with current office space standards used in our company. If you believe you will need more space in the new building please notify me by the 20th.

So that you may study the building more closely a copy of the new building's blueprint is attached. Thus your recommendation on exact space considerations will coincide with the final plan.

JOB 140/141 B. INTEROFFICE MEMO

Standard format. Apply the comma rules. Workbook 239 bottom.

[To:] Lisa L. Montgomery, [From:] Rudy T. Gable, [Subject:] Office Layout

When I received the revised office layout I realized that the space allowed for my office is 50 square feet less than I now have. If sales continue to expand as they have been expanding in the past seven years this space will be insufficient for me. As you must realize I cannot function with less than 175 square feet to accommodate files furniture and a sales research area.

Take two 2-minute timings on lines 16–20. Format: Double spacing, 5-space tab.

16   Getting up in the morning is quite a job for   10

17 me. I grab my yellow jacket and go for the bus––   20

18 just in time to miss it. Five more minutes would   30

19 have done it. Next time I will not doze so long.   40

20 I can still make it. Maybe I will beat the bell.   50

| 1 | 2 | 3 | 4 | 5 | 6 | 7 | 8 | 9 | 10   SI 1.13

FORMATTING: BLOCK CENTERING

To center a group of lines (not each line separately), use the following block-centering procedure:

1. Select the longest line in the group.
2. Backspace to center that line.
3. Set the left margin stop.
4. Begin all lines at the left margin.

Practice: Block-center each of the drills in the next column, leaving 5 blank lines between exercises. Begin on line 26 and double-space.

```
Centering a block
of lines is called
block centering.



ITEMS TO BE CENTERED
Titles of Reports
Tables
```

JOB 22 A. BLOCK CENTERING

Format the three groups of terms by block-centering each group. Use a full sheet of paper. Double-space. Begin on line 13. Leave 5 blank lines between each group.

```
keyboard
cassette tape
floppy disk
optical mark reader
light pen
```

```
video screen
printer
plotter
cassette tape
floppy disk
```

```
Read Only Memory
ROM
Random Access Memory
RAM
permanent
temporary
```

LESSON 23

■ **GOALS**
To construct fractions not on keyboard.
To type mixed numbers with constructed fractions.
To format data using mixed numbers and constructed fractions.

■ **FORMAT**
Single spacing   50-space line

KEYBOARDING SKILLS

Type each line twice.

Speed   1   She paid for a title to the island with the oaks.

Accuracy   2   Jack amazed Rex by pointing quickly to five haws.

Numbers   3   Type these: $10\frac{1}{2}$ and $29\frac{1}{4}$ and $38\frac{1}{2}$ and $47\frac{1}{4}$ and $56\frac{1}{2}$.

■ **GOALS**
To type 40/5'/5e.
To review six comma rules.
To type two memos and a speech applying comma rules.

■ **FORMAT**
Drills: Single spacing   60-space line
5-Minute Timings: Double spacing   5-space tab

NUMBERS REVIEW

Type lines 1–4 once, applying correct number style. Edit your copy as your teacher reads the answers. Then retype lines 1–4 from your edited copy.

1 I typed just fourteen letters, twelve memos, and eight reports yesterday.
2 11 complaints were received about the defective motors.
3 Sarah bought 4 texts, and Jeffrey bought 5 magazines.
4 The 6 of them will meet at Twelfth Avenue and 8th Street.

PRETEST

Take a 5-minute timing on lines 5–24. Circle and count your errors.

```
                              1                          2
5       Have you ever been on a fairly long trip by car simply      12
                    3              4
6   to find yourself bored because you did not have anything to      24
          5                  6                          7
7   do?  Actually, you have numerous options available to mini-      36
                          8
8   mize your boredom.                                                40
                                                                     —
                              9                     10
9       One answer to boredom is to read good-quality books in      12
                    11                    12
10  the car.  Purchase a paperback at your local bookstore; and      24
          13                  14                      15
11  as you read, you can obtain many hours of entertainment and      36
                          16
12  relaxing enjoyment.                                              40
                                                                     —
                              17                        18
13      But you, a passenger, can do much more than just read.      12
                    19                    20
14  There are dozens of activities and games that are enjoyable      24
          21                  22                      23
15  while traveling; magnetic checkers and chessboards may also      36
                          24
16  be quite exciting.                                               40
                                                                     —
                              25                        26
17      There are also games where passengers count particular      12
                    27                        28
18  types of signs or landmarks, or you might choose to partake      24
          29                  30                      31
19  in guessing games with other passengers.  And extra players      36
                          32
20  might add fun too.                                               40
                                                                     —
                              33                        34
21      Therefore, if you are a person who does not quite like      12
                    35                    36
22  riding along on an extended trip, plan ahead.  Think of all      24
          37                      38                      39
23  the nice activities you and others can participate in while      36
                          40
24  you are traveling.                                               40
    | 1 | 2 | 3 | 4 | 5 | 6 | 7 | 8 | 9 | 10 | 11 | 12   SI 1.50
```

PRACTICE

Take a 1-minute timing on each paragraph of the Pretest.

POSTTEST

Take another 5-minute timing on lines 5–24 to see how much your skill has improved.

CONSTRUCTING FRACTIONS

To construct a fraction, use the diagonal key.

Type each line twice.

4 1/3, 3/4, 4/8, 5/10, 6/12, 7/14, 9/18, and 24/48.
5 Now add 1/4, 4/8, 1/2, and 6/8. The answer is 2.
6 Other fractions are 4/10, 13/78, 9/25, and 11/60.

TYPING MIXED NUMBERS

Mixed numbers are whole numbers with fractions. Space between the number and a constructed fraction (9 3/16). Do not space between the number and a keyboard fraction (9½).

Type each line twice.

7 Type: 7 3/4, 8 9/12, 5 1/2, 34 6/9, and 85 3/10.
8 His Maltese weighs 13½ lb; my terrier weighs 15¼.
9 My room is 12 2/3 feet wide and 14 1/2 feet long.
10 This jar is 12 1/2 oz, but the other is 7 1/8 oz.
11 Melody worked 6 1/4 days in 3 of her 3 1/5 weeks.
12 There are 5¼ weeks left to my 2½-year assignment.

2-MINUTE TIMINGS

Take two 2-minute timings on lines 13–17. Format: Double spacing, 5-space tab.

13   When you work with people every day, you get   10
14 to know what it is that they like best. You also   20
15 find out quickly what makes them frown. A bit of   30
16 extra effort in a dozen small ways will make your   40
17 office a pleasant place in which to do your work.   50

| 1 | 2 | 3 | 4 | 5 | 6 | 7 | 8 | 9 | 10   SI 1.18

JOB 23 A. LIST

Format: Block-center. Half sheet of paper. Double spacing.

Materials needed:
9 sheets of paper, 8½ by 11 inches
3 floppy disks, 5¼ inch
1 microcomputer
1 dot-matrix printer

JOB 23 B. DIMENSION LIST

Format: Block-center. Full sheet of paper. Double spacing.

ROOM MEASUREMENTS BY FEET
Living Room: 14 3/8 by 20 7/8
Dining Room: 10 1/4 by 12 5/16
Kitchen: 10 3/4 by 14 1/8
Bedroom: 12 1/2 by 12 7/8
Bedroom: 11 3/4 by 13 5/6
Bedroom: 13 1/4 by 15 1/2
Bathroom: 7 3/4 by 12 1/2
Bathroom: 6 1/4 by 8 3/4
Family Room: 15 1/2 by 25 3/4

JOB 23 C. LIST

Format: Block-center. Half sheet of paper. Single spacing.

Supplies to buy:
2 reams of 8½- by 11-inch paper
8 system disks, 5¼ inch
8 data disks, 5¼ inch
8 microcomputers
8 letter-quality printers
1 box of 2¾- by 4½-inch labels
4 boxes of large envelopes

4. Use figures to express time with *minutes, a.m., p.m.,* and *o'clock.* (For greater formality, numbers may be spelled out with *o'clock.*) Also use figures to express years: *1986, 1988,* and so on.

> The committee meeting should take only *15* or *20 minutes*; thus we should be able to leave by *3:45 p.m.*

Type lines 5–10 once. Then repeat lines 5–10 or take a series of 1-minute timings.

```
5   Drive exactly 5 miles on Route 22; then turn left on Fifth.    12
6   Fifteen applicants were interviewed by Mrs. Mary Rodriguez.    12
7   Helen hired five clerks, two typists, and four secretaries.    12
8   Helen Greene hired 11 clerks, 2 typists, and 4 secretaries.    12
9   The meeting has been rescheduled for 2:45 p.m. on March 23.    12
10  Jack Mazer's law office is on First Avenue and 12th Street.    12
```
`|  1  |  2  |  3  |  4  |  5  |  6  |  7  |  8  |  9  |  10  |  11  |  12`

JOB 139 A. LETTER

Block format. Apply the numbers rules. Workbook 235–236. Body 98 words.

Locksmith City Service, 194 Lakeshore Drive, NE, Atlanta, GA 30324, Attention: Chief Locksmith, Gentlemen:

Last April (10/tenth) you installed the restricted access locks on all the doors of our new building. (7/Seven) keys were stolen from one of our employees on July (7/seventh), and we would like to have new locks installed on the doors for which keys are missing.

If I recall correctly, you said that each lock replacement would cost about (\$17/seventeen dollars) plus labor. Would the charge for replacing these (7/seven) locks be greater than (\$20/twenty dollars) per lock? Please let me have your estimate by August (15/fifteenth) so that we can have our locks replaced as soon as possible. Cordially yours,

R.T. Allen, Manager, cc: Ruth Richards

JOB 139 B. LETTER

Standard format. Apply the numbers rules. Workbook 237–238. Body 80 words.

```
Mrs. R. T. Allan, Manager, Baird Insur-
ance Company, 946 Pine Street, NW,
Atlanta, GA 30309-7143, Dear Mrs. Allen:
    Thank you for your letter informing
me about the keys that were stolen from
your company.  The price charged quoted you for
lock replacement was [$17/seventeen dol-
lars] including labor, and I will be able
to replace your locks by August July [15/fif-
teenth].
Will you need [2/two], [3/three], or [4/
four] duplicates of each key?  On your
original order you asked for [3/three]
duplicates.  The [3/three] duplicates for
the locks that will be replaced should be
returned to you to accompany the locks when the replacements are made.
Yours truly, Edgar H. Hartly, Chief lock smith,
PS:  I will be arriving at [10/ten] a.m.
to start replacing the locks.
```

REVIEW

■ **GOALS**
To type 25/2'/4e (25 wam for 2 minutes with 4 or fewer errors).
To block-center and center data both horizontally and
   vertically on half and full sheets of paper.
■ **FORMAT**
Single spacing   50-space line

PREVIEW PRACTICE

Type each line twice as a preview to the 2-minute timings below.

Accuracy 1 look class fixed amazing quickly exactly computer

Speed   2 report input store right lines page when make say

2-MINUTE TIMINGS

Take two 2-minute timings on lines 3–7. Format: Double spacing, 5-space tab.

3   When you use a computer to input and store a   10

4 report for a class, you can have it say just what   20

5 you want it to say and look exactly right. It is   30

6 amazing to see how quickly the lines can be fixed   40

7 and the pages changed to make the job just right.   50

   | 1 | 2 | 3 | 4 | 5 | 6 | 7 | 8 | 9 | 10   SI 1.19

JOB 24 A. CENTERING

Format: Center horizontally and vertically. Half sheet of paper. Double spacing.

PRINTER CATEGORIES

Dot matrix

Daisy wheel

Ink jet

Laser

Serial

Parallel

Chain

Band

JOB 24 B. ADVERTISEMENT

Display format. Full sheet of paper. Double spacing.

FOR SALE
5¼-inch DS, DD disks
dot matrix printer
applications software
Use on any home
microcomputer
Call 555-3748

JOB 24 C. ANNOUNCEMENT

Format: Block-center horizontally and center vertically. Half sheet of paper. Double spacing.

The Washington Township Schools
are offering an eight-week program
in both diet/exercise/nutrition and
microwave cooking. Classes will
begin the first week of October.
They will meet on Mondays at 7 p.m.

JOB 138 A. LETTER ON BARONIAL STATIONERY

Standard format. Apply the capitalization rules. Workbook 233 top. Body 75 words.

Mr. George Pera, Manager, Pera's Camera Service, 105 Wilson Avenue, Kingsford, MI 49801, Dear Mr. Pera:

I am returning the nobel camera I purchased from your west avenue store on may 2. As shown on the enclosed invoice that came with my order, the camera is just one of several pieces of nobel camera equipment that I purchased from your store.

After using four rolls of film to shoot senator barnes's campaign visit, I found that all my pictures were out of focus.

Please send me a replacement for this camera. Sincerely yours, Jeffrey S. Johnson, Photographer

JOB 138 B. INVOICE 1380

Standard format. Apply the capitalization rules. Date the invoice May 2. Workbook 233 bottom.

[*To:*] Jeffrey S. Johnson, photographer
Johnson Portraits
246 Front Street
Marquette, MI 49855

1	nobel camera, Model CR-25A @ $265.89	265.89
1	Zoom lens, 200-mm @ $150.33	150.33
1	Strobe, Model CR-44 @ $56.99	56.99
	Total amount due	473.21

LESSON 139

■ **GOALS**
To review numbers rules.
To type two letters applying numbers rules.

■ **FORMAT**
Single spacing   60-space line

CAPITALIZATION REVIEW

Type lines 1–4 once, providing the missing capitals. Edit your copy as your teacher reads the answers. Then retype lines 1–4 from your edited copy.

1 the red river is close to grand forks, wahpeton, and fargo.
2 i sent two letters to the president of the firm, earl jobe.
3 quinlan avenue is the site of our newest store in scranton.
4 al diaz, who imports spanish leather goods, is now in town.

NUMBERS REVIEW

1. Spell out numbers from 1 through 10; use figures for numbers above 10. Also spell out numbers that begin a sentence.

> We will need *three* or *four* more clerks.
> She estimates that the project will take *12* hours.
> *Eleven* committee members were invited.

When numbers above 10 *and* below 10 are mixed, use figures for numbers.

> Ellen surveyed *11* supervisors, *6* department heads, and *3* regional managers.

2. In technical copy, in dates, and for emphasis, use figures for all numbers.

> The next meeting is scheduled for May *3* at *2:30* p.m.
> The cost for *2* grams of this powder is only *$2*.

3. Spell out street names from *first* to *tenth*; use figures for street names above *tenth*. Use ordinal numbers (*11th, 21st, 42d, 53d,* and so on) for street names.

> They moved from *Fifth Avenue* to *19th Street*.

(Continued on next page)

■ **GOALS**
To type 25/2'/4e.
To demonstrate competency in block-centering and centering data both horizontally and vertically on half and full sheets of paper.

■ **FORMAT**
Single spacing   50-space line

PREVIEW PRACTICE

Type lines 1–2 twice as a preview to the 2-minute timings below.

Accuracy   1   except setting records accessed computer diskette

Speed   2   quicker making fields order laid just file box is

2-MINUTE TIMINGS

Take two 2-minute timings on lines 3–7. Format: Double spacing, 5-space tab.

3   Making up a data base on a computer diskette   10

4   is just like setting up a file box except that it   20

5   is much quicker. Each file size will vary. Each   30

6   file will have fields and records to be laid out.   40

7   The files can be accessed in more than one order.   50

| 1 | 2 | 3 | 4 | 5 | 6 | 7 | 8 | 9 | 10   SI 1.24

JOB 25 A. CENTERING

Format: Center horizontally and vertically. Half sheet of paper. Double spacing.

INFORMATION PROCESSING TASKS

Recording

Coding

Sorting

Calculating

Summarizing

Communicating

Storing

Retrieving

JOB 25 B. ANNOUNCEMENT

Display format. Full sheet of paper. Double spacing.

DEMONSTRATION
Wednesday, November 18
Integrated Software
Laser Printer
Voice Synthesizer
Register today
Room C273

JOB 25 C. ANNOUNCEMENT

Format: Block-center horizontally and center vertically. Half sheet of paper. Double spacing.

The Lincoln Heights School District
is offering a twelve-week course
in both photography and
photo development. Classes
will begin the third week of March.
They will meet on Thursdays at 7 p.m.

In Units 7 through 22 you completed 16 LABs (Language Arts for Business) that presented modern rules of punctuation and style. In Unit 23 you will review all 16 LABs and will complete more exercises related to them. Learning activities will be introduced through (1) brief reviews of the rules, (2) examples of each rule, (3) sentence applications for each rule, and (4) production applications for each rule.

CAPITALIZATION REVIEW

1. Capitalize proper nouns—the names of specific persons, places, or things. Capitalize common nouns when they are part of proper names.

Proper nouns:	Captain Ames	Kansas City	Chevrolet
Common nouns:	captain	city	car

Note: Capitalize adjectives formed from proper nouns—proper adjectives such as *American, European, French,* and *Freudian.* (One common exception is *french fries.*) Also capitalize the first word of a sentence and the word *I.*

> *She* and *I* worked for a *Greek* shipping firm.

2. Capitalize *north, south, east,* and *west* when they refer to *specific* regions, are part of a proper noun, or are within an address.

> Wesley lived in the *North* until 1982. (Specific region.)
> He worked for the *West* End Realty Company. (Part of proper noun.)
> His new address is 121 *South* Grand Avenue. (Part of address.)

> You must travel *east* on Route 122. (General direction.)
> The office is on the *south* side of the city. (General location.)

Likewise, capitalize *northern, southern, eastern,* and *western* when they refer to *specific* people or regions, not when they refer to *general* locations or directions.

> Zambia was formerly known as *Northern* Rhodesia.
> That warehouse will be built in the *southern* part of the state.

3. Capitalize official titles that precede names. Do not capitalize titles that follow names.

> We asked *Mayor* Bradley to attend the reception.
> We asked James T. Bradley, *mayor* of Scranton, to attend the reception.
> A United States *senator* will be the main speaker.

Note: The titles of some officials of very high rank are capitalized even when they follow or replace a name—for example, *President, Pope, Governor, Secretary General.*

Type lines 8–13 once. Then repeat lines 8–13 or take a series of 1-minute timings.

```
 8  Subi, a Japanese import firm, makes high-quality materials.   12
 9  Our warehouses in the East are inadequate for our purposes.   12
10  The new metals factory is in the western part of Kalamazoo.   12
11  Rex Young, a former colonel in the Marines, is our manager.   12
12  All six distributors are north of our Bogg Street terminus.   12
13  Pat lived in the Midwest before she moved south to Florida.   12
    |   1   |   2   |   3   |   4   |   5   |   6   |   7   |   8   |   9   |   10   |   11   |   12
```

LEVEL 2

GOALS

1. Demonstrate keyboarding speed and accuracy on straight copy with a goal of 32 words a minute for 3 minutes with 5 or fewer errors.

2. Demonstrate basic formatting skills on enumerations, outlines, and personal notes.

3. Demonstrate an ability to locate and correct errors.

4. Demonstrate an ability to understand proofreaders' marks by making appropriate corrections in text copy.

5. Apply rules for correct use of word division and capitalization in written communications.

Type each line twice.

```
 6  an and sand want grand angles be beg best bend bells behind
 7  cr cry crib cram crime create do dog done door doing double
 8  ea ear easy earn earth eagles fu fur fury fuel fussy future
 9  go got gown gold goods govern hi him hits hire hilly hinder
10  in pin wine grin inner inside jo jog join joke jolly joyful
11  ki kit king kind skill skiing la lad lake lash laugh lawyer
12  mi mid mine mile might middle ne net near next nerve needle
13  or ore torn more orbit orange pu put pure push pulse punish
14  qu qua quiz quip quart quorum ra raw rain rant radio rather
15  si sip site sigh sixth single te ten tell test terry tenant
16  um gum plum jump crumb summer va van vain vary vague vacant
17  wh why when whiz whole whales ex vex exit exam extra excuse
18  ye yet yelp year yeast yellow ze zee zero size zesty glazed
```

TIMINGS

Repeat the Pretest/Practice/Posttest routine on page 223.

UNIT 23 Language Arts Review
UNIT GOAL 40/5'/5e

■ GOALS
To form noun possessives correctly while typing sentences.
To review capitalization rules.
To type a letter and an invoice applying capitalization rules.

■ FORMAT
Single spacing   60-space line

LAB 16

Noun Possessives

Workbook 231–232.

Type lines 1–4 once, making possessives of the underscored words as you type each line. Edit your copy as your teacher reads the answers. Then retype lines 1–4 from your edited copy.

```
1  The Moore garage door was broken by the girl large toy.

2  Those attorneys salaries were reviewed yesterday by Diana.

3  Ms. Hastings outline was one of the best I have ever seen.

4  The actress entrance is a very critical part in the play.
```

12-SECOND TIMINGS

Type each line three times, or take three 12-second timings on each line. For each timing, type with no more than 1 error.

```
5  Is there some place where I can stop for just a short time?
6  It might rain when the sun sets and before the stars shine.
7  May I have my pen to write your name on the sheet of paper?
```

```
      5    10    15    20    25    30    35    40    45    50    55    60
```

UNIT 5 Keyboarding—The Symbols

UNIT GOAL 28/3'/5e

■ **GOALS**
To control #, $, %, and & keys by touch, holding home key anchors.
To type 28/3'/5e.

■ **FORMAT**
Drills: Single spacing   50-space line
3-Minute Timings: Double spacing   5-space tab

KEYBOARDING SKILLS

Speed

Accuracy

Numbers

Type each line twice.

1 This title to the island is the first to be kept.

2 A quick tally shows that taxi drivers whiz along.

3 Al jumped over Nos. 10, 29, 38, 47, and 56 today.

Hold Those Anchors

For # anchor A
For $ anchor A
For % anchor A
For & anchor ;

 # KEY

Shift of 3. Use D finger.

before a number means "number"; # after a number means "pounds."

Do not space between the number and the #.

Type each line twice.

4 ded de3 d3d d3#d d#d d#d #3 #33 #333 d#d d3d #333

5 Catalog #56 weighs 38#, and Catalog #2947 is 10#.

6 My favorite ones are #10, #29, #38, #47, and #56.

 $ KEY

Shift of 4. Use F finger.

Do not space between the $ and the number.

Type each line twice.

7 frf fr4 f4f f4$f f$f f$f $4 $44 $444 f$f f4f $444

8 The latest rates are $10, $29, $38, $47, and $56.

9 Who bought a $56 suit at the Fashionette for $38?

TECHNIQUE CHECKPOINT

Keep eyes on copy while typing numbers and symbols.

Type lines 10–13 once. Then repeat lines 4 and 7.

10 Item #1029 lists at $38.50 but will be reduced in   10

11 June to $34.50. Item #847, which weighs 56#, can   20

12 be bought for $74. Items #1029, #3847, and #5665   30

13 will all sell for $2 in June and $3.95 in August.   40

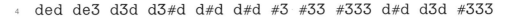

| 1 | 2 | 3 | 4 | 5 | 6 | 7 | 8 | 9 | 10

JOB 136 A. LETTER

Standard format with indented paragraphs. Workbook 227–228. Body 104 words.

Ms. Jennifer Wells, 105 Cedar Street, 11
Wayne, NE 68787, Dear Ms. Wells: 19

As you requested, I am enclosing 27
the latest copy of our sales catalog 34
for senior class rings. When you 41
place your order, please remember to 48
do the following: 52

1. Give the complete Catalog number 61
for the style of ring you wish to 69
purchase. 72

2. Indicate your ring size on the 81
order form. 84

3. Enclose a money order or check 93
for the purchase price of the ring, 102
plus a 5 percent sales tax. 108

We would appreciate your sharing 117
the catalog with your classmates at 124
Sunnyvale Senior High School. We hope 132
you will take this opportunity to order 140
one of the finest rings on the market 147

today. Cordially yours, Christopher 161
Brandenburg, manager, Catalog Sales, 170
cc: Dolores Simpson, Samuel Bolstad 175

JOB 136 B. LETTER ON MONARCH STATIONERY

Standard format. Workbook 229–230 top. Body 53 words.

Ms. Anne B. clifton, Juneau Manager, 15
United Charities Campaign, Juneau, AK 22
99801, Dear ~~Mrs.~~ Ms. Clifton: Subject: 31
Juneau Campaign 34

Thank you for your report on ~~the~~ 41
~~Alaska~~ Juneau's fund-raising campaign. We are always 51
happy to hear that the campaign is 58
going \well/ ~~so\~~ in your region. 64

The other regions ~~in Anchorage and~~ 68
~~Fairbanks~~ are also doing quite well; 74
~~and~~ consequently; this may be a banner year for our 83
campaign. We ~~all~~ look forward to re- 90
ceiving your final report. Yours truly, 100
Ralph B. Jones, Alaska Manager 113

CLINIC

■ **GOAL**
To improve your typing skills.

■ **FORMAT**
Single spacing   60-space line

KEYBOARDING SKILLS

Type lines 1–4 once. In line 5 use the shift lock for each word in all-capital letters. Repeat lines 1–4, or take a series of 1-minute timings.

Speed	1	We should make the next year the best one we have ever had. 12
Accuracy	2	Vic quickly mixed grape juice with the frozen strawberries. 12
Numbers	3	We saw 10 bats, 29 owls, 38 rodents, 47 birds, and 56 cows. 12
Symbols	4	We paid 15% on a loan of $650; they (Sam and Jan) paid 14%. 12
Technique	5	The fruits are BANANAS and ORANGES and MELONS and APRICOTS.

| 1 | 2 | 3 | 4 | 5 | 6 | 7 | 8 | 9 | 10 | 11 | 12

Hold Those Anchors

For # anchor A
For $ anchor A
For % anchor A
For & anchor ;

 KEY

Shift of 5. Use F finger.

The % symbol is used only in statistical information. Do not space between the number and the %.

Type each line twice.

14 f5f f5% f%f f5f f5% f%f 5% 55% 15% 25% 25.5% 5.5%

15 The return rates are 10%, 29%, 38%, 47%, and 56%.

16 Annette scored 92%, Joe made 83%, and Ed had 74%.

 KEY

Shift of 7. Use J finger.

Space once before and after an ampersand (&) used between words and numbers. Do not space when used between initials.

Type each line twice.

17 j7j j7& j&j j7j j7& j&j 7 & 8 & 9 & 10 & 11 & 121

18 Jean made profits of 10% & 29% & 38% & 47% & 56%.

19 Joan worked at H&S Company and then Rex & Penrod.

TECHNIQUE CHECKPOINT

Keep eyes on copy while typing numbers and symbols.

Type lines 20–23 once. Then repeat lines 14 and 17.

20 The rates given by L&S Loan Company are 15% for a   10

21 short term and 18% for a long term. P&W Loan Co.   20

22 offered 14% for short term and 17% for long term.   30

23 Dawes & Kipp has the best deals with 13% and 16%.   40

| 1 | 2 | 3 | 4 | 5 | 6 | 7 | 8 | 9 | 10

3-MINUTE TIMINGS

Using Speed Markers

The numbers in this timing are *speed markers*. At the end of the timing, the number you reach will tell you your wam speed, because the total words have already been divided by 3. For example, if you end the timing on the last letter of *which* on line 31, you typed 26 wam.

Take two 3-minute timings on lines 24–32.

24   I would really like to join a club at school   10

25 this year. There are so many from which to pick.   20

26 I just cannot make up my mind. There is the Swim   30

27 Club and the Ski Club; I could try out for a play   40

28 or try chess. Debate has quite a record for hard   50

29 work, and the jazz band should be an exciting new   60

30 venture too. Now which one shall I choose? Will   70

31 my friends want to help? Tell me which club will   80

32 be the best for me?   84

| 1 | 2 | 3 | 4 | 5 | 6 | 7 | 8 | 9 | 10 SI 1.09

■ GOALS
To form noun possessives correctly while typing sentences.
To type 39/5'/5e.
To type two letters.

■ FORMAT
Drills: Single spacing   60-space line
5-Minute Timings: Double spacing   5-space tab

LAB 16

Noun Possessives

Type lines 1–4 once, making possessives of the underscored words as you type each line. Edit your copy as your teacher reads the answers. Then retype lines 1–4 from your edited copy.

1   Your <u>car</u> engine did not start for last <u>week</u> final race.
2   Both <u>partners</u> shares equal less than half the total stock.
3   Ms. <u>Holmes</u> eraser is worn so badly that it wouldn't work.
4   The <u>Simmons</u> factory is located near the west edge of town.

PREVIEW PRACTICE

Accuracy
Speed

Type each line twice as a preview to the 5-minute timings below.

5   search typing ability personal employer carefully emotional
6   always public mature touch adept loyal might work such when

5-MINUTE TIMINGS

Take two 5-minute timings on lines 7–23.

7   When employers search for a new office worker, they do   12
8   so by looking at several things. The worker must have good   24
9   skills that very well may be quite hard to locate. For in-   36
10   stance, the adept office worker must work quickly and care-   48
11   fully. Also, the valued office worker must be at ease with   60
12   other personnel as well as with the general public. If you   72
13   wish to have employment in an office, touch up your skills.   84
14   You must improve your professional skills such as typ-   96
15   ing, shorthand, and mathematics; personal skills, including   108
16   initiative, being on time, and working with others; and, of   120
17   course, emotional skills such as working with stress, being   132
18   loyal to your employer, and "keeping the business of an of-   144
19   fice in an office." Whenever a mature employee works in an   156
20   office, these skills are rather easily observed and identi-   168
21   fied. Just by being aware of the very nature of work in an   180
22   office, you'll conduct all your work with zeal and soon be-   192
23   come a winner.   195

| 1 | 2 | 3 | 4 | 5 | 6 | 7 | 8 | 9 | 10 | 11 | 12 | SI 1.49

■ **GOALS**
To control *, ___,), and (keys by touch, holding home key
   anchors.
To type 28/3'/5e.

■ **FORMAT**
Drills: Single spacing   50-space line
3-Minute Timings: Double spacing   5-space tab

KEYBOARDING SKILLS

Speed
Accuracy
Numbers
Symbols

Type each line twice.

1 If Helen owns this land, she may wish to sell it.
2 Zeke was quite vexed about the joke made by Carl.
3 Type dates as April 5, 1988, or 4/5/88 or 4-5-88.
4 When J&R orders it at a 3.6% discount, #1 is $29.

Hold Those Anchors

For * anchor ;
For ___ anchor J
For) anchor J
For (anchor J

 KEY

Shift of 8. Use K finger.

Do not space between the word and the *.

Type each line twice.

5 ki8 ki* k*k k*k My style manual* is a great help.
6 Rules in the reference book* help solve problems.
7 He recommends this manual* for grammar and style.

 KEY

Shift of - (hyphen). Use Sem finger.

Workbook 21–22.

 On some computers or word processors, you do not type the underscore. Instead, you code the word to be underscored and the printer does the work.

To underscore a word or a group of words: (1) type the word or words, (2) backspace to the first letter of the word or words to be underscored, (3) depress the shift lock, and (4) strike the underscore key repeatedly until all the words have been underscored. On some typewriters, the underscore key may operate continuously, like the space bar. Make sure you stop in time. **Note:** Do *not* underscore the punctuation or the space following an underscored word or phrase. (**Exception:** If the punctuation is part of a title—as in <u>Oklahoma!</u>—then the punctuation *is* underscored.) *Do* underscore the punctuation or the space *within* a group of words to be underscored. See, for example, lines 9 and 10 below.

Type each line twice.

8   ;p_ ;p_ ;_; ;_; Mary <u>did</u> say she would <u>not</u> drive.
9   It is <u>not</u>, Linda claims, <u>very, very well written</u>.
10 Sara read her class the book <u>Alice in Wonderland</u>.

TECHNIQUE CHECKPOINT

In figuring speed, count underscored words triple.

Type lines 11–14 once. Then repeat lines 5 and 8.

11 A reference manual* is valuable for all of us who   10
12 write letters, memos, and reports. A manual will   20
13 help to solve problems in using <u>who</u> and <u>whom</u>, for   33
14 example, and in using punctuation marks properly.   43

    | 1 | 2 | 3 | 4 | 5 | 6 | 7 | 8 | 9 | 10

FORMATTING LETTERS ON BARONIAL AND MONARCH STATIONERY
Workbook 218.

Some firms have their short letters typed on either baronial stationery (5½″ by 8½″) or monarch stationery (7¼″ by 10½″).

1. To format letters on baronial stationery:
   a. Date: line 12.
   b. Inside address: line 16 (↓ 4).
   c. Line length: 4-inch (40P/50E).
2. To format letters on monarch stationery:
   a. Date: line 14.
   b. Inside address: line 19 (↓ 5).
   c. Line length: 4- or 5-inch (40P/50E, 50P/60E).

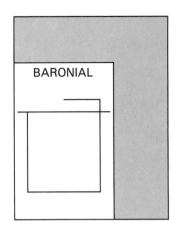
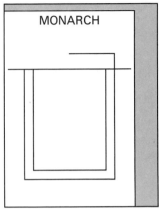

JOB 135 A. LETTER ON BARONIAL STATIONERY
Standard format. Workbook 223–224 top. Body 66 words.

Ms. Roberta Kile, Office Administration Department,   18
Mayville State College, Mayville, ND 58257, Dear   28
Ms. Kile :   31

     We are pleased to be able to take part in your   41
survey on reading and writing skills. I have completed   52
your school's survey and am returning it as you   62
requested in your letter.   67

     My colleagues and I had some comments on   76
the issues you raised in your survey, and our   86
reactions appear on the enclosed sheet.   94

     We look forward to receiving a copy of the   103
survey results. Yours truly, Frank S. James,   118
Chairperson   125

JOB 135 B. LETTER ON MONARCH STATIONERY
Standard format. Workbook 225–226. Body 65 words.

Mr. James P. Hill, Manager, Lomax Sales Associates, 20627 Hawthorne Boulevard South, Torrance, CA 90503, Dear Mr. Hill: 17 24 32

     Thank you for the catalog showing your line of office supplies. We were indeed interested in looking at the quantities of metric supplies in your store's inventory. ¶Next week Ms. Lang   42 52 61 71 from our Long Beach store will be in Torrance to view your line of metric supplies. ¶You will be receiving our fall order by the end of the week. Thank you again for the catalog. Very truly yours, Karen T. Booker, Office Manager   81 91 101 112 127

JOB 135 C. LETTER ON BARONIAL STATIONERY

Retype Job 135 A with the following change: Delete the final paragraph, and compose a new one that says that you would like to meet with Ms. Kile to discuss the survey results. Standard format. Workbook 223–224 bottom.

Hold Those Anchors

For * anchor ;
For __ anchor J
For) anchor J
For (anchor J

 KEY

Shift of 0 (zero). Use Sem finger.

Space once after a closing parenthesis; do not space before it.

Type each line twice.

15 ;p; ;p) ;); ;); 10) 29) 38) 47) 56) ½) ½) ;p; ;);
16 We included 1) skis, 2) coats, 3) hats, 4) boots.
17 My rates are 1) 5%, 2) 7%, 3) 9%, 4) 16%, 5) 18%.

KEY

Shift of 9. Use L finger.

Space once before an opening parenthesis; do not space after it.

Type each line twice.

18 lol lo(l(l l(l (10) (29) (38) (47) (56) (½) (1¼)
19 My speech (it is not too long) will cover skiing.
20 Your car (the convertible) is our favorite color.

TECHNIQUE CHECKPOINT

Keep eyes on copy while typing numbers and symbols.

Type lines 21–24 once. Then repeat lines 15 and 18.

21 When typing a symbol, follow the steps: (1) cap,   10
22 (2) strike, and (3) home. They help you feel the   20
23 motions of (1) cap, (2) strike, and (3) home in a   30
24 smooth rhythm——(1) cap, (2) strike, and (3) home.   40

| 1 | 2 | 3 | 4 | 5 | 6 | 7 | 8 | 9 | 10

3-MINUTE TIMINGS

Take two 3-minute timings on lines 25–33. Use the speed markers to figure your speed.

25   When you want to mail a letter or a package,   10
26 you have a choice as to the way you want it sent.   20
27 If you want a package to be sent very fast, place   30
28 it in Express Mail. If you are not in a rush for   40
29 it to be sent, you can send it third class. Most   50
30 letters are mailed first class, but they just may   60
31 go quicker by special delivery. The size and the   70
32 weight may mean that you must change the way that   80
33 an item may be sent.   84

| 1 | 2 | 3 | 4 | 5 | 6 | 7 | 8 | 9 | 10   SI 1.13

JOB 134 B. LETTER

Block format (see page 224). Workbook 221–222. Body 66 words.

Mr. Jonathan Shield ;

ˌShield Home Inspection*Inc.;* 1800 South Elm Street, Grand Forks, ND

58201, Dear Mr. Shield: Subject: Home Repairs Check

ˌ*home* buyerˌ; Mrs. Anna Shirek, has asked that I contact you to

arrange for an inspectionˌ *of the foundation* on a home that we repᵢared last *year* ~~March.~~

(Please send all charges for this inspection to my office.)

At the buyer's request, | *I ~~will~~ would like you to inspect the basic*

workmanship and materials used | in ~~renovating~~ *repairing* the foundation for the

house at 1210 South Elm (St.) Sincerely yours, Gordon H. *Hall ;*

Building Contractor, cc: Mr. & Mrs. Ralph M. Ernst, ˌbcc: Kay

West) *P S : Please let me know the exact day on which you plan*

to make the inspection so that I may inform the present owners.

■ **GOALS**
To identify the possessive forms of nouns while typing sentences.
To format and type letters on baronial and monarch stationery.

■ **FORMAT**
Single spacing   60-space line

LAB 16

Noun Possessives

Type lines 1–4 once. Then repeat lines 1–4 or take a series of 1-minute timings.

1 Her boss's answer was different from their bosses' answers.   12
2 This clerk's records are neater than other clerks' records.   12
3 One child requested six toys in that children's department.   12
4 The Rizzo's van left already, but the Joneses' van has not.   12

  | 1 | 2 | 3 | 4 | 5 | 6 | 7 | 8 | 9 | 10 | 11 | 12

30-SECOND "OK" TIMINGS

Type as many 30-second "OK" (errorless) timings as possible out of three attempts on lines 5–7. Then repeat the effort on lines 8–10.

5 James swung my ax quite rapidly, chopping five logs to size   12
6 before it was time to quit for lunch. At this rate, he may   24
7 finish chopping all the big logs before the day is through.   36

8 One thing of which we are quite sure is never to expect our   12
9 speed to jump or zip higher for three minutes before we can   24
10 type with the same degree of skill for about half a minute.   36

  | 1 | 2 | 3 | 4 | 5 | 6 | 7 | 8 | 9 | 10 | 11 | 12

GOALS
To control ', !, and " keys by touch, holding home key anchors.
To type 28/3'/5e.

FORMAT
Drills: Single spacing   50-space line
3-Minute Timings: Double spacing   5-space tab

KEYBOARDING SKILLS

Speed   1 It is the duty of the girls to cut down the bush.
Accuracy   2 Joel quickly fixed five zippers while she waited.
Numbers   3 Now read this new order: 10, 29, 38, 47, and 56.
Symbols   4 A copy of The Style Book* should be on each desk.

Hold Those Anchors

For ' anchor J
For ! anchor J
For " anchor J

 KEY

Next to ; key. Use Sem finger.

Do not space before or after an apostrophe.

Type each line twice.

5 ;'; ;'; ''' It's Mia's job to get Lynn's lessons.
6 Wasn't Paul going? Isn't Jim here? Help us now.
7 We're so happy. Aren't you pleased? It's not I.

 KEY

Shift of 1. Use A finger.

Or next to P. Use Sem finger.

Or construct. (See below.)

Type each line twice. Type either line 8A or 8B.

8A aql aq! a!a a!a Watch! Watch them! Watch those!
8B ;;; ;!; ;;; ;!; Watch! Watch them! Watch those!
9   Look! Look there! Look there! Look everywhere!
10 She paced: Five! Four! Three! Two! One! Go!
11 Look at the sky! You can see it from here! Wow!

CONSTRUCT AN EXCLAMATION POINT

Space twice after an exclamation point only at the end of a sentence.

If your machine has no exclamation point, you may construct one: (1) strike the period, (2) backspace, and (3) strike the apostrophe. Type each line once.

12 That song must have taken many months to compose!
13 My, how well she plays! She's a superb musician!
14 His accompaniment is superb! He's a new pianist!

 KEY

Shift of ' key. Use Sem finger.

Type each line twice.

15 ;"; ;"; """" "Here," she cried. "I am over here."
16 The signal is "blue" for up and "green" for down.
17 "Stop!" they shouted. The painting was a "fake."

Plural nouns that end in *s* show ownership by adding an apostrophe.

both sisters' husbands   those managers' offices   two secretaries' desks

30-SECOND SPEED TIMINGS

Take two 30-second speed timings on lines 5 and 6. Then take two 30-second speed timings on lines 7 and 8. Or type each sentence twice.

5 The cash was used to buy a new tape, but she soon found out   12
6 that the tape was not any good and could not be run at all.   24
7 She will have to find some other way to get a new tape, and   12
8 it must be at least by the time she needs to tape the song.   24

| 1 | 2 | 3 | 4 | 5 | 6 | 7 | 8 | 9 | 10 | 11 | 12

FORMATTING A POSTSCRIPT (PS:)
Workbook 217.

A postscript (*PS:*) is an additional message typed in paragraph form at the end of a letter. To format a postscript:

1. Double-space after the last item in the letter.

2. Type the postscript at the left margin if paragraphs were blocked; indent it if paragraphs were indented.

3. Type *PS:*, leave 2 spaces, and type the message.

Production Practice. Set margins for a 6-inch line. Set a 5-space and center tab. Single spacing. Clean sheet of paper. Use Job 134 A below.

Space down to line 7. Tab to the center. Type the complimentary closing. Return four times. Tab to the center. Type the writer's name. Return once and tab to the center. Type the writer's title. Return twice. At the left margin type your initials. Return twice. Tab for the paragraph indention. Type the postscript. Check your work. Remove

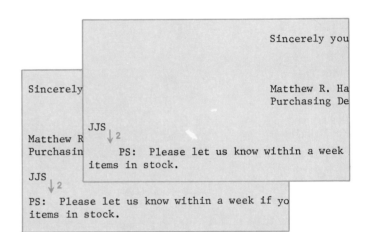

your paper from the typewriter, and reinsert it upside down.

Repeat the practice using block format—all lines typed at the left margin. Check your work after you finish.

JOB 134 A. LETTER
Standard format with indented paragraphs. Workbook 219–220. Body 89 words.

Central High School, 2389 Highland Avenue, Fall River, MA 02720, Attention: High School Seniors, Ladies and Gentlemen: 22   38

To sign up for concurrent enrollment at Salem State College, it is necessary to complete the following procedure: 50   58

1. Schedule a meeting with your adviser so that you can plan your complete summer course load.   76   84

2. Complete the Enrollment Form that is enclosed with this letter.   101

3. Send an official copy of your high school transcript to the Admissions Office at Salem State College.   117   127

We look forward to seeing you this summer. If you have any questions, please feel free to write to us any time prior to your arrival. Sincerely, J. W. Holmes, Admissions Director, PS: Please bring your SAT test score with you when you register.   143   162   191   197

QUOTATION MARKS

Workbook 23–24.

Quotation marks are used in pairs. Often the second quotation mark is used with another punctuation mark, as shown in lines 18–22 below.

Follow these rules when using quotation marks with other punctuation:

1. Place commas and periods *before* the second quotation mark (see A and B).

2. Place colons and semicolons *after* the second quotation mark (see C and D).

3. Place question marks and exclamation points *before* the second quotation mark *only if* the entire quotation is a question or an exclamation (see E). In all other cases, place the question mark or exclamation point *after* the second quotation mark (see F and G).

Practice: Type lines 18–22 once. Format: Double spacing, 5-space tab.

```
18        "Good morning ," said Joe.   "Come in ."
                          Ⓐ                      Ⓑ
19        I did as he "offered":  I went in.  He
                                Ⓒ
20   said that I seemed "excited"; he listened.
                                Ⓓ
21        "What's your news?" he asked.  "Tell me!"
                            Ⓔ                      Ⓔ
22   Did he already "know"?  I think he "guessed"!
                          Ⓕ                      Ⓖ
```

TECHNIQUE CHECKPOINT

Keep eyes on copy while typing symbols.

Type lines 23–26 once. Then repeat lines 5, 8, and 15 (page 48).

```
23   It's not very often that we hear the words "thank   10
24   you" or "please."  Is it that we don't "care" and   20
25   "feel," or is it that we just don't "think" to be   30
26   courteous?  We all "know" that we "ought" to try!   40
     |  1  |  2  |  3  |  4  |  5  |  6  |  7  |  8  |  9  |  10
```

3-MINUTE TIMINGS

Take two 3-minute timings on lines 27–35. Use the speed markers to figure your speed.

```
                      1                  2              3
27        The end of a semester would be just great if   10
                 4              5            6
28   it were not for the tests.  It is a joy to finish   20
             7              8            9          10
29   the term, to have the course done, to have a hold   30
                   11              12             13
30   on things we have mastered, etc.  The lone shadow   40
              14              15              16
31   is the course exam.  But, on the other hand, some   50
            17              18              19         20
32   students like tests; they see tests as the chance   60
                     21              22             23
33   to prove how much they have learned.  Things that   70
              24              25              26
34   are a puzzle to some of us are quite clear to all   80
              27              28
35   those lucky persons.                               84
     |  1  |  2  |  3  |  4  |  5  |  6  |  7  |  8  |  9  |  10   SI 1.15
```

FORMATTING LETTERS IN BLOCK STYLE

Another style that is used to format letters is known as the *block style,* where *all* letter parts begin at the left margin. Margins and vertical spacing remain the same.

JOB 133 A. LETTER
Block format. Workbook 215–216. Body 73 words.

Ms. Audrey L. Simms, Knight Insurance Com 16
pany, 204 Pine Ridge Road, Boston, MA 23
02181, Dear Ms. Simms: Subject: Carpet Clean 34
ing 35

    As we discussed on the telephone today, we 45
will be able to clean the carpeting on the fourth 55
floor of your building on Saturday, March 3. 64

    Our people will be at your office at 6 p.m. on 74
Friday, March 2, to move out the furniture and 84
vacuum the carpet before cleaning and sham 92
pooing on Saturday. 96

    Thank you for doing business with us. Yours 107
truly, Archie T. Maisley, Manager 118

LESSON 134

■ **GOALS**
To recognize the possessive forms of nouns while typing sentences.
To type letters in modified-block and block styles.
To format and type postscript notations.

■ **FORMAT**
Single spacing   60-space line

LAB 16

Noun Possessives

Type lines 1–4 once. Then repeat lines 1–4 or take a series of 1-minute timings. As you type each line, note the noun possessives.

```
1  The manager's reply was extremely helpful to Jackie Quimby.   12
2  The managers' replies were very helpful to Fred and Maxine.   12
3  A new employee's chart must be sent to a dozen departments.   12
4  New employees' charts must be duplicated by your secretary.   12
   |  1  |  2  |  3  |  4  |  5  |  6  |  7  |  8  |  9  |  10  |  11  |  12
```

To form the possessive of a singular or plural noun not *ending* in an *s* sound, add an *apostrophe* plus *s* to the noun.

  a person<u>'s</u> personal property   a state<u>'s</u> natural boundary   the children<u>'s</u> school

To form the possessive of a singular noun *ending* in an *s* sound, add an *apostrophe* plus *s* to the noun. However, if the addition of an extra syllable would make an *s*-ending word hard to pronounce, add the apostrophe only.

  my boss<u>'s</u> calendar   Mr. Phillips' pen

(Continued on next page)

■ **GOALS**
To control ¢, @, =, and + keys by touch, holding home key anchors.
To construct special symbols.

■ **FORMAT**
Single spacing   50-space line

KEYBOARDING SKILLS

Type each line twice.

Speed   1 The firm that they own may make a big profit now.

Accuracy   2 Her job was to pack a dozen equal boxes by night.

Numbers   3 Mark will order 10, 29, 38, 47, and 56 varieties.

Symbols   4 It's not "up" but "down"! He saw Jane's new car.

Hold Those Anchors

For ¢ anchor ;
For @ anchor F
For ± anchor J

¢ **KEY**

Shift of 6. Use J finger.

Do not space between the number and the ¢.

Type each line twice.

5 jy6 jy¢ j¢j j¢j Is it 10¢, 29¢, 38¢, 47¢, or 56¢?

6 Lisa has too many for 67¢ and not enough for 20¢.

7 The sales taxes total 56¢, 47¢, 38¢, 29¢, and 1¢.

@ **KEY**

Shift of 2. Use S finger.

@ means "at."

Space once before and after an @.

Type each line twice.

8 sw2 sw@ s@s s@s She wants 21 @ 11¢, not 11 @ 21¢.

9 Pat and Ted sold them for 20 @ 14¢, not 14 @ 20¢.

10 How much are 10 apples @ 12¢ and 14 lemons @ 10¢?

TECHNIQUE CHECKPOINT

Keep eyes on copy while typing symbols and numbers.

Type lines 11–14 once. Then repeat lines 5 and 8.

11 The following increases were noted: cereal, 10¢;   10

12 milk, 29¢; bread, 38¢; sugar, 47¢; and beef, 56¢.   20

13 A dozen apples @ 15¢ each is also a big increase,   30

14 but buying oranges @ 20¢ is an even larger total.   40

| 1 | 2 | 3 | 4 | 5 | 6 | 7 | 8 | 9 | 10

Take a 5-minute timing on lines 5–21. Circle and count your errors.

```
5       Have you ever felt run-down, tired, and fatigued?  The      12
6   symptoms just identified are experienced by many people to-     24
7   day.  They affect our job performance, they limit enjoyable     36
8   times with our families, and they quite possibly can affect     48
9   our health.  The following paragraph suggests a few ways to     60
10  minimize these problems as we become more active persons in     72
11  all our activities.                                             76
12      It is essential that we get plenty of sleep so that we      88
13  are rested when we get up each morning.  We must eat a good     100
14  breakfast so that we can build up energies for the day that     112
15  follows.  Physical exercise is needed, and it might well be     124
16  the one most important ingredient in building up our energy     136
17  reserves.  We must take part in exercises that make us per-     148
18  spire, make our hearts beat faster, and cause our breathing     160
19  rate to increase appreciably.  All these things can help us     172
20  to increase our energies and become healthier people.  Life     184
21  will be more enjoyable if we can focus on these actions.        195
    |  1  |  2  |  3  |  4  |  5  |  6  |  7  |  8  |  9  |  10  |  11  |  12    SI 1.49
```

In the chart below find the number of errors you made on the Pretest. Then type each of the designated drill lines four times.

Pretest errors	0–1	2–3	4–5	6+
Drill lines	25–29	24–28	23–27	22–26

Accuracy
```
22  have tired exercise fatigued important enjoyable ingredient
23  run ever energies physical essential identified appreciably
24  felt down increase possible breakfast breathing experienced
25  just many suggests minimize healthier paragraph performance
```

Speed
```
26  family people times limit today rate ways with they and the
27  become health build sleep these help well that more our job
28  person active heart thing cause life take must most all get
29  things plenty focus might quite each beat make part for day
```

Take another 5-minute timing on lines 5–21 to see how much your skill has improved.

Hold Those Anchors

For ¢ anchor ;
For @ anchor F
For ± anchor J

 **KEYS**

+ is shift of =.
Next to hyphen. Use
Sem finger.

Type each line twice.

15 ; =; === ; =; === = A = 40, B = 35, C = 25, D = 20.
16 ; +; +++ ; +; +++ 0 + 10 + 29 + 38 + 47 + 56 = 180.
17 Yes, 3 + 3 = 6 and 9 + 9 = 18; but 3 + 18 = what?

TECHNIQUE CHECKPOINT

Space once before
and after the + and
the =.

Be sure to hold
anchors while making
long reaches to the
top row.

Type lines 18–21 once. Then repeat lines 15–16.

18 If 2 + 2 = 4 and 7 + 7 = 14, how much is 14 + 14? 10
19 Watch the ball go! It's a home run for the team! 20
20 If 4 + 6 = 10 and 6 + 4 = 10, what will 5 + 5 be? 30
21 Watch the beautiful eagle! It's building a nest! 40

| 1 | 2 | 3 | 4 | 5 | 6 | 7 | 8 | 9 | 10

SPECIAL SYMBOLS

Many keys on the keyboard can be used to represent special symbols. Some are typed "as is," some are typed off the line of writing, and others are typed in combination with other symbols. The most common of these special symbols are shown below. Using the procedures given in Column 3, type Column 2 centered on a full page. Use double spacing.

Column 1	Column 2	Column 3
22. Roman numerals	Chapter XVIII	Capitals of I, V, X, L, C, D, and M.
23. Feet and inches	Mary is 5' 2"	For feet, apostrophe; for inches, quotation mark.
24. Minutes, seconds	Time: 3' 15"	For minutes, apostrophe; for seconds, quotation mark.
25. Times, by	What is 4 x 5	Expressed by the small letter X.
26. Minus	140 − 56 = 84	Expressed by a single hyphen; space before and after.
27. Ellipsis	He . . . also He I	Three periods, spaced apart (but four periods if there is a sentence ending within the omitted material).
28. Degrees	32°F (or 0°C)	Small letter O, raised slightly (turn cylinder by hand).
29. Superscript	$8^2 + 6^2 = 10^2$	Type number or letter above line (turn cylinder by hand).
30. Subscript	H_2O is water.	Type number or letter below line (turn cylinder by hand).
31. Equals	11 x 11 = 121	Two hyphens, one below the other (turn cylinder by hand).
32. Plus	87 $\neq$ 18 = 105	Hyphen, intersected by diagonal or apostrophe.
33. Divided by	120 ÷ 10 = 12	Colon, intersected by hyphen.

FORMATTING LETTERS WITH INDENTED PARAGRAPHS

The letters that you have typed in this course have all been formatted in *modified-block style,* with the date, complimentary closing, and writer's name or name and title indented to the center. A variation of this style is to also indent the first line of each paragraph 5 spaces.

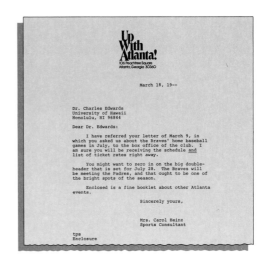

Up With Atlanta!
106 Peachtree Square
Atlanta, Georgia 30360

March 18, 19--

Dr. Charles Edwards
University of Hawaii
Honolulu, HI 96844

Dear Dr. Edwards:

I have referred your letter of March 9, in which you asked us about the Braves' home baseball games in July, to the box office of the club. I am sure you will be receiving the schedule and list of ticket rates right away.

You might want to zero in on the big double-header that is set for July 28. The Braves will be meeting the Padres, and that ought to be one of the bright spots of the season.

Enclosed is a fine booklet about other Atlanta events.

Sincerely yours,

Mrs. Carol Heinz
Sports Consultant

tps
Enclosure

JOB 132 A. LETTER

Standard format with indented paragraphs. Workbook 209–210. Body 82 words.

Dr. Sheng Y. Hwang, 12678 Kimball	15
Avenue, Waterloo, IA 50701, Dear	22
Dr. Hwang:	24
Thank you for your recent request	33
for a copy of a memorandum written by	41
Dr. Carolyn Jankowski to Congresswoman	48
Kathryn Caulfield.	52
As chairperson of the committee	61
that used that memo as evidence in	68
the case Jernigan v. Mayberry, I must	76
inform you that I am not permitted	82

to reveal the contents of the memo	89
until the case is closed.	95
Mr. Lee Hart, who was also	102
involved in this case, may be able	109
to assist you. He worked with	115
Dr. Jankowski at that time. Yours	125
truly, W. L. Safranski, Member of	139
Congress	142

JOB 132 B. COMPOSED LETTER

Standard format with indented paragraphs. Workbook 211–212.

Compose a letter for Dr. Hwang to Mr. Lee Hart, 11234 Douglas Avenue, Des Moines, IA 50322, as suggested in Job 132 A. Ask for his assistance.

LESSON 133

■ **GOALS**
To form plurals of nouns correctly while typing sentences.
To type 39/5'/5e.
To format and type a letter in block style.

■ **FORMAT**
Drills: Single spacing   60-space line
5-Minute Timings: Double spacing   5-space tab

LAB 15

Plurals

Workbook 213–214.

Type lines 1–4 once, making plurals of the underscored words. Edit your copy as your teacher reads the answers. Then retype lines 1–4 from your edited copy.

1 The <u>company</u> represented at least a dozen northern <u>city</u>.
2 Janet will make several <u>journey</u> to the <u>oversea</u> <u>country</u>.
3 My <u>sister-in-law</u> saw two one-act <u>play</u> last Tuesday night.
4 She <u>rely</u> on the reputations of the <u>attorney</u> on the case.

LESSON 30

■ **GOALS**
To review the symbol-key controls.
To type 28/3'/5e.

■ **FORMAT**
Drills: Single spacing   50-space line
3-Minute Timings: Double spacing   5-space tab

KEYBOARDING SKILLS

Type each line twice.

Speed   1 She may wish to amend the form when she signs it.
Accuracy   2 Jackey's vague quip amazed and vexed her brother.
Numbers   3 Your fingers can now find 10, 29, 38, 47, and 56.
Symbols   4 Do 10 + 29 + 38 + 47 + 56 = 180? Yes! It's 180.

REVIEW

Type each line twice.

( )   5 He listed items (10), (29), (38), (47), and (56).

+   6 Millie counted 10 + 29 + 38 + 47 + 56 to get 180.

=   7 Grades: 10 = D, 29 = C, 38 = B, 47 = A, 56 = A+.

$ 8 My special rates are $10, $29, $38, $47, and $56.

¢   9 I collected 10¢, 29¢, 38¢, 47¢, and 56¢ for them.

@   10 They saw 12 pears @ $1.28 and 12 bananas @ $1.39.

TECHNIQUE CHECKPOINT

Keep eyes on copy while typing numbers and symbols.

Type lines 11–12 once. Then repeat any of lines 5–10 that contain symbols you need to practice.

11 Anna, did you know that (9 + 9)(8 + 8) = 18 x 16?   10

12 Buy 8 @ 75¢ and 26 @ 25¢; total (plus 4%) is $13.   20
    | 1 | 2 | 3 | 4 | 5 | 6 | 7 | 8 | 9 | 10

REVIEW

Type each line twice.

13 Carpet remnants were #10, #29, #38, #47, and #56.

%   14 New rates: 1% to 10%, 29% to 38%, or 47% to 56%.

!   15 Shout! Up! No! Down! There! Yes! Here! Oh!

:   16 Times listed: 10:29, 11:38, 2:47, 1:56, or 2:01.

&   17 Pair them as follows: 10 & 29, 38 & 47, 56 & 29.

An asterisk (*) follows a punctuation mark.

*   18 Which is the right date: 1929,* 1947,* or 1956?*

"   19 "Isn't it fine!" she exclaimed. "Look at it go!"

'   20 It's not that he won't speak; it's that he can't.

___ 21 Please send Return of Lassie or Call of the Wild.

Alternate-Hand	13	One of the criteria we should use is capability. Will	12
Reaches	14	the equipment perform the functions important to our needs?	24
	15	If we select equipment that's able to perform more than our	36
	16	needs, we may be spending much more than we should. There-	48
	17	fore, cost is one factor to think about. Lastly, it is im-	60
	18	portant that we think about the quality of service that can	72
	19	be secured with our equipment.	78

```
|  1  |  2  |  3  |  4  |  5  |  6  |  7  |  8  |  9  |  10  |  11  |  12
```

PRACTICE

In which timing did you make more errors? If in the first one (lines 6–12 on page 220), type lines 20–23 four times and lines 24–27 two times. If most of your errors were in the second timing (lines 13–19), reverse the procedure.

Double-Letter	20	comma falls foods annoys annual asleep banner booths borrow
Reaches	21	sheep shell sleep bottle bottom button caller cannon cannot
	22	smell sorry spell commit common copper cotton dinner galley
	23	tells tooth upper happen keeper manner middle mirror occupy
Alternate-Hand	24	abide black cable absent blamed carpet damage eighty favors
Reaches	25	dealt ended flaps gladly hauled island jacket ladies league
	26	gleam habit lakes manage namely oblige parked purple ranges
	27	names stake tapes scheme theory urgent visual widely wished

POSTTEST

Repeat the Pretest on page 220 and above to see how much your skill has improved.

LESSON 132

UNIT 22 Formatting Correspondence

UNIT GOAL 39/5'/5e

■ **GOALS**
To form plurals of nouns correctly while typing sentences.
To format and type letters in indented-paragraph style.

■ **FORMAT**
Single spacing   60-space line

LAB 15
Plurals

Type lines 1–4 once, making plurals of the underscored words. Edit your copy as your teacher reads the answers. Then retype lines 1–4 from your edited copy.

1 Two district attorney quietly talked with the free agent.

2 Those secretary--Liza, Jane, and Alex--work on annuity.

3 All editor in chief must post jobs on the bulletin board.

4 Send dictionary to your copywriters in these territory.

12-SECOND TIMINGS

Type each line three times, or take three 12-second timings on each line. For each timing, type with no more than 1 error.

5 The tree fell down just a short time after it began to die.

6 We can win the long race if we work hard for days and days.

7 Will she be able to get the job done by the end of the day?

```
5      10      15      20      25      30      35      40      45      50      55      60
```

TECHNIQUE CHECKPOINT

Keep eyes on copy while typing numbers and symbols.

Type lines 22–24 once. Then repeat any of lines 13–21 (page 52) that contain symbols you need to practice.

22 Their #4 and #7 sizes are 30% to 40% higher here.   10
23 K&D arrived at 1:30.   L&W came later on at 2:45.*   20
24 "It's Oklahoma!" Jean said.   "Let's buy tickets!"   34
   | 1 | 2 | 3 | 4 | 5 | 6 | 7 | 8 | 9 | 10

3-MINUTE TIMINGS

Take two 3-minute timings on lines 25–33. Use the speed markers to figure your speed.

25   A jigsaw puzzle is such fun. To fit all the   10
26 shapes is a game. At first it is a game of hues,   20
27 and then it is a game of sizes, and at the last a   30
28 game of fits. Each piece looks as though it will   40
29 fit, but just one piece will do so. You can push   50
30 and squeeze all day, but only the right shape and   60
31 proper size will drop into place. Many pieces do   70
32 look equal to the holes, but only the exact match   80
33 fits in the puzzle.   84
   | 1 | 2 | 3 | 4 | 5 | 6 | 7 | 8 | 9 | 10   SI 1.13

LESSON 31

CLINIC

■ GOALS
To review the number-key controls.
To build skill in typing numbers by touch, holding home key anchors.

■ FORMAT:
Drills: Single spacing   50-space line

KEYBOARDING SKILLS

Type each line twice.

Speed   1 The girls may wish to go to the city for a visit.
Accuracy   2 Jodie will quickly fix seven big pizzas for them.
Numbers   3 Add 10 and 29 and 38 and 47 and 56 and 74 and 83.
Symbols   4 He paid $3.60 (80% of 6 @ 75¢) for #10 envelopes.

PRETEST

Take two 2-minute timings on lines 5–9. Proofread your copy and circle your errors.

5 0101 0202 0303 0404 0505 0606 0707 0808 0909 1010   10
6 1111 1212 1313 1414 1515 1616 1717 1818 1919 2020   20
7 2121 2222 2323 2424 2525 2626 2727 2828 2929 3030   30
8 3131 3232 3333 3434 3535 3636 3737 3838 3939 4040   40
9 4141 4242 4343 4444 4545 4646 4747 4848 4949 5050   50
  | 1 | 2 | 3 | 4 | 5 | 6 | 7 | 8 | 9 | 10

pocket. A desktop unit can be purchased from many different suppliers. Many of these units operate with cartridges or cassette tapes; you can dictate, transcribe, or perform both functions on these machines.[2]

Some offices have centralized systems that use private wire connections to all dictators. Sometimes a telephone system can be used for a word processing dictation system. The number of people capable of using this system at one time is limited only by the number of telephone extensions in use in the office.

FOOTNOTES

1. Marilyn K. Popyk, <u>Word Processing, Essential Concepts,</u> 2d ed., McGraw-Hill Book Company, New York, 1986, p. 4.

2. Marilyn K. Popyk, <u>Word Processing and Information Systems,</u> 2d ed., McGraw-Hill Book Company, New York, 1986, pp. 58–59.

LESSON 131

CLINIC

■ **GOALS**
To improve your typing skills through the Selective Practice routine.

■ **FORMAT**
Drills: Single spacing   60-space line
2-Minute Timings: Double spacing   5-space tab

KEYBOARDING SKILLS

Type lines 1–4 once. In line 5 use the shift lock for each word in all-capital letters. Repeat lines 1–4, or take a series of 1-minute timings.

Speed	1	These short, easy words help you when you build your speed.	12
Accuracy	2	Jacqueline was glad her family took five or six big prizes.	12
Numbers	3	If I need 56 points, then 47, 29, 38, or 10 would not help.	12
Symbols	4	I concluded that 1/2 of $28 = $14 and that 20% of $10 = $2.	12
Technique	5	See if ONE and TWO work; don't try THREE and FOUR and FIVE.	

| 1 | 2 | 3 | 4 | 5 | 6 | 7 | 8 | 9 | 10 | 11 | 12

PRETEST

Take a 2-minute timing on lines 6–12; then take a 2-minute timing on lines 13–19 on page 221. Circle and count your errors on each.

Double-Letter Reaches

6   Word processing has suddenly become very valued in the   12
7 office of today. We have all seen the advent of terminals,   24
8 disk drives, letter-quality printers, and added features in   36
9 the office the past few years. It appears there are liter-   48
10 ally dozens of models offered for all our needs and equally   60
11 as many vendors too. What factors should be looked at when   72
12 we choose to update equipment?   78

| 1 | 2 | 3 | 4 | 5 | 6 | 7 | 8 | 9 | 10 | 11 | 12

(Continued on next page)

Type lines 10–14 three times. Proofread your copy and circle your errors.

```
10  1 aql aql aql l ll lll ll l ll lll ll l ll lll ll
11  0 ;p0 ;p0 ;p0 0 10 100 10 0 01 001 01 0 10 100 10
12  2 sw2 sw2 sw2 2 20 220 20 2 02 022 02 0 20 220 20
13  9 lo9 lo9 lo9 9 93 939 93 9 39 399 09 9 39 999 90
14  3 de3 de3 de3 3 33 332 38 3 38 383 03 3 38 323 30
```

Type lines 15–19 three times. Proofread your copy and circle your errors.

```
15  8 ki8 ki8 ki8 8 82 882 80 8 28 288 08 8 82 882 80
16  4 fr4 fr4 fr4 4 43 432 42 4 44 489 04 4 44 474 40
17  7 ju7 ju7 ju7 7 78 747 47 7 74 787 07 7 74 747 70
18  5 ft5 ft5 ft5 5 54 535 25 5 75 557 05 5 55 535 50
19  6 ju6 ju6 ju6 6 67 686 65 6 56 667 07 6 56 656 60
```

Type lines 20–24 three times. Proofread your copy and circle your errors.

```
20  we 23 24 25 we 23 24 25 – up 70 71 72 up 70 71 72
21  re 43 44 45 re 43 44 45 – or 94 95 96 or 94 95 96
22  ow 92 93 94 ow 92 93 94 – it 85 86 87 it 85 86 87
23  ie 83 84 85 ie 83 84 85 – ru 47 48 49 ru 47 48 49
24  qu 17 18 19 qu 17 18 19 – ye 63 64 65 ye 63 64 65
```

POSTTEST

Take two 2-minute timings on lines 5–9 (page 53). Proofread your copy and circle your errors. Note your improvement.

LESSON 32

UNIT 6 Introduction to Production Typing

UNIT GOAL 30/3'/5e

■ GOALS
To type 30/3'/5e.
To use the bell to make line-ending decisions.
To use the margin release to type outside set margins.

■ FORMAT
Drills: Single spacing   60-space line
3-Minute Timings: Double spacing   5-space tab

KEYBOARDING SKILLS

Type each line twice.

Speed   1 She may wish to go to the lake to ice-fish or to ice-skate.
Accuracy   2 Five or six big jet planes zoomed quickly by the new tower.
Numbers   3 We need 16 pens, 24 pencils, 50 paper clips, and 38 stamps.
Symbols   4 Did he read or see <u>Treasure Island</u> (the book or the movie)?

PREVIEW PRACTICE

Type each line twice as a preview to the 3-minute timings on page 55.

Accuracy   5 for amazed friend special whether hobbies thoughts choosing
Speed   6 also joke gift your will when what that how you may has the

JOB 129/130 A. (CONTINUED)

<u>October.</u> The Rock Medley Concert, direct from London, will accent this month's activities. Three separate shows are scheduled on October 10, 11, and 12. All shows will run from 8 p.m. to 10:30 p.m. This will be our biggest event, with a total audience of 60,000 for the combined performances. Special attention will be given to the sound system in the Convention Center—several additional amplifiers and speakers will have to be installed for the concert.

[**Students:** You are to compose the last two paragraphs for the newsletter article, including main attractions for November and December. Use the information given below when you draft your composition.]

Month: November
Event: Arts and Crafts Show
Dates: 17th through the 30th
Audience: 7000
Special Attention: 500 exhibit booths to display the artists' works

Month: December
Event: National Antique Show
Dates: 5th through the 11th
Audience: 10,000
Special Attention: Security will have to be increased to protect some of the valuable items.

JOB 129/130 B. MULTIPAGE REPORT
Standard format. Footnotes on page 220.

THE ADVENT OF WORD PROCESSING
By Don Martin

HISTORY

The concept of word processing has been with us for quite a few years, back to 1868 when C. L. Sholes from Wisconsin received a patent for the first typewriter.[1] The touch system (1889) used on the typewriter was responsible for changing the outlook of the modern office in terms of the amount of work that could be done by a typist who used all the fingers working at the task instead of just two or four fingers. Dictating machines were also responsible for causing rapid changes in the office.

Thus, like its predecessors, word processing systems have had great influence on the amount of work produced in the office of today. The completion of more work is made possible through the use of such equipment as the automatic typewriter and the cathode ray tube. Magnetic tape and magnetic card typewriters are able to capture on tape or card all that is placed into the machine and change or delete those words or sections that must be revised before the final copy is typed. The cathode ray tube shows on a screen above the keyboard what is being placed into the storage unit of the typewriter. The keyboard of this machine allows for changes to be made very easily in the text. The evolution of word processing, then, has progressed through a number of important events since 1868, as revealed in the table below.

EVOLUTION OF WORD PROCESSING
1868–1986

Manual Typewriter	1868
Electric Typewriter	1933
Selectric Typewriter	1961
MT/ST	1964
Display Word Processor	1971
Floppy Disk System	1973
Memory Typewriter	1974
Electronic Typewriter	1978
Personal Computer	1981

Source: Marilyn K. Popyk, <u>Word Processing, Essential Concepts</u>, 2d ed., McGraw-Hill Book Company, New York, 1986, p. 73.

DICTATION EQUIPMENT

Many different kinds of input dictation equipment for word processing are available. You can buy portable units that can be carried away from your desk, and these units are small enough to fit into your coat

(Continued on next page)

3-MINUTE TIMINGS

Take two 3-minute timings on lines 7–14. Use the speed markers to figure your speed.

```
              1                2              3                4
 7    When you choose a gift for a friend, how do you decide     12
            5             6              7               8
 8  what it will be?  You will be amazed at the hours which you   24
              9             10             11          12
 9  spend choosing the exact gift.  You may choose a gift to be   36
             13            14             15            16
10  worn, or you may choose a gift to be read.  The gift may be   48
           17              18             19             20
11  a joke which brings a smile.  You could also note whether a   60
            21           22             23            24
12  friend is active or quiet, and you could check hobbies that   72
         25             26             27              28
13  your friend has.  The gift will show those special thoughts   84
           29             30
14  that you have for your friend.                               90

    |  1  |  2  |  3  |  4  |  5  |  6  |  7  |  8  |  9  |  10  |  11  |  12    SI 1.10
```

RIGHT MARGIN BELL Workbook 27–28.

To help make the right margin lines end close to the desired right margin, a bell rings when the carriage or carrier approaches the margin. Depending on the machine, the bell may ring as few as 8 or as many as 15 spaces before the margin. (Check *your* machine. How many spaces before the margin does it ring?)

Assume that your machine will ring 8 spaces before the right margin. Assume, too, that you have set your right margin at 80. The bell will ring when you reach 72. When the bell rings, you must decide how best to end the line closest to 80—preferably without dividing words. Here are some typical line-ending decisions:

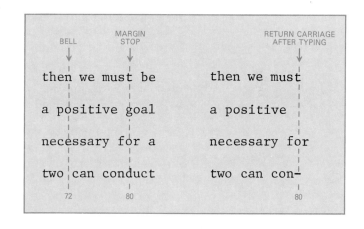

JOB 32 A. MAKING LINE-ENDING DECISIONS

Type the following paragraphs, making line-ending decisions as you type. Do not go beyond the right margin, and do not divide any words. Format: Double spacing, 50-space line, 5-space tab.

Computers and word processors have automatic word wraparound. At the end of a line of keyboarding, the cursor automatically drops down to the next line without the use of a carriage return. If the last word will not fit on a line, that word is automatically entered as the first word of the next line.

It is time to realize that it is not through chance that the lines in your timings seem to end straight. Each line has been changed a number of times, some as many as six times, just to be sure that all lines are equal in length.

The reason that lines are written to be even is simply to help you in checking your work. Any line, other than the last one of a paragraph, not ending with the others must contain an error; and knowing this, you can check work in less time.

TYPING BEYOND THE MARGIN

A formatting technique.

Sometimes, in order to make good line-ending decisions, you must type a few characters beyond the right margin. In order to type beyond the right margin without resetting it, you can use the margin release key. The margin release key is usually located in the upper left section of the keyboard. When you depress the margin release key, it temporarily unlocks the margin and allows you to continue typing. You should not exceed your set margin by more than 3 or 4 spaces. (You also should not stop more than 3 or 4 spaces before the desired margin.)

Practice. Retype lines 1–4 (Keyboarding Skills) on page 54. Leave your margins set for a 50-space line. Use the margin release key so that you can finish each drill line.

■ GOALS
To identify plural forms of nouns while typing sentences.
To type 39/5'/5e.
To type a newsletter article with composed paragraphs and a
report with a table and footnotes.

■ FORMAT
Drills: Single spacing   60-space line
5-Minute Timings: Double spacing   5-space tab

LAB 15

Plurals

Type lines 1–4 once. Then repeat lines 1–4 or take a series of 1-minute timings.

1 Peter Zak wrote essays on the subject for my English class.   12
2 The armies of the nine nations have signed a unique treaty.   12
3 The mothers-in-law in our neighborhood have a weekly class.   12
4 Several companies have tried to have the taxes lowered now.   12

   | 1 | 2 | 3 | 4 | 5 | 6 | 7 | 8 | 9 | 10 | 11 | 12

12-SECOND TIMINGS

Type each line three times, or take three 12-second timings on each line. For each timing, type with no more than 1 error.

5 They would like to drive in their car when they go to town.
6 We would like to sign the memo when it is sent in the mail.
7 She wants to do all of that work by the end of the workday.

        5   10   15   20   25   30   35   40   45   50   55   60

PREVIEW PRACTICE

Type lines 1 and 2 on page 208 twice as a preview to the 5-minute timings on page 208.

5-MINUTE TIMINGS

Take two 5-minute timings on lines 3–22 on page 208.

JOB 129/130 A. NEWSLETTER ARTICLE

Two paragraphs at the end of the article must be composed. Draft at the typewriter those two paragraphs before you type the article. Standard format.

CONVENTION CENTER SCHEDULE
By (*Your name*)

Scheduling for the Convention Center has been completed, and we look forward to another fall of maximum use of our facility. To keep you informed of latest developments, this month's company newsletter will provide a summary of activities from August to December. The following paragraphs reveal main attractions for the fall period.

August. The main attraction for this month will be the Southwest Computer Show. The dates for the show will be August 14–22. Anticipated attendance is 12,000; special attention will have to be given to the electrical hookups because of the 250 exhibitors who will be displaying their systems.

September. Highlighting this month will be the Travel Home Convention, scheduled to run on two different weeks: September 4–10 and September 22–28. We expect 2500 people during each week, for a total of 5000. Special attention will have to be given to the entrances and exits to be certain our west doors will accommodate some of the larger travel homes.

(Continued on next page)

JOB 32 B. MAKING LINE-ENDING DECISIONS

Type the following paragraph, making line-ending decisions as you type. Use your margin release key to type beyond your right margin where necessary. Do not divide words. Format: Double spacing, 50-space line, 5-space tab.

This paragraph was designed to help you learn how to make line-ending decisions and to give you practice in using the margin release key. Several spaces after the bell rings, the carriage or carrier will lock at the margin. You should try to end the typing as close as possible to the margin. Try to keep your typing within four spaces of your margin. (That is, you may stop four spaces short or go over by four spaces.) To type beyond your right margin without changing it, all you have to do is depress the margin release key. If you made all the right line-ending decisions, you had to use your margin release key five times while typing this paragraph.

LESSON
33

■ **GOALS**
To type 30/3'/5e.
To correct errors using a variety of techniques.
To format and type enumerations.

■ **FORMAT**
Drills: Single spacing   60-space line
3-Minute Timings: Double spacing   5-space tab

KEYBOARDING SKILLS

Type each line twice.

Speed
Accuracy
Numbers
Symbols

1 On the shelf he may find the map for the lake and the land.
2 Sew the azure badge on my velvet jacket before the banquet.
3 Type 1 or 2 or 3 or 4 or 5 or 6 or 7 or 8 or 9 or 10 or 11.
4 Pay 80% of $2.59 for #7 ledgers at Owens & Barnes Supplies.

PREVIEW PRACTICE

Type each line twice as a preview to the 3-minute timings below.

Accuracy
Speed

5 text dizzy covers neatly errors liquid corrects typewriter.
6 nice look will when page from take hole your have that sign

3-MINUTE TIMINGS

Take two 3-minute timings on lines 7–14.

```
                1                2                3                4
 7      When you correct an error that you have typed, you are    12
                5                6                7                8
 8  to do it as neatly as you can.  A smear or a hole in a page   24
                    9                10               11           12
 9  is a sign that you do not take pride in the text that comes   36
                13               14               15               16
10  from your typewriter.  If you make a page dizzy with liquid   48
                17               18               19               20
11  corrections, the page will not look nice at all.  That tape   60
                21               22               23               24
12  which covers is fine, but you must be sure that you are not   72
                25               26               27               28
13  able to see where you used it.  Chalk will do on some jobs,   84
                29               30
14  but it will rub off with time.                               90
     |  1  |  2  |  3  |  4  |  5  |  6  |  7  |  8  |  9  |  10  |  11  |  12    SI 1.11
```

7:30 p.m., EST — Arrive Atlanta Airport.

8:00 p.m. — Depart Atlanta Airport, Delta Air Lines Flight 556.

9:15 p.m. — Arrive Lexington.

Accommodations: Sheraton Inn. Guaranteed arrival.

Monday, October 3

9:00 a.m. — Meet with Chris Bloomfield, Schofield Hall, University of Kentucky.

1:00 p.m. — Convention at Rupp Arena.

Tuesday, October 4

9:25 a.m., EST — Depart Lexington, Delta Air Lines Flight 983, snack served.

11:14 a.m., CST — Arrive Dallas, DFW Airport.

2:30 p.m. — Meeting with Kathryn Davis.

JOB 128 B. MAGAZINE ARTICLE

Standard format (p. 215). Edit the copy as you type. (That is, correct spelling, capitalization, and punctuation errors.)

Computer Processing Speeds by michael s. johnson
(lines of 50 spaces)

Improvements that have taken place in computer technology can be segmented into a series of different stages of development. These individual segments are known as generations. The first generation computers, which used vacuum tubes, were popular up until about 1959; there capabilitys exceeded a thousand calculations a second. The unit of time given to this speed is millisecond. To give you some sense as to how fast a millisecond is, a plain flying at 200 mile an hour would travel less than 1 inch in a millisecond.

The second generation computers came to us about 1959 or 1960. They were 10 times as fast as the first generation computers and the heart of this system was the transistor. they were much smaller in size than the first generation computers.

The 3d generation computers were introduced by various companys in 1964. The heart of these computers was the miniature electronic circuit. They operated at the rate of 1 million operations a second. The unit of time given to this speed is microsecond. To give you some sense as to how fast this is, a spaceship traveling toward the planet mars at 100,000 miles an hour would move less than 2 inches in a microsecond.

Fourth generation computer came to us in the 1970s, and the heart of these systems is the silicon chip. These computers are used today in almost every segment of business--in doctors' offices in attorneys' offices in government in education, etc. They operate in nanoseconds (one billion operations per second) and picoseconds (one trillion operation per second). A nanosecond is an extremely small unit of time; in fact, there are as many nanoseconds in one second as there are seconds in thirty years. Another way of saying it is that there are as many nanoseconds in a minute as there are minutes in 1100 centurys. A picosecond is the smallest unit of time asociated with computers. In this unit of time, light would move less than 1/50th of an inch. A picosecond is to a second what a second is to about 32,000 years.

CORRECTING ERRORS

One way to correct errors on a computer or word processor is to position the cursor at the point of the incorrect letter. Type the correct letter over the incorrect one. This is called the strikeover method.

Errors may be corrected in a number of ways: erasing, using correction fluid to cover errors, using correction tape or paper to cover up or lift off errors, or using the correcting mechanism on a typewriter.

To erase errors:

1. Turn the paper so that the error will be at the top of the cylinder.
2. Using the margin release, move the carriage or carrier as far left or right as possible (to keep eraser grit out of the operating parts of the machine).
3. Press the paper tightly against the cylinder with your fingertips.
4. With a typewriting eraser, erase each letter to be deleted; use light up-and-down strokes.
5. Turn the paper back to the writing line.
6. Insert the correction.

To correct errors using correction fluid:

1. Turn the paper so that the error will be at the top of the cylinder.
2. Use short, light dabs to cover the error. Let the fluid dry.
3. Roll the paper back and type the correction.

To correct errors using correction paper:

1. Backspace to the error.
2. Insert the correction paper.
3. Strike the incorrect letter. The paper will cover up or lift off the incorrect letter.
4. Remove the correction paper.
5. Backspace and type the correction.

To use correction tape on draft copy:

1. Press the correction tape over the copy to be deleted.
2. Type the correct copy on the tape.

To correct errors using the typewriter correcting mechanism:

1. Position the carrier in the space following the error.
2. Press the correcting key. This will move the carrier 1 space backwards and will engage the correction tape.
3. Strike the incorrect letter. The tape will cover up or lift off the error.
4. Type the correction. Do *not* backspace before typing the correction; the correcting mechanism will hold the carrier until the correction is made.

Practice

Type this: There are four rules to remember. Try to learn then today.

Correct it to: There are five rules to remember. Try to learn them today.

FORMATTING ENUMERATIONS

An enumeration is a series of numbered or lettered words, phrases, or sentences. An enumeration may be typed in *hanging-indented format,* where the numbers or letters stand by themselves in the margin. Or it may be typed in *paragraph format,* where paragraphs are indented and begin with a number or a letter.

To format enumerations:

1. Set margins for a 5-inch line (50-pica spaces/60 elite spaces). You may use a longer or shorter line depending on the length of the enumerated items.
2. Center the enumeration vertically if it is on a page by itself, or begin it on line 13.
3. Use single spacing, and leave 1 blank line between paragraphs.
4. Follow the numbers or the letters with a period and 2 spaces.
5. In the hanging-indented format, turnover lines (those lines not beginning with a number or letter) are indented 4 spaces from the left margin.
6. In the paragraph format, the first line (the one beginning with the number or letter) is indented 5 spaces from the left margin. Turnover lines block at the margin.

Formatting Titles

1. Center the title over the copy.
2. Type the title in all-capital letters.
3. Leave 2 blank lines below the title.

■ **GOALS**
To recognize plural forms of nouns while typing sentences.
To type an itinerary and a magazine article.

■ **FORMAT**
Single spacing   60-space line

LAB 15
Plurals

Type lines 1–4 once. Then repeat lines 1–4 or take a series of 1-minute timings.

1 Persons in local governments serve the cities and counties.   12
2 Her brothers-in-law went to the studio to do a job quietly.   12
3 The ladies work as volunteers at the exits at the city zoo.   12
4 Dr. Perry's attorneys are working on the case for Mrs. Lee.   12
   | 1 | 2 | 3 | 4 | 5 | 6 | 7 | 8 | 9 | 10 | 11 | 12

When a singular noun ends in *y* preceded by a consonant, the plural is formed by changing the *y* to *i* and adding *es* to the singular.

company, companies   authority, authorities

But when a singular noun ends in *y* preceded by a vowel, the plural is formed by adding *s* to the singular.

attorney, attorneys

The plurals of compound nouns spelled with a hyphen or as two words are formed by making the chief element of the compound plural.

brother-in-law, brothers-in-law
account receivable, accounts receivable

30-SECOND "OK" TIMINGS

Type as many 30-second "OK" (errorless) timings as possible out of three attempts on lines 5–7.

5 Judge Zoller requires the work to be typed with extra care,   12
6 because it will have to be retyped if any errors are found.   24
7 I remember quite vividly the last time we had to retype it.   36
   | 1 | 2 | 3 | 4 | 5 | 6 | 7 | 8 | 9 | 10 | 11 | 12

JOB 128 A. ITINERARY
Standard format.

Itinerary

J. R. Reynolds

(Dallas -- Lexington)

October 2, 19--

Sunday, October 2
4:50 p.m., CST

Depart Dallas, DFW Airport, Delta Air Lines Flight 748, dinner served.

(Continued on next page)

Some jobs have arrows and numbers to help you space vertically. For example, ↓3 means "go down 3 lines." (Leave 2 lines blank, and type on the third line.)

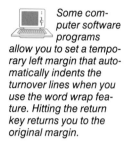 *Some computer software programs* allow you to set a temporary left margin that automatically indents the turnover lines when you use the word wrap feature. Hitting the return key returns you to the original margin.

From now on, use a full sheet of paper unless told otherwise.

JOB 33 A. ENUMERATION
Hanging-indented format. Full sheet of paper. 4-space tab.

HANGING–INDENTED ENUMERATION

↓3

A. An enumeration can be a set of steps or a series of num—
   bered or lettered words or statements.

B. It is arranged so that the numbers or letters stand by
   themselves in the margin.

C. Each number or letter is followed by a period, and the
   period is followed by two spaces.

D. All lines that do not start with a number or a letter
   are tabbed in four spaces.

E. This job uses letters to separate the items, but numbers
   would be just as good.

JOB 33 B. ENUMERATION
Paragraph format. Full sheet of paper. 5-space tab. Retype Job 33 A making the following changes: (1) use numbers instead of letters. (2) Change the title to PARA-GRAPH-STYLE ENUMERATION. (3) Substitute the paragraph below for paragraph B. (4) Delete paragraph D. (5) Switch the words *letters* and *numbers* in paragraph E. Hint: Make the changes on your copy of Job 33 A; then type from the corrected copy.

   2. Indent the first line of each enumerated item, and
type turnover lines at the left margin.

LESSON
34

■ **GOALS**
To type 30/3'/5e.
To correct errors by squeezing and spreading characters and
   spaces.
To type enumerations.

■ **FORMAT**
Drills: Single spacing   60-space line
3-Minute Timings: Double spacing   5-space tab

KEYBOARDING SKILLS

Type each line twice.

Speed   1 Dick may wish to type the forms with the aid of some codes.
Accuracy   2 My lazy, gray dog curled up very quietly and went to sleep.
Numbers   3 Kay had to try 546 samples before she found any of No. 329.
Symbols   4 He read "How to Type" in Max's August issue of Office News.

PREVIEW PRACTICE

Type each line twice as a preview to the 3-minute timings on page 59.

Accuracy   5 new jazz music sounds country classical different depending
Speed   6 like tune have fast slow beat show rock mind much tale rich

Take a 1-minute timing on each paragraph of the Pretest on page 214.

Take another 5-minute timing on lines 6–25 on page 214 to see how much your skill has improved.

FORMATTING ARTICLES

Some magazines contain articles written only by staff members. However, many others accept articles written by people outside of the organization. Also, some companies publish in-house newsletters to keep their employees informed about business and company activities. To format articles for magazines or newsletters:

1. Use double spacing and a 50-space line.

2. Use the top margins used in other reports—begin the title on line 13; begin page numbers (beginning with page 2) on line 7.

3. Under the byline, indicate the line length used and the number of lines in the article. (You will have to insert the number of lines after you have finished typing the article.) This line helps editors determine how long the article is and how well it will fit into the magazine or newsletter.

4. Bottom margins should contain 6 to 9 blank lines.

5. Except on page 1, type the writer's name before the page number, separating the two items with a diagonal—for example: Perez / 5

Note: If you are submitting an article to a specific magazine or newsletter, you may want to use the same line length as used in the magazine or newsletter. To find the exact length, copy 10 full lines and average them; do not exceed that line by more than 2 spaces.

JOB 127 A. ARTICLE FOR A NEWSLETTER
Standard format.

```
              ADDITIONS
  NEW EQUIPMENT MODIFICATIONS                  14

           By Jean McDonald               26
         ( Lines of 50 Spaces)            42

    This year has been an active one      51

for the purchase of new equipment.        59

We are very fortunate to have been        66
selected
named   as recipients of the Graham       73

Johnson grant provided by Equipment       80

Systems Inc.  This grant has enabled us   88

this year to purchase some much-needed)   94
                              plant
equipment for our Greenville division     103

    In March we added 45 ACTV Micro-      111

system Terminals to the Sales Division.   119

in Greenville  These terminals have       123

CP/M capabilities and hard disk stor-     130
                     a
age.  They are very versatile systems     138

in that we can use them off-line as       145

micro processors, or we may use them      152

in Room DP-22 to communicate directly)    157

with our main frame computers located     168
                        plant was
¶In June our printing capabilities were   175
                                    15
enhanced with the addition of fifteen     181

microprinters, Model PRT-2580.  These     189

printers are very sophisticated and       196

are equipped with the following spe-      203

cial capabilities:  (1) microspacing,     211

(2) superscript/subscript printing,       218

(3) eight-position vertical adjust-       225
          (4)
ment, graphics printing, and (5) high-    233

quality dot matrix print.                 239

    In October we will spend the          245
         rest
remaining portion of the grant on the     250

purchase of new $oftware for our          257

equipment design division.                262
```

3-MINUTE TIMINGS

Take two 3-minute timings on lines 7–14.

```
                  1               2              3            4
 7      Which kind of music do you like best?  A jazz tune can   12
                5           6              7           8
 8   have a fast or a slow beat, depending on the mood the tunes   24
               9            10            11            12
 9   are meant to show.  Rock music has a different beat and can   36
              13          14           15           16
10   bring a new set of moods to mind.  Much of folk music has a   48
              17          18           19           20
11   tale of joy or grief as its text.  Country tunes are like a   60
             21           22           23           24
12   folk tune, but they are a blend of other types.  Music that   72
             25           26           27           28
13   is classical has rich tones of quiet or blaring sound.  The   84
                29           30
14   choice is as wide as you wish.                               90
```
| 1 | 2 | 3 | 4 | 5 | 6 | 7 | 8 | 9 | 10 | 11 | 12 | SI 1.14

CORRECTING ERRORS

Workbook 29–30.

 *Spreading and squeezing corrections on computers and word processors is very easy. All you have to do is press the insert key to add an extra space or press the delete key to remove an extra space.*

Problem: In making a correction, how can you squeeze in an extra letter?

Answer: Move the word a half space to the *left* so that only a half space precedes and follows it.

To do this, you must keep the carriage or carrier from spacing normally. You can use one of three ways to control the carriage or carrier movement: (1) press your fingertips against the end of the platen or carrier, (2) depress the halfspace key if your machine has one, or (3) partly depress the backspace key.

Practice: Type lines *a* and *b exactly* as shown; then insert *said* in each of the two blank areas in line *b*.

```
a   You say that you will help us.  You say that you will work.
b   You      that you will help us.  You      that you will work.
```

Problem: How do you spread a word so that it will occupy an extra space?

Answer: Move the word a half space to the *right* so that 1½ spaces precede and follow it. This requires your controlling the carriage or carrier just as you did in the preceding exercise.

Practice: Type lines *c* and *d exactly* as shown; then insert *say* in each of the two blank areas in line *d*.

```
c   You said that you will help.  You said that you will do it.
d   You      that you will help.  You      that you will do it.
```

JOB 34 A. ENUMERATION

Paragraph format (see page 57). 5-space tab.

ATTENTION ALL STUDENTS

Volunteers are needed for the marathon to serve in the following capacities:

1. We need drivers who will pick up handicapped people, bring them to the race, and take them home at the end of the race. The drivers must be able to assist with wheelchairs.

2. We need people to serve at the registration desk. This job would involve being at the high school parking lot at 8:30 a.m. the day of the race, checking credentials of the runners, and staying to count the money after the race.

3. We need people to serve as guides in the parking lot; that is, direct drivers to a space, keep the cars parked within the painted guidelines, direct people to the refreshments, and answer questions. To volunteer, call Marilyn Lewis, 555-8786.

■ **GOALS**
To type 39/5'/5e.
To format and type an article for a newsletter.

■ **FORMAT**
Drills: Single spacing   60-space line
5-Minute Timings: Double spacing   5-space tab

KEYBOARDING SKILLS

Type lines 1–4 once. Then do what line 5 tells you to do as you type it. Repeat lines 1–4, or take a series of 1-minute timings.

Speed   1 A whole kernel of corn was picked up by the hen last night.   12
Accuracy   2 Did Liz give Weldon your picturesque jukebox for Christmas?   12
Numbers   3 Fires raged all night at 1029 Pine, 3847 Oak, and 5610 Elm.   12
Symbols   4 We found out that 1/5 of $20 = $4 and that 10% of $40 = $4.   12
Technique 5 Use your return key after every word as you type this line.

| 1 | 2 | 3 | 4 | 5 | 6 | 7 | 8 | 9 | 10 | 11 | 12

PRETEST

Take a 5-minute timing on lines 6–25. Circle and count your errors.

6   Today, a quick method of getting to other locations is   12
7   by airplane. You can choose a variety of airlines for your   24
8   flight. Airlines throughout the country provide flights to   36
9   most locations.   39

10   If you have never before flown on commercial airlines,   12
11   you should plan to arrive at the terminal approximately one   24
12   hour prior to departure to permit time for checking in your   36
13   extra baggage.   39

14   When flying on a commercial airline, you may choose to   12
15   sit in the smoking or the nonsmoking section. You can tell   24
16   the airline agent in which part of the plane you would like   36
17   to be seated.   39

18   Are your ears bothered by changes in air pressure? If   12
19   changes in pressure cause your ears to plug, consider chew-   24
20   ing gum. The right time to start chewing is during a take-   36
21   off or landing.   39

22   If you are flying cross-country or to another country,   12
23   take along a magazine or other reading materials. Airlines   24
24   provide limited reading materials that can occupy your time   36
25   on long flights.   39

| 1 | 2 | 3 | 4 | 5 | 6 | 7 | 8 | 9 | 10 | 11 | 12   SI 1.49

JOB 34 B. ENUMERATION
Hanging-indented format.

BETTER COMMUNICATION

Here are three practical suggestions to help make
your conversation more interesting and effective:
1. Listen attentively. Almost all of us need to be
   better listeners. Don't be preoccupied with
   your own thoughts.
2. Ask the right questions. A good question
   indicates a genuine interest in the other person.
3. Learn how to disagree. It isn't what you
   say but how you say it that often makes
   all the difference.

LESSON 35

■ **GOALS**
To type 30/3'/5e.
To format and type outlines.

■ **FORMAT**
Drills: Single spacing   60-space line
3-Minute Timings: Double spacing   5-space tab

KEYBOARDING SKILLS

Type each line twice.

Speed   1   They did not have time to go to the movies or to play golf.

Accuracy   2   My ax just zipped through the fine black wood quite evenly.

Numbers   3   We get a discount if we order 15, 30, 45, 75, or 150 boxes.

Symbols   4   I don't believe it! She said to me, "You were the winner!"

PREVIEW PRACTICE

Type each line twice as a preview to the 3-minute timings on page 61.

Accuracy   5   quite other means nicely change around expanding attractive

Speed   6   page make from just such that they some type both line them

Production Practice. Set margins for a 70-space line. Set tabs at 5 spaces from the left margin, at 25 spaces from the left margin, and at the center. Single spacing. Clean sheet of paper. Use Job 126 A below.

A. Heading. Space down to line 13. Tab to the center. Backspace-center and type the word *ITINERARY*. Space down 2 lines. At the left margin type the name *M. J. Donaldson*. Move the carriage or carrier to the right margin. Backspace for the date (December 10, 19--). Type the date. Return twice. Tab to the center. Backspace-center and type the words (*Memphis--San Francisco*). Return twice.

B. First Body Entry. Starting at the left margin, type the words *Sunday, December 10*. Move the carriage or carrier back to the left margin, and underscore the day/date line. Return twice. Tab to the first tab stop. Type the time (9:35 a.m., CST). Tab to the second tab stop. Type the first line of the departure information. Return once. Tab to the second tab stop. Indent 2 spaces before typing the turnover line. Return twice.

C. Second Body Entry. Tab to the first tab stop. Type the time. Tab to the second tab stop. Type the first line of the arrival information. Return once. Tab to the second tab stop. Indent 2 spaces before typing the turnover line. Return twice.

D. Fourth Body Entry. Tab to the second tab stop. Type the first line of the accommodations information. Return once. Tab to the second tab stop. Indent 2 spaces before typing the turnover line.
Check your work.

JOB 126 A. ITINERARY
Standard format.

```
                              ITINERARY

     M. J. Donaldson                            December 10, 19--
                                              c
                        (Memphis--San Franciso)
                                             ^

     Sunday, December 10

          9:35 a.m., CST     Depart Memphis, United Air Lines Flight 433
                             lunch served
          1:02 p.m., PST     Arrive San Francisco, San Francisco Interna-
                                tional Airport.

          5:30 p.m.          Depart hotel for Chinatown visit.

                             Accommodations:  Mark Hopkins hotel, (1)Nob
                                Hill.

     Monday, December 11

          9 a.m. - 5 p.m.    Convention at Mark Hopkins Hotel.

          Reminder           Call Pat Wolton to confirm dinner arrange-
                                ments for Tuesday

                                             Mark
          Tuesday, December 12

          9 a.m.-5 p.m.      Convention at Hopkins Hotel.
                                        ^
          7 p.m.             Dinner with Pat Wolton

     Wednesday, December 13

          10:30 a.m.         Depart hotel for airport.
                                noon                San Francisco
          12 p.m., PST       Depart San Francisco, International Airport,
                                United Air Lines Flight 700, lunch served.

          7:15 p.m., CST     Arrive Memphis.
```

Take two 3-minute timings on lines 7–14.

```
                1               2               3               4
 7        To format words on a page means to make them look just  12
                5           6               7            8
 8  as attractive as you can.  It also means that you plan them   24
             9           10              11          12
 9  in such a way that they are easily read.  One way to change   36
                13            14            15            16
10  a format of a page is to type some parts in all caps and to   48
             17          18            19            20
11  type other parts in both caps and lowercase.  Expanding the   60
          21              22            23            24
12  letters in a line or two makes them stand out from the maze   72
             25              26            27            28
13  of words quite nicely.  The use of a box around word groups   84
             29          30
14  makes it simple to read a page.                              90
    |  1  |  2  |  3  |  4  |  5  |  6  |  7  |  8  |  9  |  10  |  11  |  12   SI 1.17
```

FORMATTING OUTLINES

To format an outline of, for example, a term paper, follow these rules:

1. Set your margins so that the outline will be approximately centered horizontally. Or if you wish, use the same margins as those used in your term paper.
2. Center the outline vertically, or type the title on line 13 if you are using a full sheet of paper.
3. Align the periods after roman numerals, like this:

    I.
    II.
    III.
    IV.

Use the margin release key and backspace from the left margin for roman numerals that take more than 1 space.

4. Use single spacing, but leave 2 blank lines before and 1 blank line after a line that begins with a roman numeral.
5. Indent each subdivision 4 more spaces.

    I.##
        A.##
            1.##
                a.##
                    (1)##(etc.)

Remember: If you are using a computer, you can use a temporary left margin.

JOB 35 A. OUTLINE

Standard format. 50-space line. Set tab stops 4, 8, and 12 spaces from your left margin.

FORMING A BICYCLE TOURING CLUB ↓3

Align periods after roman numerals.

```
I.    PLAN A SHORT TRIP.
                       ↓2
      A.  Take a one—day city tour.
      B.  Take a weekend trip.
          1.  Go to a state park.
              a.  Eat at a country inn.
              b.  Camp overnight.
          2.  Go to Lake Aurora.
                               ↓3
```

Leave 2 blank lines before and 1 blank line after lines that begin with roman numerals.

```
II.   PLAN A LONG TRIP.
                      ↓2
      A.  Write to other clubs in our country.
      B.  Write to clubs in foreign countries.
                                             ↓3

III.  TAKE CLASSES IN BIKE SAFETY.
```

■ **GOALS**
To form plurals of nouns correctly while typing sentences.
To format and type an itinerary.

■ **FORMAT**
Single spacing   60-space line

LAB 14

Plurals

Type lines 1–4 once, making plurals of the underscored words. Edit your copy as your teacher reads the answers. Then retype lines 1–4 from your edited copy.

1 The child working at the computer can check it quickly.
2 The waitress should add some radish to today's lunch.
3 After the accountant checked, the clerk left for the day.
4 The woman drove to the new office next to the lazy river.

30-SECOND SPEED TIMINGS

Take two 30-second speed timings on lines 5 and 6. Then take two 30-second speed timings on lines 7 and 8. Or type each sentence twice.

5 We want to buy that new car, but we do not have the cash to   12
6 pay for it on this day. We may buy it sometime next month.   24

7 Here it is a week later, and we still have not been able to   12
8 buy that new car. I do not think we will ever buy the car.   24

    | 1 | 2 | 3 | 4 | 5 | 6 | 7 | 8 | 9 | 10 | 11 | 12

FORMATTING AN ITINERARY

An *itinerary* is an outline of the details of a planned trip. It includes departure and arrival times, meeting times, flight plans, and other essential information. To format an itinerary on plain paper:

1. Set your margins for a 6-inch line (60P/70E).

2. Set 5-space and 25-space tabs.

3. Type the itinerary heading as follows:
  a. Type *ITINERARY* centered on line 13.
  b. Double-space, and at the left margin type the name of the person for whom the itinerary is prepared.
  c. On the same line as the person's name, type the date on which the trip will begin. Backspace this date from the right margin.
  d. Double-space, and then center the name(s) of the city(ies) to be visited; begin with the departure city. Use a dash (two hyphens) to separate the city names.

4. Double-space after the heading information, and begin typing the day-to-day schedule. Beginning at the left margin, type the day, month, and date. Underscore the day/date information.

5. Double-space. Indent all time and reminder notes 5 spaces from the left margin. Whenever time zones are changed, specify the time zone after each time.

6. Indent 25 spaces to type the description information for each notation in the left column. Indent any turnover lines 2 spaces from the 25-space tab.

7. Underscore departure and arrival cities and the word *Accommodations*.

8. For itineraries longer than 1 page, leave a bottom margin of 6 to 9 lines. Type page numbers on all pages except the first, beginning on line 7 at the right margin.

JOB 35 B. OUTLINE
Standard format. Block-center.

COMPUTERS IN OUR LIVES

I. Computers in Government
  A. The Census Bureau
  B. The Internal Revenue Service
    1. Accuracy of returns
    2. Printing out refund checks
II. Computers in Banks
  A. Customer automatic deposits
  B. Customer withdrawals
  C. Customer monthly statements
  D. Electronic tellers
  E. Check processing

III. Computers in Hospitals
  A. Patient monitoring
  B. Computerized X-rays
  C. Billing
    1. Patient
    2. Insurance company
IV. Computers at Home
  A. Money management
  B. Games
  C. Word processing
    1. Letters
    2. Reports
  D. Inventories
    1. Household items
    2. Investments

LESSON 36

■ **GOALS**
To type 30/3'/5e.
To type an enumeration and an outline.
To revise an outline.

■ **FORMAT**
Drills: Single spacing   60-space line
3-Minute Timings: Double spacing   5-space tab

KEYBOARDING SKILLS

Type each line twice.

Speed	1	Alene's neighbor owns six or eight antique autos right now.
Accuracy	2	Five lizards very quickly jumped into the box on the table.
Numbers	3	we 23 up 70 to 59 or 94 it 85 yi 68 et 35 op 90 ur 74 re 43
Symbols	4	File cards (unlined) sold as a pack of 500 @ $2.70 in June.

PREVIEW PRACTICE

Type each line twice as a preview to the 3-minute timings on page 63.

Accuracy	5	who senior others flowers citizen service students projects
Speed	6	their time work with some done take read like and the to by

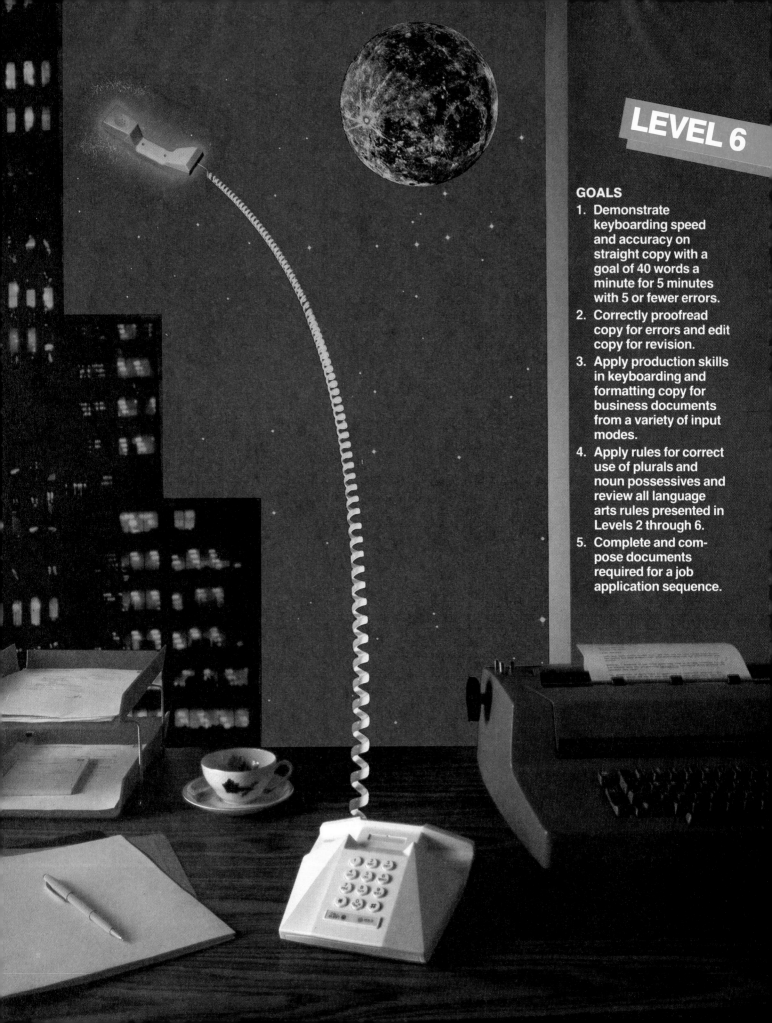

GOALS

1. Demonstrate keyboarding speed and accuracy on straight copy with a goal of 40 words a minute for 5 minutes with 5 or fewer errors.
2. Correctly proofread copy for errors and edit copy for revision.
3. Apply production skills in keyboarding and formatting copy for business documents from a variety of input modes.
4. Apply rules for correct use of plurals and noun possessives and review all language arts rules presented in Levels 2 through 6.
5. Complete and compose documents required for a job application sequence.

Take two 3-minute timings on lines 7–14.

```
                1              2              3              4
7       Many students give hours of their time to work for the    12
          5              6              7              8
8    service projects in their towns.  Some jobs are done with a   24
              9            10             11            12
9    group, while some are not.  Students work with kids at some   36
          13             14             15             16
10   parks, and they work with kids who are ill.  They take food   48
          17             18             19             20
11   to senior citizens and read to those who are blind.  Bright   60
          21             22             23             24
12   flowers and green trees are planted, and trash is picked up   72
          25             26             27             28
13   by some students.  These nice young people like helping out   84
                     29             30
14   others in many different ways.                                90

    |  1  |  2  |  3  |  4  |  5  |  6  |  7  |  8  |  9  | 10  | 11  | 12     SI 1.20
```

JOB 36 A. ENUMERATION

Hanging-indented format (see page 57). Half sheet of paper. 4-inch line. 4-space tab.

VERTICAL CENTERING
↓ 3

1. Count the number of lines needed.
2. Subtract the needed lines from the number of lines available on the paper.
3. Divide the difference by 2 to find the line on which to start.
4. If a fraction is left, drop it.
5. Check center by folding the paper from top to bottom.

JOB 36 B. OUTLINE

Standard format (see page 61). Half sheet of paper. 30-space line.

```
MAKING FRIENDS
I.     Join a Club
A.     School Clubs
1.     The Business Club
2.     Junior Achievement
3.     Y-Teens
B.     Out-of-School Clubs
II.    Get a Pen Pal
III.   Take Up a Sport
A.     Join a Team
B.     Learn a New Sport
1.     Tennis
2.     Golf
3.     Skiing
```

JOB 36 C. REVISED OUTLINE

Word processors (and computers with word processing software) can automatically insert or delete characters, words, or paragraphs if certain function keys are used.

Retype Job 36 B making the changes below: 40-space line. Hint: Make the changes on your copy of Job 36 B; then type from the corrected copy.

Under	Insert
I. B. Out-of-School Clubs	1. Community Art Groups
	2. Computer Clubs
	a. Local
	b. National
II. Get a Pen Pal	A. In Eastern or Western U.S.A.
	B. In a Foreign Country
III. B. Learn a New Sport	Three sports you like or are interested in (**delete** Tennis, Golf, and Skiing)
	IV. Be a Friendly Person
	A. Be a Good Listener
	B. Smile

JOB 124/125 B (CONTINUED)

I have enclosed our latest listing of homes in the Concord area and have circled those homes priced in the $70s and $80s which I think would meet the needs of your employees. The Northwest Addition and Carlton Heights are the two most desirable locations for most newcomers because of their proximity to schools and hospitals. We have over 30 listings in these two areas.

The Chamber of Commerce will be sending you additional information on Concord; and it will include the names and addresses of schools, churches, hospitals, zoos, and other places of interest.

Please call me or write to me if there is any other information I can provide. Concord Real Estate looks forward to the opportunity of serving the housing needs of your employees. Thank you for your interest in our firm. / Sincerely, / Roxanne Dalhart / Sales Manager / [*Your initials*] / Enclosure / cc: Carole Dunn / Christopher Roberts

JOB 124/125 C. MEMO
Standard format. Workbook 203.

(Today's date) / [TO:] L. Dunbar, M. Gibson, W. Jaralowski, T. Jennings, D. Madeley, C. Rozell, G. Tate, L. Westmoreland / [FROM:] Lyndon Powell / [SUBJECT:] Visitation Schedule

The Quality Control Team from the Southeast district will be at our facility on Monday, June 10. They are here, as you know, at our request to help us isolate the contamination of Sector D.

At 8 a.m. they will begin their inspection tour of our Division in Bldg. 220. Every half hour thereafter they will visit Buildings 240, 260, 270, & 290. At 10:30 a.m. they will reach our research lab and will spend the rest of the morning at that location. We look forward to some positive suggestions from the team. / LP / (Your initials)

JOB 124/125 D. PURCHASE REQUISITION
Workbook 205 top.

Purchase Requisition 2675. Date of requisition: April 5, 19--. Jill McDaniel, Sporting Goods Department, 3d Floor, needs the following by May 9: 4 polyester sleeping bags, Cat. No. 60-73445; 6 nylon water-resistant backpacks, Cat. No. 60-36422; and 2 lightweight pup tents, Cat. No. 60-98633. Order from Sporting Supplies Inc., 5924 Boston Avenue, Orlando, FL 32811. To replenish stock.

JOB 124/125 E. PURCHASE ORDER
Workbook 205 bottom.

Purchase Order 1856. Date of order: three days after date of requisition. Use information from the purchase requisition in Job 124/125 D to prepare this requisition. The unit price for each of these items is as follows: sleeping bags—54.75; backpacks—22.89; tents—164.99. Calculate a total order price.

JOB 124/125 F. INVOICE
Workbook 207.

Invoice 3970. Date of invoice is two weeks after date of order. Sporting Supplies responds to Palo Vista Department Store's purchase order by sending the complete order. Add a 5 percent sales tax when completing the invoice for this order.

LESSON 37

CLINIC

■ **GOALS**
To build typing speed.
To type 30/3′/5e.

■ **FORMAT**
Drills: Single spacing   60-space line
3-Minute Timings: Double spacing   5-space tab

KEYBOARDING SKILLS

Type each line twice.

Speed   1 The eight may make a profit if they handle the forms right.
Accuracy 2 Quietly pick up the box with five dozen gum and candy jars.
Numbers   3 On May 29 and June 10, I will use 38, 47, and 56 if we can.
Symbols   4 Jarris & Sons buys from Wilson & Harris and M&E in Houston.

12-SECOND TIMINGS

Type each line three times, or take three 12-second timings on each line. For each timing, type with no more than 1 error.

5 She works with them and with the boss in this small office.
6 They put a box down the chute and into a van waiting there.
7 Now is the hour to come to the aid of those of us who work.

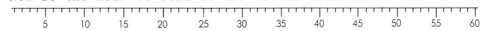
```
       5    10    15    20    25    30    35    40    45    50    55    60
```

30-SECOND SPEED TIMINGS

Take two 30-second speed timings on lines 8 and 9. Then take two 30-second speed timings on lines 10 and 11. Or type each sentence twice.

8   Each of us must sit down and think about what we wish to do   12
9   with our lives so that we can set goals and make our plans.   24

10 Goals may be just for today or for next year, but we always   12
11 must set a firm time by when we expect to meet these goals.   24
```
| 1 | 2 | 3 | 4 | 5 | 6 | 7 | 8 | 9 | 10 | 11 | 12 |
```

PRETEST

Take a 3-minute timing on lines 12–19. Circle and count your errors.

```
                  1              2                 3                  4
12        High school students can be an active part of politics    12
                5                 6              7                8
13  if they choose.  They can keep up with the news for the day     24
              9              10             11              12
14  and know what issues are at hand.  They can type letters to     36
             13               14              15              16
15  be put in papers to question and express points of view for    48
             17               18              19              20
16  the public to read.  If they choose to be more active, then    60
              21               22              23              24
17  they may want to join a campaign team and work for a person    72
             25               26              27              28
18  who seeks an office.  All students realize that their votes    84
              29              30
19  will also be the way to speak.                                 90
```
```
| 1 | 2 | 3 | 4 | 5 | 6 | 7 | 8 | 9 | 10 | 11 | 12 |   SI 1.20
```

JOB 124/125 A. SPEECH
Standard format.

REPORT HEADINGS FORMATS 14
Presented to the Office Personnel Association 44
By Leslie Brown 56

Thank you very much for the invi- 66
tation to speak to your group at the 73
June luncheon. Because we have so 80
little time together today, I will be 88
very brief with my comments on 94
report headings formats. 99

The two categories of headings 106
most often used in reports are 113
main headings and minor headings. 120

SLIDE 1 126

This slide shows the three most 133
typical lines that are used in the 140
main heading: title line, sub- 146
title line, and byline. As you 153
can see, the title line always 159
appears first, and it is typed in all 167
capitals. The line appearing below the 175
main title is called the subtitle, 182
and a typist will normally type 188
a subtitle with both uppercase and 195
lowercase letters. The last line 202
included in the main heading is 208
a byline, and its basic purpose 215
is to tell who prepared the report. 222

The lines of a main heading are 230
double-spaced. They are separated 237
from the body of the report by 2 243
blank lines. 246

SLIDE 2 252

The second category of headings, 260
minor headings, may include a side 267

heading and a paragraph heading. 274
This slide reveals both of these 280
styles. A side heading is preceded by 288
2 blank lines and is followed 294
by 1 blank line. It may be 300
centered or typed at the left margin. 308
A paragraph heading, which is in- 314
dented and underscored, is typed at 321
the beginning of a paragraph. The 328
main purpose of a minor heading is to re- 336
veal the content of major sections. 344

Either or both of these heading 351
formats may be used in the typing 358
of a report. It is not necessary to 365
include both formats within the 372
body of one report, but it is per- 378
missible. 380

I thank you for these few 387
brief moments together today so 393
that I could present an overview 400
of report heading formats. If 406
you have any questions on this 412
topic, I will be happy to 417
visit with you after the con- 423
clusion of your meeting this 429
afternoon. 431

JOB 124/125 B. LETTER
Workbook 201–202. Body 166 words.

May 25, 19— / Mr. Leon Walker / Personnel 12
Manager / 2438 Forecastle Drive / New Port 20
Richey, FL 33552 / Dear Mr. Walker: / Subject: 31
Real Estate Listing 35

Thank you for your letter of May 10 in which 45
you request a real estate listing for some of your 55
employees who will be moving to the Concord 64
area next year. 67

(Continued on next page)

PRACTICE

Type each line three times, or take a series of 1-minute timings on each line, working to increase your speed.

20 tool well soon keep look fill need less been eggs ebbs burr 12
21 ball miss mill pass good pool feel sees toss seem will book 12
22 wall door hood food ooze buff mitt cuff putt miff mutt full 12

23 She may make the girls do the theme for their eighth panel. 12
24 Both the men may go to town if he pays them for their fuel. 12
25 They paid for the pen and the box, so I paid for the forks. 12
    | 1 | 2 | 3 | 4 | 5 | 6 | 7 | 8 | 9 | 10 | 11 | 12

POSTTEST

Take another 3-minute timing on lines 12–19 (page 64) to see how much your skill has improved.

LESSON 38

UNIT 7 Introduction to Correspondence
UNIT GOAL 32/3'/5e

■ **GOAL**
To apply some rules of word division.

■ **FORMAT**
Single spacing   60-space line   5-space tab

KEYBOARDING SKILLS

Type lines 1–4 once. Read line 5; then do what it tells you to do as you type it. Repeat lines 1–4, or take a series of 1-minute timings.

Speed   1 If they handle the work right, the eight may make a profit. 12
Accuracy   2 Our packing the dozen boxes for fresh jam was quite lively. 12
Numbers   3 We counted 38, 47, and 56; they counted 10, 29, 38, and 47. 12
Symbols   4 Mark 38¢, 49¢, and 50¢ after each item shown with a # sign. 12
Technique   5 Return the carriage or carrier after each word as you type.
              | 1 | 2 | 3 | 4 | 5 | 6 | 7 | 8 | 9 | 10 | 11 | 12

30-SECOND SPEED TIMINGS

Take two 30-second speed timings on lines 6 and 7. Then take two 30-second speed timings on lines 8 and 9. Or type each sentence twice.

6 As you look to the future, you may wonder about the ways it 12
7 is going to differ from the world we enjoy living in today. 24

8 You can get ready for the future by keeping up with all the 12
9 new and super things that come into our world each new day. 24
  | 1 | 2 | 3 | 4 | 5 | 6 | 7 | 8 | 9 | 10 | 11 | 12

RULES OF WORD DIVISION

When your typewriter bell rings, you must often decide whether you have space to complete a word or whether you should divide it. To divide words, follow the rules given below and on page 66; additional rules will be given in Lesson 39.

1. Divide only between syllables. If you are not sure where a syllable ends, use a dictionary. Never guess—some words are tricky.

Examples: syl-la-ble prod-uct chil-dren knowl-edge
pres-ent (a gift) pre-sent (to make a gift)

(Continued on next page)

X   46   The excommunicated xylophonist excerpted the right example.
Y   47   Your yellow yacht's yawl was yawing yesterday in Yorkshire.
Z   48   Dazed by the haze, Zeta zigzagged her way to my jazz class.

LESSONS 124/125

TEST

- **GOALS**
  To type 38/5'/5e.
  To demonstrate competency in typing a speech, a letter, a memo, and three forms.
- **FORMAT**
  Double spacing   60-space line   5-space tab

PREVIEW PRACTICE

Type each line twice as a preview to the 5-minute timings below.

Accuracy   1   dozens vacancies excellent recognize employment foreseeable
Speed   2   that they must very the one are you may and for new out job

5-MINUTE TIMINGS

Take two 5-minute timings on lines 3–22.

3   Locating a suitable job is one of the important things   12
4   you'll accomplish in a lifetime. There are dozens of posi-   24
5   tions which may appeal to you and for which you have proper   36
6   training.   38
7   A large number of people find good jobs through ads in   50
8   their local newspapers. The ads may often quote the skills   62
9   and background needed for a position for which you may like   74
10   to apply.   76
11   Your friends may also be an excellent source for hear-   88
12   ing about openings that exist. They may possibly hear that   100
13   a new job is coming in the foreseeable future for which you   112
14   may apply.   114
15   The next source for identifying a good position may be   126
16   some companies that are aware of job vacancies. Employment   138
17   firms are excellent at finding out about positions that are   150
18   in demand.   152
19   You might possibly consider these various sources when   164
20   you search for a new job. It is critical to recognize that   176
21   you must seek a number of options to be assured of the very   188
22   best job.   190

| 1 | 2 | 3 | 4 | 5 | 6 | 7 | 8 | 9 | 10 | 11 | 12 | SI 1.47

Many word processors have an automatic hyphenation feature that will divide words automatically or highlight those words so that the operator can insert a hyphen at the appropriate division point.

2. Do not divide:
  a. A word pronounced as one syllable: *shipped, strength, tire.*
  b. A word of 5 or fewer letters: *about, into.*
  c. Any contraction: *couldn't, can't, o'clock.*
  d. Any abbreviation: *dept., UNICEF, a.m.*

3. Leave a syllable of at least 2 letters on the upper line.

Line 1: to-   ab-   around   **not** a-
Line 2: gether   solute   round

4. Carry to the next line a syllable of at least 3 letters (or 2 letters and a punctuation mark that follows the word).

Line 1: full–   cov–   teacher   **not** teach–
Line 2: est   er.   er

JOB 38 A. WORD DIVISION PRACTICE

Type lines 10–12. Then study each word and draw a vertical line on your paper between syllables if the word may be divided. Check your answers. Then retype lines 10–12 from your edited copy, inserting hyphens at the correct division points.

```
10   knowledge doesn't children worthwhile tricky; settle profit

11   stop leading steamed mfg. p.m. UNESCO planned signed worthy

12   around, court; mixer, sixty, shouldn't, service area; into.
```

JOB 38 B. WORD DIVISION PRACTICE

Type the paragraph below. Some words will have to be divided at the end of the line, so listen for the bell. If you make the correct line-ending decisions, all lines except for the last will end evenly. Format: Double spacing, 50-space line, 5-space tab.

If your word processor or computer software does not have an automatic hyphenation feature, you must depress the return key to make the lines end exactly where you want them to.

Do not divide words at end of more than 2 consecutive lines.

13   All of us need to watch our diets to maintain good health. If you
14   do not know much about nutrition, then you should start to learn--
15   now. Eating habits can destroy good health or can help you attain
16   good health, so be sure to eat wholesome food at every meal. If you
17   would like to read some information on nutrition, visit your library or
18   your local bookstore. Also, be sure to learn how vitamin supplements
19   ensure that we receive the minimum daily requirements of vitamins and
20   minerals.

JOB 38 C. WORD DIVISION

Type lines 21–28. When you reach the italicized word in each sentence, decide whether it may be divided. If the word may be divided, do so at the correct division point, return, and complete the sentence. If the word should not be divided, type it, return, and complete the sentence. Format: 40-space line, double-space between sentences.

21   Clarence worked hard until his *strength* was weakened by age.
22   Alexis tried each day to be the *ideal* assistant to the president.
23   The company had a reputation for *service* within 24 hours.
24   The equipment has security that *doesn't* permit access to nonemployees.
25   Many automobiles are frequently *abused* and lose their resale value.
26   In our high-tech world of *information,* workers need computers.
27   Please be sure that your workers *record* the hours that they work.
28   As I understand the plans, this *project* should take 16 days.

5-MINUTE TIMINGS

What Increases Your Accuracy
Sitting right and not moving.

Typing with fingers ONLY.

Keeping arms and wrists quiet.

Typing steadily, not speedily.

Thinking each letter to yourself.

Keeping your wits about you.

Keeping calm about your errors.

Take two 5-minute timings on lines 7–22.

```
                        1                              2
 7      Looking for a place to live can be frustrating as well    12
               3                         4
 8   as exciting; many different points must be examined before,   24
         5                       6                        7
 9   during, and after this search.  In order to make what seems   36
                    8                        9
10   to be a hazy issue clear, construct a detailed list of pros   48
              10                      11                   12
11   and cons for all apartments that you see.  Needless to say,   60
               13                      14
12   you should consider important points when making this list;   72
           15                         16
13   it's imperative that each point be in its perspective.       83
                    17                   18                   19
14      In making your list of pros and cons, quiz yourself on    95
                       20                        21
15   the following aspects:  How long will you have to travel to   107
                    22                       23
16   get to work?  If you don't own an auto, how near are public   119
         24                      25                       26
17   transportation lines?  Is your apartment furnished, or must   131
                  27                         28
18   you provide the furniture?  Are you responsible for all the   143
             29                      30                        31
19   utilities?  What kinds of recreational facilities might you   155
                       32                       33
20   have available?  Must you sign a lease, or can you just pay   167
                       34                       35
21   rent every month?  How large a security deposit is required   179
           36                       37                       38
22   prior to your occupancy?  How much rent will you pay?        190
     |  1  |  2  |  3  |  4  |  5  |  6  |  7  |  8  |  9  |  10 |  11 |  12   SI 1.47
```

ACCURACY PRACTICE

Type lines 23–48 once. Proofread your copy and circle your errors. Repeat two times those lines in which you made errors.

A 23 Ample accusations are always apparent among all applicants.
B 24 Big boats brought beautiful blooming bouquets by black bag.
C 25 Cowboys can corral carefully chosen cattle conscientiously.
D 26 Deprived daffodils and dandelions were dampened by the dew.

E 27 Every evening eleven enormous elephants escaped extinction.
F 28 Five fox were found fleeing from the forest fire on Friday.
G 29 Gray ganders gained ground on growing great goose feathers.
H 30 Her husband had heartaches while he handled health hazards.

I 31 Idle ibex intuitively inhabited isolated inclines in India.
J 32 Jumbo jetliners were justified in joining the Japan jaunts.
K 33 Kindly Katherine knowingly kidnapped the kaiser's knapsack.
L 34 Little lonely lambs loped lightly on Lealand's lovely land.

M 35 My many meals are made mostly of meat, mushrooms, and milk.
N 36 None of the ninety nearby neighbors noted the noisy nomads.
O 37 Only in October ought Ollie occasionally obtain one orchid.
P 38 Pat paid appropriate prices for paper to the proper people.

Q 39 Queen Quita quickly quipped a quaint quote in a quiet quiz.
R 40 Rural carriers were irregular in preserving their reorders.
S 41 Sandra's steady shears silently slit Sylvia's shorn shreds.
T 42 Three little letters told the story—a matter of attitudes.

U 43 Ursula unfairly upset Ula until unnecessary ulcers erupted.
V 44 Vivacious voters value vision, verve, and very vivid vigor.
W 45 We want a welcome when we work westward with new waterways.

(Continued on next page)

LESSON 39

■ **GOALS**
To type 32/3'/5e.
To apply additional rules of word division.

■ **FORMAT**
Drills: Single spacing   60-space line
3-Minute Timings: Double spacing   5-space tab

KEYBOARDING SKILLS

Type lines 1–4 once. Then do what line 5 tells you to do. Repeat lines 1–4, or take a series of 1-minute timings.

Speed   1 Helen paid the city firm for the land she owns by the lake.   12
Accuracy 2 Quickly fix the seven wires that jeopardized the big camps.   12
Numbers   3 Please vote, when you can, for Laws 10, 29, 38, 47, and 56.   12
Symbols   4 Use these percentages when you write a chart: 38% and 56%.   12
Technique 5 Center your name; then center your teacher's name below yours.

| 1 | 2 | 3 | 4 | 5 | 6 | 7 | 8 | 9 | 10 | 11 | 12 |

PRETEST

Take a 3-minute timing on lines 6–14. Circle and count your errors.

```
                 1              2            3           4
 6       Do you want to get better grades in school?  Then here   12
           5          6             7           8
 7  are a few tips you should follow for doing good work in all    24
         9          10
 8  courses, no matter which ones they are.                        32
      11         12            13            14
 9       You should prepare for each class so that you might be    12
       15         16            17            18
10  able to respond when there is any chance to discuss a major    24
       19         20          21
11  issue or a point made by another student.                      32
           22           23          24          25
12       Discover what all your teachers expect of each student    12
       26           27          28          29
13  in and out of class.  Listen.  Be exact in all answers that    24
       30          31           32
14  you give on a quiz.  Know all the facts.                        32
```

| 1 | 2 | 3 | 4 | 5 | 6 | 7 | 8 | 9 | 10 | 11 | 12 | SI 1.25

PRACTICE

Take a 1-minute timing on each paragraph of the Pretest.

POSTTEST

Take another 3-minute timing on lines 6–14 to see how much your skill has improved.

MORE RULES OF WORD DIVISION

Workbook 33–34.

Rule	Preferred	Avoid
1. Divide a compound word between the whole words that it contains. Similarly, divide a hyphenated compound word after the hyphen.	business– men under– stand father– in-law clerk– typist	busi– nessmen un– derstand fa– ther-in-law clerk-typ– ist
2. Divide after a one-letter syllable unless it is part of a suffix. Divide between two consecutive, separately pronounced vowels.	sepa– rate simi– lar radi– ation valu– able	sep– arate sim– ilar rad– iation valua– ble
3. When dates, personal names, street names, and long numbers must be broken, do not separate parts that must be read as units. Follow preferred examples.	June 10, / 1982 Ms. Elsie / Berndt 132 Eastern / Road 1,583,– 000,000	May / 21 Mr. / Swenson 132 / Eastern Road 27,– 567

(Continued on next page)

67   LESSON 39   **67**

_{again}

Thank you, Mr. Braum, for agreeing 106
to take part in our annual meeting. / 113
_{R.}
yours very truly, / Ms. Jane Windom / 127
President/(Your initials) / Enclosure / 133
cc: Scott Webb / Brenda McDaniel 142

JOB 122 B. MEMO
Workbook 199.

[To:] Jo Anne Jones, Richard Weeks, Gabriel Sanchez, Patsy Holder, Maureen Reinholtz, Samuel Crocker, Cecelia Brown/ [Date:] (Today's date) / [From:] Barbara Jensen / [Subject:] Fund Drive for Children's Home.

Thank you for your excellent reports on the Children's Home. All of you did a great job, and I know now that I made an excellent decision in asking each of you to help me on this project.

It is good to know that the entire community supported the drive and that we went over our goal of $3000. Be sure to turn in all your collections by the 15th so that we can close the books on this project by the end of the month.

Once again, thank you for all your hard work. I hope we can be as successful in next year's drive. See you at the campaign party. /BJ/[Your initials]

LESSON 123

■ **GOALS**
To form plurals of nouns correctly while typing sentences.
To type 38/5'/5e.
To improve your keyboarding accuracy.

■ **FORMAT**
Drills: Single spacing   60-space line
5-Minute Timings: Double spacing   5-space tab

LAB 14

Plurals

Type lines 1–4 once, making plurals of the underscored words. Edit your copy as your teacher reads the answers. Then retype lines 1–4 from your edited copy.

1 The <u>employee</u> moved the <u>desk</u>, <u>typewriter</u>, and huge <u>box</u>.
2 Jo took the <u>mix</u> from the <u>bag</u> located near the <u>terminal</u>.
3 The <u>charge</u> listed on the <u>invoice</u> cannot be quoted to him.
4 The <u>bus</u> left the depot by noon, followed by Zelda's <u>van</u>.

PREVIEW PRACTICE

Type each line twice as a preview to the 5-minute timings on page 207.

Accuracy 5 quiz travel security exciting utilities examined imperative
Speed 6 provide during prior make what pros work sign auto when say

	Rule	Preferred	Avoid
4.	Divide after a prefix or before a suffix.	super– sonic legal– ize	su– personic le– galize
5.	Avoid dividing the last word on a page.		

JOB 39 A. WORD DIVISION PRACTICE

Clear your tabulator; then set tab stops 20 spaces and 40 spaces from the left margin. Type lines 15–19, which show all syllable breaks for the words given. Draw a line on your paper through the best division point for each word. Then retype lines 15–19, showing only the *best* division point for each word.

```
15   sep-a-rate      in-tro-duce     re-ad-just
16   crit-i-cal      grad-u-a-tion   ret-ro-ac-tive
17   time-ta-ble     le-gal-ize      care-less-ness
18   eye-wit-ness    pre-ma-ture     val-u-a-ble
19   reg-u-late      su-per-star     cen-ter-piece
```

JOB 39 B. WORD DIVISION PRACTICE

Using the same margins and tabs as in Job 39 A, type lines 20–23. Then decide on the *best* division point for each term given. Some words or phrases cannot be divided.

```
20   Dr. Hamill        radiation        international
21   1,265,610,000     May 31, 1984     cross-reference
22   masterpiece       $265.22          facilitate
23   September 21      Ms. E. Swenson   23 Mulberry Avenue
```

LESSON 40

■ **GOALS**
To recognize how words are capitalized while typing sentences.
To format and type informal notes.

■ **FORMAT**
Single spacing   60-space line   5-space tab

LAB 1

Capitalization

Type lines 1–4 once. Then repeat lines 1–4 or take a series of 1-minute timings.

```
1   Jane's instructor, Ms. Patterson, teaches in New York City.   12
2   Gerald hopes to travel to Mozambique and Germany next year.   12
3   Dr. Frey, the new museum director, bought a rug in Bangkok.   12
4   Today, Global Airlines travels to most countries in Europe.   12
    | 1 | 2 | 3 | 4 | 5 | 6 | 7 | 8 | 9 | 10 | 11 | 12
```

Capitalize a proper noun (the name of a specific person, place, or thing): *Ms. Patterson, Germany, New York, Kleenex, Spanish, January.*

Note: Common nouns such as *museum, high school,* and *city* are also capitalized when they are part of proper names: *Carnegie Museum, Patterson High School, New York City.*

Capitalize the first word of a sentence.

Corporations in the city contribute to public museums.

■ GOALS
To identify the plural forms of nouns while typing sentences.
To type a letter and a memo.
■ FORMAT
Single spacing   60-space line

LAB 14

Plurals

Type lines 1–4 once. Then repeat lines 1–4 or take a series of 1-minute timings.

1 Several businesses stay open late; thus Janice may be late. 12
2 Seventy typists and programmers attend college every night. 12
3 The dentist checked the teeth of ten children in West Farm. 12
4 Alice heard the buzzes of the saws and quickly rushed home. 12

| 1 | 2 | 3 | 4 | 5 | 6 | 7 | 8 | 9 | 10 | 11 | 12

12-SECOND TIMINGS

Type each line three times, or take three 12-second timings on each line. For each timing, type with no more than 1 error.

5 Those birds did not sing very long after the sun went down.
6 We have to push the car so that we can make it up the hill.
7 You have to put it on my desk now so that I can pick it up.

5   10   15   20   25   30   35   40   45   50   55   60

30-SECOND SPEED TIMINGS

Take two 30-second speed timings on lines 8 and 9. Then take two 30-second speed timings on lines 10 and 11. Or type each sentence twice.

8 If you want to run in that race, you must work out at least 12
9 five or six times each week to build up to your best speed. 24
10 The best time for her to run is early in the day before the 12
11 hot sun gets too high in the sky and before the wind blows. 24

| 1 | 2 | 3 | 4 | 5 | 6 | 7 | 8 | 9 | 10 | 11 | 12

JOB 122 A. LETTER
Standard format. Workbook 197–198. Body 79 words.

(Today's date) / Mr. Roger Braum / 2476 12

Flora Avenue / SanJose, CA 95103 / Dear 21

Mr. Braum: / Subject: July 14 Luncheon 29

        It was a real pleasure to learn that 38

you will be our guest speaker for the 44

July 14 luncheon meeting. Your presen- 52

tation, "The New Office of the 90s," 58

will be well recieved by all our members. 67

        The luncheon tickets enclosed are 75

for you and your wife, the program will 83

begin at 1 p.m., and you'll have about 91

fifty 50 minutes for your talk. 97

(Continued on next page)

12-SECOND TIMINGS

Type each line three times, or take three 12-second timings on each line. For each timing, type with no more than 1 error.

5 If the order is a big one, we will make a profit this year.
6 We will do all we can to help them win the big prize today.
7 He cannot go there if he is to come here first for an hour.

```
     |     5    10    15    20    25    30    35    40    45    50    55    60
```

30-SECOND SPEED TIMINGS

Take two 30-second speed timings on lines 8 and 9. Then take two 30-second speed timings on lines 10 and 11. Or type each sentence twice.

8 Each time you step out of your house, you are likely to see   12
9 a bird of some kind, which adds much to our love of nature.   24
10 If you like to watch birds and plan to take a field trip, a   12
11 wide area must be seen so that you can study lots of birds.   24

```
| 1 | 2 | 3 | 4 | 5 | 6 | 7 | 8 | 9 | 10 | 11 | 12
```

FORMATTING NOTES

Informal notes are short and therefore are usually typed on a half sheet of paper. To format informal notes:

1. Use a 5-inch line.
2. Begin date at the center on line 7.
3. Leave 4 blank lines between date and salutation.
4. Type salutation at the left margin.

5. Leave 1 blank line between salutation and body (the message).
6. Indent paragraphs 5 spaces from the left margin.
7. Single-space each paragraph, but double-space between paragraphs.
8. Type the closing a double space below the body, beginning at the center.

INFORMAL NOTES

JOB 40 A. INFORMAL NOTE
Standard format. Half sheet of paper.

DATE
↓7
October 14, 19--
↓5

SALUTATION
Dear Club Member:
↓2

BODY
    We have planned a special program on diving techniques for our next Swim Club meeting. Last year's city diving champion, Lisa Cammero, will demonstrate proper diving for all of us.
↓2
    The meeting will be held in the pool area of the Civic Center at 7 p.m., Wednesday, October 24. You will not need a pass to enter. We are making arrangements for everyone to swim free at this meeting.
↓2

CLOSING
Always sign correspondence in ink.
SIGNATURE
                              Your president,

                              Gloria

```
- -    10   39 - 28 - 47 - 56 - 10 - 39 - 28 - 47 - 56 - 10 - 390 - 280
' "    11   '39' '28' '47' '56' '10' '39' "28" "47" "56" "10" "39" "28"
/ ?    12   39 / 28 / 47 / 56 / 10 / 39 / 28 ? 47 ? 56 ? 10 ? 39 ? 28 ?
: ;    13   39: 28: 47: 56: 10: 39: 28; 47; 56; 10; 39; 280; 470;
! ¢    14   39! 28! 47! 56! 10! 39! 28¢ 47¢ 56¢ 10¢ 39¢ 280¢ 470¢
```

PRETEST Take a 5-minute timing on lines 15–31. Circle and count your errors.

```
                                  1                            2
15       Can you remember how easy it was when you were younger    12
              3                              4
16   and did not have to worry about money?  In those years your   24
          5                        6                        7
17   parents paid for what you needed or what you couldn't quite   36
                        8                         9
18   do without; you didn't even have to give a thought to where   48
                  10                      11                    12
19   that money had originated.  Now, though, you have dozens of   60
                            13                       14
20   places where your limited amount of earnings must be spent.   72
                    15                    16
21   Most of us know exactly how much money we can spend, and we   84
          17                      18                      19
22   must make wise decisions and set realistic priorities about   96
23   spending.                                                     98
                     20                  21                     22
24       Because you must make these wise, realistic judgments,   110
                       23                      24
25   it is best to plan a budget.  You, the wage earner, must be  122
                  25                      26
26   careful enough to plan ahead.  Items such as food, housing,  134
          27                      28                      29
27   transportation, and any other necessities must be taken out  146
                  30                       31
28   first.  Only after all of these have been taken care of can  158
              32                      33                      34
29   you afford to turn your attention to such items as clothing  170
                        35                      36
30   and entertainment.  Then you should also think about saving  182
                  37                  38
31   some of the money you earned by working.                     190
     | 1 | 2 | 3 | 4 | 5 | 6 | 7 | 8 | 9 | 10 | 11 | 12     SI 1.45
```

PRACTICE In the chart below find the number of errors you made on the Pretest. Then type each of the designated drill lines four times.

Pretest errors	0–1	2–3	4–5	6+
Drill lines	35–39	34–38	33–37	32–36

Accuracy
```
32   careful because thought younger remember clothing attention
33   about worry limited without couldn't originated necessities
34   easy when exactly parents earnings realistic transportation
35   money spending judgments decisions priorities entertainment
```
Speed
```
36   needed though dozens those quite where think were have days
37   places amount budget spent spend these yours paid what even
38   earner enough afford ahead items other makes have give that
39   should saving worked taken first after plans wise best been
```

POSTTEST Take another 5-minute timing on lines 15–31 to see how much your skill has improved.

JOB 40 B. INFORMAL NOTE
Standard format. Half sheet of paper. Sign your own name.

January 20, 19--

Dear Dr. Reshmi,

The Redcreek Valley High School Biology Club appreciates your coming to speak to us last week. Your presentation on acid rain was very informative, and all of us learned a great deal.

Thank you for sharing your expertise with us.

Sincerely yours,

LESSON 41

■ **GOALS**
To identify how words are capitalized while typing sentences.
To type 32/3'/5e.
To type informal notes.
To compose an informal note.

■ **FORMAT**
Drills: Single spacing   60-space line
3-Minute Timings: Double spacing   5-space tab

LAB 1

Capitalization

Type lines 1–4 once. Then repeat lines 1–4 or take a series of 1-minute timings.

1   Our supervisor, Mrs. Jezarian, is flying to Peru next year.   12
2   El Duo Corporation, a Spanish company, does this work best.   12
3   Lincoln Center will feature a hula dance group from Hawaii.   12
4   My French teacher will visit the Grand Canyon during March.   12

| 1 | 2 | 3 | 4 | 5 | 6 | 7 | 8 | 9 | 10 | 11 | 12

PRETEST

Take a 3-minute timing on lines 5–13. Circle and count your errors.

5   Jazz and blues music have the same roots from the past   12
6   in black gospel singing; slaves had just religion and music   24
7   to lessen the hardships of their lives.   32

8   When days were bad, captives wrote and sang the blues.   12
9   When life was freer, jazz was sung to express joy. Both of   24
10 these are popular with all races today.   32

11   Whether played and sung by a lone guitarist or done by   12
12 a quintet, the music and the mood are sensed best by people   24
13 if they grasp the meaning of the words.   32

| 1 | 2 | 3 | 4 | 5 | 6 | 7 | 8 | 9 | 10 | 11 | 12   SI 1.26

a certain number of ~~activities~~ *projects* each   385
year.   Whatever funds we are able to   392
generate should be ~~categorized for~~ use   397
as eiter (development) ~~or~~ interest bear-   402
ing funds.   407

CLOSING REMARKS *AND ADJOURNMENT*   415

    Several Council members ~~PARTICI-~~   421
~~PATED in a discussion on~~ *discussed* the develop-   426
ment program, and Mr. Pulaski suggested   435

that we conduct a drive to harness sup-   441
port from our alum ni.   446

    The next Council meeting will be   454
held ~~in the~~ on November 12.   A specific   461
time will be set ~~and communicated~~ in   465
September.   467

¶ The meeting was adjourned at 12:25 p.m.   477

        Sharon Lawson, Secretary   485

LESSON 121

■ **GOALS**
To recognize the plural forms of nouns while typing
  sentences.
To build skill in typing symbols.
To type 38/5'/5e.

■ **FORMAT**
Drills: Single spacing   60-space line
5-Minute Timings: Double spacing   5-space tab

LAB 14

Plurals

Type lines 1–4 once. Then repeat lines 1–4 or take a series of 1-minute timings. As you type each line, note the noun plurals.

1 The businesses and churches in our town are assisting Jack.   12
2 Thursday the new bands will perform in two quaint villages.   12
3 The girls and boys of the community like puzzles and flags.   12
4 For many years our taxes have been increased by our county.   12

| 1 | 2 | 3 | 4 | 5 | 6 | 7 | 8 | 9 | 10 | 11 | 12

Plurals are regularly formed by adding *s* to the singular form.

  bank, banks worker, workers typist, typists

However, when the singular ends in *s, x, ch, sh,* or *z,* the plural is formed by adding *es* to the singular.

  business, businesses tax, taxes inch, inches

The plurals of some nouns are formed in irregular ways.

  woman, women child, children tooth, teeth

SYMBOLS PRACTICE

Type each line twice to find out which symbol keys are the most difficult for you. Force yourself to type rapidly—push yourself to your fastest rate. Circle each symbol in which an error was made, and then repeat the lines in which those errors occur.

@ #   5   3 @ 28 @ 47 @ 56 @ 10 @ 39 @ 28 #39 #28 #47 #56 #10 #39 #28
$ %   6 $39 $28 $47 $56 $10 $39 $28 $39 28% 47% 56% 10% 39% 28% 47%
& *   7   3 & 28 & 47 & 56 & 10 & 39 & 28 *47 *56 *10 *39 *28 *47 *56
( )   8   (39) (28) (47) (56) (10) (39) (28) (47) (56) (10) (39) (28)
= +   9   39 = 28 = 47 = 56 = 10 = 39 = 28 + 47 + 56 + 10 + 390 + 280

(Continued on next page)

PRACTICE Take a 1-minute timing on each paragraph of the Pretest (page 70).

POSTTEST Take another 3-minute timing on lines 5–13 (page 70) to see how much your skill has improved.

JOB 41 A. INFORMAL NOTE
Standard format. Half sheet of paper.

December 5, 19--

Dear Fred,

Several of us are planning a trip for the spring break. We want to come to the beach. Our break falls in the last week of March this year. Is this the same week that you will have off? We hope that we can get together with you if it is.

Would you recommend some motels where we might stay for the week? We need to make our plane reservations before Christmas, and we would like to make our motel plans at the same time.

See you soon.

Rick

A period follows the complimentary closing because it is a complete sentence.

JOB 41 B. HARD COPY OF ELECTRONIC MESSAGE
Ms. Bowman's printer is broken; she has asked you to type a hard copy of the electronic message shown below. A *hard copy* is simply the text printed on a sheet of paper. Format the message as an informal note. For the salutation, use *Dear Mr. Salvato:*. For the closing, use *Regards,*. Do not use all-capital letters. Standard format for informal notes. Half sheet of paper.

 Computers can communicate with each other electronically. Computer-based message systems use some type of message form on the terminal screen. The message form guides you as to what you should type. In the illustration, the message form guides are DATE, TO, FROM.

```
DATE:    APRIL 10, 19--
TO:      TONY SALVATO
FROM:    GERALDINE BOWMAN

THANK YOU FOR APPROVING THE SCHEDULE FOR
THE REGIONAL SPEECH TOURNAMENT AT CLOVER
HILL HIGH SCHOOL.  IT IS AN HONOR FOR US
TO HOST THE TOURNAMENT, AND YOUR SUPPORT
OF IT WILL MAKE IT THE BEST TOURNAMENT
EVER.

FRAN RICHARDS WILL CONTACT YOU NEXT WEEK
TO EXPLAIN THE OPENING ASSEMBLY.  WE
APPRECIATE YOUR VOLUNTEERING TO MAKE THE
OPENING INTRODUCTIONS.
```

6   15   On 6/6/86 and 6/16/86 we sold 66 units of Item 66 for $666.
7   16   On the 17th we bowled scores of 77, 117, 171, 177, and 207.
8   17   Series 8 was used in 88 high schools in the area on 8/8/86.
9   18   Their winning numbers are 9919, 9929, 9939, 9949, and 9959.
0   19   The metric system is founded on tens: 10, 20, 30, 40, etc.

POSTTEST   Repeat the Pretest on page 201 to see how much your skill has improved.

JOB 120 A. MINUTES OF A MEETING
Standard format (p. 175).

Department of Business   5
MINUTES OF THE BUSINESS COUNCIL   11
Apr. 7, 19--   15

OPENING REMARKS   19

The meeting was opened by Alex   27
Thomas, Chairman of the Business Advisory   34
Council, at 9:00 a. m. Members   40
present were as follows: Linda Blakely, Kenneth   49
Carnes, Sharon Lawson, Daniel Day,   56
Rita Morales, Jeanine Sanderson, James   63
Tresvandt, and Robert Pulaski. Opening   69
ductory remarks were made by Mr.   76
Thomas, Council Chair, and by Ms.   83
Morales, Head of the Business   89
Department Program   91

ACADEMIC PROGRAM REVIEW   97

Mr. Daniel Day reviewed the prog-   104
ress being made on the department's   111
current review of the general studies   119
program. He also presented a few brief   127
comments on the structure of general   134
education within the center for general   142
studies.   144

External Activities   149

Ms. Sanderson gave a review of current   158
departmental activities that included the following: 166
external activities for credit (health   174
care program, student internship, and   181
free enterprise workshop) and external   189
activities for no credit.   194

Mr. Tresvandt presented an over-   205
view of the Placement Office's activi-   209
ties. Since he was recently appointed   215
as Director of Placement, Mr. Tresvandt   222
shared with the Council his own goals   229
for the Placement Office. In summary,   234
he believes that we should think about   242
the objectives of placement in order   250
to create a sound career development   257
concept and that we should improve the way   266
we present it.   269

DEVELOPMENT ACTIVITIES   274

Ms. Morales opened the discussion   283
on development activities by announc-   290
ing that Mr. Thomas has proposed to   297
make a contribution to the department   305
of business as an initial donation for   313
the endowment fund. The contribution   320
will be matched by the companies for   328
which Mr. Thomas serves as a member of   336
the Board of Trustees.   340

Ms. Morales discussed fundrais-   348
ing goals for the department and sug-   355
gested that the department should not wait   363
for the accumulation of the entire   370
fund; instead, we should start funding   378

(Continued on next page)

COMPOSING AT THE KEYBOARD

It is a proven fact that people can keyboard faster than they can write in longhand. Therefore, it makes good sense to compose many types of written communications directly at the keyboard.

To compose at the keyboard, keep these points in mind:

1. Organize your ideas mentally—do not write them down.

2. Use the correct format for the document you are composing.

3. Try to keyboard a final copy on the first try.

4. You may look at what you are composing, but do not look at your keys.

5. Proofread, and edit if necessary.

JOB 41 C. COMPOSED INFORMAL NOTE

Assume you are Fran Richards. Compose a note to Mr. Salvato telling him that the opening assembly for the speech tournament will be Wednesday, April 25, 19—. Tell him that his opening remarks will be delivered at 10 a.m. in the main assembly hall. Invite him to stay for lunch. Parking is available at the rear of the building. Standard format.

LESSON 42

■ **GOALS**
To capitalize words correctly while typing sentences.
To type 32/3'/5e.
To format and type informal notes with enumerations.

■ **FORMAT**
Drills: Single spacing   60-space line
3-Minute Timings: Double spacing   5-space tab

LAB 1

Capitalization

You have to provide the missing capitals as you type this exercise.

Type lines 1–4 once, providing the missing capitals. Edit your copy as your teacher reads the answers. Then retype lines 1–4 from your edited copy.

1   Their teacher, ms. quartz, hopes to visit sicily this year.

2   The buhl planetarium in pittsburgh is a great place to see.

3   The president of our company also serves the jacox company.

4   He bought a swiss clock at the st. louis auction last week.

PREVIEW PRACTICE

Type each line twice as a preview to the 3-minute timings on page 73.

Accuracy   5   junk vases quite amazes buyers anxious sometimes neighbor's

Speed   6   happens market their right make that they else glad may rid

```
P   26   peg pit put pale plan push pearl plant point parade picture
Q   27   quay quid quip quit quiz quart quick quaint quarter quintet
R   28   rat red rug rank risk road reign rinse rough ramble reverse
S   29   sag ski sub sift slip soft scope short slice sphere slender
T   30   tap toy two take that tone taunt trail twist target trailer

U   31   urn use ugly undo urge used unit unite until unfold upright
V   32   van vie vow very veto vote valid vowel vocal victim variety
W   33   was why win wait wear work waist weigh wrong wrench warning

X   34   axe fix six next text taxi extra relax toxic influx expense
Y   35   yes yet you yawn yowl your yucca yummy yearly yellow yonder
Z   36   zig zip zoo zest zinc zone zebra zesty zippy zenith zigzags
```

POSTTEST   Repeat the Pretest on page 200 to see how much your skill has improved.

LESSON 120

■ **GOALS**
To build skill in keyboarding numbers.
To type the minutes of a meeting.

■ **FORMAT**
Drills: Single spacing   60-space line
2-Minute Timings: Double spacing

KEYBOARDING SKILLS

Type lines 1–4 once. In line 5 backspace and underscore each word containing double letters immediately after typing it. Repeat lines 1–4, or take a series of 1-minute timings.

```
Speed       1   The key to the problem with both their maps is their shape.   12
Accuracy    2   Jack bought five exquisite bronze bowls at Pam's yard sale.   12
Numbers     3   We set our tabs at 10, 29, 38, 47, and 56 for the problems.   12
Symbols     4   Only 9% of #47 and 8% of #56 were sold on the 1st (Monday).   12
Technique   5   They, too, shall give three good yells when the bell tolls.
                |  1  |  2  |  3  |  4  |  5  |  6  |  7  |  8  |  9  |  10  |  11  |  12
```

PRETEST

Take a 2-minute timing on lines 6–9, or type them twice to find out which number keys are the most difficult for you to type. Keep your eyes on your copy as you type. Circle each digit where an error was made.

```
6   4703 6051 8954 5607 1283 7626 5316 0914 9065 7283 9413 8972   12
7   3145 2364 5603 8917 4823 0543 7951 2541 7068 6079 7286 9012   24
8   8942 5613 7084 9508 5263 7420 8162 7395 9481 5369 4327 6110   36
9   4378 6250 9064 1357 7072 1431 5923 7045 8968 2648 9019 8123   48
    |  1  |  2  |  3  |  4  |  5  |  6  |  7  |  8  |  9  |  10  |  11  |  12
```

PRACTICE

Type lines 10–19 once. Then repeat any of the lines that stress the digit errors you circled in the Pretest.

```
1   10   I have 1 tulip, 1 rose, 11 zinnias, 11 violets, and 1 iris.
2   11   We donated 2 quarters, 2 dimes, 22 nickels, and 22 pennies.
3   12   When multiplying 3 times 13, we get 39; 3 times 3 equals 9.
4   13   Study page 44 in Chapter 4 and read page 444 in Chapter 14.
5   14   The mileage between cities was 5, 45, 85, 95, 125, and 165.
```

(Continued on next page)

Take two 3-minute timings on lines 7–15.

```
                 1              2              3              4
7      Have you ever gone to a flea market?  At flea markets,    12
          5              6              7              8
8   people try to sell their crafts, junk items, or things they  24
          9             10
9   no longer can keep or store in an attic.                     32
      11            12             13            14
10      Often it happens that one person can use any old thing   44
     15            16            17            18
11  that someone else seems most anxious to dispose of.  Such a  56
     19           20            21
12  sale makes both buyers and sellers glad.                     64
          22            23            24            25
13      Sometimes it amazes people to find that what they hate   76
         26            27            28            29
14  so much, others like.  A vase you do not like in your house  88
        30            31            32
15  may be quite right in a neighbor's home.                     96
    |  1  |  2  |  3  |  4  |  5  |  6  |  7  |  8  |  9  |  10  |  11  |  12    SI 1.24
```

FORMATTING ENUMERATIONS WITHIN OTHER DOCUMENTS

Enumerations are often contained in the body of other documents—letters, memos, reports. The format you use will depend on the length of the enumerated items.

Hanging-Indented Format. If the items are short (one or two lines), use the hanging-indented format. To format:

1. Display the enumeration by indenting it 5 spaces from the left and right margins.

2. Single-space the items; double-space between items; indent turnovers.

3. Leave 1 blank line above and below the enumeration.

Paragraph Format. If any item in the enumeration takes three or more lines, use the paragraph format. To format:

1. Use the same margins as are used in the document.

2. If the document is double-spaced, double-space the enumeration. Do not leave any extra blank lines.

3. If the document is single-spaced, single-space the enumeration. Leave 1 blank line above and below the enumeration and between items.

Note: If the paragraphs in the document are blocked (begin at the left margin), use the hanging-indented format, but do *not* indent the left and right margins.

JOB 42 A. INFORMAL NOTE WITH ENUMERATION

Standard format (hanging indented). Half sheet of paper.

[Today's date]

Dear Students,

We are making a survey to study the physical fitness of our students. Will you please answer the following questions:

1. What exercises do you do to keep fit?
2. What games do you play regularly?
3. What do you eat for breakfast?

Thank you,

[Sign your name]

LESSON 119

UNIT 20 Skill Building
UNIT GOAL 38/5'/5e

■ **GOALS**
To use colons correctly while typing sentences.
To build skill on the alphabetic keyboard.

■ **FORMAT**
Single spacing   60-space line

LAB 13

Colons

Workbook 195–196.

Type lines 1–4 once, providing the missing colons. Edit your copy as your teacher reads the answers. Then retype lines 1–4 from your edited copy.

1 Gregory Ashton quoted these prices $4.16, $31.78, $90.82.
2 Choose one of these subjects management, finance, or tax.
3 Type it like this single spacing, 50-space line, no tabs.
4 Katy Venezia ordered these items inks, ribbons, and pens.

12-SECOND TIMINGS

Type each line three times, or take three 12-second timings on each line. For each timing, type with no more than 1 error.

5 They have made a big profit on the big order they now made.
6 The class can be taken by all who want to get a better job.
7 She will work at it for an hour and get the job done right.

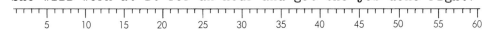

```
        5    10   15   20   25   30   35   40   45   50   55   60
```

PRETEST

Type lines 8–10 twice to find out which alphabetic keys are the most difficult for you. Force yourself to type rapidly—push yourself to your fastest rate. Circle each letter in which an error is made.

8 Jeff amazed the audience by quickly giving six new reports.
9 Jacqueline was glad her family took five or six big prizes.
10 Judy gave a quick jump as the zebra and lynx wildly fought.

PRACTICE

Type lines 11–36 once. Then repeat any of the lines that stress the letter errors you circled in the Pretest.

A 11 aid air apt army aunt able abide aimed alone adjust amazing
B 12 buy bad bag bike blow bold baked below block baking belongs
C 13 cat cob cot cent clog cold check clock close cancel capitol
D 14 dad den dot disk drew drop doing drill dream dinner destroy
E 15 eel elf elm east easy ends exact enter equip enable examine

F 16 fig for fun film foot form fills films flint filing fiction
G 17 gag gem get grew girl give going great guide guilty gathers
H 18 hat hem hop hand help hope happy habit haven height hastily
I 19 ink ill inn into idle iron ideas incur issue income illness
J 20 jab jet job joke jump just jelly jewel judge justly journey

K 21 keg key kit knee knew knot knack keeps kitty knight keeping
L 22 lap let log line lone lost limit locks looks linens leisure
M 23 map men mob milk mile mind meter merit merge merger mission
N 24 nap new nor name neat noun niece noise nurse nephew nervous
O 25 oak out owl once oust over often opera ought ordeal outline

(Continued on next page)

JOB 42 B. INFORMAL NOTE WITH ENUMERATION
Standard format (paragraph). Full sheet of paper.

Rick,

Plans for our spring vacation in Florida are almost complete. These are the hotels that have space available for the dates we want.

1. The Southern Star. Rates are $39 per person for a double room with twin beds. The hotel is located one block from the beach.

2. The Tidewater. Rates are $44 per person for a twin double. The hotel is located right on the beach.

3. The Beachcomber. Rates are $48 per person for a twin double, which includes breakfast. This hotel is also located right on the beach.

Let me know which hotel you prefer.

Fred

LESSON 43

CLINIC

■ **GOALS**
To build typing accuracy.
To type 32/3'/5e.

■ **FORMAT**
Drills: Single spacing   60-space line
3-Minute Timings: Double spacing   5-space tab

KEYBOARDING SKILLS

On computers the caps lock only capitalizes the alphabet keys. You must still depress the shift key to type the quotation and question marks.

Speed
Accuracy
Numbers
Symbols
Technique

Type lines 1–4 once. Then do what line 5 tells you to do. Repeat lines 1–4, or take a series of 1-minute timings.

```
 1  It is his fault if he does not help us find the six orders.   12
 2  Jumping quickly from the taxi, Hazel brushed a woven chair.    12
 3  Please get some price tags for 10¢, 29¢, 38¢, 47¢, and 56¢.    12
 4  "Why must I leave?" she asked.  "Well," we said, "why not?"     12
 5  Depress the shift lock and type line 4 in all-capital letters.
    |  1  |  2  |  3  |  4  |  5  |  6  |  7  |  8  |  9  | 10  | 11  | 12
```

PRETEST

Take a 3-minute timing on lines 7–15 on page 73. Circle and count your errors.

PRACTICE

Type lines 6–9 three times. Then type lines 10–13 three times.

```
 6  sws swim swam swell swaps swish sweeps swanky sweats sweets
 7  kik skim skid kindly skinny skimpy killer skips skins skimp
 8  lol long love loosen clouds sloppy floods loyal along loses
 9  ded deer deck dealer seeded headed leaded ceded deeds deuce

10  waw wade wage awake waist waxen awards warden waxers wander
11  lil like lilt clips light slips lilies flight limber slices
12  drd draw drab draft drama drawn drills droopy drives dreads
13  nkn inks pink skunk ankle chunk linked banker tanker dunker
```

POSTTEST

Take another 3-minute timing on lines 7–15 on page 73 to see how much your skill has improved.

LESSON 118

■ GOAL
To improve your keyboarding skills using the Selective
   Practice routine.

■ FORMAT
Drills: Single spacing   60-space line
2-Minute Timings: Double spacing   5-space tab

KEYBOARDING SKILLS

Type lines 1–4 once. Then do what line 5 tells you to do. Repeat lines 1–4, or take a series of 1-minute timings.

Speed   1 She paid Laurie to fix the ivory box that the visitor made.   12
Accuracy   2 A frozen bird squawked vigorously as Joseph coaxed him out.   12
Numbers   3 Players 29, 38, 47, and 56 all scored 10 points last night.   12
Symbols   4 On 1/31 they received a 9% raise, from $1200/week to $1308.   12
Technique   5 Strike your return key after typing each word in this line.

| 1 | 2 | 3 | 4 | 5 | 6 | 7 | 8 | 9 | 10 | 11 | 12

PRETEST

Take a 2-minute timing on lines 6–12; then take a 2-minute timing on lines 13–19. Circle and count your errors on each.

Consecutive Right-   6   If you've had an opportunity to visit a haunted house,   12
Hand Reaches   7 I am certain you would really enjoy going back. I have not   24
                       8 had the opportunity to do so. You may believe I'm a little   36
                       9 curious about what is in store for me if such a wish should   48
                      10 come true some day. I envision monsters chasing me rapidly   60
                      11 around the house or out a window. Or I may envision myself   72
                      12 all alone with them.   76

Consecutive Left-   13   Exactly what causes those fears to overcome us? Where   12
Hand Reaches   14 do we first begin to be afraid? When thinking about it, we   24
                      15 really have to laugh at ourselves. We quickly observe just   36
                      16 how foolish we were to be afraid. Ghosts and monsters come   48
                      17 from fantasy. Actually, many of these fears probably came,   60
                      18 for the first time, when our older brothers or sisters were   72
                      19 always teasing us.   76

| 1 | 2 | 3 | 4 | 5 | 6 | 7 | 8 | 9 | 10 | 11 | 12   SI 1.45

PRACTICE

In which timing did you make more errors? If in the first one (lines 6–12), type lines 20–23 four times and lines 24–27 two times. If most of your errors were in the second timing (lines 13–19), reverse the procedure.

Consecutive Right-   20 coin copy inks know knox mind mine nine none noun omit pine
Hand Reaches   21 pink pins pipe pius pond pops pump sink tiny unit upon your
                      22 among ankle axiom bonus bound count doing don't donor equip
                      23 found going inlay input knock known lemon minds miner minor

Consecutive Left-   24 crew ever feel fees have here mart mass mere nest next owes
Hand Reaches   25 pads part pave rest sack save seek seem sees tree ward warm
                      26 affix aired alert arrow asset await award aware birds blast
                      27 board buses chart chest class coast cover dress dwell error

POSTTEST

Repeat the Pretest to see how much your skill has improved.

LESSON 44

UNIT 8 Skill Building/Production Review

UNIT GOAL 32/3'/5e

■ **GOALS**
To capitalize words correctly while typing sentences.
To type from rough drafts.

■ **FORMAT**
Single spacing   60-space line

LAB 1

Capitalization

Type lines 1–4 once, providing the missing capitals. Edit your copy as your teacher reads the answers. Then retype lines 1–4 from your edited copy.

1 I hope that ms. sajovic and ms. quinn fly to great britain.

2 We met mr. and mrs. dextor when they visited san francisco.

3 We wrote to the peking art museum about the chinese sketch.

4 A big american flag was flying atop new zenith high school.

12-SECOND TIMINGS

Type each line three times, or take three 12-second timings on each line. For each timing, type with no more than 1 error.

5 If the wind hits the leaves, they will come down very soon.

6 We know that he had the spools when he left here about six.

7 The new moon went over the hills and out of sight too soon.

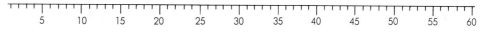

PROOF-READERS' MARKS

Workbook 37–38.

When corrections must be made in copy, professional writers, editors, proofreaders, and typists use proofreaders' marks. These symbols are quick and easy to use, and they make typing from a rough draft faster and easier for the typist. Study the proofreaders' marks shown below.

Proofreaders' Mark	Draft	Final Copy	Proofreaders' Mark	Draft	Final Copy
SS Single-space	SS [first line / second line]	first line / second line	O→ Move as shown	it is (not)	it is
ds Double-space	ds [first line / second line]	first line / second line	∩ Transpose	(is/it) so	it is not so
⌐ Move to left	⌐ let us	let us	⌒ Omit space	to⌒gether	together
⌐ Move to right	it is so ⌐	it is so	ℓ Delete letter	errorx	error
5 Indent 5 spaces	5 Let it be	Let it be	ℓ Delete word	it may be	it may
] [Center	] TITLE [	TITLE	word Change word	and if it	and so it
¶ Paragraph	¶ If he is	If he is	↗ Delete and close up	judgement	judgment
O Spell out	the only ①	the only one	⋯ Don't delete	can we go	can we go
= Capitalize	mrs. Wade	Mrs. Wade	# Insert space	Itmay be	It may be
/ Lowercase letter (make letter small)	Business	business	∧ Insert word or letter	and it	and so it
			V or ∧ Insert punctuation mark	Shes not	She's not,
			⊙ Insert a period	other way	other way.

■ **GOALS**
To use colons correctly while typing sentences.
To type 38/5′/5e.
To type purchase requisitions and purchase orders.

■ **FORMAT**
Drills: Single spacing   60-space line
5-Minute Timings: Double spacing   5-space tab

LAB 13
Colons

Type lines 1–4 once, providing the missing colons. Edit your copy as your teacher reads the answers. Then retype lines 1–4 from your edited copy.

1 Get these items a daisy wheel, an element, and a typebar.
2 James has done the following problems 10, 11, 12, and 14.
3 Please pick up these items bananas, carrots, and oranges.
4 She possesses these skills typing, shorthand, and filing.

**PREVIEW
PRACTICE**
Accuracy
Speed

Type lines 5 and 6 twice as a preview to the 5-minute timings.

5 quite didn't dozens exactly couldn't priorities necessities
6 spending spent when paid with make also turn them such work

**5-MINUTE
TIMINGS**

Take two 5-minute timings on lines 15–31 on page 204.

JOBS 117 A AND 117 B. PURCHASE REQUISITIONS
Standard format (p. 197). Use today's date. Workbook 189 bottom and 191 top.

Sarah Carpenter, Hardware Department, Ground Floor, needs the following tools by October 12 to restock inventory: 3 Handymate 1 1/2-hp Routers, Catalog No. A841-7628; 20 rust-resistant router bits, 5 each of Models A, C, D, and F; and 1 Handymate 2.25-hp Circular Saw, Catalog No. A841-6308. Order from Consolidated Hardware Inc., 2276 Fairview Avenue, Casper, WY 82601.

Ms. Carpenter needs the following tools by November 15 to restock inventory: 10 Handymate 1/2-inch variable speed drills, Catalog No. A841-3370; 5 Handymate 7-inch polishers, Catalog No. A841-7528; 7 Handymate 3-inch by 21-inch belt sanders, Catalog No. A841-3682. Use the same supplier as that used in Job 117 A.

JOBS 117 C AND 117 D. PURCHASE ORDERS
Standard format (p. 197). Use today's date. Workbook 191 bottom and 193 top.

Quality Products Inc., 1457 Bradley Avenue, Cheyenne, WY 82001. 2 20-foot aluminum ladders, Catalog No. L380-5723, @ 155.99 = 311.98; 8 W-370 paint sprayers, Catalog No. P598-7744, @ 125.99 = 1007.92; 8 W-375 paint roller extensions, Catalog No. P590-3211, @ 55.99 = 447.92. Total = 1767.82.

Order from the same supplier as that used in Job 117 C. 5 Handymate garage door openers, Model SGO-1357, Catalog No. A841-6671, @ 249.99 = 1249.95; 1 exterior window shutter, Model SWS-2468, Catalog No. W112-7230, @ 15.99 = 15.99; 3 24-gauge steel storage cabinets, Model SSC-9078, Catalog No. C450-5321, @ 67.99 = 203.97. Total = 1469.91.

JOB 44 A. ROUGH-DRAFT PARAGRAPH

Format: Double spacing, 60-space line, 5-space tab. Half sheet of paper. Center title on line 7.

<u>Cooking Chinese Style</u>

¶ The chinese cook ~~foods~~ so that neither the color nor vitamins are lost

in the pan. So, if you want to cook chinese style, make sure that you

cook your vegetables in a Wok (with a touch of oil) rather than in a skillet

and do not over cook. With a Wok, the cook can toss food about so that the heat

is evenly spread. ¶The chinese like their vegetables to be crisp

and very fresh. Have you ever tasted foods cooked in a Wok?

JOB 44 B. ROUGH-DRAFT ENUMERATION

Hanging-indented format (see page 57). 40-space line. Half sheet of paper.

<u>do you read bumper stickers?</u>

ds
1. Some ask questions: "Have you Hugged your Child today?"

2. Some give answers: "Don't follow me. I'm lost too."

3. Some are serious: "60 is Thrifty."

4. Some are for small cars: "I'm Pedaling As Fast As I can."

JOB 44 C. ROUGH-DRAFT INFORMAL NOTE

Standard format (see page 69). Half sheet of paper.

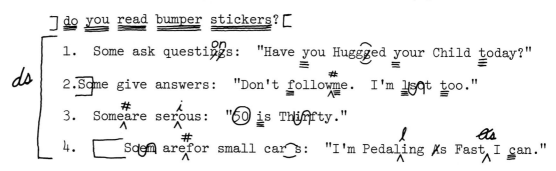

(Today's date)

Dear Sally and Joe,

As you know, Ann & I became members of our local 4-H
club. The judging of our annual projects will take place ~~on~~ July 25
at the Allen County Fairgrounds.

We would like you to come see to our projects. Ann has an
especially well-fed steer; I am going to compete in the ~~ad~~
advanced ~~cook~~ bake-off.

See you at the fair!

Ed

FORMATTING PURCHASE REQUISITIONS

Purchasing goods or services is a two-step procedure in most companies: First a *purchase requisition* is completed and sent to the purchasing department. Then the purchasing department completes an *official purchase order,* and sends it to the supplier.

To format a purchase requisition:

1. Align the heading fill-ins with the guide words.

2. Begin typing the body a double space below the ruled line.

3. Visually center the quantity in the *Quantity* column.

4. Begin the description 2 spaces after the vertical rule. Single-space items that take more than one line. Double-space between items.

5. Insert the suggested supplier's name and address as an address block, 2 spaces after the vertical rule.

6. Do not fill in the bottom portion of the form. This will be completed by the purchasing department.

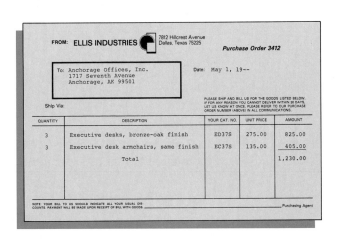

JOB 116 A. PURCHASE REQUISITION

Standard format. Use today's date. Workbook 187 top.

Larry McClure, Computer Department, 2d Floor, needs the following items by June 4 to replenish supplies: 20 boxes of 5 1/4″ diskettes, single-sided, double density; 15 boxes of carbon printing ribbons, Catalog No. ES82143; and 3 sound covers for the Model PSM-18 printer. Order from Crandel Supplies, 2754 Roxbury Street, SW, Seattle, WA 98126.

FORMATTING PURCHASE ORDERS

When a purchase requisition has been approved, the purchasing department completes a purchase order.

To format a purchase order:

1. Use the standard format for invoices.

2. Visually center the catalog number in the column marked "Catalog No."

3. Type the word *Total* aligned with the *D* in *Description.*

Remember: Dollar signs are not needed in the Unit Price and Amount columns because only dollar amounts are listed there.

JOB 116 B. PURCHASE ORDER

Standard format. Use today's date. Workbook 187 bottom.

Home Shopper Inc., 739 Rim Drive, Everett, WA 98204. 1 Carpet, Style 2698, 12′ × 20′ ($7/sq ft), Cat. No. CPT98, @ 1680.00; 10 Office chairs, Model 275A, Cat. No. CHO75, @ 55.00 = 550.00; 1 Executive chair, Model 970EX, Cat. No. CHE70, @ 145.00. Total 2375.00.

JOB 116 C. PURCHASE ORDER

Standard format. Use today's date. Workbook 189 top.

Restock your inventory by placing an order for the following items: 3 Carpets, 12′ × 20′; 5 Office chairs; and 3 Executive chairs. Use descriptions, catalog numbers, and prices as given in JOB 116 B.

■ GOALS
To type 32/3'/5e.
To type from rough-draft copy.

■ FORMAT
Drills: Single spacing   60-space line
3-Minute Timings: Double spacing   5-space tab

KEYBOARDING SKILLS

Type lines 1–4 once. Then do what line 5 tells you to do. Repeat lines 1–4, or take a series of 1-minute timings.

Speed   1 Then the boys moved with their friends to the right corner. 12
Accuracy 2 Jack Drew and Vera Lopez quietly bought six new farm tools. 12
Numbers   3 The May 2 group included 38 men, 47 women, and 56 children. 12
Symbols   4 Contracts were sent to L&R and to T&W but not to Rod & Loo. 12
Technique 5 As you retype line 2, underscore all proper nouns in it.

| 1 | 2 | 3 | 4 | 5 | 6 | 7 | 8 | 9 | 10 | 11 | 12

PRETEST

Take a 3-minute timing on lines 6–13. Then circle and count your errors.

                    1   2   3   4
6   Outer space is an exciting new place about which we do 12
                5   6   7   8
7 not know very much. Science has tried to guess some of the 24
                9   10   11   12
8 answers to the questions, but we need more facts. We have, 36
               13   14   15   16
9 of course, done amazing feats in space, such as land on the 48
               17   18   19   20
10 moon and shake hands during a walk in space among the stars 60
               21   22   23   24
11 and planets; but there are vast areas still to be explored. 72
               25   26   27   28
12 Do you think that you would like to take a fun journey into 84
               29   30   31   32
13 outer space? Would you be afraid to encounter the unknown? 96

| 1 | 2 | 3 | 4 | 5 | 6 | 7 | 8 | 9 | 10 | 11 | 12   SI 1.26

PRACTICE

In the chart below find the number of errors you made on the Pretest. Then type each of the following designated drill lines three times.

Pretest errors	0–1	2–3	4–5	6+
Drill lines	17–21	16–20	15–19	14–18

Accuracy 14 walk feats areas space tried place amazing unknown exciting
          15 land shake among outer hands facts answers science explored
          16 not stars guess about would course afraid journey encounter
          17 be you has there hands which think during planets questions

Speed   18 know very much into new the but and you fun not is an we do
          19 some need more like have done such that moon vast take area
          20 space tried facts feats areas land know much into are be to
          21 hands outer place would shake walk more some like has if so

POSTTEST

Take another 3-minute timing on lines 6–13 to see how much your skill has improved.

Take a 1-minute timing on each paragraph of the Pretest on page 195.

POSTTEST
Take another 3-minute timing on lines 5–16 on page 195 to see how much your skill has improved.

JOB 115 A. INVOICE 43-107
Standard format. Use today's date. Workbook 185 top.

[To:] Ms. Annette Pierce / Pierce Enterprises / 4680 First Street / Wayne, NE 68787

12 Model GC18 secretarial desks @ 358.99 = 4307.88

 5 Model GC27 executive desks @ 575.84 = 2879.20

12 Model EZ18 secretarial chairs @ 115.25 = 1383.00

 5 Model EZ27 executive chairs @ 215.55 = 1077.75

Amount due 9647.83 / Delivery charges 55.00 / Total amount due 9702.83

JOB 115 B. INVOICE 43-108
Standard format. Use today's date. Compute the figures for the Amount column. Workbook 185 bottom.

[To:] J. K. Gilmore and Son Inc. / 2112 Longhorn Building / 1800 West Fourth Street / Houston, TX 77007

10 reams of 16# white bond typing paper @ 8.25

 1 carton of No. 821 transparent tape @ 11.25

 6 bottles of Prime Drawing Ink @ 1.15

 4 8″ scissors, Model 2A-R17 @ 35.00

Total amount due

LESSON 116

■ **GOALS**
To identify how colons are used while typing sentences.
To format and type a purchase requisition and purchase orders.

■ **FORMAT**
Single spacing   60-space line

LAB 13
Colons

Type lines 1–4 once. Then repeat lines 1–4 or take a series of 1-minute timings.

1 Bring the following: two pencils, exam, and answer sheets. 12
2 Pack these car parts: valves, spark plugs, and fuel gauge. 12
3 I need these supplies right now: paper, pens, and pencils. 12
4 The car has several extras: clock, roof rack, and air bag. 12
  | 1 | 2 | 3 | 4 | 5 | 6 | 7 | 8 | 9 | 10 | 11 | 12

30-SECOND "OK" TIMINGS

Type as many 30-second "OK" (errorless) timings as possible out of three attempts on lines 5–7.

5 Judy weaves quickly at large beaches for extra prize money, 12
6 and just last week she found out that all the money she had 24
7 collected was enough to pay for her travels to the Midwest. 36
  | 1 | 2 | 3 | 4 | 5 | 6 | 7 | 8 | 9 | 10 | 11 | 12

JOB 45 A. HANDWRITTEN ROUGH DRAFT

Format: Double spacing, 60-space line, 5-space tab. Half sheet of paper. Center the title on line 7.

Smoking and Sleeping

¶ Smoking has been linked to many health problems, including lung cancer and heart disease. Now it also appears to cause sleeping problems. ¶ a recent 2-year study in Washington of 100 smokers and non-smokers found that non smokers fall asleep after an average of 30 minutes, while it takes smokers about 50 to 70 minutes. That's because the nicotine in cigarettes is a stimulant. #

JOB 45 B. ROUGH-DRAFT ENUMERATION

Hanging-indented format. Block-center. Half sheet of paper.

] common computer languages [

SS There are more than 200 computer languages.
The following are the most common.

1. COBOL--mainly for business use.
2. RPG--programs for writing report.
3. basic--simplest of languages.
4. FORTRAN--scientific/mathematical use.

JOB 45 C. ROUGH-DRAFT ANNOUNCEMENT

Display format.

SPECIAL Announcement
] The 11:00 a.m. Typewriting Class [
CHALLENGES
Invites
Typewriting
All Other Classes

To a

TYPING SPEED CONTEST

to be held on
Friday
Thursday, April 9

■ **GOALS**
To recognize how colons are used while typing sentences.
To type 38/3'/3e.
To type invoices.

■ **FORMAT**
Drills: Single spacing   60-space line
3-Minute Timings: Double spacing   5-space tab

LAB 13

Colons

Type lines 1–4 once. Then repeat lines 1–4 or take a series of 1-minute timings.

1 Please pack the following: visor, cosmetics, and six jars. 12
2 You need these personal traits: tact, quick wit, and zest. 12
3 We had three visitors: Mr. White, Ms. Zonn, and Ms. Yates. 12
4 Jan's set of silver is small: 6 forks, 6 knives, 6 spoons. 12

| 1 | 2 | 3 | 4 | 5 | 6 | 7 | 8 | 9 | 10 | 11 | 12

When a clause contains a word or phrase such as *the following, as follows, this,* or *these* (or even if these words or phrases are implied, not stated) and is followed by a series of words, phrases, or clauses, use a colon between the main clause and the series.

Include the following: item number, description, and cost.

Buy these items: rubber bands, paper clips, and markers.

Format the report like this: double spacing, 6-inch line, margins moved 3 spaces to the right.

PRETEST

Take a 3-minute timing on lines 5–16. Circle and count your errors.

5 　　　Selecting the right software for your computer is just 12
6 one of a maze of decisions you must make when you have your 24
7 own system. It is a task to which you must give very care- 36
8 ful thought. 38

9 　　　For example, you must find out how good the documenta- 12
10 tion is so that you can get answers to questions about your 24
11 software. The documentation for your software can help you 36
12 immensely. 38

13 　　　You should also consider the price of the software and 12
14 the ease with which you can use the software. A final con- 24
15 sideration is whether your operating system will match your 36
16 software. 38

| 1 | 2 | 3 | 4 | 5 | 6 | 7 | 8 | 9 | 10 | 11 | 12   SI 1.43

LESSON 46

■ **GOALS**
To recognize how words are capitalized while typing sentences.
To type enumerations and an informal note.

■ **FORMAT**
Single spacing   60-space line

LAB 2

Capitalization

Type lines 1–4 once. Then repeat lines 1–4 or take a series of 1-minute timings.

```
1  North Dakota and South Dakota are states north of Nebraska.   12
2  Just five bankers went to the West to tour Northern Realty.    12
3  Jo Proxmire is moving from West Virginia to the West Coast.    12
4  Go quickly to 1700 East Graham, on the south side of Azusa.    12
   |  1  |  2  |  3  |  4  |  5  |  6  |  7  |  8  |  9  | 10  | 11  | 12
```

Capitalize *north, south, east,* and *west* when they refer to definite regions; are part of a proper noun; or are within an address.

in the West   West Company   610 West Carson Street

Do not capitalize *north, south, east,* and *west* when they merely indicate direction or general location.

Drive *west* on Hatteras Street.
We live in the *south* part of Italy.

30-SECOND "OK" TIMINGS

This version of a 30-second timing is used to build your accuracy on alphabetic copy. Try to type as many 30-second "OK" (errorless) timings as possible out of three attempts on lines 5–7. Then repeat the effort on lines 8–10.

```
5  There is no quick way to learn to spell.  But if you are an   12
6  expert typist, there is one very good method for you.  Just   24
7  teach your fingers to spell as you zip through the lessons.    36
8  Nothing exceeds the damage to your hearing than that caused   12
9  by very loud noises.  If you work quite near a machine that   24
10 is noisy, you may get dizzy or perhaps injure your hearing.    36
   |  1  |  2  |  3  |  4  |  5  |  6  |  7  |  8  |  9  | 10  | 11  | 12
```

JOB 46 A. ROUGH-DRAFT ENUMERATION
Hanging-indented format.

HINTS FOR HELPING THE NEW DRIVER

1. keep in mind that the new driver needs more time to deal with traffic.

2. inform a new driver well in advance of the need to make a turn at a certain corner.

3. give the new driver an opportunity to practice driving in bad weather.

4. make sure the driver has enough practice in parking the car.

FORMATTING QUANTITY COLUMNS WITH WORDS

Sometimes the Quantity column contains words as well as numbers. The numbers must align at the right just as they would in a plain number column. The entire entry (both number and word) should be visually centered in the Quantity column. Use the longest number and the longest word.

QUANTITY	DESCRIPTION
3 boxes	Paper clips
1 pkg.	Carbon paper
125	Envelopes

FORMATTING ADJUSTMENTS TO INVOICES

Adjustments such as delivery charges, sales taxes, and discounts are typed before *Total amount due* and aligned with it, as shown at the right. First type *Amount due* (a subtotal) a double space below the last entry. Then type the adjustment line (or lines) single-spaced below *Amount due,* with a rule under the last adjustment entry. Double-space and then type *Total amount due.*

```
Amount due              343.35
Sales tax 6%             20.60
Delivery charges         15.00
                        _____
Total amount due        378.95
```

JOB 114 B. INVOICE

Standard format. Use today's date. Workbook 183 bottom.

To: Raymond Hensley, Treasurer, The Computer Club
Westside High School
10833 Castelar Street
Omaha, NE 68144

30 cans	Cola, grape soda, and fruit juice @ .50	15.00
4 packs	Napkins @ 1.23	4.92
6 packages	Forks, spoons, and knives @ .72	4.32
3 dozen	Sandwiches @ .70	25.20
	Amount due	49.44
	Sales tax 3.5%	1.73
	Total amount due	51.17

JOB 46 B. ROUGH-DRAFT ENUMERATION

Paragraph format.

]HOME COMPUTER GAMES[

2# ⟶

What should you∧ask for in a home computer ga∧me? #

      1. a̲ home computer game should∧ not be designed to make the game↑impossib̲l̲e̲↑ to beat.

      2. i̲t should use all∧the Ꞧesources∧ of the comput∫er # and do th̲e things the com͡puter does well.

5│3. It should be an∧excellent past͡ ty∫me--the play itself should # be exciting and not ⌐merely∫serve⌐ as an∧excuse to show the pro- # grammer's expertise ⦸off⦸.

JOB 46 C. COMPOSED INFORMAL NOTE

Compose an informal note to a friend inviting him or her to take a course with you at Utica College. Include in your note the courses offered, as shown on the screen at the right. Tell your friend the three courses you are most interested in and why. Standard format.

COLLEGENET
UTICA COLLEGE, NORTH MONTOUR CAMPUS
FALL NONCREDIT COURSES

CHINESE COOKING 1, COMPUTER LITERACY,
DANCERCISE, FAMILY LIFE, ICE SKATING,
MANAGING STRESS, MEMORY DEVELOPMENT,
NUTRITION, PERSONAL COMPUTING,
PHOTOGRAPHY 1, PRACTICAL WRITING,
SENSATIONAL JAZZ, SKIING, SPEED READING,
SWIMMING 1, THEATRE, WOMEN ON THE MOVE

LESSON 47

■ **GOALS**
To identify how words are capitalized while typing sentences.
To type an enumeration and outlines.
To divide words correctly.

■ **FORMAT**
Single spacing   60-space line

LAB 2

Capitalization

Type lines 1–4 once. Then repeat lines 1–4 or take a series of 1-minute timings.

1 On Saturday he will zip to South Carolina for the election. 12

2 Back East in our hometown of Quincy, Maine, we like to ski. 12

3 In order to reach Georgia, Jacob will have to travel south. 12

4 Fay moved from 16 East Sixth Street, New York, to the West. 12

  | 1 | 2 | 3 | 4 | 5 | 6 | 7 | 8 | 9 | 10 | 11 | 12

FORMATTING INVOICES
Workbook 179–182.

An *invoice* is a bill sent by one company or organization for materials it sold or services it rendered to another company or organization. Invoices vary in size, length, and complexity, but all have the same general format, as shown below. A printed invoice form includes the company name and its return address, the guide words *To:* and *Date:* and the word *Invoice.* For ease in typing invoices, the column areas are ruled. To format invoices:

Heading. Begin typing the name and the date 2 spaces after the guide words. Align the bottom of the typed words with the bottom of the guide words.

Quantity, Unit Price, and Amount Columns. The entries in these columns should be centered visually within each ruled area. Type an underscore under the last entry in the Amount column. The underscore should be as long as the longest entry. **Remember:** Columns of numbers align at the right. Set margin or tab stops for the length of the entry most frequently used, and backspace or space in for other entries.

Description Column. Set a tab 2 spaces to the right of the vertical rule. Double-space between entries. Single-space turnovers when an entry is more than one line. Indent turnovers 3 spaces.

Total Amount Due Line. Type the words *Total amount due* in the Description column, approximately aligned with the *D* in the word *Description.* Type the numbers in the Amount column.

Spacing. Begin the body of the invoice a double space below the horizontal rule. Single-space each entry; double-space between entries, including the Total amount due line.

Note: Dollar signs are not needed in the Unit Price and Amount columns because only dollar amounts are listed there.

JOB 114 A. INVOICE
Type a copy of the invoice shown below. Standard format. Workbook 183 top.

SWISSVALE HIGH BUSINESS CLUB
1036 HIGHLAND AVENUE
SWISSVALE, PA 13821

TO: Ms. Marion Mertz
    Music Department

DATE: June 11, 19--

INVOICE 1096

QUANTITY	DESCRIPTION	UNIT PRICE	AMOUNT
300	2-page concert programs	.06	18.00
2	Offset masters	1.10	2.20
800	1-page handouts	.03	24.00
1	Stencil	.75	.75
40	Invitations	.08	3.20
	Total amount due		48.15

12-SECOND TIMINGS

Type each line three times, or take three 12-second timings on each line. For each timing, type with no more than 1 error.

5 Once the boy began to laugh, all of us began to laugh also.
6 Where in the world can we find an island on which to relax?
7 Now is the time for all of us to rush and join a good team.

| | | | | | | | | | | | |
5 10 15 20 25 30 35 40 45 50 55 60

30-SECOND SPEED TIMINGS

Take two 30-second speed timings on lines 8 and 9. Then take two 30-second speed timings on lines 10 and 11. Or type each sentence twice.

8 All of us need to relax our minds each day. Some of us use   12
9 yoga, while others jog, join a spa, or take up a new hobby.   24
10 We can all have true feelings of peace and joy if we try to   12
11 think of happy events in our lives and keep a cheery smile.   24

| 1 | 2 | 3 | 4 | 5 | 6 | 7 | 8 | 9 | 10 | 11 | 12

 Some word processors and word processing software include special symbols such as accent marks that can be inserted during typing.

JOB 47 A. ROUGH-DRAFT ENUMERATION
Hanging-indented format.

REPORT ON FLORIDA

1. St. Augustine is the oldest city in the continental United States. It was founded in 1565 by Pedro Menéndez de avilés.

2. Florida was sold to America in 1819, but the transfer took 2 years.

3. Florida oranges were developed by the botanist Lue Gim Gong in 1898.

4. The word florida means "flowery" in spanish.

5. Florida was sighted by Ponce De León in 1513.

JOB 47 B. COMPOSED OUTLINE
Standard format.

MICROCOMPUTERS

I. Popular Makes
   [*List three or more names of computer brands—use* A., B., C., *and so on. Under at least one brand, list two or more models—use* 1., 2., *and so on.*]

II. Uses of Personal Computers
   [*List three or more uses, such as word processing.*]

III. Programming Languages
   [*List three or more names of languages, such as* BASIC.]

(Continued in next column)

IV. Function Keys
   [*List three or more key names, such as* Reset.]

JOB 47 C. REVISED OUTLINE
Retype Job 47 B. Insert a new category between roman numerals II and III. Standard format.

III. Software
A. WordStar
1. Easy to Learn
2. Advanced Functions
a. MailMerge
b. SpellStar
B. Jazz

JOB 113 B. THREE-COLUMN TABLE

Arrange the file cards you typed in Job 113 A on page 191 in alphabetic order (by last name). Then type the table, arranging the names alphabetically. Standard format. Full sheet of paper.

FORMATTING BUSINESS MAILING LABELS

Workbook 175.

When using sheets of labels, type the left-hand labels first; then move the margin stop and type the right-hand labels. Start each name and address 1 inch (10P/12E) from the left edge and estimate the vertical center for each entry.

JOB 113 C. BUSINESS MAILING LABELS

Type a mailing label for each person in Job 113 A on page 191, using the illustration to the right as your format. Workbook 177–178.

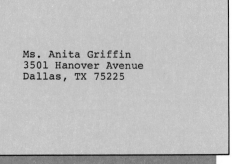

```
Ms. Anita Griffin
3501 Hanover Avenue
Dallas, TX 75225
```

LESSON 114

■ GOALS
To format and type invoices.
To format and type quantity columns with words.
To format and type adjustments in invoices.

■ FORMAT
Single spacing   60-space line   Tabs every 7 spaces

KEYBOARDING SKILLS

Type lines 1–4 once. In line 5 use your tabulator key to advance from one number to the next through the entire line. Repeat lines 1–4, or take a series of 1-minute timings.

Speed 1 They may go to the fair; they must come back home in a day. 12
Accuracy 2 The old, gray boxer won seven unique prizes from lazy Jack. 12
Numbers 3 If they wait 56 days, then 10, 29, 38, or 47 is not enough. 12
Symbols 4 With our 7% return, she bought 4 pounds of #29, #38, & #56. 12
Technique 5 574   483   392   201   164   574   483   392   201
| 1 | 2 | 3 | 4 | 5 | 6 | 7 | 8 | 9 | 10 | 11 | 12

30-SECOND SPEED TIMINGS

Take two 30-second speed timings on lines 6 and 7. Then take two 30-second speed timings on lines 8 and 9. Or type each sentence twice.

6 It is nice to know that Joan can come to our party; she may 12
7 be able to bring along a few of her very close friends too. 24

8 They might all come to the party if it is the only one that 12
9 day and if they do not have any other plans they have made. 24
| 1 | 2 | 3 | 4 | 5 | 6 | 7 | 8 | 9 | 10 | 11 | 12

JOB 47 D. WORD DIVISION PRACTICE

Two divisions for each word are listed below. Type the division of each word that you consider correct or preferred.

1. busi-nessman   business-man
2. intro-duce   in-troduce
3. su-personic   super-sonic
4. circum-stances   cir-cumstances
5. trimmed   trim-med
6. Mrs. West   Mrs. / West
7. bacter-ia   bacteria
8. pian-o   piano
9. ad-journ   adjourn
10. checkup   check-up
11. ad-min.   admin.
12. couldn't   could-n't
13. converti-ble   convert-ible
14. practi-cable   practica-ble
15. 16 / East Beach   16 East / Beach
16. $265.22 $265.-22

LESSON 48

■ GOALS
To capitalize words correctly while typing sentences.
To type 32/3'/5e.
To type enumerations and an informal note.

■ FORMAT
Drills: Single spacing   60-space line
3-Minute Timings: Double spacing   5-space tab

LAB 2

Capitalization

Type lines 1–4 once, providing the missing capitals. Edit your copy as your teacher reads the answers. Then retype lines 1–4 from your edited copy.

1 Jean Azar moved from the northeast in april or may of 1980.
2 During the Civil War, the north attacked southern shipping.
3 Our south side high school is two miles south of knoxville.
4 The northern and southern railroad travels north to quebec.

PREVIEW PRACTICE

Accuracy

Speed

Type each line twice as a preview to the 3-minute timings below.

5 quick Japan Brazil widely players beloved reflexes required
6 spirit women since both this such many that men and had too

3-MINUTE TIMINGS

Take two 3-minute timings on lines 7–14.

```
                1              2                3            4
7       Strong legs, quick reflexes, and great team spirit are   12
            5            6              7            8
8  what it takes to play the really fast game of soccer.  Both   24
           9          10            11          12
9  men and women can play, since skill, not size, is required.   36
          13            14              15          16
10 Long the most widely played sport in Europe, soccer in this   48
             17            18            19          20
11 country is growing fast.  It is beloved in other countries,   60
          21            22            23          24
12 too, such as Brazil and Japan.  Some high schools that have   72
           25            26            27          28
13 had football as a major team sport have dropped the game in   84
           29            30            31          32
14 favor of soccer, since players are less likely to get hurt.   96
   |  1  |  2  |  3  |  4  |  5  |  6  |  7  |  8  |  9  |  10 |  11 |  12   SI 1.28
```

UNIT 19 Formatting Forms
UNIT GOAL 38/5'/5e

■ **GOALS**
To use semicolons correctly in compound sentences while typing.
To format and type alphabetic file cards.
To type a three-column table.
To format and type business mailing labels.

■ **FORMAT**
Single spacing   60-space line

LAB 12

Semicolons in Compound Sentences

Workbook 169–170.

Type lines 1–4 once, providing the missing semicolon in each of the compound sentences. Edit your copy as your teacher reads the answers. Then retype lines 1–4 from your edited copy.

1 Jim Mazer is the new manager ask him for more information.

2 This quarter was very rewarding we made a million dollars.

3 Carole gave explicit instructions see her October 12 memo.

4 You and I will discuss this with Bart let's meet at 2 p.m.

FORMATTING ALPHABETIC FILE CARDS
Workbook 175.

Names and addresses that are frequently referred to are often kept on 5 by 3 cards for quick reference. If the cards are arranged in alphabetic order by last name, they are called *alphabetic file cards*.
   To format alphabetic file cards:

1. Start typing the person's name on line 2, 4 spaces from the left edge of the card.

2. Type the person's last name first, followed by the first name and middle initial or middle name (if any). Separate the last and first names by a comma.

3. Type titles such as *Miss, Ms., Mrs., Mr.,* and *Dr.* in parentheses after the name.

4. Type the address a double space below the name, indented 3 spaces.

```
1 2 3 4
1
2   Griffin, Anita (Ms.)
3
4      3501 Hanover Avenue
5      Dallas, TX 75225
```

JOB 113 A. ALPHABETIC FILE CARDS
Type a card for each name in the table below. Standard format. Workbook 171–173.

NEW-CUSTOMER LIST
Second Quarter, 19--

Mr. Wilbur M. Mandrell	429 Holley Circle	Provo, UT 84601
Ms. Juanita T. Zabell	780 Maple Lane	Provo, UT 84601
Dr. J. D. Genetti	1356 Williams Avenue	Salt Lake City, UT 84105
Mrs. Yvonne Scott	3409 Tyler Avenue	Ogden, UT 84403
Dr. Carmen T. Chavez	287 Windsor Street	Salt Lake City, UT 84102
Mr. Cecil Gentry	156 Jackson Avenue	Salt Lake City, UT 84103
Ms. Barbara Perez	375 Palmer Way	Sandy, UT 84070
Ms. Pamela R. Duquette	240 Oak Lane	Provo, UT 84601

JOB 48 A. ROUGH-DRAFT ENUMERATION
Paragraph format.

COURSE DESCRIPTIONS FROM UTICA COLLEGE

1. DANCERCISE--8 Thursdays, 7:30-9 p.m.

Exercise doesn't have to be boring. Dancercise incorporates both dance and exercise in 1 class. The emphasis will be on toning the body and weight control. Aerobic dance will be taught as well.

Elsa Parrish, instructor.

2. COMPUTER LITERACY--8 Mondays, 6:30-8 p.m.

If you've always been a bit afraid of the computer, take this course. You'll wind up as the master of the machine. This course is designed for the beginners. Absolutely no experience is needed. Basic Language. Roger Chung, Instructor.

3. NUTRITION--5 Wednesdays, 6:30-8:30 p.m.

Research on the role of nutrition in maintaining optimal health and longevity. Topics to be discussed include: proper diet, nutrition and heart disease, nutrition and Western foods, nutrition and obesity.

Siamak C. Abidi, M.D., Instructor.

JOB 48 B. ENUMERATION
Paragraph format.

DINING OUT

A new survey of 155 chefs and restaurateurs shows the following findings:

1. New York City has the best restaurants (49 percent), followed by San Francisco (19 percent), New Orleans (10 percent), Chicago (4 percent), and Los Angeles (3 percent).

2. Seafood, veal, and fish are each chosen by 21 percent of all customers, followed by chicken (19 percent) and beef (18 percent).

3. Broccoli is the number one vegetable (30 percent), followed by asparagus (13 percent).

4. Vegetable soup and seafood chowders tied for the top appetizer at 23 percent each.

JOB 48 C. INFORMAL NOTE
Standard format.

[Today's date] Dear [Use a friend's name], How do you like the way this note looks? I am typing it in my typing class. We are writing to friends who live in other states. I will type another note to a friend who lives in the East.

Our teacher says that we will learn how to type reports soon. Then I can type all my papers for my English class. Until next time, [Sign your name]

14   Travel can provide you with exciting, fun experiences.   12

15 The skills you might gain from travel can make you a better   24

16 person regardless of where you are--at home, at work, or at   36

17 play.   37

18   While at work, you will come into contact with men and   49

19 women from every walk of life. The various people that you   61

20 meet while traveling will prepare you for new and different   73

21 jobs.   74

22   When you travel, you may sometimes find yourself among   86

23 people speaking different languages than you do. The chal-   98

24 lenge this situation presents will very likely be useful to   110

25 you.   111

26   At school you can share many of your travels with your   123

27 classmates and teachers. You might tell them all about the   135

28 colorful, historical national shrines that you were able to   147

29 visit.   148

30   It might be that the quality of your leisure time will   160

31 improve. Consider all the dozens of new, unique dances and   172

32 other activities that you learned that you could share with   184

33 others.   185

| 1 | 2 | 3 | 4 | 5 | 6 | 7 | 8 | 9 | 10 | 11 | 12   SI 1.44

POSTTEST

Take another 5-minute timing on lines 14–33 to see how much your skill has improved.

TAB AND MARGIN RELEASE REVIEW

Set your left margin at 20 and your right margin at 62. Set a tab every 10 spaces. Type lines 34–45 below. Use the tabulator key to move from column to column. Use the margin release key to complete the typing of the last word in each line.

34 abide	bevel	crude	ditch	eaves
35 groan	hinge	igloo	judge	knock
36 meter	mourn	ounce	prowl	quart
37	slack	toast	until	venue
38	fixed	youth	zebra	adorn
39	clock	doubt	every	fable
40		heart	imply	joist
41		learn	music	north
42		phase	query	react
43			tempt	union
44			worry	exams
45			zings	again

TEST

- **GOALS**
  To type 32/3'/5e.
  To demonstrate competency in typing enumerations,
  announcements, informal notes, and outlines.
- **FORMAT**
  Double spacing   60-space line   5-space tab

PREVIEW PRACTICE

Type each line twice as a preview to the 3-minute timings below.

Accuracy 1 jolt spray quick simply canyon hazards waterways excitement
Speed   2 sometimes through world, rocky flows with down that and has

3-MINUTE TIMINGS

Take two 3-minute timings on lines 3–11.

3   You simply do not go rafting down the quick river that   12
4 flows through the Grand Canyon without skills and plenty of 24
5 help. The many hazards are truly great.   32
6   It's one of the longest waterways in the world, and it   44
7 has rapids that are fearsome to hear, see, and run; but the 56
8 first trip can be filled with excitement.   64
9   The lovely canyon is rocky, thorny, and hot in summer.   76
10 Sometimes it is so windy that the spray and sand hit you in 88
11 the face with a brisk and stinging jolt.   96

| 1 | 2 | 3 | 4 | 5 | 6 | 7 | 8 | 9 | 10 | 11 | 12 | SI 1.28

JOB 49/50 A. ENUMERATION

Hanging-indented format. Title: Rules for the Hugo High School Marathon.

1. ~~Each~~ *Every* runner must have a signed statement of approval
    from a qualified physician.

2. ~~Every~~ runner must wear approved clothing and shoes.

3. All runners must be present in the parking lot of Hugo
    high school, one-half hour before ~~the~~ starting time.
    at 9:30 a.m.

4. Runners cannot leave the designated course for any reason.
    Any runner leaving the course will be disqualified.

5. A runner cannot interfere with ~~the~~ other runners; viola-
    tors will be disqualified.

6. Sponsors ~~of the race~~ *will* cannot be responsible for *any* medical
    expenses of runners caused by personnel injuries.
    First aid will be available.

7. The decision of the judges at the end of the race will
    be final.

JOB 111 B. LETTER
Standard format. Workbook 167–168. Body 68 words.

(Today's date) / Public relations De-   12
partment / A. B. Morgan, Inc. / 284 Main   19
Street / Yankton, SD 57087 / Attention: 28
Department Manager / Ladies and Gen-   35
tlemen: / Subject: Luncon Speaker / It   45
was a [pleasure real] to learn that one   53
of the members of your staff will be   60
speaking at our July 14 luncheon meet-   67
ing.   The program will *begin* ~~start~~ at 2:00   74

the speaker
p.m.; ~~you~~ will have about 60 minutes   83
in which to give ~~your~~ *the* talk. ¶ Thank   91
you again for agreeing to supply us   98
with a speaker.   Please let us know   105
the speaker's name as soon as you have   113
~~have~~ it available. / Your very truly, /   122
~~Ms.~~ Jessie Seals / President / (Your   134
initials) / *bcc : Brad Morgan /*   141
Brenda Novak   145

LESSON 112

CLINIC

■ **GOALS**
To type 37/5'/5e.
To review tabulator key and margin-release-key operations.

■ **FORMAT**
Drills: Single spacing   60-space line
5-Minute Timings: Double spacing   5-space tab

KEYBOARDING SKILLS

Type lines 1–4 once. Then practice shift-key control by capitalizing the proper nouns in line 5. Repeat lines 1–4, or take a series of 1-minute timings.

Speed   1 The right height of the slope is kept firm with such signs. 12
Accuracy   2 Mack played the jukebox while Fritz sang a very quick song. 12
Numbers   3 If 56 days are left, then May should use 47, 29, 38, or 10. 12
Symbols   4 With a 5% raise I can buy 7 cartons of #32 and #48--really! 12
Technique 5 Akron Linda Butte Cadiz Davis Janis Fulda Ortiz Koloa Wells

| 1 | 2 | 3 | 4 | 5 | 6 | 7 | 8 | 9 | 10 | 11 | 12

PRETEST

Take a 5-minute timing on lines 14–33 on page 190. Circle and count your errors. In the chart below find the number of errors you made on the Pretest. Then type each of the designated drill lines four times.

Pretest errors	0–1	2–3	4–5	6+
Drill lines	9–13	8–12	7–11	6–10

PRACTICE

Accuracy 6 people shrine provide quality presents exciting experiences
          7 with dozen likely demand whether improve sometime different
          8 skill person useful unique leisure teacher learned presents
          9 dance school prepare shrines schools national opportunities

Speed   10 might while touch with gain from when find very come can in
         11 women walks among make life home than this able make you at
         12 share about visit work your will many with time gain fun or
         13 think other skill come that meet tell them from than the do

JOB 49/50 B. INFORMAL NOTE
Standard format.

August 15, 19—

Dear [*Insert your own name*],

Thank you for volunteering to run in the marathon race for your classmate Andy Burke, who must have money for a needed kidney transplant.

The race will be held on Saturday, September 6. Persons running in the race should meet in the Hugo High School parking lot at 9:30 a.m. The race will follow a 10-mile course through town and end in the west parking lot of the Hugo Shopping Mall.

Will you please send a note to your friends and relatives asking them to sponsor you in this worthy event? Explain that Andy needs approximately $25,000 for a kidney transplant, which will permit him to live a normal life like you and me.

Sincerely, Marilyn Lewis

JOB 49/50 C. COMPOSED INFORMAL NOTE
Type an answer to the message shown on the screen below. Address the note to Superintendent McKune; compose your own closing. Standard format.

DATE: JAN. 12, 19--
TO: ALL STUDENTS
FROM: SUPERINTENDENT MCKUNE

I WANT TO KNOW MORE ABOUT THE STUDENTS
IN MY SCHOOL DISTRICT. PLEASE WRITE ME
AN INFORMAL NOTE ABOUT YOURSELF--YOUR
FAVORITE COURSES, CLUBS, SPORTS, AND
HOBBIES. TELL ME ABOUT THE COMPUTERS AT
YOUR SCHOOL AND WHAT YOU KNOW ABOUT
THEM. THANK YOU.

JOB 49/50 D. ANNOUNCEMENT
Display format. Spread last line.

ATTENTION RUNNERS AND SPONSORS
10-Mile Marathon for Andy Burke
Saturday, September 6, 10 a.m.
Hugo High School Parking Lot
All Proceeds to Aid Andy Burke
BE THERE!

JOB 49/50 E. REVISED OUTLINE
Type the outline below. After each rule, type a colon followed by 2 spaces. Insert a word (and hyphen if appropriate) that illustrates each rule (see I. A.). Try to think of your own words, or select them from those provided below the outline. Standard format. 50-space line.

RULES OF WORD DIVISION
I.   Where to Divide Words
A.   Between Syllables: num-bers
B.   Between Compound Words
1.   Hyphenated Compound Words
2.   One-Word Compounds
C.   After Prefixes
D.   Before Suffixes
II.   What Not to Divide
A.   Words
1.   One-Syllable Words
2.   Words of 5 or Fewer Letters
3.   Contractions
4.   Abbreviations
B.   Word Groups
1.   Dates
2.   Addresses
3.   Proper Names
4.   Numbers

sacrifice	numbers	checkbook
tablecloth	weight	shake
can't	shouldn't	pretaped
untrue	careless	stopped
July 22, 19—	Mr. Goodshall	61 East Bay Road
dept.	glass	self-examine
laughable	clerk-typist	1,234,567
525	August 7	medicine

Type each line twice as a preview to the 5-minute timings below.

Accuracy 5 positive drizzles extended obviously frequently suggestions
Speed   6 friends surely today rains visit clean when this job for an

5-MINUTE TIMINGS

Take two 5-minute timings on lines 7–23.

```
                          1                           2
 7     The laws in this country permit us to drive an automo-    12
            3                           4
 8  bile; many of us do so prior to finishing high school.  The  24
       5                    6                    7
 9  majority of us today believe that we must own an automobile  36
                      8                      9
10  to search for a new job, entertain ourselves, or visit good  48
            10                    11                       12
11  friends.  When we have an automobile, we must check for re-  60
                             13                   14
12  pairs frequently.  Here are six quick suggestions to follow  72
13  carefully.                                                   74
          15                    16                      17
14     We must be quite positive that we have checked the oil    86
                    18                   19
15  level, the quantity of gas in the car, and the air pressure  98
          20                    21                         22
16  in the tires.  Obviously, we must clean the windshield with  110
                    23                         24
17  care so that our view is not obstructed.  We should observe  122
              25                        26
18  the condition of the windshield wipers in case we need them  134
       27                    28                      29
19  if it drizzles or rains.  Finally, it is very important for  146
                30                        31
20  us to inspect the drive belts carefully for wear.  Should a  158
          32                        33                      34
21  belt break on an extended trip, we could possibly find our-  170
                          35                      36
22  selves stranded for hours while waiting for someone to give  182
              37
23  us assistance.                                               185
    |  1  |  2  |  3  |  4  |  5  |  6  |  7  |  8  |  9  | 10  | 11  | 12    SI 1.44
```

FORMATTING ROUTING LISTS FOR MEMOS

A routing list is used to send the same memo to several persons. To be sure that all addressees read the memo, each person initials his or her name and passes the memo on to the next person on the list. The last person on the list often returns the memo to the person who circulated it.

A routing list is formatted very much like a distribution list. To format a routing list:

1. Type the words *See below* after the guide word *To:*.

2. Type the word *Route:* over the list instead of the word *Distribution:*.

3. Type four underscores after each name to allow each person to write his or her initials.

JOB 111 A. MEMO WITH ROUTING LIST
Standard format. Workbook 165.

[*Today's date*] / [ROUTE:] Audrey Brooks, J. W. Day, Eva McBride, Joel Robnett, Stella Yen / [FROM:] Kenneth Frazier / [SUBJECT:] Promotion List

Attached is the promotion list for the Southeastern Division. As we discussed at the last meeting, only 75 percent of all recommended promotions were granted.

Please check the list closely; then ensure that all your respective personnel promotions are included. Pass the list on to the next person on the list until all managers have had the opportunity to review the names. / KF / [*Your initials*] / Attachment

LEVEL 3

GOALS

1. Demonstrate keyboarding speed and accuracy on straight copy with a goal of 35 words a minute for 3 minutes with 5 or fewer errors.
2. Demonstrate improved skill in the control of the nonprinting parts of the typewriter.
3. Demonstrate basic formatting skills on reports, correspondence, and tables for personal use.
4. Detect, mark with proofreaders' marks, and correct errors in typewritten copy.
5. Apply rules for correct use of numbers and punctuation in written communications.

FORMATTING ATTACHMENT NOTATIONS

Items enclosed in an envelope are called *enclosures*. When those items are clipped or stapled to a letter or memo, they are called *attachments*. Format attachment notations the same way you format enclosure notations.

JOB 110 B. MEMO WITH DISTRIBUTION LIST
Standard format. Workbook 163.

(Today's date) / [TO:] N. Booker, L. Edinger, R. Lopez, W. Money, B. O'Neal, J. Symarek R. Wong / [FROM:] Gail Morgan / [SUBJECT:] Annual Goals

Attached you will find a working draft of our annual goals. I hope you will all have an opportunity to review the draft prior to our meeting on the 16th. We look forward to any suggestions or ideas you may have.

My sincere thanks to those of you who sent in materials from which this draft was prepared. See you Friday morning in Conference Room 216. / G M / [Your initials] / Attachment

- GOALS
To use semicolons correctly in compound sentences while typing.
To type 37/5'/5e.
To format and type routing lists for memos.
To type a letter.

- FORMAT
Drills: Single spacing   60-space line
5-Minute Timings: Double spacing   5-space tab

LAB 12

Semicolons in Compound Sentences

Type lines 1–4 once, providing the missing semicolon in each of the compound sentences. Edit your copy as your teacher reads the answers. Then retype lines 1–4 from your edited copy.

1 Alex made copies for everyone he mailed them the next day.
2 Katie traveled to Brazil she plans to stay there one week.
3 Call Diane quickly write her a letter explaining the idea.
4 File just these five or six copies discard all the others.

LESSON 51

■ **GOALS**
To capitalize words correctly while typing sentences.
To format and type one-page reports.

■ **FORMAT**
Single spacing   60-space line

LAB 2

Capitalization

Workbook 39–40.

Type lines 1–4 once, providing the missing capitals. Edit your copy as your teacher reads the answers. Then retype lines 1–4 from your edited copy.

1   I moved to james plaza, which is south of butternut square.
2   The hotel is on north valley drive, just north of oak road.
3   On my birthday we may fly north to vermont for some skiing.
4   We will drive to the west coast next week for a short rest.

12-SECOND TIMINGS

Type each line three times, or take three 12-second timings on each line. For each timing, type with no more than 1 error.

5   The man and woman got a day off and went to the west beach.
6   Did you see that our new red car is in the lot, out of gas?
7   It is not at all clear to us why he is to get a part of it.

    5   10   15   20   25   30   35   40   45   50   55   60

FORMATTING ONE-PAGE REPORTS

Many reports are short enough to fit on one page. To format one-page reports:

1. Set margins for a 6-inch line (60P/70E).

2. Leave a 2-inch top margin—center the title on line 13. Type the title in all-capital letters.

3. Center the **subtitle** a double space below the title. Use *initial caps,* that is, capitalize the first letter of each important word. The subtitle may further explain the title or may be a *byline*—the name of the author of the report. Triple-space after typing the subtitle or byline.

4. Double-space the body of the report.

5. Indent paragraphs 5 spaces.

 When preparing a double-spaced document, like a report, on a computer, you may double-space or quadruple-space after the title as a triple space would require special coding.

Production Practice.   Set your margins for a 6-inch line (60P/70E). Set tabs at 5 and center. Single spacing. Clean sheet of paper. Use the report illustrated on page 88.

Space down to line 13, and center the title. Space down 2 lines (double-space), and center the subtitle. Space down 3 lines (triple-space), and set your typewriter for double spacing. Type the first three lines of the text. Check your work.

Remove your paper from the typewriter, and insert it upside down. Set your typewriter for single spacing. Repeat the practice. Check your work.

JOB 51 A. ONE-PAGE REPORT

Type the report shown on page 88. Standard format.

FORMATTING MULTIPLE ADDRESSEES IN MEMOS

A memo that is being sent to several people should contain all the names in the heading (do not use a copy notation). To format multiple addressees in memos:

1. Insert the names after the guide word *To:*, separating each name with a comma.

2. Be sure to leave 1 blank line (a double space) between the last name and the next line of typing.

Note: Use an initial instead of a first name to save space when several names need to be inserted or the amount of space is limited.

```
                 M E M O R A N D U M

To:  Theresa Blake, Jonathan Gainer,    From:  Audrey Dupont
     Charlotte Thomas

Subject:  Work Schedule                 Date:  May 5, 19--
```

```
                  MEMORANDUM


    TO:  T. Blake, J. Gainer, C. Thomas    DATE:  May 5, 19--

    FROM:  Audrey Dupont

    SUBJECT:  Work Schedule
```

JOB 110 A. MEMO
Standard format (page 152). Workbook 161.

[*Today's date*] / [TO:] John Burkett, Nona Osborne, Peggy Williams, Dennis Wright / [FROM:] Kay Thompson / [SUBJECT:] Course Approval 13 24

    All new course requests were approved at this month's curriculum meeting; however, we have to make some minor changes in our request for an additional 11 microcomputers for our word processing lab. ¶ It was suggested at the meeting that we obtain new bids for our microcomputers, since our latest request was based on bids that we received last August. The decline in microcomputer prices that we have seen in the past two months is not reflected in our request. ¶ Please have your revised bids ready for next month's meeting. / KT / [*Your initials*] / cc: Paula Davis / Jerome Perry 40 54 69 83 99 112 128 143 144

FORMATTING DISTRIBUTION LISTS IN MEMOS

Because of the number of people who might be receiving the memo, it is not always possible to type their names in the space provided at the top of the memo after the guide word *To:*. In this instance the names should be placed at the bottom of the memo. To format a distribution list in a memo:

1. Type the words *See distribution below* after the guide word *To:* at the top of the memo.

2. Type the word *Distribution:* at the left margin a triple space below the last notation. Underscore the word (but not the colon).

3. Begin the list of names at the left margin, a double space below the word *Distribution:*.

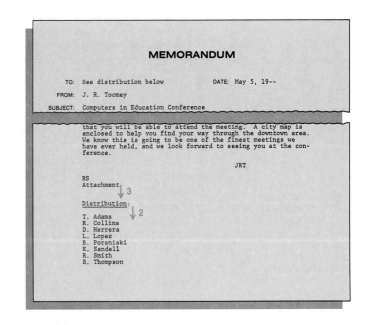

MARGINS
6-inch line

TITLE
Centered, all caps

SUBTITLE
Centered, initial caps

BODY
Double-spaced

↓ 13

HOW COMPUTERS DEVELOPED

↓ 2

By Jane Baxter

↓ 3

The first computer was the abacus. The abacus is from the Orient and is more than 5000 years old. It is still the primary form of "number crunching" in many parts of the world.

The next major breakthrough in computers came in 1642, when a Frenchman, Blaise Pascal, invented an "arithmetic machine" to help in his father's business. A high-level computer language--Pascal--was named after him.

In 1694 a German, Gottfried Leibniz, invented the Stepped Reckoner. Leibniz used a system consisting of only two symbols (0 and 1), which was called binary (bi meaning "two").

In 1801 a Frenchman named Jacquard invented a punched card system for controlling the threads on his weaving looms. Charles Babbage followed in 1833 with his invention, which could perform calculations automatically using punched cards.

ONE-PAGE REPORT IN PICA TYPE (REDUCED)

If *you* cannot correct the defect, ~~we~~ *I* will have to give the owner 113
a new watch. / Yours Truly, / Leslie E. Lauson / Manager, Dallas 132
Region / (Your initials) / Enclosure / cc: Mr. Conrad White 138
Paul Spencer

FORMATTING A BLIND COPY NOTATION

Workbook 157–158.

When you do not want the addressee to know that a copy is being sent to someone else, use a blind copy (*bcc*) notation on all copies but *not* on the original letter or memo. To format a *bcc* notation:

1. Open the paper release, and remove the original copy and the first sheet of carbon paper; close the paper release.
2. Type the *bcc* notation at the left margin, a double space below the last notation you typed (initials, enclosure, or cc:).

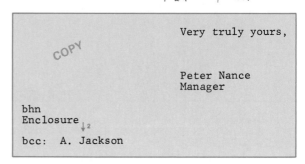

Very truly yours,

Peter Nance
Manager

bhn
Enclosure ↓2

bcc: A. Jackson

3. Use the same style for the *bcc* notation as you would for a *cc* notation.

JOB 109 B. LETTER

Standard format. Workbook 159–160.

Retype Job 109 A on page 184 with the following changes:

1. Replace the last paragraph in the letter with one that asks if the watch can be sent to the main office in Toronto if the defect cannot be fixed.
2. Change the *cc* notation to Paul Spencer.
3. Send a *bcc* to Kathryn Lloyd.

LESSON 110

■ **GOALS**
To identify how semicolons are used in compound sentences while typing.
To format and type memos with multiple addressees, distribution lists, and attachment notations.

■ **FORMAT**
Single spacing   60-space line

LAB 12

Semicolons in Compound Sentences

Type lines 1–4 once. Then repeat lines 1–4 or take a series of 1-minute timings.

1 I may be able to help you with this; Vera may also be free. 12
2 Yes, Joan types quickly; she is also an expert in spelling. 12
3 Max Dubron prefers the new procedures; Ella Zeldon doesn't. 12
4 Ken works in our Dallas office; he may be transferred soon. 12
   | 1 | 2 | 3 | 4 | 5 | 6 | 7 | 8 | 9 | 10 | 11 | 12

12-SECOND TIMINGS

Type each line three times, or take three 12-second timings on each line. For each timing, type with no more than 1 error.

5 We had a kit of tools that we could use to fix the engines.
6 The two of them sat in the soft sand and soaked up the sun.
7 All they want to do is to sit in the shade of the big oaks.

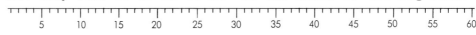

JOB 51 B. ONE-PAGE REPORT
Standard format.

WHAT MESSAGE ARE YOU SENDING?
By [*Your name*]

Without your saying a word, your posture and your walk might tell people what is on your mind. Although your walking style may not tell the whole story, it can send a message about your moods.

Check the way you walk.

When you walk at a slow pace, with your head down and hands in your pockets, you tell others that you want to be alone. If your shoulders are drooped, your head is downcast, and your gait is a kind of shuffle, you are telling others that you feel sad. But when you walk at a brisk pace, hold your head up, look relaxed, swing your arms, and use your entire body, you express a sense of openness to everyone.

LESSON 52

■ **GOALS**
To type 34/3'/5e.
To format and type a one-page report with side headings.

■ **FORMAT**
Drills: Single spacing   60-space line
3-Minute Timings: Double spacing   5-space tab

KEYBOARDING SKILLS

Type lines 1–4 once. Then do what line 5 tells you to do. Repeat lines 1–4, or take a series of 1-minute timings.

Speed
Accuracy
Numbers
Symbols
Technique

1 Kay got the forms for the firm at the south mall near here. 12
2 Six jumbo elephants quickly moved the wagon from the blaze. 12
3 You can take the 1:38 bus, the 4:56 bus, or the 8:47 train. 12
4 Grant & Harris developed the Kenyan, Ramos & Blake project. 12
5 Retype line 3. Underscore only the times—not the words.

```
| 1 | 2 | 3 | 4 | 5 | 6 | 7 | 8 | 9 | 10 | 11 | 12
```

PRETEST

Take a 3-minute timing on lines 6–14. Circle and count your errors.

6   The Inca Indians lived hundreds of years ago near what 12
7 is now Peru; they were a great nation well known for unique 24
8 buildings, which can still be seen in jungle ruins. 34

9   The temples that stand can be searched for clues about 12
10 these people and their way of life. Some knowledge exists, 24
11 for we know that they were a people of many skills. 34

12   The Incas still have lots of secrets which are lost in 12
13 the haze of their culture. The best-kept secret is why the 24
14 Incas vanished. In time, we may learn the secret. 34

```
| 1 | 2 | 3 | 4 | 5 | 6 | 7 | 8 | 9 | 10 | 11 | 12   SI 1.26
```

ASSEMBLING A CARBON PACK

Carbon packs consist of ① the sheet of paper or letterhead on which your original is to be typed, ② the carbon paper containing the carbon ink that transfers to the copy paper, and ③ the onionskin or some other thin paper on which you wish to make a copy.

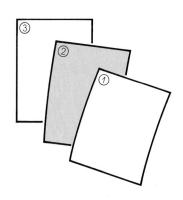

When assembling a carbon pack, make sure the carbon (shiny) side faces the copy paper—not the original.

To insert a carbon pack into your typewriter: Ⓐ Straighten the sides and top of the carbon pack so that all edges are even. Ⓑ Hold the carbon pack with your left hand with the carbon side (and the copy paper) facing you. Ⓒ Turn the cylinder smoothly with your right hand. Continue turning the cylinder until you have advanced to the vertical position where you want to start typing.

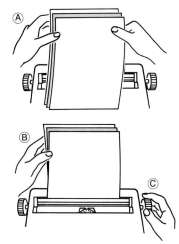

FORMATTING A COPY NOTATION

When a copy of a letter or memo is sent to someone in addition to the addressee, a copy (*cc*) notation is typed on the original and all copies. To format a *cc* notation:

1. One line below the reference initials (or below the enclosure notation, if there is one), type *cc:*, space twice, and type the name of the person receiving the copy.
2. Type each additional name on a separate line, aligned with the name on the first line. Do not repeat *cc:* before each name.
3. Type a title before the person's name only if you do not have a first name or initial.

Production Practice. Set a center tab. Single spacing. Clean sheet of paper. Use Job 109 A below.

Space down to line 7. Tab to the center. Type the complimentary closing. Space down 4 lines and tab to the center. Type the writer's name. Space down 1 line and tab to the center. Type the writer's title. Space down 2 lines.

Note: The letters "cc" are used whether the copy is made with carbon paper or on a copying machine.

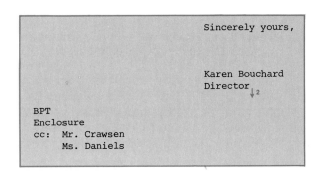

At the left margin, type your initials. Single-space and type the enclosure notation. Single-space and type the copy notation. Check your work.

Remove your paper from the typewriter, turn it upside down, and reinsert it into the machine. Repeat the practice. Check your work.

JOB 109 A. LETTER

Standard format. Workbook 155–156. Body 76 words.

(Today's date) / Mr. Rick Menlo / Timekeeper watches / Co. / 225   16

Eighth Ave. / New York, NY 10011 / Dear Mr. Menlo: 27

Subject: Defective Watch   34

    Enclosed is the defective Timekeeper watch to wich I refered   47

in my recent letter of May 10. We have had this watch in our re-   59

pair shop on ④ different occassions; we have been unable to resolve   73

the problem. ¶Would you, Mr. menlo, please ask your repair shop to   87

isolate the cause of the problem--a stem date that does not release   101

(Continued on next page)

Take one 1-minute timing on each paragraph of the Pretest (page 89).

Take another 3-minute timing on lines 6–14 (page 89) to see how much your skill has improved.

FORMATTING SIDE HEADINGS IN REPORTS

When preparing a double-spaced report on a computer, you may double-space or quadruple-space before side headings as a triple space would require special coding.

Side headings divide reports into sections. To format side headings:

1. Type the side headings in all-capital letters.

2. Triple-space (leaving 2 blank lines) before a side heading.

3. Double-space (leaving 1 blank line) after a side heading.

Production Practice. Set your margins for a 6-inch line (60P/70E). Set a tab stop 5 spaces from the left margin. Double spacing. Clean sheet of paper. Use the report illustrated on page 91.

Space down 7 lines. Type the first paragraph of the report. Return the carriage or carrier once (a double space); then roll the paper up 1 full line space by turning the platen knob by hand (2 + 1 = triple space). Depress the shift lock key. Type the side heading WRITING A PROGRAM. Return your carriage or carrier once, release the shift lock, and type the second paragraph. Check your work.

Remove your paper from the typewriter, and insert it upside down. Repeat the practice. Check your work.

JOB 52 A. REPORT WITH SIDE HEADINGS

Type the one-page report with side headings on page 91. Standard format (page 87 and above).

LESSON 53

■ **GOALS**
To recognize how numbers are expressed while typing sentences.
To format and type one-page reports with side and paragraph headings.

■ **FORMAT**
Single spacing   60-space line

Number Style

Type lines 1–4 once. Then repeat lines 1–4 or take a series of 1-minute timings.

```
1  Jack ordered five boxes of pads and eight boxes of pencils.   12
2  This aircraft will hold 152 passengers and 12 crew members.   12
3  Fourteen members of the panel voted in favor of my quizzes.   12
4  That room is precisely 8.5 meters long and 4.7 meters wide.   12
   |  1  |  2  |  3  |  4  |  5  |  6  |  7  |  8  |  9  | 10  | 11  | 12
```

Spell out numbers from *1* through *10*; use figures for numbers above *10*. (**Exception:** Spell out any number that begins a sentence.)

Only *three* offices have been painted.
Send *12* brochures and *75* order forms to Ms. Ames.
Fifteen applicants were interviewed today.

In technical copy and for emphasis, use figures for numbers: *4 p.m., 3 liters, 2.5 miles, 7 spaces, 12 lines, page 9, $8.*

6 people buying quickly sidewalk features different advantage
7 grass tennis usually dazzling business commuting appliances
8 quite travel minimal assigned carpeted enjoyable suggestion
9 next major offer living complex residing possible apartment

Speed

10 latest people could found sauna make many wide they bus are
11 latest modern often close since will find work easy the not
12 duties safely house these live home when edge very most and
13 before chance might paint some time your life that have one

POSTTEST

Take another 5-minute timing on lines 9–23 on page 180 to see how much your skill has improved.

JOB 108 A. LETTER
Standard format. Workbook 153–154. Body 74 words (plus 40 words for attention line and subject line).

(Today's date) / All World Travel / 238 12
White Pond Drive / Akron, Oh 44331 / 19
Attention: Cruise Manager / Ladies and 28
Gentlemen: / Subject: Cruise To France 37
/ We received May 4, today, confirma- 45
tion from your office for our June 30 53
through July 20 cruise to France. We 60

would like to clarify two points you 68
mentioned in your letter. First, we 76
are to fly to Paris on a Luxury Jet, 83
not on the Super Jet that you mentioned 91
in your letter. Second, we have a 98
garanteed arrival time of 9 p.m., Paris 107
time, instead of the 8 p.m. arival time 115
you stipulate. / Very sincerely yours, 124
/ Claire C. Baker / Employee Travel 136
Group / (Your initials) 139

LESSON 109

■ **GOALS**
To recognize how semicolons are used in compound sentences while typing.
To learn how to use carbon packs.
To format and type *cc* and *bcc* notations.

■ **FORMAT**
Single spacing   60-space line   5-space tab

LAB 12

Semicolons in Compound Sentences

Type lines 1–4 once. Then repeat lines 1–4 or take a series of 1-minute timings.

1 Ms. Wall is our personnel director; she is now on vacation. 12
2 Jeff must go to Zurich quickly; May is on her way to Zaire. 12
3 Alex's report is due next week; he has nearly completed it. 12
4 Bertha is in charge of this project; give her all my bills. 12
| 1 | 2 | 3 | 4 | 5 | 6 | 7 | 8 | 9 | 10 | 11 | 12

In LAB 7, page 134, you learned to use a comma before *and, but, or,* and *nor* in compound sentences. When no conjunction is used, place a semicolon between the two independent clauses.

Larry took a bus; Mary went by plane. (No conjunction joins the two independent clauses. A semicolon is needed.)

We have an office in New York; we will have one in Boston soon.

COMPUTER PROGRAMS

By Gordon MacIntosh

There is a great difference between running a program and writing a program. Running a program is simple; writing a program for a computer requires a lot of work.

WRITING A PROGRAM

First, you must learn a computer language. Computers have their own languages--Basic, Fortran, Pascal, and so on.

Second, computers are exacting and precise. One character out of place can cause a program not to run.

Third, the programmer never knows quite how the program is going to turn out until it is finished.

RUNNING A PROGRAM

Computer programs are easy to run. All you do is put a disk in a disk drive--or a cassette in a cassette player-- and push a button. Programs that are easy to learn are called "user-friendly."

ONE-PAGE REPORT IN PICA TYPE (REDUCED) WITH SIDE HEADINGS

Production Practice. Single spacing. Use the same sheet of paper you used for the other production practice. Use Job 107 B below.

Space down to line 20. Type the inside address. Space down 2 lines and type the salutation. Space down 2 lines and type the subject line. Space down another 2 lines and type the first line of the letter. Check your work.

Remove your paper from the typewriter, turn it upside down, and reinsert it into the machine. Space down to line 20. Type the inside address, but do *not* type Mr. Abernathy's name in the inside address. Space down 2 lines and type an attention line—*Attention: Mr. Paul Abernathy.* Space down 2 lines and type a salutation—*Gentlemen:.* Space down another 2 lines and type the subject line. Space down another 2 lines and type the first line of the letter. Check your work.

JOB 107 B. LETTER
Standard format. Workbook 151–152. Body 68 words (plus 20 words for subject line).

[Today's date] / Mr. Paul Abernathy / 12
Nightlight Hotel Inc. / 2670 Blue 18
Bird Drive / Great Neck, NY 11023 / 25
Dear Mr. Abernathy: / Subject: 33
Sales Meeting 36
Last year we had the pleasure 43
of holding our sales meeting at 49
your hotel. Our meeting was a 55
big success; and a large part of 62
our good fortune was due, of course, 69
to the excellent services we received 77
from your hotel. 80
We would like to return to your 88
hotel for our next meeting. Would you, 96
therefore, please let me know what your 104
group rates are for this year. / Sincerely, / 114
J. J. Reynolds / Program Chairperson / 126
[Your initials] 128

■ **GOALS**
To type 37/5′/5e.
To type an attention line and a subject line in a letter.

■ **FORMAT**
Drills: Single spacing   60-space line
5-Minute Timings: Double spacing   5-space tab

KEYBOARDING SKILLS

Type lines 1–4 once. In line 5 backspace and underscore each underlined word immediately after typing it. Repeat lines 1–4, or take a series of 1-minute timings.

Speed   1 It is easy for them to type this short, brief line of type. 12
Accuracy 2 If we find the precise quiz, just give Bob an exam quickly. 12
Numbers   3 On 10/29/85 we drove 36 miles to Waco and 47 miles to Hico. 12
Symbols   4 Is #47 selling @ $.38 or $.56? It sold for $.45 (20% off). 12
Technique 5 They <u>may</u> soon <u>know</u> how <u>good</u> they are as <u>they</u> type <u>the</u> work.

          | 1 | 2 | 3 | 4 | 5 | 6 | 7 | 8 | 9 | 10 | 11 | 12

PRETEST

Take a 5-minute timing on lines 9–23 on page 180. Circle and count your errors.

PRACTICE

Use the chart below to find the number of errors you made on the Pretest. Then type each of the designated drill lines on page 183 four times.

Pretest errors	0–1	2–3	4–5	6+
Drill lines	9–13	8–12	7–11	6–10

Take two 30-second speed timings on lines 5 and 6. Then take two 30-second speed timings on lines 7 and 8. Or type each sentence twice.

```
5  A job or copy that the students type must not cause them to   12
6  just stop working; students need to get one job done right.   24
                                                                 —
7  Success is very much needed by all students who are trying,   12
8  to the best of their abilities, to get all their work done.   24
   |  1  |  2  |  3  |  4  |  5  |  6  |  7  |  8  |  9  | 10 | 11 | 12
```

FORMATTING PARAGRAPH HEADINGS IN REPORTS

Paragraph headings further subdivide a report. To format paragraph headings:

1. Type paragraph headings at the beginning of a paragraph in initial caps.

2. Underscore paragraph headings.

3. Follow paragraph headings with a period and 2 spaces.

JOB 53 A. REPORT WITH SIDE AND PARAGRAPH HEADINGS
Standard format. (If you need review, check pages 87 and 90.)

ABOUT APPLES

PICKING APPLES

If you live near apple-growing farms, you can get the very freshest fruit, along with some fresh air and exercise, by going to a pick-your-own orchard. These fruit farms often post signs on roads or run ads in local papers. Call in advance to see if you need to bring baskets and to check on the kinds of apples they grow.

RATING APPLES

Big apples may look solid, but often they are mealy and mushy inside. Small- or medium-sized fruit may taste better. Here are some names of apples and their features to help you get the right kind of apple for your needs.

Northern Spy. This kind of apple is somewhat tart and is best for baking because it holds its shape well when cooked.

Cortland. This apple is somewhat tart too, but it has a nice crunch. It is best for salads because it will not discolor as fast as some others.

Red and Golden Delicious. Both kinds are good to eat; both kinds are sweet and juicy.

Remember that paragraph headings are typed in initial caps at the beginning of a paragraph, underscored, and followed by a period and 2 spaces.

JOB 53 B. REPORT WITH SIDE AND PARAGRAPH HEADINGS
Retype the report on page 91, creating paragraph headings as follows: Under the side heading WRITING A PROGRAM, change First, Second, and Third to paragraph headings by underscoring and putting a period after each. Standard format.

FORMATTING AN ATTENTION LINE

When a letter is addressed directly to a company, an attention line may be used to route it to a particular person or department. To format an attention line:

1. Type the attention line in initial caps at the left margin, a double space below the inside address and a double space above the salutation. Use a colon after the word *Attention.*

2. After an attention line, use the salutation *Ladies and Gentlemen:, Gentlemen:,* or *Ladies:.*

3. On the envelope, type the attention line (an on-arrival direction—see page 105) in capital and lowercase

```
United Charities Campaign
258 North Star Drive
Anchorage, AK 99503

Attention:  Campaign Manager

Ladies and Gentlemen:
```

letters on line 9, 5 spaces from the left edge. Also underscore it.

Note: Because the attention line will add two lines (one typed, one blank), add 20 words to the body count to determine placement.

Production Practice. Single spacing. Clean sheet of paper. Use Job 107 A below.

Space down to line 20 (15 plus 5) and type the inside address. Space down 2 lines (double-space). Type the attention line (remember to space twice after the colon).

Space down 2 lines and type the salutation. Check your work.

Remove your paper from the typewriter, turn it upside down, and reinsert it into the machine. Repeat the practice. Check your work. Save this sheet of paper.

JOB 107 A. LETTER

Standard format. Workbook 149–150. Body 139 words (plus 20 words for attention line).

May 10, 19— / Concord Real Estate / 3470	12
Madison Street / Concord, NH 03301 / Atten-	20
tion: Sales Office / Ladies and Gentlemen:	30
Our company will be starting a branch office	40
in the Concord area next year, and nearly 100	49
employees will be moving to your city. We	58
would like to receive a real estate listing from	67
your agency so that our employees can start	76
looking for houses that will suit their needs. We	86

would like to have this data no later than the end	97
of this month, May 31.	101
Most of our employees are looking for homes	111
in the $70s and $80s price range with no fewer	121
than three bedrooms. We also need some infor-	130
mation on schools and hospitals and the names,	139
addresses, and telephone numbers of lending	148
institutions in Concord.	153
Please send any information you have to me	163
so that I can share it with the employees who	172
will be moving to Concord next year. We look	181
forward to hearing from you. / Sincerely, / Leon	196
Walker / Personnel Manager / [*Your initials*]	204

FORMATTING A SUBJECT LINE

A subject line briefly identifies the main topic of a letter. To format a subject line:

1. Type the subject line in initial caps at the left margin between the salutation and the body of the letter. Leave 1 blank line before and after the subject line.

2. Follow the word *Subject* with a colon and 2 spaces.

Note: The subject line, like the attention line, occupies two lines—add 20 words to the body count to determine placement.

```
Dear Ms. King:

Subject:  Battlefield Charity Dance

I am pleased that you thought of our firm in
tion with your charity dance.  We have found
```

LESSON 54

■ GOALS
To identify how numbers are expressed while typing sentences.
To type 34/3'/5e.
To format and type run-in references.

■ FORMAT
Drills: Single spacing   60-space line
3-Minute Timings: Double spacing   5-space tab

LAB 3

Number Style

Type lines 1–4 once. Then repeat lines 1–4 or take a series of 1-minute timings.

```
1  Eighty-eight students will tour Europe for five long weeks.   12
2  Just mix 12.5 grams of powder in 10.5 liters of the liquid.   12
3  I will purchase 13 pairs of socks, 15 blazers, and 22 ties.   12
4  Yes, 14 students from my college are among the 77 scholars.   12
   | 1 | 2 | 3 | 4 | 5 | 6 | 7 | 8 | 9 | 10 | 11 | 12
```

PREVIEW PRACTICE

Accuracy

Speed

Type each line twice as a preview to the 3-minute timings below.

```
5  basic require explore zestful preserve exercises ridiculous
6  sensible natural health dairy their time when that make but
```

3-MINUTE TIMINGS

Take two 3-minute timings on lines 7–15.

```
                1                2                3                4
7       Health foods may seem ridiculous to some of us; but if    12
            5              6                7              8
8  you enjoy pure and natural foods, you know what a change it    24
                9            10              11
9  makes in your life when you eat all-natural foods.            34
          12           13              14              15
10      It is a fact that most people who eat health foods all    46
          16            17              18              19
11  the time require less medical care.  If you play a sport or   58
        20              21              22
12  exercise and get plenty of rest, you are sensible.           68
        23            24            25            26
13      Explore health foods like fruits, fresh produce, nuts,   80
        27            28            29            30
14  grains, and dairy foods; they make up a basic diet that all  92
        31            32            33            34
15  need to preserve their strength for zestful lives.          102
   | 1 | 2 | 3 | 4 | 5 | 6 | 7 | 8 | 9 | 10 | 11 | 12    SI 1.26
```

FORMATTING RUN-IN REFERENCES

When you are writing a report in which you refer to or quote an idea, fact, or statement of someone else, you should give your readers the source of this information. In this way, you give credit to the original author. You also aid your readers, who may want to find additional information on the subject about which you are writing.

In this lesson you will practice using run-in references. A run-in reference is one that is typed in the body of the report.

Format a **book reference** as follows: Author, book title, publisher, place of publication, year of publication, page number if reference is being made to a specific page. Note the underscored book title.

(John Speer, <u>Flying</u>, Aviation Books, Inc., New York, 1986, p. 10.)

(Continued on next page)

Take a 5-minute timing on lines 9–23. Circle and count your errors.

9   To some, living in an apartment is enjoyable. At some time in your life,   16

10   it is quite possible that you might have a chance to live in an apartment   31

11   complex before buying your home.   37

12   When residing in an apartment complex, you do not have to mow lawns,   15

13   paint a house, or edge the grass next to your sidewalk. Your apartment   29

14   manager is usually assigned these duties.   37

15   Very often an apartment is close to the business area, and you will find   15

16   that your commuting time to work is quite minimal. One suggestion is to   30

17   travel quickly and safely by a bus.   37

18   You will find it easy to make friends in an apartment, since so many   15

19   different people live next door or very close to your home. This could be a   30

20   major advantage of apartment life.   37

21   Most apartments can be found with the latest in modern appliances; they   16

22   are carpeted; and they offer a wide choice of dazzling features like pools,   31

23   sauna rooms, or new tennis courts.   37

| 1 | 2 | 3 | 4 | 5 | 6 | 7 | 8 | 9 | 10 | 11 | 12 | 13 | 14 | 15 | SI 1.41

PRACTICE

Take a 1-minute timing on each paragraph of the Pretest.

POSTTEST

Take another 5-minute timing on lines 9–23 to see how much your skill has improved.

LESSON 107

UNIT 18 Formatting Correspondence
UNIT GOAL 37/5'/5e

■ GOALS
To use commas correctly to set off appositives while typing
sentences.
To format and type an attention line in a letter.
To format and type a subject line in a letter.

■ FORMAT
Single spacing   60-space line

LAB 11

Commas With Appositives

Workbook 147–148.

Type lines 1–4 once, providing the missing commas for each line. Edit your copy as your teacher reads the answers. Then retype lines 1–4 from your edited copy.

1   I thank you Ms. Heilman for all your help on our project.
2   Our employer the Quincey Corporation is moving to Boston.
3   Gregg Hanley's office the huge corner office was painted.
4   Ask our manager John Appezzatto to send five dozen boxes.

Format a reference to a **magazine article** as follows: Author [*if known*], "article title," name of magazine, volume number [*if applicable*], date, page number. Note the quotation marks for the article title and the underscored magazine title.

(Beth Zeiman, "The Friendly Skies," Pilot's Quarterly, Vol. 6, Spring 1986, p. 88.)

Practice: Type each of the preceding references three times. When backspacing to underscore the titles, use a different method each time. (1) Depress the backspace key once for each letter and space in the title. (2) Depress the backspace key hard enough to engage the repeat mechanism. Be sure to stop in time! (3) Push the carriage or carrier back by hand, or use the express key if you have one. Decide which is the best method for long and short titles.

JOB 54 A. REPORT WITH RUN-IN REFERENCES
Standard format.

A HISTORY OF PARACHUTING
by Grace ackerman

There are clues that many years ago the chinese tried to invent a sort of "roof tent" for jumping. But the parachute as we know it was not made until the 1700s. (Ted Terrance, A History of Flying, Glenmore Press, New York, 1980, p. 104.) Balloonists worked to build a type of parachute because they needed a safe way to land if the balloon burst.

invention
In france a man by the name of garnarin made the first drop in a cone-shaped parachute. (Scot Webber, "Sky Diving," Sports Today, May 1981, pp. 5-6.) He made many jumps but got air sick because of the wobbly ride down. Then a friend told him to cut a hole in the top of the chute, allowing air to flow through. This cone shape with a hole in the top is still used today.

modern uses
With the use of air planes in world war I, we were able to drop supplies by parachute to our forces deep in hostile lands. the parachute pack has saved the lives of many pilots. Today there are all kinds of people who enjoy the sport of sky diving.

Note that *May 1981* (rather than *May, 1981,*) is the modern style for month/year dates. Also note that *p.* indicates one page; *pp.*, more than one page.

JOB 105 A. MINUTES OF A MEETING

Standard format. Retype Job 104 A (pages 176–177) with these changes:

1. Minutes are to be typed for the June meeting.

2. The Marketing Director is Philip Crane.

3. The following members were present:

John Lee
Annette Foresta
Jean Smith
Neal Tinley
Diane Sanchez
Don Pride
May Fong
Donna Schultz
Ron Blakely
Philip Crane

4. The minutes for the May meeting were approved as read.

5. The only other item of UNFINISHED BUSINESS was as follows: The marketing plan that was presented during the May meeting was discussed. It was decided that $40,000 be directed toward this plan and that Ms. Schultz be named as the chairperson of the Marketing Planning Committee.

6. Mr. Blakely recommended that the revisions scheduled on the data processing text be moved ahead one year to coincide with the revised information processing texts due for publication the year after next.

7. Claire T. Stark remains as secretary.

LESSON 106

CLINIC

■ **GOALS**
To improve your keyboarding skills.
To type 37/5'/5e.

■ **FORMAT**
Drills: Single spacing   60-space line   Tabs every 8 spaces
5-Minute Timings: Double spacing   5-space tab

KEYBOARDING SKILLS

Type lines 1–4 once. In line 5 use your tabulator key to advance from one word to the next through the entire line. Repeat lines 1–4, or take a series of 1-minute timings.

Speed	1	If an auditor signs the key amendment, I may work for them.	12
Accuracy	2	Have five more wax jugs been glazed quickly for two people?	12
Numbers	3	With 56 precincts tallied, Graber had 3847; Green had 2910.	12
Symbols	4	Interest on the $247 loan was 9 3/4%, which came to $24.08.	12
Technique	5	and den for the mop nor let you	

| 1 | 2 | 3 | 4 | 5 | 6 | 7 | 8 | 9 | 10 | 11 | 12 |

30-SECOND "OK" TIMINGS

Type as many 30-second "OK" (errorless) timings as possible out of three attempts on lines 6–8. Then repeat the effort and try to improve on the first score.

6 Vicky placed a dozen jugs from Iraq on the waxed tabletops,   12

7 and all the guests who came to her party wanted to know how   24

8 they could purchase some of this pottery for their own use.   36

| 1 | 2 | 3 | 4 | 5 | 6 | 7 | 8 | 9 | 10 | 11 | 12 |

LESSON 55

■ **GOALS**
To express numbers correctly while typing sentences.
To format and type a two-page report.

■ **FORMAT**
Single spacing   60-space line

LAB 3
Number Style

Type lines 1–4 once, correcting any errors in number-style rules. Edit your copy as your teacher reads the answers. Then retype lines 1–4 from your edited copy.

1 Joann listed 100 items to be discussed at the next meeting.

2 The engineer said that the precise diameter is 1.75 meters.

3 We need 10 samples, but they shipped us only 4 or 5.

4 426 women attended the huge convention.

30-SECOND "OK" TIMINGS

Type as many 30-second "OK" (errorless) timings as possible out of three attempts on lines 5–7.

5 To be an expert in typing, you need to spend quite a lot of   12

6 time on drill work, which at times can be a big job. Three   24

7 or four drills done well can bring you victory and a prize.   36

 | 1 | 2 | 3 | 4 | 5 | 6 | 7 | 8 | 9 | 10 | 11 | 12

FORMATTING MULTIPAGE REPORTS

Workbook 41.

Word processors have an automatic page-break feature. The machine will end each page at the appropriate point to provide the correct bottom margin and then space down to begin the next page, leaving the correct top margin, automatically numbering the pages.

Reports of two or more pages usually contain side headings and/or paragraph headings.

The first page of a long report is formatted in the same manner as a one-page report: (1) the title is typed on line 13; (2) margins are set for a 6-inch line; and (3) the body of the report is double-spaced. The bottom margin for any full page should contain a minimum of 1 to 1½ inches—6 to 9 blank lines.

To format continuation pages in a long report:

1. Type the page number (the word *Page* is unnecessary) on line 7 at the right margin. (Do not type a page number on the first page.)

2. Begin the text of the report on line 10, a triple space below the page number.

3. Leave at least 2 lines of a paragraph at the bottom of a page, and carry at least 2 lines of a paragraph to the top of a page.

Visual Guide: A visual guide is very useful in helping you maintain the proper side, top, and bottom margins. You may use the visual guide on page 41 of your workbook, or your teacher may give you instructions for making one of your own.

↓7
2 ↓3

BOTTOM MARGINS

     The bottom margin on each page should be a minimum of 6

or a maximum of 9 lines deep. On standard paper with 66 lines,

■ **GOALS**
To use commas correctly to set off appositives while typing sentences.
To type 37/5'/5e.
To type minutes of a meeting.

■ **FORMAT**
Drills: Single spacing   60-space line
5-Minute Timings: Double spacing   5-space tab

LAB 11

Commas With Appositives

Type lines 1–4 once, providing the missing commas for each line. Edit your copy as your teacher reads the answers. Then retype lines 1–4 from your edited copy.

1   The best runner is Phil Jones a new student at Maxim High.

2   If you have questions, call our service manager Ann Smith.

3   Get in touch with the dean Dr. Leonard for an assignment.

4   Will Liz be available on Tuesday August 21 for a meeting?

PREVIEW PRACTICE

Type each line twice as a preview to the 5-minute timings below.

Accuracy   5   size assess several inquire ascertain graduation acceptable
Speed   6   identify specific program total many wish cost also for may

5-MINUTE TIMINGS

Take two 5-minute timings on lines 7–22.

7   If you attend college upon graduation from high school   12
8   next year, choose the school you feel will be acceptable to   24
9   you. Specific issues must be reviewed; and you, the gradu-   36
10 ating senior, should assess all of them very carefully. In   48
11 making a choice, it's essential that you discuss the issues   60
12 with many of your closest friends who are attending schools   72
13 you may likely attend. Travel to the college campuses that   84
14 may be of interest to you, also.   90
15   While you are in high school is the time to plan for a   102
16 program of study you wish to pursue in college. Inquire at   114
17 several schools to ascertain whether the college you'd like   126
18 to attend has the precise program of your choice. You must   138
19 also identify just where you'd like to go to school. Would   150
20 you prefer staying quite close to home, or would you prefer   162
21 going to college in another state, far away from home? You   174
22 ought to consider your total cost and the school size.   185

| 1 | 2 | 3 | 4 | 5 | 6 | 7 | 8 | 9 | 10 | 11 | 12   SI 1.41

Production Practice. Set your margins for a 6-inch line (60P/70E). Double spacing, 5-space tab. Clean sheet of paper. Place a small pencil mark 1 inch from the bottom of the paper and another mark 1½ inches from the bottom of the paper. Use the report below.

1. Space down to line 50 (25 returns). Type the fourth paragraph—the one beginning with the paragraph heading *Other Pages.* Use the pencil marks to help you decide where to end the page. Remove the paper from the machine and check your work. Are there between 6 and 9 blank lines in the bottom margin?

 Turn the paper upside down and make small pencil marks at 1 and 1½ inches from the bottom. Reinsert it in the machine. Space down 55 lines and repeat the practice. Remove your paper from the machine and check your work. Are there between 6 and 9 blank lines in the bottom margin? Turn your paper over and reinsert it in the machine.

2. Space down to line 7. Move the carriage or carrier to the space before the right margin locks. Type the number 2. Space down 3 lines (return once and turn the platen knob by hand 1 full line space). Type the fifth paragraph—the one beginning with the side heading BOTTOM MARGINS. Check your work.

JOB 55 A. TWO-PAGE REPORT
Standard format. Underscore words in italics (except *Your name*).

FORMATTING LONG REPORTS ON A TYPEWRITER

A Report for Typing I

By [*Your name*]

A long report is one that takes more than one page. To prepare long reports that are consistent and attractively arranged, follow the guidelines given in this paper.

GENERAL RULES

A long report is typed on a line of 60 pica or 70 elite spaces, with the body double-spaced. The main title, subtitle (optional), and author's name are centered. Side headings are typed at the left margin in all caps, preceded by 2 blank lines.

HEADINGS AND TOP MARGINS

First Page. The main heading of two or three double-spaced lines (as shown above) begins on line 13, leaving a top margin of 2 inches. The main heading is followed by 2 blank lines. This page is counted, but no page number is typed on page 1.

Other Pages. The heading of each other page consists of the page number (usually without the word *Page*). The page number is typed at the right margin on line 7, leaving 6 blank lines in the top margin. The page number is followed by 2 blank lines, so the body of the report will always resume on line 10 on each continuation page.

BOTTOM MARGINS

The bottom margin on each page should be a minimum of 6 or a maximum of 9 blank lines. On standard paper with 66 lines, the last line of typing should appear on line 57, 58, 59, or 60. If it is necessary to break a paragraph, at least 2 lines should be typed on the first page and 2 lines on the following page.

To avoid typing in the bottom margin, use one of these techniques:

Counting. Count the lines; stop on line 57, 58, 59, or 60.

Marking. Before inserting the paper, draw a very light pencil line at the right edge about 2 inches from the bottom as a caution signal; erase the line when you finish after removing the page from the typewriter.

Using a Visual Guide. On a separate sheet of paper, draw heavy lines to show where the margins should be. Put this visual guide under the paper on which you type; the lines will show through to help you maintain correct margins on every page of the report.

JOB 104 A (CONTINUED)

Mark(t)eing Director, presided at the
meeting. The following *members* were present:
~~at the meeting:~~

Mr. Frank Souza
Mr. Wayne Hall
Ms. Donna Shultz
Ms. Cathy Cooper
Dr. A. R. Wang
Mrs. Anne Krouse
Mr. E. G. Moore
Mr. Paul E. Santini
Ms. Mae Lopez
Claire T. Stark

arrange alphabetically in two columns

UNFINISHED BUSINESS

The secretary read the minutes of
the ~~March~~ *February* meeting, and they were approved as read.

Ms. Moore reported on the progress
of the new text on auto repair. Contracts for the text were drawn up and
sent to the authors on March 1. First
drafts of the text material ~~are to~~ *would* be
completed one year from the date of
the contract.

New Business

Ms. Schultz suggested that the
information processing texts be revised
one year earlier than planned because
of the rapid changes that had taken
place *in this area* in the past (2) years. A committee
was formed to study these changes and *to*
come up with a reco*m*mendation at next
month's meeting. Ms. Schultz would
chair this committee.

Claire T. Stark, *Secretary*

JOB 104 B. SPEECH
Standard format (page 171).

WORK MEASUREMENT	10
Presented to the Office Products Division	38
By Sharyl Corsi	50

Business likes to know how good its employ- 61
ees are and how skilled they are in the work they 71
do. On a production line it is easy to measure 81
output by the number of units that are produced 90
in an hour, a day, a week, or a month. A similar 100
technique can be used to measure the output of 110
work in an office, and a record of this work is 119
often placed on a log sheet. This sheet is used to 130
record work entering and leaving a word pro- 138
cessing center. 142

LOG SHEET PROFILE 154
Although a number of formats can be used to 164
design a log sheet, a few items are often com- 173
mon to many of them. First of all, there is room 183
for the name of the author of the work as well as 193
the name of the department in which that person 203
works. There is also a place for the type of out- 212
put, such as a letter, memo, or report. It is also 223
important to know when the work was received 232
by the center as well as when it was completed. 242
The person who completes the work must also 250
put his or her name on the log sheet. Lastly, 260
there must be some indication as to how long it 269
took to complete the work as well as how many 279
total lines were needed to complete the whole 288
job. 289

LINE COUNT 297
Many methods are used to compute line 306
count, but the following are three basic things to 316
consider. Some centers give extra credit for 325
work that is prepared from a rough draft. Some 335
allow extra credit for tables. Finally, some cen- 345
ters give a lower line count to partial lines in a 355
job. 356

CLINIC

■ **GOALS**
To type 34/3'/5e.
To improve your typing accuracy.

■ **FORMAT**
Drills: Single spacing   60-space line
3-Minute Timings: Double spacing   5-space tab

KEYBOARDING SKILLS

Type lines 1–4 once. Then do what line 5 tells you to do. Repeat lines 1–4, or take a series of 1-minute timings.

Speed
Accuracy
Numbers
Symbols
Technique

1 Ms. Lela Dow owns a pair of authentic ivory and clay bowls.   12
2 Next month Phil may just quit work and buy five cozy games.   12
3 Marathon runners 10, 29, and 56 had exact times of 3:38:47.   12
4 In Cruz's new book, A New Math, does 2 + 2 = 4? Of course!   16
5 As you type this line, use your return key after each word.

| 1 | 2 | 3 | 4 | 5 | 6 | 7 | 8 | 9 | 10 | 11 | 12

PRETEST

Take a 3-minute timing on lines 6–14. Circle and count your errors.

```
              1               2               3             4
6        A batik is a dyed cloth that has hot wax painted on it    12
              5           6              7              8
7  to form a design.  The artist melts wax, tints it different    24
              9             10            11
8  colors, paints a design, and then dyes each cloth.             34
           12             13            14             15
9        But some artists paint the cloth with clear wax.  Then   46
           16             17            18            19
10 the batik is dyed again and again, using many colors.  Just    58
           20          21            22
11 the part not coated with that wax is then colored.             68
           23          24            25            26
12       The second method requires more work on the part of an   80
           27          28            29            30
13 artist, but the colors in the finished batik will have more    92
           31          32            33            34
14 zest and look brighter to those who see the cloth.            102
```

| 1 | 2 | 3 | 4 | 5 | 6 | 7 | 8 | 9 | 10 | 11 | 12   SI 1.26

PRACTICE

Type each line once. Then practice twice each line that corresponds to the letters you missed in the Pretest.

15 aa arrow appeal annual affairs attract apparent attached aa
16 bb books barrel bubble biggest blabber bulletin baseball bb
17 cc class career cattle collect correct connects commence cc

18 dd drill dinner dollar dropped drilled dwelling deferred dd
19 ee error excess exceed effects essence employee effected ee
20 ff freed fellow fluffy footage fulfill flooring followed ff

21 gg glass gallon glossy getting grammar greeting guessing gg
22 hh hurry hooted happen hassled hurried helpless happened hh
23 ii inner inning indeed issuers issuing irritate imminent ii

(Continued on next page)

NEW BUSINESS 209
    James Brown discussed the need for planning 220
a campaign to let job applicants know of the 229
openings that now exist in our office. Steps for 239
action were planned: Miss Verne will write to all 249
the local training schools, and Mr. Kline will 258

send a note to all members of the staff to ask 268
them to look for potential job applicants. 277
    A final report of the work measurement study 288
was given by Sharyl Corsi. A copy of the entire 297
report is attached to these minutes. 305
                    Ray W. House, Secretary 313

■ GOALS
To identify how commas are used to set off appositives while
   typing sentences.
To type minutes of a meeting and a speech.

■ FORMAT
Single spacing   60-space line

LAB 11

Commas With Appositives

Type lines 1–4 once. Then repeat lines 1–4 or take a series of 1-minute timings.

1 The book I want, Principles of Management, is out of stock. 22
2 My sister, Jane Qually, is a center on the basketball team. 12
3 Your next workshop will be on Valentine's Day, February 14. 12
4 Sue Krzyskowski, our personnel manager, recruits employees. 12
   | 1 | 2 | 3 | 4 | 5 | 6 | 7 | 8 | 9 | 10 | 11 | 12

30-SECOND "OK" TIMINGS

Type as many 30-second "OK" (errorless) timings as possible out of three attempts on lines 5–7.

5 Matt had a zest for quiet living and put a lot of time into 12
6 the purchase of his new home. He wanted to be certain that 24
7 his choice of location would guarantee him peace and quiet. 36
   | 1 | 2 | 3 | 4 | 5 | 6 | 7 | 8 | 9 | 10 | 11 | 12

JOB 104 A. MINUTES OF A MEETING
Standard format.

New-Products Committee

MINUTES OF THE MARCH MEETING

] (Today's date) March 3, 19-- [

ATTENDANCE

    The March meeting of the New-Products committee was held
in the Boardroom of Sutton Publishing Company. Ms. Mae Lopez,

(Continued on next page)

```
24  jj jazzy jobber jarred jubilee jamming jettison jaggedly jj
25  kk knees kennel kidded knotted keepers kangaroo kindness kk
26  ll looks lesson ladder luggage legally lollygag lollipop ll

27  mm merry matter missed muffler mammoth molasses millions mm
28  nn noons needed narrow nibbled needles normally nineteen nn
29  oo offer office occurs overall omitted opposite occasion oo

30  pp pulls proofs passes putting pressed passport planning pp
31  qq quell quills queens quarrel quizzes quelling quarried qq
32  rr roots roller runner repress running repeller referral rr

33  ss stood street sudden stopped success supposed sessions ss
34  tt teeth tooled teller traffic totally tomorrow thirteen tt
35  uu upper unless unnail usually utterly umbrella unfilled uu

36  vv veers vessel vacuum village vaccine verbally vendetta vv
37  ww woods winner weekly willing written withheld warranty ww
38  xx exert exceed excess exposes express expelled excelled xx

39  yy yells yammer yesses yapping yelling yellowed yearbook yy
40  zz zooms zagged zipper zoology zillion zucchini zeppelin zz
```

POSTTEST

Take another 3-minute timing on lines 6–14 on page 97 to see how much your skill has improved.

LESSON 57

UNIT 10 Formatting Correspondence
UNIT GOAL 34/3'/5e

■ **GOALS**
To express numbers correctly while typing sentences.
To format and type a personal-business letter.

■ **FORMAT**
Single spacing   60-space line

LAB 3

Number Style

Type lines 1–4 once, correcting any errors in number-style rules. Edit your copy as your teacher reads the answers. Then retype lines 1–4 from your edited copy.

```
1  Over 250 people attended the party for Jacqueline and Gary.
2  90 pens were left on the desk for their art instructor.
3  About 5 or 6 members of the club attended the meeting.
4  6 students helped the 120 senior citizens plan that tour.
```

12-SECOND TIMINGS

Type each line three times, or take three 12-second timings on each line. For each timing, type with no more than 1 error.

```
5  The circus show begins with a march around the center ring.
6  He likes the animals and the very funny clowns most of all.
7  He is saving all his money so that he can go to the circus.
```
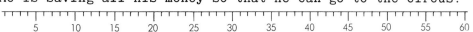
```
    5    10   15   20   25   30   35   40   45   50   55   60
```

```
       1                2               3              4
 5   Have you ever dreaded taking a long trip by automobile  12
          5                  6            7            8
 6   because of those cramped quarters you find yourself in?  It  24
         9              10            11         12
 7   might be an amazing experience if you ride those miles in a  36

 8   van.                                                     37
          13             14             15            16
 9   A van allows you to relax as you ride because you will  12
        17           18          19            20
10   be able to tilt back your seat or turn it around so that it  24
       21             22            23             24
11   is possible for you to visit with others in the rear of the  36

12   van.                                                     —
            25               26            27            28
13   When riding in a van, it will also be possible for you  12
        29           30           31            32
14   to enjoy such modern home conveniences as a television set,  24
      33              34             35             36
15   a stereo, and kitchen appliances that work like magic on dc  36
       37
16   power.                                                   37
```

    | 1 | 2 | 3 | 4 | 5 | 6 | 7 | 8 | 9 | 10 | 11 | 12 | SI 1.40

FORMATTING MINUTES OF A MEETING

Minutes of a meeting are usually saved in a three-ring binder. To format minutes:

1. Set margins for a bound report (60P/70E, shifted 3 spaces to the right).

2. Type the title on line 7 of page 1. Type page numbers on line 7 of additional pages.

3. Single-space.

4. Type side headings in all-capital letters. Double-space before and after side headings.

5. Begin closing at the center. Leave 3 blank lines for the signature.

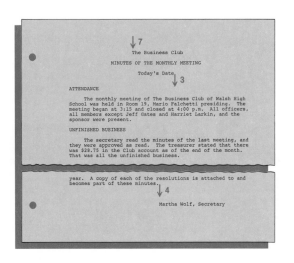

JOB 103 A. MINUTES OF A MEETING
Standard format.

Office Products Division   15
MINUTES OF THE MAY MEETING   33
May 10, 19—   44

ATTENDANCE   48

The May meeting of the Office Products Division was held on May 10, 19—, in Room 224 of A. L. Day Products Inc. The meeting began at 1:30 p.m. and was adjourned at 3:30 p.m. Anne Yeung, Division Manager, presided at the meeting. All members except Beth English and Don   59 68 77 86 95 105

Bright were present. Mr. Bright was represented by Jane Fields.   114 118

UNFINISHED BUSINESS   123

The secretary read the minutes of the April meeting. After two minor changes suggested by Juan Diante were accepted, the minutes were approved.   134 143 152 154

Celeste Young gave a report on the survey she is working with on the need for advanced training on our computer network that was installed last month. Ms. Young will continue her work on this study and present a final paper at the June meeting.   165 174 184 193 203 205

(Continued on next page)

HEADING
Writer's address
Date

OPENING
Name
Inside address
Salutation

BODY

CLOSING
Complimentary
 closing
Signature always
 in ink.
Writer's name

↓ 13

672 Greenwood Avenue
Yuma, AZ 85364
April 10, 19—— ↓ 5

Mrs. Violet Logan
LaVista High School
2400 Highland Avenue
San Luis, AZ 85349 ↓ 2

Dear Mrs. Logan: ↓ 2

Last fall I was a student in an advanced course in
typing that you taught at the high school on Monday
evenings, starting September 4. I received a grade
of A for the course. ↓ 2

Perhaps you will remember that you helped me get a
typing job at the Mesa Clinic. I have been working
for two months now for Dr. Joel Weiss, and I enjoy
my work a great deal. But I find that I need more
practice in typing medical terms and filling out
forms for patients. ↓ 2

Do you know where I can take a course in typing for
medical office workers? I would be grateful if you
would send any brochures about such a course to my
home. The address is at the top of this letter. ↓ 2

Sincerely yours, ↓ 4

Nadine Hooper

Nadine Hooper

In address blocks
(return address or
inside address), use
the two-letter state
abbreviation or spell
out the name of the
state (**example:** AZ
or Arizona). Two-
letter abbreviations
are used only with
ZIP Codes and are
typed in capital
letters with no
periods or space
between the letters.
Leave 1 space
between the state
and the ZIP Code.

***PERSONAL-BUSINESS LETTER, STANDARD FORMAT
MODIFIED-BLOCK STYLE***

and so forth. We do this when we 420
talk to people, and the pronouns 426
can have the same effect on people 433
when they are used in the body 439
of a letter. 442

SLIDE 4 449
The last suggestion I have 455
for personalizing your letter 461
is to choose your closing care- 467
fully. Some closings, such as 473

"Sincerely," are less formal 479
than others, such as "Very 484
truly yours." 487

I thank you for the opportu- 494
nity to speak to you on the 499
topic of personalizing your 505
letters. The suggestions I have 512
given you will help you do exactly 519
that. 520

LESSON 103

■ **GOALS**
To recognize how commas are used to set off appositives
  while typing sentences.
To type 37/3'/3e.
To format and type minutes of a meeting.

■ **FORMAT**
Drills: Single spacing   60-space line
3-Minute Timings: Double spacing   5-space tab

LAB 11

Commas With Appositives

Type lines 1–4 once. Then repeat lines 1–4 or take a series of 1-minute timings.

1 Our educational consultant, Jan Newby, is highly qualified. 12
2 Mr. Williams, our resident expert, was amazed at this idea. 12
3 We have planned to hold the next meeting on Monday, May 27. 12
4 It is best for you, our client, to know everything we know. 12
   | 1 | 2 | 3 | 4 | 5 | 6 | 7 | 8 | 9 | 10 | 11 | 12

An *appositive* is a word or a phrase that further describes or identifies a person or a thing. Use two commas to separate an appositive within a sentence. Use one comma if the appositive ends the sentence.

Mrs. Baker, *the national sales manager,* approved the raises.
(The words *the national sales manager* further identify *Mrs. Baker.*)

This account was handled by a local firm, *Adams & Fells.*

The seminar has been rescheduled for next Monday, *August 12.*

PRETEST

Take a 3-minute timing on lines 5–16 on page 175. Circle and count your errors.

PRACTICE

Take a 1-minute timing on each paragraph of the Pretest on page 175.

POSTTEST

Take another 3-minute timing on lines 5–16 on page 175 to see how much your skill has improved.

FORMATTING PERSONAL-BUSINESS LETTERS

A letter from an individual to a department store concerning a personal bill or to a company asking for a job interview is called a *personal-business letter.* A personal-business letter has these standard parts:

Heading. The heading consists of a return address (the writer's address) and the date.

Opening. The opening is the inside address (the name and address of the person or firm to whom the letter is being sent) and the salutation or greeting.

Body. The message of the letter.

Closing. A complimentary closing, such as *Yours truly,* or *Sincerely yours,* and the name of the writer.

To format a personal-business letter:

1. Use standard-size paper (8½ by 11 inches).
2. Set margins for a 5-inch line (50P/60E).
3. Begin the return address on line 13, at the center.

4. Type the date on the line below the return address, aligned with it.
5. Type the inside address 5 lines below the date, at the left margin.
6. Type the salutation, followed by a colon, a double space below the inside address.
7. Begin the body a double space below the salutation. Single-space paragraphs, but double-space between them. Block paragraphs at the left margin.
8. Type the complimentary closing, followed by a comma, a double space below the body, beginning at the center.
9. Type the writer's name 4 lines below the complimentary closing, beginning at the center. This space is for the writer's signature.

The format described here (and illustrated on the previous page) is the most commonly used letter style and is considered to be the standard format. This style is known as *modified-block style.*

Production Practice. Set your margins for a 5-inch line (50P/60E). Set a center tab. Single spacing. Clean sheet of paper. Use the letter illustrated on page 99.

1. Space down 13 lines. Tab to the center. Type the return address and the date. Space down 5 lines. Type the inside address. Double-space and type the salutation. Check your work.

   Remove your paper from the typewriter, and insert it upside down. Repeat Practice 1 using your own address and today's date in the heading (return address and date section). Check your work.

2. Remove your paper; turn it over. Reinsert it in the typewriter. Space down 7 lines. Type the last paragraph in the letter. Double-space; tab to the center. Type the complimentary closing. Space down 4 lines; tab to the center. Type the writer's name. Check your work.

   Remove your paper from the typewriter, and insert it upside down. Repeat Practice 2 using your own name as the writer's name. Check your work.

JOB 57 A. PERSONAL-BUSINESS LETTER
Type the letter shown on page 99. Standard format.

LESSON 58

■ **GOALS**
To type 34/3'/5e.
To format and type small envelopes.
To type a personal-business letter.

■ **FORMAT**
Drills: Single spacing   60-space line
3-Minute Timings: Double spacing   5-space tab

KEYBOARDING SKILLS

Type lines 1–4 once. Then do what line 5 tells you to do. Repeat lines 1–4, or take a series of 1-minute timings.

Speed	1	If they give him a good price, he might take a lot of them.	12
Accuracy	2	Jeff quickly amazed the audience by giving six new reports.	12
Numbers	3	The years to remember are 1910, 1929, 1938, 1947, and 1956.	12
Symbols	4	Please find #2938, #4756, #1029, #1038, and #1947 for them.	12
Technique	5	Retype line 3. Underscore each of the years.	

| 1 | 2 | 3 | 4 | 5 | 6 | 7 | 8 | 9 | 10 | 11 | 12 |

Type as many 30-second "OK" (errorless) timings as possible out of three attempts on lines 6–8.

```
6  You do not expect to save time when you indent with the tab   12
7  key; but if a tab stop is set, you will soon recognize that   24
8  each tab is quite uniform and each indention is just right.    36
   |  1  |  2  |  3  |  4  |  5  |  6  |  7  |  8  |  9  |  10  |  11  |  12
```

JOB 102 A. SPEECH
Standard format (page 171).

The Personality of a Letter — 16
By Carol T. Preston — 31

I was asked to speak today on the topic of letter writing, and I have chosen as the title for my speech "The Personality of a Letter." In all my years of speaking and writing, I have never found a topic as interesting as this one. I would like to share with you today some of the ideas I have gained in letter writing that will make letters more personable. — 40, 47, 53, 61, 68, 75, 82, 90, 96, 104, 106

SLIDE 1 — 113

My talk to you today will focus on developing a personality for the letters you write by examining the three basic parts of a letter: (1) the inside address, (2) the body, and (3) the closing. Let us look briefly at each of these sections to see how they can individually personalize your letters. — 120, 129, 137, 145, 153, 160, 167, 174

SLIDE 2 — 180

One of the first things a letter reader will notice is whether his or her name is spelled correctly. This is especially true these days because — 188, 195, 203, 210

a large number of letters are created in bulk by a word processing system and have not been typed as individual letters. Be certain, therefore, that the name in the salutation matches the name you have typed in the inside address. It is permissible to use a person's first name in the salutation if you are writing to a personal friend or a close business associate. Above all, seek every means possible to find out the name of the person to whom you are writing rather than address a letter to "Personnel Manager" or "Marketing Director." You will much more likely get a response to your letter if you use a name rather than just the title of a person. — 216, 223, 229, 235, 243, 250, 257, 264, 270, 278, 286, 293, 300, 307, 314, 322, 329, 335, 342

SLIDE 3 — 348

One suggestion to remember when you attempt to personalize the body of your letter is to use the person's name (either the person's first name or the last name with a title, depending on how well you know that person) as you write the letter. Another suggestion is to use personal pronouns such as I, you, we, they, — 356, 363, 371, 378, 385, 393, 400, 406, 413

(Continued on next page)

Take a 3-minute timing on lines 6–14. Circle and count your errors.

```
           1            2            3            4
6      High tech is the name given to a basic and useful type    12
       5            6            7            8
7  of design that is changing the concept of modern living and   24
       9            10           11           12
8  things we use daily.  It has long enjoyed a quiet appeal in   36
       13           14           15           16
9  places like stores and restaurants, but now it is coming to   48
       17           18           19           20
10 be used in homes.  High tech designs are not expensive, and   60
       21           22           23           24
11 they are built to last.  They come in a wide range of zany,   72
       25           26           27           28
12 bright colors; things such as water pipes, tire rubber, and   84
       29           30           31           32
13 window glass are often used with style in high tech designs   96
       33           34
14 and are fun to own and to use.                               102
   |  1  |  2  |  3  |  4  |  5  |  6  |  7  |  8  |  9  | 10  | 11  | 12    SI 1.26
```

PRACTICE

In the chart below find the number of errors you made on the Pretest. Then type each of the designated drill lines three times.

Pretest errors	0–1	2–3	4–5	6+
Drill lines	18–22	17–21	16–20	15–19

Accuracy

```
15  own basic quiet stores design concept expensive restaurants
16  built style pipes range bright rubber window appeal designs
17  use and are they tech living modern useful designs changing
18  now but used come water things colors coming places enjoyed
```

Speed

```
19  glass daily wide zany such tire come like home with has not
20  homes given high tech name type long used they last now are
21  appeal living useful given basic things daily long type use
22  colors bright stores water pipes style glass range zany are
```

POSTTEST

Take another 3-minute timing on lines 6–14 to see how much your skill has improved.

FORMATTING SMALL ENVELOPES (NO. 6 3/4)

Envelopes contain two addresses—the *writer's return address* and the *mailing address,* to which the letter is sent.

1. To format a return address, begin ½ inch (5P/6E) from the left edge, on line 3. Single-space.
2. To format the mailing address, begin the addressee's name and address 2 inches (20P/24E) from the left edge, on line 12. Single-space.

In all addresses, type the city, state, and ZIP Code on one line. Remember to leave 1 space between the state and the ZIP Code.

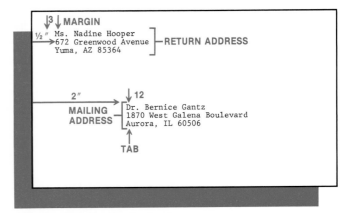

No. 6¾ (6½ by 3⅝ inches)

In 1980, 26 vendors were busy ⟨169⟩
selling there 80 different systems. In ⟨177⟩
1981 there were 56 vendors ~~selling 174~~ ⟨185⟩
~~models.~~ In 1985 there were over 75 ⟨192⟩
vendors selling over 200 models, and ⟨200⟩
this year the number of vendors has ⟨207⟩
exceeded 100. *TRANSPARENCY 2* ⟨210⟩
5 In 1980 there were not more than ⟨220⟩
1 million ~~1,000,000~~ word processing keyboards ⟨235⟩
in this country. In 1985 that number ⟨243⟩
had reached close to 2 million. Today, ⟨259⟩
nearly ④ out of every ⑤ white-collar ⟨268⟩
workers will use a keyboard device, and ⟨276⟩
nearly every manager will have the ⟨283⟩
power of a computer at his or her desk. ⟨291⟩
It has been said by some that ~~people~~ *I believe, those* ⟨301⟩
who know nothing about computers will ⟨308⟩
be as handicapped as those who do not ⟨316⟩
In 1990 we will reach close to 3 million.

possess the skills to read, to write, ⟨324⟩
or to do simple math problems. ¶A ⟨331⟩
bright future awaits those who choose ⟨339⟩
word processing as a career ~~in life.~~ A ⟨345⟩
career in this field offers good pay, ⟨353⟩
good working conditions, and the change ⟨361⟩
to work ~~yourself~~ *one* self up the career ladder. ⟨369⟩

<u>Transparency 3</u> ⟨379⟩
Here are some want ads from this ⟨387⟩
mornings paper that will show you, ⟨394⟩
for instance, just how many job opportunities are *out* ⟨405⟩
there each day that require someone ⟨412⟩
who has word processing skills. ⟨419⟩
Please share this information with ⟨426⟩
your ~~good~~ friends who you think might ⟨432⟩
want to apply for one of these jobs. ⟨440⟩
I thank you for inviting me here ⟨448⟩
~~today~~ to play a part in your meeting. ⟨455⟩
I wish you the best in the coming year. ⟨463⟩

LESSON 102

- **GOAL**
  To type a speech from handwritten copy.
- **FORMAT**
  Single spacing   60-space line

KEYBOARDING SKILLS

Type lines 1–4 once. In line 5 backspace and underscore each underlined word immediately after typing it. Repeat lines 1–4, or take a series of 1-minute timings.

Speed	1	It was not my duty to pay the bill when it was given to me.	12
Accuracy	2	Calm Rex Whit quit many jobs before driving for a park zoo.	12
Numbers	3	They hoped for 3856; only 2947 came. Those 10 did not pay.	12
Symbols	4	An asterisk (*) showed the loss to be $7946.50 as of 12/18.	12
Technique	5	It <u>is</u> not <u>up</u> to <u>us</u> to <u>pay</u> the <u>bill</u> by <u>the</u> time <u>we</u> get <u>home</u>.	

| 1 | 2 | 3 | 4 | 5 | 6 | 7 | 8 | 9 | 10 | 11 | 12

FOLDING LETTERS FOR SMALL ENVELOPES

To fold a letter for a small envelope, bring the bottom edge up to ⅜ inch (10 mm) from the top edge, fold the right-hand third toward the left, fold the left-hand third toward the right. Then insert the last crease into the envelope.

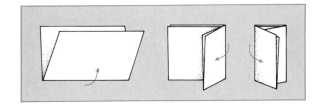

JOB 58 A. SMALL ENVELOPES

Address two envelopes as follows: (1) as shown in the illustration of the small envelope on page 101, and (2) for the letter in Job 57 A (page 99). Workbook 45.

JOB 58 B. PERSONAL-BUSINESS LETTER AND ENVELOPE

Standard format (page 100). Address a small envelope. Envelope: Workbook 47 top. Body 132 words.

Notice that the number 5 has been circled—the proofreaders' mark for spelling out a numeral.

/ means start a new line.
¶ means start a new paragraph.

618 Riverview Avenue/Parkersburg, WV 26101/November 19, 19--/LaViva Foods, Inc./1200 Grant Street/Trenton, NJ 08609/Ladies and Gentlemen:/Yesterday I bought ⑤ LaViva frozen pizzas for a party I had last night. Although I baked the pizzas as directed, the crust was tough, and the sauce was so bitter that we could not eat them. I had to throw them out. ¶Today I took my receipt to the Fair Price Market where I bought the pizzas. The manager gave me a refund; then he asked me to write to you because he thought that you should know about this problem. ¶I hope that you will check this matter so that your food products will always be up to your usual high standards. The code number on the boxes was CX-463./Yours truly,/Peggy Hamner

LESSON 59

■ GOALS
To recognize how numbers are expressed while typing sentences.
To type a personal-business letter.
To format and type a business letter.

■ FORMAT
Single spacing   60-space line

LAB 4

Number Style

Type lines 1–4 once. Then repeat lines 1–4 or take a series of 1-minute timings.

```
1   They have fine new offices at 171 Seventh Avenue in Queens.    12
2   The Orin Building is located at 56th Street and West Fifth.    12
3   They built a new zoo at 462 Sixth Avenue--or is it Seventh?    12
4   Our jet departs at 11:45 a.m. and arrives 30 minutes later.    12
    |  1  |  2  |  3  |  4  |  5  |  6  |  7  |  8  |  9  |  10  |  11  |  12
```

■ **GOALS**
To use commas correctly to set off nonessential elements while typing sentences.
To format and type a speech.

■ **FORMAT**
Single spacing   60-space line

LAB 10

Commas for Nonessential Elements

Workbook 145–146.

Type lines 1–4 once, providing the missing commas for each line. Edit your copy as your teacher reads the answers. Then retype lines 1–4 from your edited copy.

1 When will you and Marge arrive in Sacramento Mrs. Sanchez?
2 This is as you indicated your last chance to participate.
3 We look forward to hearing you speak to our group Dr. Lon.
4 The treasurer must therefore resign no later than Friday.

12-SECOND TIMINGS

Type each line three times, or take three 12-second timings on each line. For each timing, type with no more than 1 error.

5 Where in the world can we find an island on which to relax?
6 Once the rain began to pour, it just went on and on and on.
7 Now is the right time for you to buy all of the small toys.

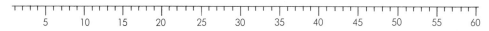

   5   10   15   20   25   30   35   40   45   50   55   60

FORMATTING SPEECHES

A speech is formatted very much like a report (see pages 87 and 95), but with a few changes:

1. Margins: 50-space line. (Use standard top and bottom margins for page 1 and for continuation pages.)

2. Triple-space for easier reading.

3. If audiovisual materials such as transparencies are used, indicate in the copy where they occur by centering TRANSPARENCY 1, TRANSPARENCY 2, and so on.

JOB 101 A. SPEECH
Standard format.

ds [THE STATUS OF WORD PROCESSING   18
         By (Your name)   34

(It's) a pleasure to be here in   43

Misoula for the Rocky Mountain Busi-   50

ness Conference. The title of my   57

speech, "The Status of Word Process-   64

ing", is one that, in all my years of   72

speaking, is the most enviable of all.   80

     Here we are just a few years be-   87

fore the turn of the century, experi-   94

encing today what many have entitled   102

an explosion *information* in information. Much of   109

this change in information *moreover,* has been   118

brought about by the advent of word   125

processing. let me give you *just a few* some   133

facts today to let you know ~~just~~ how   140

pronounced word processing has been   147

in the last few years.   152

         Transparency *1*   162

(Continued on next page)

Spell out street names from *first* through *tenth*; use figures for street names above *tenth*. Also use figures for all house numbers except *one: One Third Avenue, 12 West 22 Street, 7 Fifth Avenue.*

Use figures to express most periods of time: *45 minutes, 10:15 a.m., 7 o'clock, 30 days.* Use figures for dates: *May 9, 1989.*

30-SECOND SPEED TIMINGS

Take two 30-second speed timings on lines 5 and 6. Then take two 30-second speed timings on lines 7 and 8. Or type each sentence twice.

```
5  We hope to get a big order from one of the firms near here,   12
6  but we may not be lucky with them because of the bad times.   24
7  Sue did her best to get a pup that we can keep with us when   12
8  we take our trip to the coast the week after school is out.   24
   |  1  |  2  |  3  |  4  |  5  |  6  |  7  |  8  |  9  |  10  |  11  |  12
```

JOB 59 A. PERSONAL-BUSINESS LETTER
Standard format. Use your own return address and today's date; use your name as the writer. Address an envelope. Envelope: Workbook 47 bottom. Body 122 words.

Mr. Edward L. Brown, Manager / The Skyline Motel / Mercer, PA 16137 / Dear Mr. Brown: / Last week my two friends and I stayed at your motel for a weekend of skiing in the area. As members of the Skyline Ski Club and guests at your motel, we were to be given free ski-tow passes. ¶ When I got home, however, I checked the bill dated _____ [*Fill in last Sunday's date*] and discovered that we were charged $36 for the use of the ski tow. Since we are all members of the Skyline Ski Club, we should not have been charged for the use of these facilities. ¶ I would appreciate your taking the time to correct our bill and send me a check for the sum of $36, the amount of the overcharge. My address is at the top of this letter. / Sincerely,

FORMATTING BUSINESS LETTERS
Workbook 49–51.

A business letter represents a company, not an individual, and is therefore typed on official company stationery—"letterhead"—on which are printed the company's name, address, and, often, the telephone number.

The parts of the business letter—heading, opening, body, closing—are similar to the parts of the personal-business letter. However, there are some differences.

1. Most of the heading information is already included in the letterhead; only the date must be typed.

2. In a business letter the closing includes not only the writer's name but also his or her business title. (To-gether, the name and title lines are called the *writer's identification*.)

3. The closing in a business letter includes the typist's initials at the end (see page 104).

When formatting a business letter: (1) Type the date on line 15, beginning at the center. (2) Type the writer's title on the line below the writer's name, aligned with it. (3) Type the initials of the typist at the left margin, a double space below the writer's title. Type the initials without periods in either lowercase letters or all-capital letters.

This format is the one most commonly used in business and is considered to be the standard format. It is known as *modified-block style.*

JOB 59 B. BUSINESS LETTER
Type the letter on page 104. Standard format. Use your own initials as the typist. Workbook 53–54. Body 178 words.

GOALS

1. Demonstrate keyboarding speed and accuracy on straight copy with a goal of 38 words a minute for 5 minutes with 5 or fewer errors.

2. Correctly proofread copy for errors and edit copy for revision.

3. Apply more advanced production skills for formatting business documents from a variety of input modes.

4. Apply rules for correct use of commas, semicolons, colons, and plurals in written communications.

LaViva Foods

1200 Grant Street • Trenton, N J 08609

↓ 15

November 29, 19—

↓ 5

Ms. Peggy Hamner
618 Riverview Avenue
Parkersburg, WV 26101

↓ 2

Dear Ms. Hamner:

↓ 2

We are very sorry to learn that you could not eat the five LaViva frozen pizzas you bought at your local store last week. Thank you for writing to us about this matter. We want all our customers to be pleased with our products.

↓ 2

When our pizzas leave our plant, they are fresh, with all the flavor frozen in; but sometimes the shipper or the grocer does not put the pizzas in the freezer right away. The food begins to defrost, and when at last the pizzas are put in the freezer case, they have lost their true flavor. There is nothing we can do about this.

↓ 2

We want to give you a gift for trying to help us. If you will take this letter to your Fair Price store, your grocer will give you free $10 worth of LaViva frozen foods of your choice. We hope that you will enjoy these great foods and that you will continue to buy our pizzas.

↓ 2

Sincerely yours,

↓ 4

Dominic Sparanta

Dominic Sparanta
Vice President

↓ 2

CLOSING
Writer's name
and job title

kmk

**BUSINESS LETTER, STANDARD FORMAT
MODIFIED-BLOCK STYLE**

JOB 99/100 D. TWO-PAGE LETTER
Standard format. Workbook 143–144.

[Today's date] / Ms. Roberta T. Blake / Chair-person / Technology Fair / 5302 Belle Crest Lane / Silver Spring, MD 20906 / Dear Ms. Blake: / Peter Lee, president of Lee Business Schools, wants you to know that he is in full support of the program your group has planned to sponsor this coming summer. The concept that you outlined in your letter sounds most exciting, and Mr. Lee is pleased to accept your invitation to serve on the planning group that you have set up. He will attend the meeting that you have planned for next Monday noon. ¶ In giving some thought to your proposal, Mr. Lee talked with each of the directors of the three Lee Business Schools in the Washington area. Each would be proud to have his or her school take part in the fair, and each felt that the school could prepare for the fair at the same time it is preparing for the annual career day with which the Lee Business Schools close the term. Depending on how we could best help you, our schools could do something with you individu-ally or as a group. ¶ In answer to some of the questions raised in your letter, it is important to get the support of the entire business, lay, and civic community. Therefore, you should consider having a broad group of advisers to get the project under way. It may also be wise to appoint one individual to be chairperson of the advisory group. This, of course, should be a very capable man or woman who would make sure that all details are right. ¶ There will be a great deal of paperwork in this project, and there is a need for someone to keep up with it. Therefore, you will need to hire someone to handle the clerical and office duties. ¶ Again, please be assured that the staff and directors of the Lee Business Schools are excited about the prospects of a Technology Fair. It is felt that this type of project will be good for our area in many ways. Mr. Lee pledges his support for this task and will be glad to serve on the planning group and on any other task force to which you, Ms. Blake, may assign him. / Sincerely yours, / Marvin Conrad / Assistant to the President / [Your initials]

JOB 99/100 E. THREE-COLUMN TABLE
Standard format. Double-space on a full sheet of paper.

AFRICA'S LARGEST LAKES

Name of Lake	Square Miles	Location
Victoria*	26,828	Southeast Uganda
Tanganyika	12,700	Southeast Zaire
Nyasa	11,100	Southwest Tanzania
Chad	6,300	North-Central Africa
Rudolph	3,475	Northwest Kenya

Source: Information Please Almanac.
*Situated on the equator.

LESSON 60

■ **GOALS**
To identify how numbers are expressed while typing sentences.
To format and type large envelopes.
To type a business letter.

■ **FORMAT**
Single spacing   60-space line

LAB 4

Number Style

Type lines 1–4 once. Then repeat lines 1–4 or take a series of 1-minute timings.

1 My jet should depart at 10:47 a.m. and arrive at 12:34 p.m.   12
2 Eighty-six people will attend the workshop on September 21.   12
3 Meet Bart at 12 o'clock on 142d Street near Seventh Avenue.   12
4 Amy lives quietly on Third Avenue, but she prefers Seventh.   12

| 1 | 2 | 3 | 4 | 5 | 6 | 7 | 8 | 9 | 10 | 11 | 12

30-SECOND "OK" TIMINGS

Type as many 30-second "OK" timings as possible out of three attempts on lines 5–7.

5 All of us must make decisions every day. Some of these are   12
6 quite routine, but others can be of major importance. Good   24
7 citizens work at always making logical and exact decisions.   36

| 1 | 2 | 3 | 4 | 5 | 6 | 7 | 8 | 9 | 10 | 11 | 12

FORMATTING LARGE ENVELOPES (NO. 10)
Workbook 55–56.
To format a large envelope:

1. (*a*) Type a return address. Begin ½ inch from the left edge, on line 3. Single-space the address. **Or:** (*b*) If the envelope already has a printed return address,

FORMATTING SPECIAL DIRECTIONS
To format special directions:

1. Type an on-arrival direction (such as *Personal* or *Confidential*) on line 9, aligned at the left with the return address. Use capital and small letters, underscored.

type the sender's name on the line above the address. Block the name if the address is blocked; center the name if the address is centered.

2. Begin the mailing address 4 inches (40P/50E) from the left edge, on line 14. Single-space the address; leave only 1 space between the state and ZIP Code.

2. Type a mailing direction (such as *Special Delivery* or *Registered*) on line 9, ending about ½ inch from the right edge of the envelope. Use all-capital letters. Do not underscore.

The format used for this illustration is recommended by the U.S. Postal Service for automated handling. The address is typed in all-capital letters with no punctuation; the ZIP + 4 Code is also illustrated.

This format is faster to type on a computer because you do not have to release the shift lock for the numbers.

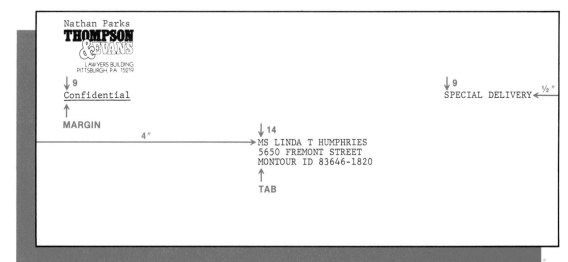

No. 10 (9½ by 4⅛ inches)

JOB 99/100 A. LONG REPORT
Space-saving format.

CREATURES FROM "DOWN UNDER"
By Sharon T. Cole

The most curious creature that lives on the other side of our globe is none other than the kangaroo. Kangaroos are well known for their sturdy, powerful hind legs and for their secluded pouches in which they carry their young. This report will reveal some of the important facts about this "rabbitlike" mammal.

PHYSICAL CHARACTERISTICS
Kangaroos have either gray or red fur, stand close to 7 feet tall when full grown, and weigh close to 200 pounds. They travel by jumping on their powerful hind legs, sometimes leaping at the rate of nearly 30 miles per hour for short distances. Their tails act as levers when they are running at a fast pace and as stools on which they may rest when they are standing still.

FAMILY LIFE
The male kangaroo accepts no responsibility for the newborn kangaroo. It is the mother's responsibility to feed and shelter the baby. The kangaroo's family life appears to be rather casual, and there are seldom any long-term commitments to any one group. Kangaroos live 7 years, with a few of them surviving until they are 20 years old. The greatest enemy of the kangaroo is drought, but some of the species are killed by hunters and wild dogs.

LIVING HABITS
Kangaroos live both in tropical forests and on the plains. They have very sharp teeth that enable them to eat the grasses much closer to the ground than most other mammals can eat. They are a nuisance to stock raisers because they eat the grass that is needed for the raising of livestock such as sheep and cattle.

JOB 99/100 B. MEMORANDUM
Standard format. Use today's date. Workbook 141.

(To:) Sue Booth, president, South Side High Business Club / (From:) Tom Dunn, President, Green High Business Club / (Subject:) Joint Meeting

I have enclosed a copy of the rough draft of the program for the next joint meeting of our clubs, which we discussed on the telephone last week. Notice, Sue, that I have moved the date from March 10 to April 6 because of a conflict with a basketball game. ¶ Please talk over the events planned with your officers and make any changes you like. Then call me before the end of the week so that I can get my members working on the details. / TD / (Your initials) / Enclosure

JOB 99/100 C. TABLE WITH LEADERS
Standard format. Half sheet of paper. 40-space line.

AVERAGE MILES PER GALLON
(TOTAL DISTANCE TRAVELED: 9000 MILES)

MONTH	MILES PER GALLON
JANUARY	25.6
FEBRUARY	27.3
MARCH	25.8
APRIL	26.9
MAY	24.7
JUNE	23.1
AVERAGE	25.6

FOLDING LETTERS FOR LARGE ENVELOPES

To fold a letter for a large envelope, fold up the bottom third of the paper, fold the top third over the bottom third, and insert the letter into the envelope, with the last crease going in first.

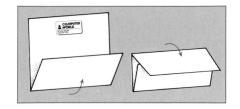

JOB 60 A. LARGE ENVELOPES
Address two envelopes, using the copy given in (1) the illustration on page 105 and (2) the letter on page 104. Workbook 57.

JOB 60 B. BUSINESS LETTER
Standard format. Workbook 59–60. Body 111 words.

Remember:

Titles of books and magazines are underscored with an unbroken line.

[*Today's date*] / Ms. Jane Petit / 3434 Paris Avenue / New Orleans, LA 70122 / Dear Ms. Petit: / Thank you for your letter telling us how much you enjoyed the story that appeared in the June issue of <u>Young Views</u> about new careers in the health field. ¶ We are sending you the booklet you asked for, <u>Your Future as a Health Worker</u>. There is, of course, no charge for the booklet. ¶ We hope that you will continue to follow your plans to train for a job in the health professions. If we can be of any further service to you, please write to us or call our toll-free number: (800) 555-6000. / Very truly yours, / Henry J. Templer / Editor in Chief / [*Your initials*]

LESSON 61

■ **GOALS**
To express numbers correctly while typing sentences.
To type 34/3'/5e.
To format and type business letters with enclosures.

■ **FORMAT**
Drills: Single spacing   60-space line
3-Minute Timings: Double spacing   5-space tab

LAB 4

Number Style

Type lines 1–4 once, correcting any errors in number-style rules. Edit your copy as your teacher reads the answers. Then retype lines 1–4 from your edited copy.

1. His jet from Mexico to Quebec leaves at eight-fifteen p.m. today.
2. You are invited to attend our sorority meeting at two-thirty p.m.
3. She bought 2 new skirts and 3 blazers on December fifteenth.
4. I walked down 6th Avenue last evening looking for a taxi.

PREVIEW PRACTICE

Type lines 5–6 twice on page 93 as a preview to the 3-minute timing on page 93.

3-MINUTE TIMINGS

Take two 3-minute timings on lines 7–15 on page 93.

FORMATTING SOURCE NOTES

A source note explains where the information used in a table originated. It is typed exactly like a footnote in a table, except the word *Source:* precedes the note instead of an asterisk or some other symbol.

JOB 98 B. TABLE WITH LEADERS

Type the table in the column to the right. Standard format.

CLIMATIC Extremes

Measurement	Extreme
Highest Temperature · · · · · ·	136 degrees
Lowest Temperature · · · · · · ·	-127 degrees
Greatest rainfall · · · · · · · ·	74 inches*
Longest hotspell · · · · · · · ·	862 days**
Greatest snowfall · · · · · · · ·	76 inches*

Source: Information Please Almanac.

* In 24 hours.
** 100 degrees Fahrenheit or above.

LESSONS 99/100

TEST

- **GOALS**
  To type 36/5'/5e.
  To demonstrate competency in typing a report, a memo, a leadered table, a letter, and a ruled table.

- **FORMAT**
  Double spacing   60-space line   5-space tab

PREVIEW PRACTICE

Type each line twice as a preview to the 5-minute timings below.

Accuracy 1 physical equipment processor expensive component definition
Speed   2 byte home make that this used want what when will word your

5-MINUTE TIMINGS

Take two 5-minute timings on lines 3–17.

```
 3       In a previous timing you were given the definitions of    12
 4  the words "boot" and "byte" as they pertain to computers or    24
 5  word processors.  In this timing you will be presented with    36
 6  definitions for hardware and software, two terms that exist    48
 7  in an office and that are used often in the computer world.    60
 8       Hardware is the physical equipment that is used in the    72
 9  computer system.  It may refer to the terminal, the screen,    84
10  the disk drive, the printer, or any physical component used    96
11  for the system.  Hardware is often the most expensive item.  108
12       Software refers to written programs that make the com-   120
13  puter do what you want it to do.  Software can aid you when   132
14  you must type a letter, add or subtract a long list of num-  144
15  bers, organize a home file, draw a picture, or create a new  156
16  program.  The price of software for your use can range from  168
17  just over ten dollars to hundreds of dollars for a package.  180
```

| 1 | 2 | 3 | 4 | 5 | 6 | 7 | 8 | 9 | 10 | 11 | 12 | SI 1.44

FORMATTING ENCLOSURE NOTATIONS

Whenever an item is sent with a letter, the word *Enclosure* is typed on the line below the reference initials. The enclosure notation reminds the sender to include the item, tells the receiver to look for the item, and serves as a record on the file copy. For more than one item, type *2 Enclosures, 3 Enclosures,* and so on.

```
                              John Harman Jones
                              President

TCW
3 Enclosures
```

JOB 61 A. BUSINESS LETTER WITH ENCLOSURE

Standard format (see page 103). Prepare two envelopes. Address a large envelope to the addressee of the letter (Mr. Martino). Address a small envelope to Mr. Alfred J. Leary to be enclosed with the letter. Use the address on the letterhead. Workbook 61–62. Body 87 words.

[Today's date]/Mr. Rudolph Martino/ 121 Newton Street/Jackson, MS 39209/Dear Mr. Martino:/ We are pleased that you plan to enter our pizza bake-off contest and test your skills in making pizza. ¶ The first round of the bake-off will be on Sunday, May 10, at 1 p.m. at the Chicago Food Show. You must be eighteen years old or under to enter, and we ask that you bring all your own supplies. Twenty-six persons have already entered. ¶ If you will need a hotel room in Chicago, please use the enclosed envelope to send me your reservation request. Good luck next Sunday./ Sincerely yours,/ Alfred J. Leary / Director of Public Relations /[Your initials]/ Enclosure

JOB 61 B. BUSINESS LETTER WITH ENCLOSURE

Standard format. Prepare the enclosure in Job 61 C. Workbook 63–64. Body 77 words.

(Today's date)/Mrs. Horton A. Smithworth/ Pleasantview Avenue/Falmouth, MA 02540/ 41 Banksville Road/

Dear Mrs. Smithworth:/We have enclosed a listing some of our informal pretrip study programs. the price of pretrip classes are included in the price of any trip you decided to take advanttage. We think that you will want to take advantage of this unique opportunity to enrich your knowledge and understanding of various country by joining one of our groups. ¶ To register, just circle the pretrip class of your choice on the enclosed listing and return it to our office./sincerely yours,/Helene Lindsey Lee/(Your initials) /Enclosure

JOB 61 C. ENCLOSURE

Format attractively on a full sheet of paper.

```
PRETRIP CLASSES
Gulliver's Travels
Spring, 19--
Morocco:  The Land of Many Moods
India:  A Vacationer's Nirvana
Cruise the Yangtze Inland Cities of China
Galapagos Islands Wildlife Sanctuary
Ancient Greece and Jerusalem
The Adriatic Sea and Yugoslavia
Fly to Egypt and Sail the Red Sea
```

Take two 5-minute timings on lines 7–21.

```
                                    1                          2
7        We have heard in recent years that our nation needs to        12
          3                          4
8   conserve its energy.  This is, of course, quite a task, and        24
     5                      6                              7
9   we must contribute in whatever way we can to this activity.        36
                          8                      9
10       For energy conservation to work, please realize we are        48
          10                  11                          12
11  requiring sacrifices.  We may not be able to keep our homes        60
                      13                      14
12  as warm in the winters or as cool in the summers as before.        72
                  15                      16
13       Putting better insulation in our houses will also help        84
     17                  18                      19
14  in the conservation program.  By doing so, we let less heat        96
                  20                          21
15  escape through walls and ceilings.  Insulating stops waste.        108
              22                      23                      24
16       To help save energy, all of us should turn off all the        120
                          25                      26
17  extra lights in our houses when the rooms are not occupied.        132
                  27                      28
18  Over a period of months, a great deal of fuel can be saved.        144
          29                      30                      31
19       We should also save energy by carpooling when going to        156
                      32                      33
20  work.  If just four of us ride together on the way to work,        168
          34                      35                      36
21  we will use only a quarter of the gas used if we all drove.        180
    | 1 | 2 | 3 | 4 | 5 | 6 | 7 | 8 | 9 | 10 | 11 | 12    SI 1.39
```

FORMATTING TABLES WITH LEADERS

Workbook 139.

You learned to use leaders in a table of contents. Leaders are often used in tables to spread a table to fill a specific line length, or they are used when the entries in the first column vary greatly in length. Leaders are especially helpful in financial statements, programs, and menus.
  To format leadered tables:

1. Set the left margin and tab stops for the table.

2. Find the point on the scale where the final period on each line of leaders will be typed. The final period should be 1 blank space before the longest item in the second column.

3. Type the first item in the first line, space once, and type the line of periods. Remember to stop 1 space before the item in the second column.

4. Repeat Step 3 for each item.

JOB 98 A. TWO-COLUMN TABLE WITH LEADERS

Standard format. Half sheet of paper. 40-space line.

SCHOOL LUNCH ENTREES

Greenville High School

Monday .... Turkey with dressing

Tuesday .... *Hot beef sandwich*

Wednesday .... Tacos and beans

Thursday .... *Barbecue with chips*

Friday .... *Tuna Casserole*

LESSON 62

■ **GOALS**
To improve keyboarding of numbers.
To type 34/3'/5e.

■ **FORMAT**
Drills: Single spacing   60-space line
3-Minute Timings: Double spacing   5-space tab

KEYBOARDING SKILLS

Type lines 1–4 once. Then do what line 5 tells you to do. Repeat lines 1–4, or take a series of 1-minute timings.

Speed
Accuracy
Numbers
Symbols
Technique

1 The man is to go to town and then make six panels for them.   12
2 My fine black ax just zipped through the wood quite evenly.   12
3 The 56 boys and 38 girls ate 29 pies and 47 pancakes today.   12
4 These forms cost 10¢, 29¢, and 38¢ each, depending on size.   12
5 Type line 3; then underscore the words but not the numbers.

| 1 | 2 | 3 | 4 | 5 | 6 | 7 | 8 | 9 | 10 | 11 | 12

PRETEST

Take a 2-minute timing on lines 6–10. Circle and count your errors.

6 woe 293 per 034 tot 595 pet 035 tip 580 owe 923 pow 092 092   12
7 tip 580 yip 680 row 492 tow 592 you 697 tie 583 tee 533 533   24
8 wet 235 pie 083 rip 480 pit 085 rut 475 pop 090 too 599 599   36
9 were 2343 your 6974 tire 5843 pour 0974 weep 2330 pity 0856   48
10 wire 2843 pout 9075 toot 5995 peep 0330 type 5603 pyre 0643   60

| 1 | 2 | 3 | 4 | 5 | 6 | 7 | 8 | 9 | 10 | 11 | 12

PRACTICE

Type each line once; then repeat the lines for number keys you missed in the Pretest.

11 1221 1331 1441 1551 1661 1771 1881 1991 1001 1231 1901 1561
12 and 12 and 13 and 14 and 15 and 16 and 17 and 18 and 19 and

13 2112 2002 2332 2992 2442 2882 2552 2772 2662 2390 2487 2576
14 were 2343 wire 2843 weep 2330 wipe 2803 wiry 2846 writ 2485

15 3113 3003 3223 3993 3443 3883 3553 3663 3773 3483 3563 3783
16 tee 533 err 344 ewe 323 eye 363 wee 233 peep 0330 pier 0834

17 4114 4004 4224 4994 4334 4884 4554 4774 4884 4293 4583 4740
18 rope 4903 rout 4975 root 4995 rote 4953 ripe 4803 wore 2943

19 5115 5005 5225 5995 5335 5885 5445 5665 5775 5394 5465 5803
20 tire 5843 tree 5433 tore 5943 toot 5995 type 5603 trip 5480

21 6116 6006 6226 6996 6336 6886 6446 6776 6556 6394 6582 6702
22 eye 363 yew 632 yet 635 you 697 yip 680 yore 6943 your 6974

23 7117 7007 7227 7997 7337 7887 7447 7667 7557 7392 7463 7850
24 rut 475 pup 070 our 974 put 075 out 975 true 5473 pure 0743

25 8118 8008 8228 8998 8338 8778 8448 8668 8558 8340 8473 8605
26 wire 2843 pity 0856 pipe 0803 wipe 2803 wiry 2846 writ 2485

27 9119 9009 9229 9889 9779 9339 9449 9669 9559 9450 9382 9704
28 to 59 or 94 too 599 our 974 ore 943 row 492 owe 923 woo 299

29 0110 0990 0220 0880 0330 0770 0440 0660 0550 0260 0837 0462
30 pity 0856 pipe 0803 poor 0994 prop 0490 putt 0755 prey 0436

JOB 97 B. THREE-COLUMN TABLE
Standard format.

SEVEN WONDERS OF THE WORLD
By Sharon Thompson

Structure	Location	Date of Construction*
Colossus	Rhodes (Greece)	280 B.C.
Hanging Gardens	Babylon (Iraq)	600 B.C.
Mausoleum	Halicarnassus (Turkey)	350 B.C.
Pharos	Alexandria (Egypt)	270 B.C.
Pyramids	Giza (Egypt)	2800 B.C.
Statue of Zeus	Olympia (Greece)	500 B.C.
Temple of Artemis	Ephesus (Turkey)	350 B.C.

*Dates listed are approximate.

LESSON 98

■ GOALS
To use commas correctly to set off nonessential elements while typing sentences.
To type 36/5'/5e.
To format and type leadered tables.
To format and type source notes in tables.

■ FORMAT
Drills: Single spacing   60-space line
5-Minute Timings: Double spacing   5-space tab

LAB 10

Commas for Nonessential Elements

Type lines 1–4 once, providing the missing commas. Edit your copy as your teacher reads the answers. Then retype lines 1–4 from your edited copy.

1 Petersen Industries in my opinion should handle this job.
2 We must of course be certain to submit our bid by June 4.
3 If the projects are late however they will not be graded.
4 When you arrive in San Jose Mr. Sands they will meet you.

PREVIEW PRACTICE

Accuracy

Speed

Type each line twice as a preview to the 5-minute timings on page 166.

5 quite extra realize quarter occupied requiring conservation
6 energy nation might those also turn fuel work ride this and

Take another 2-minute timing on lines 6–10 on page 108 to see how much your skill has improved.

3-MINUTE TIMINGS

Take two 3-minute timings on lines 31–39.

```
                    1              2              3              4
31        The Leeds firm now has 54 stores, located in 30 cities    12
              5              6              7              8
32   in the West.  Leeds has a staff of 147 women and 138 men, a    24
              9             10             11             12
33   total of 285 workers, in its stores.  The products that are    36
             13             14             15             16
34   sold are supplied by some 90 firms, located in more than 26    48
             17             18             19             20
35   states.  These facts are pretty exciting when you know that    60
             21             22             23             24
36   the unique firm did not get into business until after 1967.    72
             25             26             27             28
37   In spite of so late a start in the field, this firm now has    84
             29             30             31             32
38   a strong hold on a large portion of the market.  Leeds tops    96
                    33             34
39   its competitors in most cities.                               102
     |  1  |  2  |  3  |  4  |  5  |  6  |  7  |  8  |  9  | 10  | 11  | 12    SI 1.25
```

UNIT 11 Formatting Tables
UNIT GOAL 35/3'/5e

■ GOALS
To express numbers correctly while typing sentences.
To format and type two- and three-column tables.

■ FORMAT
Single spacing   60-space line

LAB 4

Number Style

Workbook 67–68.

Type lines 1–4 once, correcting any errors in number-style rules. Edit your copy as your teacher reads the answers. Then retype lines 1–4 from your edited copy.

1   Should Jack go to 6th Street or to 8th Avenue for fun?
2   They live near 16th Street; she lives closer to twenty-third Street.
3   Their plane stopped for forty-five minutes in Iraq around 6:30 a.m.
4   18 zealots have studied for the bar exams since 1985.

SKILL DEVELOPMENT DRILL

Type each line twice.

Speed
5   Did she pay the neighbor to fix the oaken box for the coal?
6   I am to go to work for the audit firm by the end of August.

Accuracy
7   Jeff amazed the audience by quickly giving six new reports.
8   Five bright boys could work extra now to pass a major quiz.

Numbers
9   We sold 2938 on May 2, 3847 on June 9, and 5620 on July 15.
10 Those flights leave at 10:29 a.m., 2:47 p.m., and 6:38 p.m.

Symbols
11 The five maple boards measured 10", 29", 38", 47", and 56".
12 I bought 10 shares @ 29, 38 shares @ 47, and 56 shares @ 1.

30-SECOND "OK" TIMINGS

Type as many 30-second "OK" (errorless) timings as possible out of three attempts on lines 5–7.

```
5  Jack, you know, gave two of his prize boxers to his friend,    12
6  but he was not willing to give up any of his pet dachshunds    24
7  or terriers because he had invested a lot of hours in them.    36
   |  1  |  2  |  3  |  4  |  5  |  6  |  7  |  8  |  9  | 10 | 11 | 12
```

FORMATTING TABLES WITH FOOTNOTES

Workbook 137–138.

When a footnote appears in a table, it is typed much the same as a footnote in a report. To format footnotes in unruled and ruled tables:

Tables Without Ruled Lines. (1) Separate the footnote from the body of the table with a 1-inch (10P/12E) underscore. (2) Single-space before typing the underscore; double-space after it. (3) Type an asterisk or some other symbol at the beginning of a footnote to indicate its use in the table. (4) Type short footnotes beginning at the left margin; single-space between footnotes. (5) Indent the first line of long (2-line) footnotes 5 spaces; type turnover lines beginning at the left margin; double-space between footnotes. (Do not mix styles in the same table—if one footnote is long, use the long format for all footnotes.)

Tables With Ruled Lines. (1) Type the footnote a double space below the final rule. (2) Follow Steps 3 through 5 under "Tables Without Ruled Lines."

Note: The symbol used in the body of a table to indicate a footnote reference (such as an asterisk) should be counted as part of the key line if it follows the longest entry in the column.

Production Practice. Set the left margin at 20, a tab at 40, and a tab at 60. Single spacing. Clean sheet of paper. Use the table illustrated below.

Space down to line 7, and type the last line of the table. Return the carriage or carrier once. Type a rule that extends from the left margin to 3 spaces after the last character in column 3. Return twice. Type the footnote. Check your work.

Remove your paper from the typewriter, and insert it upside down. Space down to line 7, and type the last line of the table. Return once. Type a 1-inch rule. Return twice. Type the footnote. Check your work.

JOB 97 A. THREE-COLUMN TABLE
Standard format. Half sheet of paper.

STATES BORDERING PERU

(Listed Alphabetically)

Country	Position of Border	Length of Border*
Bolivia	East	450
Brazil	East	850
Chile	South	90
Columbia	North	600
Ecuador	North	600

*In miles.

FORMATTING TABLES

A table lists data in columns and rows. For quick understanding and easy reference, tables are worded concisely.

A table can be included as part of a letter, memo, or report, or it can be displayed on a separate sheet of paper.

When a table is typed on a separate sheet of paper, standard formatting instructions apply: center the table horizontally and vertically, and double-space unless directed otherwise.

To format the body of a table horizontally, follow these steps:

1. Clear the margins and tabs on the machine.

2. Identify a "key line." Find the longest entry in each column and add 6 spaces between the columns, as shown in Job 63 A below.

(**Note:** Six spaces are standard, but you may use any number of spaces that will make the table attractive and easy to read.)

3. From the center of the page, backspace-center the key line and set the left margin stop at the point to which you backspaced.

4. Space across the paper to the start of the next column (the width of column 1 plus 6 spaces) and set a tab stop. No matter how many columns there are in the table, use the margin stop for the first column and a tab stop for each additional column.

5. When you type a table, use the tabulator to move from column to column as you type each line.

Production Practice. Clear all margins and tab stops. Single spacing. Clean sheet of paper. Use the table illustrated below.

Move the carriage or carrier to the centering point. Backspace-center the key line—*To Kill a Mockingbird######Shakespeare.* Set the left margin stop at the point to which you backspaced. Space once for every letter and space in the words *To Kill a Mockingbird.* Space once for each of the 6 spaces between the columns. Set a tab stop at the point to which you spaced. Return the carriage or carrier to the left margin.

Space down to line 7. Move the carriage or carrier to the centering point. Backspace-center the title of the table—*CLASSICS FOR TEENAGERS.* Triple-space (return the carriage or carrier three times). Set your machine for double spacing. Type the first line in column 1—*Animal Farm.* Press the tabulator to reach the tab stop set for column 2. Type the first line in column 2—*Orwell.* Return the carriage or carrier. Type the fifth line in column 1—*Romeo and Juliet.* Tab to column 2. Type the fifth line in column 2—*Shakespeare.*

Remove your paper from the typewriter. Fold the paper in half and check your horizontal centering. Clear all margins and tab stops. Reinsert your paper upside down. Redo the practice. Check your work.

JOB 63 A. TWO-COLUMN TABLE
Standard format. Half sheet of paper.

TITLE	CLASSICS FOR TEENAGERS	
BODY WITH TWO COLUMNS	Animal Farm	Orwell
	Frankenstein	Shelley
	Lord of the Flies	Golding
Column width is determined by longest item in a column.	Moby Dick	Melville
	Romeo and Juliet	Shakespeare
	To Kill a Mockingbird	Lee

	↓ Margin	↓ Tab
KEY LINE	To Kill a Mockingbird	Shakespeare
	123456	

JOB 96 A. FOUR-COLUMN TABLE

Standard format. Type the table to the right.

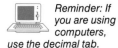 *Reminder: If you are using computers, use the decimal tab.*

CHEMICAL ELEMENTS
(Noble Gases)

Name	Chemical[8] Symbol	Atomic Weight	Date of Discovery [9]
Argon	Ar	39.948	1894
Helium	He	4.0026 [8]	1895
Krypton [7]	Kr	83.80	1898
Neon	Ne	20.183	1898
Radon	Rn	122.00	1900
Xenon	Xe	131.30	1898

JOB 96 B. FIVE-COLUMN TABLE

Standard format.

ESTIMATED POPULATION GROWTH
(Population in Millions)

City	1986 Population [10]	2000 Population [10]	Percent Increase [8]	2000 Rank [4]
Cairo	9.1	26.7	193.4	5
Jakarta	9.2	27.3	196.7	4
Karachi	8.2	23.3	184.1	6
Mexico City [11]	17.3	30.1	74.0	1
São Paulo	17.2	29.8	73.3	2
Shanghai	13.3	29.7	123.3	3
AVERAGES	12.4	27.8	140.8	—

LESSON 97

■ GOALS
To identify how commas set off nonessential elements while typing sentences.
To improve accuracy on "OK" timings.
To format and type tables with footnotes.

■ FORMAT
Single spacing   60-space line

LAB 10

Commas for Nonessential Elements

Type lines 1–4 once. Then repeat lines 1–4 or take a series of 1-minute timings.

```
1  Please let me know, Dr. Chen, if I can do anything for you.   12
2  She will not, therefore, buy it without a service contract.   12
3  You should be aware of all of the qualifications, Ms. Lund.   12
4  Dr. Robert T. Ellinger will, I expect, accept the position.   12
   |  1  |  2  |  3  |  4  |  5  |  6  |  7  |  8  |  9  |  10  |  11  |  12
```

JOB 63 B. THREE-COLUMN TABLE
Standard format.

HOME TEAMS IN VARIOUS STATES

Florida	Miami	Dolphins
Georgia	Atlanta	Falcons
Illinois	Chicago	Bears
Indiana	Indianapolis	Colts
Missouri	St. Louis	Cardinals
New York	Buffalo	Bills
Texas	Houston	Oilers
Washington	Seattle	Seahawks
Wisconsin	Green Bay	Packers

LESSON 64

■ **GOALS**
To type 35/3'/5e.
To format and type tables with subtitles, numbers, and decimals.

■ **FORMAT**
Drills: Single spacing   60-space line
3-Minute Timings: Double spacing   5-space tab

KEYBOARDING SKILLS

Type lines 1–4 once. Then do what line 5 tells you to do. Repeat lines 1–4, or take a series of 1-minute timings.

Speed   1 When we go to town, we may very well visit our best friend. 12
Accuracy   2 Ask Jack Sworcz if he can quickly fix five machines for us. 12
Numbers   3 Betty left her office at 38 First Street at 6:10 on May 29. 12
Symbols   4 For $9 more (plus tax) she can get 32% more grain––only $9! 12
Technique   5 Retype line 3, underscoring each of the numbers in the sentence.

| 1 | 2 | 3 | 4 | 5 | 6 | 7 | 8 | 9 | 10 | 11 | 12

PRETEST

Take a 3-minute timing on lines 6–14. Circle and count your errors.

```
                     1               2               3               4
6        Quilts, or padded covers used on top of beds as lovely   12
              5           6               7              8
7    spreads or just bedding, have a long history.  Quilting has   24
                      9             10            11
8    been done worldwide and has been considered as an art.        35
          12            13              14              15
9        A large part of the social life of our rural folks was    12
          16              17              18              19
10   built around a group party, like a quilting bee.  The women   24
          20          21              22          23
11   in a village often met and made many new, warm quilts.        35
                  24              25              26              27
12       Quilts that were made of strips of cloth of all colors    12
              28              29              30              31
13   and of crooked shapes were called crazy quilts.  These were   24
                  32              33              34              35
14   a part of the exciting days of our early Western life.        35
```

| 1 | 2 | 3 | 4 | 5 | 6 | 7 | 8 | 9 | 10 | 11 | 12   SI 1.27

LESSON 96

■ **GOALS**
To recognize how commas set off nonessential elements while typing sentences.
To format and type tables with two-line column headings.
To format and type decimals in tables.

■ **FORMAT**
Single spacing   60-space line

LAB 10

Commas for Nonessential Elements

Type lines 1–4 once. Then repeat lines 1–4 or take a series of 1-minute timings.

```
1  It is, however, not the exact model she would like to have.  12
2  You will, nonetheless, be required to operate the computer.  12
3  Jackie, in any event, will take the word processing course.  12
4  Paul will, therefore, be the new secretary of our fan club.  12
   |  1  |  2  |  3  |  4  |  5  |  6  |  7  |  8  |  9  |  10  |  11  |  12
```

Words, phrases, or clauses that are not essential to the meaning of a sentence are set off by commas. Names in direct address are also considered nonessential. Use two commas to set off nonessential elements within a sentence. Use one comma if a nonessential element appears at the end or at the beginning of a sentence.

We are planning, *as you know,* to reject their offer.
A quantity discount is available, *of course.*
Lisa requested, *moreover,* that the catalog be reprinted.
You will receive a copy, *Mrs. James,* with your next invoice. (Direct address)

FORMATTING TWO-LINE COLUMN HEADINGS

When a column heading is much longer than any item in the column, the column heading may be typed on two (or more) lines.

To format two-line column headings:

1. Center each line. Subtract (*a*) the number of characters in the shorter line from (*b*) the number of characters in the longer line.

2. Divide that answer by 2 (drop any fraction), and indent the shorter line by that number of spaces. In the example, $9 - 5 = 4$, and $4 \div 2 = 2$.

Indent the shorter line 2 spaces, as in this example:

Suggested ←9
Price ←5

3. Underscore the words in each line of the heading in open tables; do not underscore in ruled tables.

4. If the table contains both one- and two-line headings (such as in Job 96 A), align the one-line heading with the second line of the two-line heading.

FORMATTING DECIMALS IN TABLES

Numbers usually align at the right; however, in decimals, the decimal points must be aligned. If the numbers following the decimal point are not the same number of digits, the key line may have to be a combination of two lines, as illustrated in Job 96 A on page 163, where the width of column 3 is *122.* plus *0026.*

PRACTICE

Take a 1-minute timing on each paragraph of the Pretest (page 111).

POSTTEST

Take another 3-minute timing on lines 6–14 on page 111 to see how much your skill has improved.

FORMATTING SUBTITLES IN TABLES

Workbook 69.

Subtitles in tables are formatted the same way as subtitles in other documents: (1) Center the subtitles. (2) Double-space before and triple-space after subtitles. (3) Use initial caps.

If a subtitle takes more than 1 line, single-space the lines.

NUMBERS IN COLUMNS

On computers, word processors, and electronic typewriters a decimal tab will automatically align the figures without the need to space forward or backward.

Align Numbers. Numbers are aligned at the right. If a column of numbers contains items with decimals or amounts of money with decimals, as shown at the right, the decimals should be aligned.

Key Line. Use the longest item in the column—just as you would if the column contained words. If the column contains a dollar sign, be sure to include it in the key line.

Margin and Tabs. Since spacing forward and backward will be needed to align the numbers at the right, set the margin or tab stops for the digit that requires the least forward and backward spacing (note where the margin and the tabs were set for the illustration at the right).

```
           HEMP'S DEPARTMENT STORE
                                          ↓ 2
              Fall Clearance Sale
                                          ↓ 3

   564        Silk Ties              $10. 62

    19        Belts                     1. 43

     5        Wool Sweaters           19. 95

  1500        Pairs Socks                . 75
   M          T                        T
```

Production Practice. Set your left margin stop at 40; set a tab stop at 50. Double spacing. Clean sheet of paper. Use the table illustrated above. You will type only the number columns—columns 1 and 3.

Space down to line 7. Type the first number in column 1 at the margin. Tab to the tab stop. Backspace once. Type the $ and the first number in column 3. Return. Space once and type the second number in column 1. Tab. Space once and type the second number in column 3. Return. Space twice; type the third number in column 1. Tab. Type the third number in column 3. Return. Press the margin release key and backspace once. Type the last number in column 1. Tab. Space twice and type the last number in column 3. Check your work. Do all the numbers line up at the right?

JOB 64 A. THREE-COLUMN TABLE

Type the illustration above on Hemp's Department Store. Standard format (see page 110). Half sheet of paper.

JOB 64 B. THREE-COLUMN TABLE

Standard format. Half sheet of paper.

ASTRO CONSTRUCTION
Number of Employees
June 30

Warehouse	Lima, Ohio	116
Plant	Denver, Colo.	1235
Office	New York, N.Y.	954
Branch	Seattle, Wash.	28
Branch	Chicago, Ill.	39
Branch	Atlanta, Ga.	9
Branch	Dallas, Tex.	11

```
14      If you have had an opportunity to use word processing,      12
15   you have most likely come across a number of new terms that    24
16   you have not heard before.  The number of new words that we    36
17   have acquired in word processing expands every day; the two    48
18   in this text are recognized by many.                            55
19      To "boot" means that you are getting the system going.      67
20   Before you can create any documents on the computer, you're    79
21   going to have to boot it.  When booting the system, you are    91
22   loading a series of commands and/or data into the computer;   103
23   and this data usually is sent to the computer from the disk   115
24   drive that is often attached.                                  121
25      A "byte" is one unit of data--a letter or a space, for     133
26   example.  Each letter or each space is called a byte of in-    145
27   formation.  For example, the first day of the week, Sunday,    157
28   consists of six bytes; the first month of the year consists   169
29   of seven bytes; and the current year is just four bytes.      180
```

| 1 | 2 | 3 | 4 | 5 | 6 | 7 | 8 | 9 | 10 | 11 | 12 | SI,1.39

FORMATTING TOTAL LINES IN TABLES

A total (or average) line may appear in a table to total (or average) one or more columns.

To format a total line in unruled and ruled tables:

Tables Without Ruled Lines. (1) Type an underscore directly under the last amount, on the same line. (2) Make the underscore the same width as the longest entry in the column. (3) Double-space before typing the total.

Tables With Ruled Lines. Precede and follow the total with a ruled line that extends the full width of the table.

Single-space before the ruled lines, and double-space after them.

Note: The word *total* or *average* may be typed in initial caps or in all-capital letters.

When no total (or average) is applicable to a column, type hyphens to the full width of the column. It is preferable to use the ruled format when some columns are not totaled. (See Job 95 A below.)

JOB 95 A. FOUR-COLUMN TABLE

Standard format (page 159). Double-space on a full sheet of paper.

Data Entry Equipment
(Regional Centers)

Location	Units	Total Cost	Unit Cost
Atlanta	22	$ 26,400	$ 1200
Austin	17	25,500	1500
Chicago	31	43,400	1400
New York	36	43,200	1200
San Francisco	24	38,400	1600
Seattle	28	33,600	1200
Total Value	--	$210,500	- - - -

■ GOALS
To recognize how commas are used in series while typing sentences.
To format and type tables with short column headings.

■ FORMAT
Single spacing   60-space line

LAB 5

Commas in Series

Type lines 1–4 once. Then repeat lines 1–4 or take a series of 1-minute timings.

1 The tools, parts, and tires were in the drive near the car.   12
2 I bought a new sweater, a winter jacket, and quilted boots.   12
3 The fruit rolls, pies, cakes, and donuts are most tempting.   12
4 Fritz and Helen joined John, Sally, and Maxine in the park.   12
   | 1 | 2 | 3 | 4 | 5 | 6 | 7 | 8 | 9 | 10 | 11 | 12

In a series of three or more numbers, words, phrases, or clauses, use a comma after each item in the series except the last.

Numbers: This model costs $12, $15, or $18.
Words: Abco manufactures nuts, bolts, and locks.
Phrases: We went into the plane, onto the runway, and into the air.
Clauses: Mel cooked the food, Janice made the salad, and Bob made the dessert.

12-SECOND TIMINGS

Type each line three times, or take three 12-second timings on each line. For each timing, type with no more than 1 error.

5 When you turn the pages in the book, do not make any sound.
6 The sail of the boat caught the wind, and we scooted north.
7 The red, white, and blue colors on the wall look very nice.

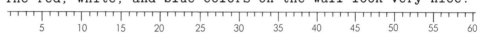

      5   10   15   20   25   30   35   40   45   50   55   60

FORMATTING SHORT CENTERED COLUMN HEADINGS

 Some computers, word processors, and electronic typewriters have a column-layout feature that automatically centers column headings over the column.

Column headings in tables clarify the data in each column and eliminate unnecessary words. In draft copies and in informal correspondence, column headings may be blocked; however, column headings are usually centered.

When a column heading is shorter than the longest line in a column, the heading should be centered over the column. Follow these formatting directions:

1. Subtract the number of spaces in the column heading from the number of spaces in the longest line in the column.

2. Divide the answer by 2 (drop any fraction), and indent the column head that many spaces.

In the column below, the heading is 4 spaces long; the longest line is 12. Thus $12 - 4 = 8$ and $8 \div 2 = 4$. Indent the heading 4 spaces from the start of the column.

3. Type a column heading in initial caps and underscore it.

4. Triple-space before and double-space after a column heading.

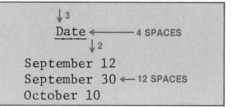

JOB 94 B. THREE-COLUMN RULED TABLE

Standard format. Double-space on a full sheet of paper.

SPORTS CAR EXHIBITS
(Final Entries)

Car	Model	Country
Corvette	Convertible	United States
Ferrari	308 GTSI	Italy
Jaguar	XJ-S	Great Britain
Nissan	300 ZX	Japan
Porsche	911	West Germany

LESSON 95

■ **GOALS**
To type 36/5'/5e.
To format and type total lines in tables.

■ **FORMAT**
Drills: Single spacing   60-space line
5-Minute Timings: Double spacing   5-space tab

KEYBOARDING SKILLS

Type lines 1–4 once. In line 5 use the shift lock for each word in all-capital letters. Repeat lines 1–4, or take a series of 1-minute timings.

Speed
1 Rush him eight bushels of corn, but make him sign for them. 12

Accuracy
2 Park my huge, bronze jet and quickly wax it for five hours. 12

Numbers
3 Our bills for the week came to $10, $29, $38, $47, and $56. 12

Symbols
4 Listen! I did <u>not</u> say 12 was 1/4 of 60.   Did <u>you</u> say that? 14

Technique
5 Go to ADAMS, not to WHITMAN or LANKIN or EDMORE or LANGDON.

| 1 | 2 | 3 | 4 | 5 | 6 | 7 | 8 | 9 | 10 | 11 | 12

PRETEST

Take a 5-minute timing on lines 14–29 on page 161. Circle and count your errors. Use the chart below to find the number of errors you made on the timing. Then type each of the designated drill lines four times.

PRACTICE

Pretest errors	0–1	2–3	4–5	6+
Drill lines	9–13	8–12	7–11	6–10

Accuracy
6 number getting example expands usually acquired opportunity
7 "boot" "byte" likely across before getting example commands
8 system you're booting current acquired computers processing
9 series letter loading consist attached documents recognized

Speed
10 terms words every have this most come week word you had use
11 means going drive term word many that year this new not day
12 often space first boot when into sent just when two the can
13 bytes month seven from disk byte each four disk and one for

POSTTEST

Take another 5-minute timing on lines 14–29 on page 161 to see how much your skill has improved.

JOB 65 A. THREE-COLUMN TABLE
Standard format. Half sheet of paper.

OAKDALE HIGH SCHOOL
Varsity Field Hockey Schedule

Date	Opponent	Site
September 12	Ellis	Home
September 21	St. Agnes	Away
September 30	Quaker Valley	Home
October 10	Keystone	Home
October 18	Winchester	Away

JOB 65 B. THREE-COLUMN TABLE
Standard format.

EXPEDITIONS TO THE NORTH POLE
By ice, air, and sea

Name	Vehicle	Year
Byrd	airplane	1926
Norge	Dirigible	1926
Nautilus	Submarine	1958
Plaisted	Snow mobile	1968
Herbert	Dog sled	1969
Arktika	Icebreaker	1979

JOB 65 C. THREE-COLUMN TABLE
Standard format. Half sheet of paper.

REQUESTED FLIGHT FARES
Fares Are Tourist
From Boise and Return

Destination	Fare	Miles
Denver	$136.00	1684
Los Angeles	146.00	1924
San Francisco	122.00	1316
Salt Lake City	82.00	732
Seattle	100.00	770

LESSON 66

■ **GOALS**
To identify how commas are used in series while typing sentences.
To format and type tables with long column headings.

■ **FORMAT**
Single spacing   60-space line

LAB 5

Commas in Series

Type lines 1–4 once. Then repeat lines 1–4 or take a series of 1-minute timings.

1 We packed our clothes, food, and a tent in the large trunk. 12
2 Joyce wrote about cities, tall buildings, and busy offices. 12
3 I very much like to play tennis, racquetball, and baseball. 12
4 We lost 38 balls, 29 bats, and 10 helmets with our luggage. 12

| 1 | 2 | 3 | 4 | 5 | 6 | 7 | 8 | 9 | 10 | 11 | 12

TABULATOR REVIEW

Type lines 5–10 once, keeping your eyes on your copy as you press the tabulator key to move from column to column. Proofread your copy and repeat lines 5–10.

5	a	l	b	2	c	3	d
6	4	e	5	f	6	g	7
7	h	8	i	9	j	0	k
8	ache	aches	bark	barks	chat	chats	drape
9	earn	earns	farm	farms	gear	gears	haste
10	lake	lakes	malt	malts	name	names	ounce

FORMATTING RULED TABLES

Workbook 135–136.

To format ruled tables, follow these guidelines:

1. Center the table horizontally and vertically.

2. Using your key line, set your left margin. Then space across for the key line as you set your tabs. This will help you determine how wide to type the ruled lines in the table.

3. Type the ruled lines (the underscores) the exact length of the key line. Single-space before each ruled line, and double-space after each ruled line.

4. End the table with a single ruled line, typed the length of the key line.

Practice: Type the table below on a full sheet of paper. Use double spacing. The table should occupy 16 lines.

SALES PERSONNEL ↓2

Southern Region ↓1

Name	City ↓1 ↓2
Kate Abramson	San Antonio ↓2
Paul Day	Dallas
Janice Taylay	El Paso
Jose Valdes	Houston ↓1

Kate Abramson123456San Antonio

FORMATTING COLUMNS WITH WORDS AND NUMBERS

You have previously learned that words align on the left and numbers align on the right. Sometimes columns contain a mixture of both words *and* numbers.

To format a column of words and numbers, align all entries at the left, as if they were all words.

JOB 94 A. THREE-COLUMN RULED TABLE
Standard format. Double-space on a full sheet of paper.

WORD PROCESSING EQUIPMENT

(Available Options)

Item	Option 1	Option 2
Disk Drive	Single	Double
Printer	Daisy Wheel	Dot Matrix
Monitor	Amber	Green
Internal Storage	64K	128K

30-SECOND SPEED TIMINGS

Take two 30-second speed timings on lines 5 and 6. Then take two 30-second speed timings on lines 7 and 8. Or type each sentence twice.

```
5  On a clear day the view from the top of a tall building can   12
6  permit men, women, and children to see the distant horizon.   24
7  The sky looks so blue that you want to jump on a plane that    12
8  will take you far away from the rush and stress of the day.    24
   |  1  |  2  |  3  |  4  |  5  |  6  |  7  |  8  |  9  | 10 | 11 | 12
```

FORMATTING LONG CENTERED COLUMN HEADINGS

Workbook 70.

When a column heading is longer than any item in the column, the column is centered under the heading. Follow these formatting instructions:

1. Subtract the number of spaces in the longest line in the column from the number of spaces in the heading.

2. Divide that answer by 2 (drop any fraction), and indent the column that number of spaces. In the example, 23 − 13 = 10 and 10 ÷ 2 = 5. Indent the column 5 spaces.

```
Some Kinds of Dinosaurs  ◄——23 spaces

    Plateosaurus
    Brontosaurus
    Brachiosaurus        ◄——13 spaces
```

3. After typing the column heading, reset the left margin or tab stop.

Note: When the column heading is longer than the column, regard the heading as part of the key line.

JOB 66 A. TWO-COLUMN TABLE
Standard format. Half sheet of paper.

DINOSAURS

A Parade Through Time

Some Kinds of Dinosaurs	Millions of Years Ago
Plateosaurus	225
Brontosaurus	185
Brachiosaurus	170
Tyrannosaurus Rex	136

JOB 66 B. THREE-COLUMN TABLE
Standard format. Half sheet of paper.

The Great Race

Distance Completed

by State Business Club Winners

School	Winner	Kilometers
Weaver High	G. Craig	12.6
Denby High	W. Lopez	10.5
Lincoln High	L. Marshall	8.0
Olliver High	R. Mercer	7.2
Gladstone High	S. poulos	6.1
Horace Mann High	A. Tyler	6.7

PRETEST

Take a 1-minute timing on lines 6–8; then take a 1-minute timing on lines 9–11. Circle and count your errors on each.

Left-Hand Reaches

6   Barbara was last seen at the new dress sale late last week.   12
7   Ada stated she had traded off the car after it was wrecked.   24
8   Gerald prefers trees that have very few leaves or branches.   36

| 1 | 2 | 3 | 4 | 5 | 6 | 7 | 8 | 9 | 10 | 11 | 12

Right-Hand Reaches

9   It is their opinion that Jimmy will join the union by noon.   12
10   Phyllis will soon shoot many photos of our immense pumpkin.   24
11   Phillip enjoys looking at and collecting only common coins.   36

| 1 | 2 | 3 | 4 | 5 | 6 | 7 | 8 | 9 | 10 | 11 | 12

PRACTICE

In which timing did you make more errors? If in the first one (lines 6–8), type lines 12–16 four times and lines 17–21 two times. If most of your errors were in the second timing (lines 9–11), reverse the procedure.

Left-Hand Reaches

12   treat severe dresses cabbage afterward addressee exaggerate
13   trade tweed wears agreed career starts assets awards better
14   cares carts darts deeds fares grade grass great reads staff
15   wash meets refer tease passes tassel assure pleases between
16   fast cases sewer meter masses letter pretty referee sixteen

Right-Hand Reaches

17   jolly imply kimono minimum million homonym opinion nonunion
18   poppy hilly onion pupil pulpy nylon milky phony plump lumpy
19   hill pink hook pool moon noon join milk mill upon look junk
20   imp import impose imposes imports improve imposing imported
21   ill chills drills fulfill willing billing goodwill waybills

POSTTEST

Repeat the Pretest to see how much your skill has improved.

LESSON
94

UNIT 16 Formatting Tables
UNIT GOAL 35/5'/5e

■ GOALS
To use commas correctly after introductory words and
    phrases while typing sentences.
To format and type ruled tables.
To format and type columns with words and numbers.

■ FORMAT
Single spacing   60-space line   Tabs every 9 spaces

LAB 9

Commas After Introductory Words and Phrases

Workbook 133–134.

Type lines 1–4 once, providing the missing commas. Edit your copy as your teacher reads the answers. Then retype lines 1–4 from your edited copy.

1   Speaking rapidly Kent explained the reasons for the delay.
2   In any event Ms. Smithe should finish before the deadline.
3   During the question-and-answer period Jan was outstanding.
4   In the first place Ms. Maizley is not a computer operator.

JOB 66 C. TWO-COLUMN TABLE
Standard format. Half sheet of paper.

PARIS

Places of Interest	Location
Eiffel Tower	Avenue de la Bourdonnais
Palais du Louvre	Quai du Louvre
Notre Dame	Ile de la Cité
Arc de Triomphe	Avenue des Champs Elysées

LESSON 67

■ GOALS
To use commas in series correctly while typing sentences.
To type 35/3'/5e.
To type tables with column headings.

■ FORMAT
Drills: Single spacing   60-space line
3-Minute Timings: Double spacing   5-space tab

LAB 5

Commas in Series

Type lines 1–4 once, providing the missing commas. Edit your copy as your teacher reads the answers. Then retype lines 1–4 from your edited copy.

1 The children played with the blocks trucks and tricycles.
2 Mr. Velez typed his quizzes tests and exams on Wednesday.
3 Jo fixed the brakes checked the oil and added antifreeze.
4 Can they make some fudge taffy popcorn and candy apples?

PREVIEW PRACTICE

Accuracy
Speed

Type each line twice as a preview to the 3-minute timings below.

5 folks watch exploit realize resources scientists quantities
6 natural things today fuels make with also coal that for and

3-MINUTE TIMINGS

Take two 3-minute timings on lines 7–15.

```
              1              2              3              4
 7        The energy from coal can do lots of jobs for us.  Coal   12
              5              6              7              8
 8   gives power for machines and heat for our homes.  Coal also   24
              9             10             11
 9   helps scientists to make things that better our lives.        35
       12             13             14             15
10        Today plastics, many drugs, and types of food dyes are   47
       16             17             18             19
11   made from coal.  With a possible fuel shortage now, a large   59
       20             21             22             23
12   effort will be made to make coal fill this urgent need.       70
              24             25             26             27
13        We realize that our search for fuels will make a drain   82
       28             29             30             31
14   on our natural resources.  So we must be on guard and watch   94
       32             33             34             35
15   that we do not let greedy folks exploit our quantities.      105
     |  1  |  2  |  3  |  4  |  5  |  6  |  7  |  8  |  9  | 10  | 11  | 12  |   SI 1.29
```

JOB 92 A. TWO-PAGE LETTER
Standard format. Workbook 131–132.
Body 455 words.

[*Today's date*] / Ms. Tina Lewis, Editor / South 14
Bend News / 21789 Douglas Road / South Bend, 22
IN 46628 / Dear Ms. Lewis: 28

Plans have now been finalized for our word 38
processing seminar to be held from June 6 46
through June 24 at the Hill Top Hotel. You asked 56
that I send you some information that you could 66
use to write a brief article for this week's <u>News</u>. 78
Select whatever you would like from the para- 87
graphs below to write your article; it is the most 97
complete data I have at this time. 104

We are going to conduct the seminar from 11 114
a.m. to 3 p.m. Monday through Friday. Partici- 123
pants will receive a total of 60 hours of instruc- 133
tion during the 15 days. Our plans at this time 143
are to have at least five different makes of word 153
processors for the seminar, and we also plan to 162
present several software packages. All in all, we 172
believe a very thorough job will be done. 181

For the first two hours of every class day for 191
the first week, a nationally known expert in 200
word processing, Ms. Helene Rowe, will pro- 209
vide a lecture on the concepts of word process- 218
ing. She will be covering a number of topics that 228
pertain to the use of word processing equipment 238
in the office. She will top off her lecture on the 248
last day by sharing with the group her thoughts 258
on the office of the future. 264

Those who attend the seminar will be ex- 273
pected to write a short paper on what they have 282
gained from the sessions as well as how they can 292
use some of what they have learned in their own 302
offices. They will also be required to demon- 311
strate at least a working knowledge of one of the 321
five pieces of hardware. The lab will be open 330
every evening during the course to allow partici- 340
pants some time to work with the processor of 349
their own choice. 353

We have been able to get a discount for the 362
rooms for those who wish to stay at the Hill Top 372
Hotel. However, there are several hotels in this 382
area; and participants may stay at these hotels if 392
they wish to. A luncheon is planned for the final 403
class day, and the seminar fee includes a ticket 412
to that luncheon. 416

If you need any further information, Ms. 425
Lewis, please feel free to write or call me. I look 436
forward to seeing your article on our seminar. / 446
Very truly yours, / Marcia T. Childress / Semi- 461
nar Director / [*Your initials*] 465

LESSON 93

CLINIC

- **GOALS**
  To improve typing skills using the Selective Practice routine.
  To type 36/2'/2e.
- **FORMAT**
  Single spacing   60-space line   Tabs every 5 spaces

KEYBOARDING SKILLS

Type lines 1–4 once. In line 5 use your tabulator key to advance from one word to the next through the entire line. Repeat lines 1–4, or take a series of 1-minute timings.

Speed	1	When it is time to go to the store, I will bring the money.	12
Accuracy	2	Quietly, six zebras jumped back over the eight brown rafts.	12
Numbers	3	Diane should not take 10, 29, and 38 in place of 47 and 56.	12
Symbols	4	On 10/29 he (Bart) paid $87, which is 36% less than I paid.	12
Technique	5	ad an as at be if in is it or to up	

| 1 | 2 | 3 | 4 | 5 | 6 | 7 | 8 | 9 | 10 | 11 | 12 |

Paper turned lengthwise has the following dimensions: width, 110 pica spaces or 132 elite spaces; depth, 51 lines.

JOB 67 A. FOUR-COLUMN TABLE
Standard format. Full sheet of paper turned lengthwise.

PORTLAND TOWN HALL
Winter Program of Events

Date	Topic	Speaker	Location
January 15	Books	L. T. Bormann 13	Downtown YMCA
January 29	Music	Sandra Chin	East End Library
February 12	Real Estate	Fred T. Hamma	South High School 13
February 26	Theater	Betty Jean Bay 14	College Club
March 10	Business	Stuart Green	Civic Hall

JOB 67 B. TWO-COLUMN TABLE
Type the copy to the right. Standard format with single spacing. Half sheet of paper.

JOB 67 C. THREE-COLUMN TABLE
Retype Job 67 B adding the name of the country as column 1. Use the column heading *Country*. Standard format. Half sheet of paper.

INTERNATIONAL
TRAVELERS' FORECAST #
Today's Projected Weather Conditions ea
2#

]City[	]Forecast[
Amsterdam	Cloudy
Frankfurt	rain
Peking	Fare
London	Heavy Fog
Mexico City	hazy
TelAviv	Claer

CLINIC

■ **GOALS**
To practice typing symbols.
To type 35/3'/5e.

■ **FORMAT**
Drills: Single spacing   60-space line
3-Minute Timings: Double spacing   5-space tab

KEYBOARDING SKILLS

Type lines 1–4 once. Then practice smooth shift-key control by capitalizing the proper nouns in line 5. Then repeat lines 1–4, or take a series of 1-minute timings.

Speed	1 He may wish to pay them if and when they go to town for us.	12
Accuracy	2 Bernard won five major prizes equal to your six big checks.	12
Numbers	3 Please order 10 cakes, 29 pies, and 38 quarts of ice cream.	12
Symbols	4 Jo may write to Dop & Co., Smith & Sons, and Howe & Blaker.	12
Technique	5 Lyle Nick Lisa Dora Lulu Mina Jack Boyd Nate Hank Jane Saul	

| 1 | 2 | 3 | 4 | 5 | 6 | 7 | 8 | 9 | 10 | 11 | 12

LESSON 92

■ **GOALS**
To use commas correctly after introductory words and
  phrases while typing sentences.
To type 36/5'/5e.
To type a two-page letter.

■ **FORMAT**
Drills: Single spacing   60-space line
5-Minute Timings: Double spacing   5-space tab

LAB 9

**Commas After
Introductory
Words and
Phrases**

Type lines 1–4 once, providing the missing commas. Edit your copy as your teacher
reads the answers. Then retype lines 1–4 from your edited copy.

1 In order to get the new disk drive we must submit our bid.
2 Yes computers will soon take over most business functions.
3 To lose weight you have to diet and to exercise regularly.
4 Actually that unit will cost less than they first thought.

**PREVIEW
PRACTICE**

Accuracy
Speed

Type each line twice as a preview to the 5-minute timings below.

5 quite boxes realize initial expensive household opportunity
6 furniture tightly town city such with big for the and it or

**5-MINUTE
TIMINGS**

Take two 5-minute timings on lines 7–21.

7   If you have ever had an opportunity to move to another   12
8 city or town, you realize that it might be quite a big job.   24
9 If you are like many others, you might try moving yourself.   36
10   The initial thing to do is to lease a truck or trailer   48
11 for moving all your household belongings. You must be sure   60
12 to get a truck or trailer just large enough for your needs.   72
13   Many large boxes and cartons must be packed and sealed   84
14 carefully. Be sure to pack all your belongings tightly for 96
15 the move so that nothing will break apart inside the boxes. 108
16   Have some of your friends assist you in carrying heavy   120
17 items such as sofas, beds, desks, and television sets. All 132
18 your large, bulky items should be put into the truck first. 144
19   As you cruise down a highway with a load of furniture,   156
20 watch carefully for any sudden stops in the traffic. Drive 168
21 slowly so that none of your expensive furniture is damaged. 180

| 1 | 2 | 3 | 4 | 5 | 6 | 7 | 8 | 9 | 10 | 11 | 12 | SI 1.38

SYMBOL PRACTICE

Take a 30-second timing on test line 6. Then type lines 7–9 twice each. Take another 30-second timing on test line 6 to see how much your skill has improved. Repeat this routine for each of the other test and drill lines.

Test Line 6   You know that 4 + 4 = 8, but what does (a + b)(a − b) mean?
( )   7   I checked items (10), (29), (38), (47), (56), (7), and (9).
+   8   Edward tallied 10 + 29 + 38 + 47 + 56 + 100 + 280 + 39 + 4.
=   9   My grading scale: 10 = D, 29 = C, 38 = B, 47 = A, 56 = A+.

| 1 | 2 | 3 | 4 | 5 | 6 | 7 | 8 | 9 | 10 | 11 | 12

Test Line 10   He got 10 @ 15¢ and 12 @ 20¢, less $1; and she got 30 @ $9.
$ 11   My contributions are $10, $28, $39, $47, and $56 for today.
¢   12   He collected 10¢, 29¢, 38¢, 47¢, and 56¢ from us in a week.
@   13   How much is 10 @ 10¢, 11 @ 29¢, 12 @ 38¢, and 13 @ only 7¢?

| 1 | 2 | 3 | 4 | 5 | 6 | 7 | 8 | 9 | 10 | 11 | 12

Test Line 14   Our #8 and #9 styles are 30% and 35% less than #29 and #47!
15   Sales are slow on #10, #29, and #38 and fast on #47 and #5.
%   16   Pay the interest ranging from 1% to 10% and about 5% to 6%.
!   17   Shout the words loudly: Type! Help! Stop! Fire! Shout!

| 1 | 2 | 3 | 4 | 5 | 6 | 7 | 8 | 9 | 10 | 11 | 12

Test Line 18   *Cox and Mendez jogged 1 mile in 10:1; R & S did it in 9:8.
:   19   Express trains leave at these times: 1:30, 6:29, and 8:45.
&   20   Haley & Parma are suing Wilcox & Byrnes; J & L is suing me.
*   21   The courses with a star are closed: AC110*, BI202*, MA11*.

| 1 | 2 | 3 | 4 | 5 | 6 | 7 | 8 | 9 | 10 | 11 | 12

Test Line 22   "Well, if it isn't Doc!" he exclaimed. "He can't eat now."
"   23   We are using "we" and "you" instead of "I," "he," or "she."
'   24   It isn't mine; maybe it's Jim's. Perhaps we'll never know.
—   25   I must get her to read Moby Dick or The Merchant of Venice.

3-MINUTE TIMINGS

Take two 3-minute timings on lines 26–34.

26   Big sale news! We think that our charge customers are   12
27   "special" customers. Therefore, starting tomorrow—and for   24
28   the next three days—you will find extra-low prices in each   36
29   department in our store. All these quality sale items will   48
30   be marked with an *. Just use your charge card; you'll get   60
31   discounts of 25–50%. Just think: you can save $9 on a $36   72
32   blouse (25% off). Most household goods will be on sale for   84
33   2 @ $1 or 50¢ each. Strauss & Sons thinks you are #1. Our   97
34   sale should = amazing bargains for you.   105

| 1 | 2 | 3 | 4 | 5 | 6 | 7 | 8 | 9 | 10 | 11 | 12   SI 1.38

JOB 91 A. TWO-PAGE MEMORANDUM ON A PRINTED FORM
Standard format. Workbook 129.

(To:) Kathy Speight, Western Division Manager / (From:) James McFeeley, Sales Manager / (Date:) September 25, 19-- / (Subject:) Return of Merchandise

It has come to my attention, in the past few weeks that our merchandise return rate has been higher in our Western Division than in the other 4 divisions. In fact, most of the returns have been in our new-products line-- and that is something we have never experienced before!

In the next month, Kathy, I want you to look into this unusual, unprecedented problem very closely in an attempt to determine its cause. We have to get to the heart of this matter soon so that we can take the appropriate action to resolve it.

As a suggestion, you might try conducting a marketing survey with some of our new customers to find out if they are experiencing any dissatisfaction with our new products. Perhaps a problem that is unique to our new-products line is causing the excessively high return rate. We conducted a similar survey 3 years ago when our Southwest Division was experiencing a dramatic decline in the sale of its mobile units. The survey revealed that a defective part was being installed in the mobile unit before it had received final approval from our Quality Control Dept. We have the final report on file in the Southwest Division office. If you would

like to review it before conducting your own survey, contact the Southwest Division manager.

You might also check, with our quality control Department to see how the changes we implemented last year are affecting the quality of our new products. Are we still strictly enforcing the 5-step quality check on all our new products, or have we resorted to a spot check on selected products only? Have we had any excessive employee turnover in the Q C Department that might be having an adverse effect on our product dependability? Is our employee morale at a high level, or is the level so low that is it affecting our quality checks? Are we continuing to purchase our internal parts from Breadford Industries, or have we changed suppliers recently? These are just a few of the questions you might want to check on, Kathy, when you conduct your investigation.

We plan to have our quarterly meeting on December 15, just before the holidays. Therefore, Would it be possible for you to have the results of your survey and any other pertinent information available for presentation at the meeting? All the other Division Managers are going to be quite interested in the findings you have to report. Please let me know by November 15 if you can present your findings. I look forward to seeing you at the December meeting. / JM

UNIT 12 Formatting a Formal Report
UNIT GOAL 35/3'/5e

■ **GOALS**
To use commas in series correctly while typing sentences.
To format and type footnotes and endnotes.

■ **FORMAT**
Single spacing   60-space line

LAB 5

Commas in Series

Workbook 73.

Type lines 1–4 once, providing the missing commas. Edit your copy as your teacher reads the answers. Then retype lines 1–4 from your edited copy.

1 I hope to go through Germany Holland and Italy next year.
2 Their figures for January are $125.50 $162.19 and $14.24.
3 Look up these numbers: 263–12 410–79 244–83 and 766–42.
4 Harold Betty Alice and Sam have worked on these quizzes.

12-SECOND TIMINGS

Type each line three times, or take three 12-second timings on each line. For each timing, type with no more than 1 error.

5 We would prefer to take a lot of quizzes, not one big exam.
6 A small tug pushed the liner into the quay and to the pier.
7 Put the sodas, lemonade, and iced tea on the picnic tables.

| | | | | | | | | | | | |
5   10   15   20   25   30   35   40   45   50   55   60

FORMATTING TEXT REFERENCES

In Lesson 54, you formatted reports with run-in references, which indicate to the reader the source of the statement cited. Run-in references were formatted in parentheses within the body of the report.

Another way to format references is to place the notes at the bottom (or the "foot") of the same page on which they occur. References formatted in this way are called *footnotes.*

A third way to format references is to place all the notes at the end of the report. References formatted in this way are called *endnotes.*

Whether footnotes or endnotes are used, the presence of a reference must be indicated in the body of the report. To indicate the presence of a reference in the body, type a superscript (raised) number immediately following the appropriate word, phrase, or sentence.

Practice: Type the sentence below. To type the superscripts, turn the cylinder back slightly with one hand and type the number with the other. Remember to return to the original line of writing before typing the next word.

    John Henry Abbott wrote the book.[1] He frequently re-
ferred to the writings of Samuel Brooks Newhouse.[2]

FORMATTING REPEATED REFERENCES

Two References in a Row. When a reference notation refers to a book or magazine article that is the same as the one immediately preceding, shorten it by using the abbreviation *Ibid.* (meaning "in the same place"). Add a page number if the page is different.

Ibid., p. 63.

Two References in the Same Work. When a reference notation refers to a book or magazine article fully identified in an earlier reference—but *not* the one immediately preceding—shorten the notation as follows: Author's surname, page number.

Speer, p. 11.

■ GOALS
To identify when commas are used after introductory words and phrases while typing sentences.
To format and type a two-page memo.

■ FORMAT
Single spacing   60-space line

LAB 9

Commas After Introductory Words and Phrases

Type lines 1–4 once. Then repeat lines 1–4 or take a series of 1-minute timings.

1 In my opinion, Joy Kim will agree to visit the Ace Company.   12
2 In the first place, Veronica Bianco plans to visit Denmark.   12
3 No, Harris Quentin will not attend next Thursday's seminar.   12
4 At our next committee meeting, Ms. Rudi will discuss taxes.   12
   | 1 | 2 | 3 | 4 | 5 | 6 | 7 | 8 | 9 | 10 | 11 | 12

12-SECOND TIMINGS

Type each line three times, or take three 12-second timings on each line. For each timing, type with no more than 1 error.

5 Their firm is paid to paint half the signs for those towns.
6 Their goal is to do all of the work by the first or second.
7 It is their wish to go to the city by auto when they do go.

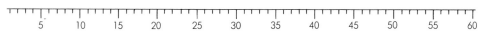

          5   10   15   20   25   30   35   40   45   50   55   60

FORMATTING TWO-PAGE LETTERS AND MEMOS Workbook 127–128.

Long business letters and memos are often continued on a second page. The second page should be a plain sheet of paper of the same quality as the letterhead or memo form used for the first page. To format:

1. Use a 6-inch line (60P/70E) for letters; follow guide words for memos.

2. Leave a bottom margin of at least 1 to 1½ inches (6 to 9 blank lines) on page 1.

3. Carry over at least 2 lines of the body to page 2.

4. Begin page 2 with a heading that includes the name of the addressee, the page number, and the date. **Style A:** Spread the heading on line 7. Type the name of the addressee at the left margin, type the page number at the center, and backspace the date from the right margin. **Style B:** Block the heading at the left margin. Type the name of the addressee on line 7; the word *Page* and page number on line 8; the date on line 9.

5. Triple-space from the heading page to the body.

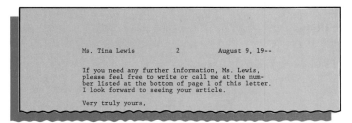

Style A: Spread.

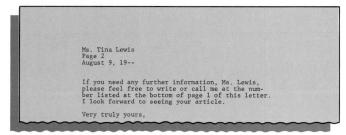

Style B: Blocked.

Production Practice. Set your margins for a 6-inch line. Set a center tab. Single spacing. Clean sheet of paper. Use the memo in Job 91 A below.

Space down to line 7, and type the name of the addressee at the left margin. Tab to the center, and type the number *2*. Move the carriage or carrier to the right margin. Backspace once for each letter and space in the date. Type the date. Return three times, and type the first two

lines of the last paragraph (column 2). Check your work.

Remove your paper from the typewriter, and reinsert it upside down. Space down to line 7. Type the name of the addressee at the left margin. Return the carriage or carrier. Type the word *Page* and the number *2*. Return. Type the date. Return three times, and type the first two lines of the last paragraph (column 2). Check your work. Which style was easier and faster to type?

FORMATTING FOOTNOTES

Footnotes must be typed on the same page as the reference to them. To format footnotes:

1. Plan ahead to determine the number of lines you must "save" at the bottom of the page for the footnotes. As you type each superscript in the text, estimate the number of lines for each footnote, and mark lightly with a pencil the point at which you should stop typing the text.

2. Single-space after the last line of text, and type a 2-inch underscore (20P/24E strokes) beginning at the left margin. This line separates the footnotes from the text.

3. Double-space, indent 5 spaces, and type the footnote number followed by a period, 2 spaces, and the reference. Use single spacing for any turnover lines needed, and begin them at the left margin, as shown in the illustration below.

Note: Some academic style manuals indicate the use of a superscript number (without a space) in footnotes as well as in text references. Example:

^{1}Barbara Anne Hemsley

4. Double-space between footnotes.

5. Always format footnotes (and the underscore) at the bottom of the page—even on the last page of a report, which may have only a few lines of text. The bottom margin below the footnote should be a minimum of 6 lines or a maximum of 9 lines.

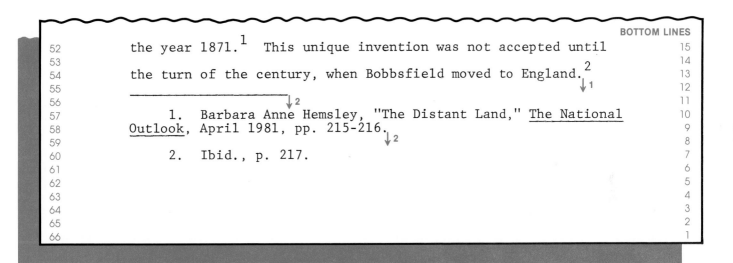

Practice: Set margins for a 6-inch line (60P/70E), 5-space tab, double spacing. Clean sheet of paper. Use the illustration above.

1. Place a small pencil mark 1 inch from the bottom of the paper. Place a second small pencil mark 1 inch (6 lines) up from the first mark (1 line for the ruled line, 1 blank line, 2 lines for footnote 1, 1 blank line, 1 line for footnote 2).

   Insert the paper and space down to line 52. Type the last two lines of the body of the report. Change to single spacing. Return the carriage or carrier once. Type a 2-inch line (20P/24E). Return the carriage or carrier twice. Tab and type the first footnote. Return twice. Tab and type the second footnote. Remove the paper and check your work. Do you have 6 blank lines below the second footnote? This is how footnotes should appear on a full page.

2. Turn the paper over and make two pencil marks at 1 inch and 2 inches from the bottom of the paper. Reinsert the paper. Change to double spacing. Space down to line 40. Type the last two lines of the body of the report. Space down to the first pencil mark, turning the platen knob by hand if necessary. Type a 2-inch line at the point where the first pencil mark appears. Return. Change to single spacing. Tab and type the first footnote. Return twice. Tab and type the second footnote. Remove the paper and check your work. Do you have 6 blank lines below the last footnote? This is how footnotes should appear on a page that is not filled.

MEMO ON PLAIN PAPER

TITLE
All caps, centered on line 7.
GUIDE WORDS
In all caps; tab 10 for copy that follows.

BODY
60P/70E, 6-inch line, single spacing.

WRITER'S INITIALS
Align at center.
TYPIST'S INITIALS
At left margin.

↓7
MEMORANDUM
↓3

DATE: March 10, 19--

TO: Helen Lowe, Department Head

FROM: James S. Pickett, Personnel Manager

SUBJECT: Interview Dates
            ↓3

The interview dates for the candidates who have applied for the sales position in our Bowling Green office have been set for March 27, 28, and 29. ↓2

Please let me know if you have any conflicts with these dates by completing and returning the enclosed form to indicate your availability. ↓2

                            JSP
                               ↓2

jt
Enclosure

MEMO ON PRINTED FORM

PRINTED GUIDE WORDS
Inserts aligned at the bottom, 2 spaces after the colons.

WRITER'S INITIALS
Aligned with date.

MEMORANDUM

TO: Philip Simek   DATE: May 21, 19--

FROM: Tracy Rushin, Editor

SUBJECT: Copy Rewrite ↓3

We received your rewrite of Chapter 15, and I would like to recommend two changes. First, we should shorten your section on personal information and lengthen your discussion on writing a letter of application. Second, we must expand our discussion questions from 15 to 20 as we planned. ↓2

To meet our production schedule of September 5, we would like to have your copy no later than the 15th of June. ↓2

                                        TR
                                          ↓2

AG

FORMATTING ENDNOTES

Endnotes are used instead of footnotes. They are placed at the end of the report.

To format endnotes:

1. Use the same margins as used in the report.

2. Follow the paragraph format for enumerations (see page 57).

3. Number the endnotes page the same way the other pages of the report are numbered.

4. Center the heading NOTES on line 13.

Note: Some academic style manuals indicate the use of a superscript number (without a space) in endnotes as well as in text references.

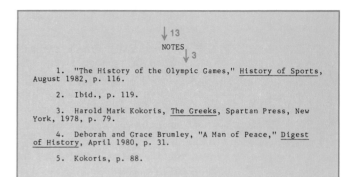

JOB 69 A. ENDNOTES

Use the footnotes for the report on pages 123–124. Standard format.

LESSONS 70/71

■ **GOALS**
To recognize how commas are used after introductory clauses while typing sentences.
To type 35/3'/5e.
To format and type long quotations and tables in reports.
To type a multipage report.

■ **FORMAT**
Drills: Single spacing   60-space line
3-Minute Timings: Double spacing   5-space tab

LAB 6

Introductory If, As, and When Clauses

Type lines 1–4 once. Then repeat lines 1–4 or take a series of 1-minute timings.

```
1  If Barte Gomez calls while we are out, just take a message.   12
2  As David quickly noticed, your extra hours are paid double.   12
3  When Yvette explained zero budgeting, she did so very well.   12
4  Although Jack left quickly, he missed the bus to Kalamazoo.   12
   |  1  |  2  |  3  |  4  |  5  |  6  |  7  |  8  |  9  |  10  |  11  |  12
```

Use a comma after an introductory clause that begins with *if, as, when, although, since, because,* or a similar conjunction. Note the examples in lines 1–4.

12-SECOND TIMINGS

Type each line three times, or take three 12-second timings on each line. For each timing, type with no more than 1 error.

```
5  As we started to dance, the lights were quickly turned off.
6  When the moon came up, the lake was a huge sheet of silver.
7  When it began to rain, they had to call a halt to the game.
```

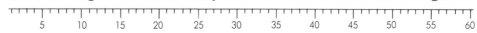

Place a comma after introductory words and phrases such as *first, in my opinion, for example,* and so on.

Yes, she is not going to purchase the microcomputer. [Word.]
Waiting for the light to turn green, Fred used his mobile telephone. [Phrase.]
In response to your letter, we honored our warranty. [Phrase.]

FORMATTING MEMOS

You can create a form on a word processor or a computer. You can then enter data on the electronic form just as you would on a typewriter. When the copy prints out, it will print out the filled-in form.

Memorandums, or memos, are letters written to people in the same organization or business. Less formal than letters, memos have no salutations and no complimentary closings; and they may be typed on half sheets or full sheets, depending on the length. Memos are used so often that most companies use standard memo forms on which the guide words *To, From, Subject,* and *Date* are printed. (The company name and other information may also be printed on the form.) However, memos can also be typed on plain paper. Look at the illustrations on page 153 as you read the formatting directions below.

To format a memo on plain paper:

1. Set margins for a 6-inch line.
2. Type the word *MEMORANDUM* in all-capital letters, centered on line 7.
3. Triple-space after *MEMORANDUM.* Type the guide words (*DATE:, TO:, FROM:, SUBJECT:*) double-spaced at the left margin in all-capital letters.

4. Type the words that follow the guide words 10 spaces from the margin (2 spaces after *SUBJECT:*).
5. Triple-space between the heading and the body of the memo. Single-space the body; double-space between paragraphs.
6. Type the writer's initials a double space below the body, beginning at the center.
7. Type any notation as in letters (a double space below the writer's initials, beginning at the left margin).

To format a memo on a printed form:

1. Set the left margin stop 2 spaces after the longest guide word, and fill in the heading information.
2. Set the right margin stop so that the right margin is approximately the same number of spaces as the left margin.
3. Align the writer's initials with the date.

JOB 90 A. MEMO ON PLAIN PAPER
Type the memo illustrated at the top of page 153. Standard format. Half sheet of paper.

JOB 90 B. MEMO ON PLAIN PAPER
Standard format. Half sheet of paper.

DATE: (Today's) / TO: Andrew Hagen, Department Head / FROM: Cheryl   27
A. Escarraz, Dean / SUBJECT: Committee Assignment / I would like you   44
to serve as committee chair of the Self-Study team that will commence   58
work next week. Therefore, please send to my office the names of five   72
other people you would like to have serve with you on this committee. ¶As   88
you know, this is a very important task; and I know that I can count on you   103
to do a superb job as chair of this important committee. / CAE [*Your*   118
initials]   120

JOB 90 C. MEMO ON PRINTED FORM
Type the memo illustrated at the bottom of page 153. Standard format. Workbook 125.

Take a 3-minute timing on lines 8–16. Circle and count your errors.

```
8      Every day the sun sends out to Earth quiet jet streams    12
9   of sunlight, which are a new and vital source of energy.  A    24
10  nation like ours could adequately fill its needs for energy    36
11  sources if the rays of the sun could be kept and stored, as    48
12  in a tank.  Solar energy could be used to heat homes and to    60
13  run engines, but more research must be done to find ways to    72
14  store the excess heat from the sun.  We all must constantly    84
15  work to save fuel; if we rely on the sun rather than oil or    96
16  coal, the possibility of a shortage is zero.                 105
    |  1  |  2  |  3  |  4  |  5  |  6  |  7  |  8  |  9  | 10 | 11 | 12    SI 1.28
```

PRACTICE

In the chart below find the number of errors you made on the Pretest. Then type each of the designated drill lines three times.

Pretest errors	0–1	2–3	4–5	6+
Drill lines	20–24	19–23	18–22	17–21

Accuracy
17 quiet could stored energy source research sunlight shortage
18 be zero earth rather nation excess sources engines research
19 we sun solar store vital every could constantly possibility
20 or jet homes needs which energy engines research adequately

Speed
21 used done heat ways fill than fuel save for run day out sun
22 rays kept find coal tank rely more ours jet its oil ray all
23 excess rather quiet store tank zero but sun and new are the
24 sources heat must from ways done used like ours jet for out

POSTTEST

Take another 3-minute timing on lines 8–16 to see how much your skill has improved.

FORMATTING DISPLAYS IN REPORTS

Long Quotations. A long quotation takes four or more typed lines. To format a long quotation in a report:

1. Indent the quotation 5 spaces from each margin. (Reset the margins before you begin and after you finish typing the quotation.)
2. Leave 1 blank line above and below the quotation.
3. Single-space the quotation.
4. Do not use quotation marks.
5. Use a paragraph indention if the original source used a paragraph indention.

Tables. To format a table in a report:

1. Center the table horizontally between the set margins. Do not go beyond the set margins; reduce space between columns if necessary.

2. Separate the table from the text copy with 3 blank lines (2 double spaces).
3. Single-space the body of the table unless told to do otherwise.
4. Use standard formatting directions for titles, column headings, and space between columns. (See pages 110, 113, and 115.)
5. Try to place the table (*a*) immediately after the point in the text where it is referred to, (*b*) at the end of the paragraph in which it is referred to, or (*c*) at the bottom of the page.
6. If the table will not fit on the page where the reference occurs, type the table at the top of the next page and insert a reference in the text indicating where the table is located, such as *the table on page 4.*

```
 9      Several kinds of printers, other than typewriters, are  12
10   found today in the office.  Two of the most common printers  24
11   are quite often recognized by some as leaders in the field.  36
12      A daisy wheel printer is one of the leaders.  The name  12
13   comes from the shape of its element, which does look like a  24
14   group of daisy petals that are joined together in a circle.  36
15      A dot matrix printer forms letters by placing a series  12
16   of dots close together on the paper.  It is much cheaper to  24
17   buy a dot matrix printer, and the printing speed is faster.  36
     |  1  |  2  |  3  |  4  |  5  |  6  |  7  |  8  |  9  |  10  |  11  |  12   SI 1.38
```

JOB 89 A. LETTER
Standard format with indented paragraphs. Workbook 121–122. Body 74 words.

```
(Today's date) / Mr. Matthew Pera /          11
2516 Washington Avenue, Apt. 243 /           18
Wilmington, DE 19805 / Dear Mr. Pera:        26
⑤  Thank you for agreeing to speak at        35
our fall meeting on the topic of the         43
office of the future.  We have had a         50
numerous, repeated
lot of requests for such a speech; and       60
I know your thoughts are going to be         67
                  much
very welcomed by our group. ¶ Please         77
send me the title of your speech as          84
```

```
soon as you can so that I can place in       92
it our program.                              95
     If you've any questions please         104
                at
call me 555-3298. / Yours sincerely, /      114
Anne clardy / Program Director / (Your      124
initials)                                   126
```

JOB 89 B. LETTER
Retype Job 89 A, adding the copy below as a new paragraph following paragraph 2. Standard format. Workbook 123–124. Body 100 words.

We would like to have you send us a copy of the handouts for your presentation so that we can duplicate enough copies for all who attend your session.

LESSON 90

■ **GOALS**
To recognize when commas are used after introductory words and phrases while typing sentences.
To format and type memos.

■ **FORMAT**
Single spacing   60-space line

LAB 9

Commas After Introductory Words and Phrases

Type lines 1–4 once. Then repeat lines 1–4 or take a series of 1-minute timings.

```
1  In any event, you will be required to leave their premises.  12
2  In my opinion, the purchase of new chairs is unjustifiable.  12
3  Just in case you would like to know, we will leave Tuesday.  12
4  During the entire rainy season, we will seldom see the sun.  12
   |  1  |  2  |  3  |  4  |  5  |  6  |  7  |  8  |  9  |  10  |  11  |  12
```

(Continued on next page)

JOB 70/71 A. MULTIPAGE REPORT WITH FOOTNOTES

Standard format. Begin typing the report, and continue in Lesson 72.

THE PERSONAL COMPUTER
By [*Your name*]

Just as the invention of typewriters, telephones, electric lights, automobiles, airplanes, and television changed our lives in the past, personal computers are changing our lives today. Word processing, accounting, inventory control, and other similar functions are handled so swiftly and easily by personal computers that within a few years microcomputers will be everywhere—in business, in school, and in the home.

According to a recent estimate, as many as half of all American workers will use display terminals in their jobs by 1990.[1] Occupations related to the new technology are growing rapidly. The table below shows the percentage of growth in employment through 1995 in America's five fastest-growing occupations.[2] Four of the five are computer-related.

FASTEST-GROWING OCCUPATIONS

Occupation	Percent Growth
Computer Service Technicians	96.8
Legal Assistants	94.3
Computer Systems Analysts	85.3
Computer Programmers	76.9
Computer Operators	75.8

Most people are first introduced to the computer through computer games, such as Pac-Man. Playing a computer game requires coordination and split-second timing, and it is a real challenge to the player to beat the machine. For instance, a student writes:

The game began. Before long the computer fell for one of my traps and let me capture one of the coveted corner squares. I pushed mercilessly, taking men. I felt an almost inhuman glee. When the last chip was played, the machine beeped once to signal the end of the game. It was all over—I beat the machine. The machine printed: ME 25. YOU 39. WANT TO PLAY AGAIN?[3]

What makes computers so fascinating? How do they work? What should everyone know about them? This paper will try to answer these questions.

THE MACHINE (HARDWARE)

The Microprocessor. Like most machines, personal computers are made of the same materials as televisions, typewriters, and tape recorders—metal, glass, paper, and plastic; so no one should feel intimidated by computers.

The first thing to know about the personal computer is the microprocessor. The processor in any computer does just that: it processes information. It sorts and resorts bits of information at speeds faster than any human can achieve. It is this speed that gives computers the edge over humans in performing certain repetitive tasks.

A microprocessor is very smart, but it has very little memory. To overcome this handicap, most personal computers have two kinds of memory combined with the central processing unit (CPU).

The first is known as "read-only memory," or ROM. This memory can be "read" by the microprocessor, but the microprocessor cannot "write" anything onto that memory. The microprocessor, then, can take information from ROM, but it cannot add information to it. The information in ROM is placed there permanently by the manufacturer. When an electric current first passes through the central processing unit, ROM is programmed to get the CPU going and to maintain certain basic functions.

The second kind of memory in a personal computer is "random-access memory," or RAM. With RAM, the CPU can read information from RAM

---

1. Russell W. Rumberger, "How Much 'Tech' Do High-Tech Workers Need?" VocEd, Vol. 59, No. 4, May 1984, p. 33.

2. Ibid., p. 34.

---

3. Peter A. McWilliams, The Personal Computer Book, 5th ed., Prelude Press, Los Angeles, 1984, p. 119.

(Continued on next page)

Third, be sure that your control cards are 201
seated firmly in the computer. If they are not 211
seated at either end, a printer malfunction may 220
occur. Reseat all the cards to see if this is 230
causing you the problem you are having with 238
your printer. 241

If the problem is not resolved after you have checked each of the above 257
items, please bring your printer to our repair shop so that we can repair it 272
for you without any unplanned, unwanted delays. / Yours truly, / Banjit 289
Laraja / Sales Representative / [*Your initials*] 299

LESSON 89

■ **GOALS**
To improve your typing accuracy on "OK" timings.
To type 36/3'/3e.
To type short letters using the placement guide.

■ **FORMAT**
Drills: Single spacing   60-space line   Tabs every 5
  spaces
3-Minute Timings: Double spacing   5-space tab

KEYBOARDING SKILLS

Type lines 1–4 once. In line 5 use your tabulator key to advance from one word to the next through the entire line. Repeat lines 1–4, or take a series of 1-minute timings.

Speed   1 They both wish to visit Japan and Turkey if they go by air. 12
Accuracy   2 Zachery joked about a group of wax squid from the carnival. 12
Numbers   3 On page 10 we saw that 47 times 56 was much less than 2938. 12
Symbols   4 Please order 480# of #5 grade @ $17.69 before September 23. 12
Technique 5 by   do   go   hi   ha   ho   ma   me   no   pa   so   to
              | 1 | 2 | 3 | 4 | 5 | 6 | 7 | 8 | 9 | 10 | 11 | 12

30-SECOND "OK" TIMINGS

Type as many 30-second "OK" (errorless) timings as possible out of three attempts on lines 6–8.

6 As we all watched the sky with amazement, five or six dozen 12
7 big jet planes zoomed quickly by the tower, and then all of 24
8 us lost sight of them as they landed on the nearby asphalt. 36
   | 1 | 2 | 3 | 4 | 5 | 6 | 7 | 8 | 9 | 10 | 11 | 12

PRETEST

Take a 3-minute timing on lines 9–17 on page 151. Circle and count your errors.

PRACTICE

Take a 1-minute timing on each paragraph of the Pretest on page 151.

POSTTEST

Take another 3-minute timing on lines 9–17 on page 151 to see how much your skill has improved.

and also write information on it. It has random access to that memory—it can erase any part of it and write some more.

But RAM has a memory problem of its own. Once the electric current is turned off, RAM forgets everything. Some form of storage media must be in place if the information is to be saved.

Storage Media. Either cartridges or magnetic media are used to save the information in RAM before the power is turned off and to load information back into RAM after the power is turned back on.

Magnetic media for personal computers come in two types—tapes and disks. Disks (also known as floppy disks or diskettes) are either 3¼-, 5¼-, or 8-inch circles of plastic. These thin circles are permanently enclosed in a cardboard envelope to protect them from dust, dirt, and fingerprints.

Another type of magnetic medium that is becoming more and more popular with users of personal computers is the hard disk. Hard disks operate very much like floppy disks, but they hold a great deal more information.[4]

Disks require a special player known as a disk drive. The disk, protective covering and all, goes into a disk drive. There, the inner plastic circle is rotated at several hundred rotations per minute, while a record/playback head moves across the disk's surface.

The Keyboard. A computer keyboard looks very much/like the keyboard on a typewriter and operates like a typewriter. With a keyboard, almost anything can be communicated to a computer.

The Screen. The video screen, or video display, on a personal computer looks just like the screen on a television set and is called a CRT (cathode ray tube), which is the same kind of tube used in a television set.

On very sophisticated personal computers, the video screens are known as monitors and are connected directly to the computer. Monitors display sharper images than television screens.

The video display can be either in color or monochrome (one color). Video color is desirable for games and graphics, but monochrome displays offer sharper characters for both words and figures.

PERIPHERALS

The Printer. The printer is the device for "outputting" information permanently. A printer is known as a peripheral because it is peripheral—useful but not necessary—to the use of the computer.

There are two kinds of printers: dot matrix and letter-quality. Dot matrix printers form characters with little dots, very much like the signs on banks that tell the time and temperature. Dot matrix printers are not commonly used for correspondence.

For correspondence (letters, reports, and such), letter-quality printers should be used. These print a bit slower and cost more than dot matrix, but the quality of their printing is similar to that of electric typewriters.

The Modem. Another popular peripheral for the personal computer is called a modem. A modem is attached to the computer and to a telephone. The computer on the receiving end requires a modem too, and when it is connected over phone lines, information can flow back and forth between the computers.

THE PROGRAM (SOFTWARE)

A program is simply a series of instructions designed to solve a problem or accomplish a task on the computer. It is not hard to program a computer—but writing a program can be difficult.[5] Just as the programs you watch on television are designed by others, the majority of the programs you run on your computer will be written by others.

Hundreds of programmers are busy writing programs for personal computers. Producing and marketing software for computers is a fast-growing business that will provide many jobs in the future.[6]

4. Marilyn K. Popyk, Word Processing and Information Systems, 2d ed., McGraw-Hill Book Company, New York, 1986, p. 79.

5. McWilliams, p. 56.

6. Fred D'Ignagio, "The World Inside Your Computer," Compute!, November 1983, p. 152.

JOB 88 A. LETTER

Standard format (pages 103–104). Workbook 115–116. Body 136 words.

[*Today's date*] / Mr. Harold R. Lehman / 195 West Broadway / Unalakleet, AK 99684 / Dear Mr. Lehman:

Welcome to the large, growing family of Best Word users. We believe our product is at the top of the charts in word processing software packages. We hope that in the next few years you will find Best Word to be all that you had hoped it would be, and we are at your service to make sure that your satisfaction is guaranteed.

As we discussed in my office on Friday, you will receive a one-year warranty on Best Word, you will be able to attend at no charge our one-week training session, and you will receive our newest version of Best Spell when it comes on the market next month.

We look forward to serving your word processing needs in the years to come. Please feel free to call me if you have any questions. / Yours truly, / Linda Hansen / Sales Manager / [*Your initials*]

LETTER-PLACEMENT GUIDE

Workbook 117.

Some employers prefer to increase the line length for very long letters. Other adjustments for very long or very short letters are shown in the chart below.

Words in Body	Line Length	Date Typed on	From Date to Inside Address	Space for Signature
Under 100	5″ 50P/60E	Line 15	5–8 lines	3–6 blank lines
100–225	5″ 50P/60E	Line 15	5 lines	3 blank lines
Over 225	6″ 60P/70E	Lines 12–15	4–5 lines	2–3 blank lines

JOB 88 B. LETTER

Standard format. Workbook 119–120. Body 228 words.

[*Today's date*] / Ms. Bette J. Calvano / 610 Eucalyptus Avenue / Santa Barbara, CA 93101 / Dear Ms. Calvano:

Thank you for choosing our store for the purchase of your new Sholes printer. As we told you when you made your purchase, we are ready to stand behind our products if any problem should ever develop. The problem you are having with your printer may be caused by one of three circumstances.

First, it may be that the daisy wheel is not secured in its holder. If this occurs, you might get a line of nonsense symbols when you give the command to print. Please remove the printwheel and reseat it in the holder to see if this is the cause of the malfunction.

Second, your interface cable from the terminal to the printer may not be working as it should. Detach the cable from both the printer and the computer. Plug it in at both ends again, and be sure to tighten the screws that hold the cable in place.

(Continued on next page)

LESSON 72

■ GOALS
To identify how commas are used after introductory clauses while typing sentences.
To format and type a bibliography and a multipage report.
■ FORMAT
Single spacing   60-space line

LAB 6

**Introductory
If, As, and
When
Clauses**

Type lines 1–4 once. Then repeat lines 1–4 or take a series of 1-minute timings.

1 When the jury was dismissed, everyone decided to celebrate. 12
2 As we walked along quickly, we spoke of their organization. 12
3 If I have time later this week, I'll check into the matter. 12
4 When you finish, let me know if the lock needs to be fixed. 12

| 1 | 2 | 3 | 4 | 5 | 6 | 7 | 8 | 9 | 10 | 11 | 12

**30-SECOND
"OK"
TIMINGS**

Type as many 30-second "OK" (errorless) timings as possible out of three attempts on lines 5–7.

5 As you know, the man at the store is very lazy and will not 12
6 be interested in putting extra effort into the sale that we 24
7 will have in January. We cannot let him squander his time. 36

| 1 | 2 | 3 | 4 | 5 | 6 | 7 | 8 | 9 | 10 | 11 | 12

FORMATTING A BIBLIOGRAPHY

A bibliography is an alphabetic listing of all the books and articles consulted by the writer, including all references cited in the footnotes.

To format a bibliography:

1. Center the heading BIBLIOGRAPHY on a clean sheet of paper, beginning on line 13.

2. Triple-space after the heading before typing the first entry in the bibliography.

3. Use the same margins as used in the report or term paper. Begin each entry at the left margin, and indent continuation lines 5 spaces.

4. Use single spacing for turnover lines, but double-space between entries.

5. Do not number the entries.

6. List the entries in alphabetic order by the authors' *last* names. For an entry that has no author, alphabetize by the title of the article or book. When alphabetizing titles, disregard *The, A,* and *An.*

7. Use six hyphens to avoid repeating an author's name after his or her first listing. (See the illustration.)

When an author has more than one title listed, arrange titles alphabetically.

8. Separate items within each entry with commas.

9. Use page numbers only if the material is part of a larger work (such as a magazine article). Use the range of pages for the entire work.

10. Number the bibliography page the same way the other pages of the report are numbered.

↓13
BIBLIOGRAPHY
↓3

Brumley, Deborah and Grace, "A Man of Peace," Digest of History, April 1980, pp. 29-36.

Drebrelis, Nichola, "In Search of Ancient Gods," Modern Science Today, November 1980, pp. 53-65.

"The History of the Olympic Games," History of Sports, August 1982, pp. 115-128.

Kokoris, Harold Mark, The Beginning of the Olympics, Dunne Publishing Company, Los Angeles, 1982.

------, The Greeks, Spartan Press, New York, 1978.

PRETEST

Take a 2-minute timing on lines 6–11; then take a 2-minute timing on lines 12–17. Circle and count your errors on each.

Alternate-Hand
Reaches

6   What activities do you like when hot temperatures come   12
7 and bring along lots of sunshine? The choice of activities   24
8 may often depend on those that are near your residence.   35
9   You may want to spend your days splashing in the water   47
10 or just dozing on the deck if there is one close by. Then,   59
11 when the temperature rises, you can take a quick dip.   70

Double-Letter
Reaches

12   Playing volleyball in the outdoors, riding a bike on a   12
13 trail, jogging with a friend, playing tennis, and reading a   24
14 terrific book are all good activities for summer days.   35
15   Whatever you choose to do with your summer, though, be   47
16 sure to seek some time for doing as little as possible. At   59
17 this time you should be planning for cool winter days.   70

| 1 | 2 | 3 | 4 | 5 | 6 | 7 | 8 | 9 | 10 | 11 | 12

PRACTICE

In which timing did you make more errors? If in the first one (lines 6–11), type lines 18–21 four times and lines 22–25 two times. If most of your errors were in the second timing (lines 12–17), reverse the procedure.

Alternate-Hand
Reaches

18 also body burn clan dial duck flap goal halt held kept lame
19 auto born bush clay dock duty foam hair hand idle keys land
20 amend blame burns civic dials eight focus handy laugh proxy
21 angle blend chair corps field fight forms ivory panel right

Double-Letter
Reaches

22 ball bell call cell door fall food foot good keen keep knee
23 miss moon noon poor roof room root soon tell well wood yell
24 alley annex bells booth broom calls cells cross ditto funny
25 fussy goods happy issue keeps motto occur proof quill rooms

POSTTEST

Repeat the Pretest to see how much your skill has improved.

5-MINUTE TIMINGS

Repeat the Preview Practice and 5-minute timing routine on page 145.

LESSON 88

UNIT 15 Formatting Correspondence
UNIT GOAL 36/5'/5e

■ GOALS
To use commas correctly between adjectives while typing sentences.
To determine letter placement using a letter-placement guide.
To type business letters.

■ FORMAT
Single spacing   60-space line

LAB 8

Commas Between Adjectives

Workbook 113–114.

Type lines 1–4 once, providing the missing commas. Edit your copy as your teacher reads the answers. Then retype lines 1–4 from your edited copy.

1 They must clean the old useless duplicator before Tuesday.
2 Cool cloudy mornings often turn into beautiful afternoons.
3 That massive well-crafted desk weighs at least 300 pounds.
4 All students must complete the long difficult exam Friday.

JOB 72 A. BIBLIOGRAPHY

Prepare a bibliography for the report you have been typing by using the footnote references (pages 123–124). Make the changes and additions shown below. If you have read any books or magazine articles on the personal computer, include them in your bibliography. Standard format.

Change the page references as follows:

Rumberger . . . pp. 32–34.

D'Ignagio . . . . pp. 150–154.

Add: Peter A. McWilliams, The Word Processing Book: A Short Course in Computer Literacy, 8th ed., Prelude Press, Los Angeles, 1984.

Focus on the Future: Special Report, McGraw-Hill, Inc., New York, 1985.

JOB 72 B. MULTIPAGE REPORT

Continue the report you started in Lessons 70/71, pages 123–124.

LESSON 73

■ **GOALS**
To use commas correctly after introductory clauses while typing sentences.
To type 35/3'/5e.
To format and type a table of contents and a cover page.

■ **FORMAT**
Single spacing   60-space line
3-Minute Timings: Double spacing   5-space tab

LAB 6

Introductory If, As, and When Clauses

Workbook 74.

Type lines 1–4 once, providing the missing commas. Edit your copy as your teacher reads the answers. Then retype lines 1–4 from your edited copy.

1 When it got very windy Joe had to call a halt to the game.
2 When you type a report be very sure that you erase neatly.
3 If I do not return in six hours please call my Azusa home.
4 As Pat started the car I realized that it was quite noisy.

PREVIEW PRACTICE

Accuracy 5 event great quite Appian streets amazing citizens exploring
Speed   6 change cities there towns name such city same and the or of

Type each line twice as a preview to the 3-minute timings on page 127.

2. Rosemary T. Fruehling and Sharon Bouchard, <u>Business Correspondence: Essentials of Communication</u>, 4th ed., McGraw-Hill Book Company, New York, 1986, p. 9. _{48 72 87 94}

3. Ibid., p. 10. ₁₀₀

4. Reid and Wendlinger, p. 208. ₁₀₈

5. Herta A. Murphy and Herbert W. Hildebrandt, <u>Effective Business Communications,</u> 4th ed., McGraw-Hill Book Company, New York, 1984, p. 95. _{118 140 148 152}

6. Fruehling and Bouchard, p. 10. ₁₆₁

FORMATTING REPORTS IN SPACE-SAVING STYLE

The space-saving format may be used when the report is long and the originator wants as few pages as possible. To format in space-saving style:

1. Margins: 65P/75E.
2. Begin the title on line 10.
3. Single-space; double-space between paragraphs.
4. Double-space before and single-space after side headings if they are used. Or, use paragraph headings instead of side headings.
5. If your typewriter is equipped with vertical half spacing, use 1/2 blank line wherever you would normally use 1 blank line.

JOB 85/86 B. MULTIPAGE REPORT

Retype Job 85/86 A with the following changes: (1) type the endnotes as footnotes and place them at the bottom of the page; (2) omit the side heading entitled READ THE LETTER and the paragraph that follows; (3) type the side heading KNOW THE PURPOSE and the paragraph that follows as a replacement for the paragraph you omitted; (4) renumber the footnotes as needed. Space-saving format.

LESSON 87

CLINIC

■ **GOALS**
To improve your typing skills using the Selective Practice routine.
To type 35/5'/4e.

■ **FORMAT**
Drills: Single spacing   60-space line
Timings: Double spacing   5-space tab

KEYBOARDING SKILLS

Type lines 1–4 once. Then type line 5 using your return key after each word. Repeat lines 1–4, or take a series of 1-minute timings.

Speed 1 Their big problem is half their profit is spent for enamel. 12
Accuracy 2 Have my six dozen quails joined two big flocks of sparrows? 12
Numbers 3 Shirley got Nos. 10 and 29; Wesley got Nos. 38, 47, and 56. 12
Symbols 4 Fox & Day ordered 25# of cheese (mellow) @ $3.09 per pound. 12
Technique 5 You should always operate the return key or lever by touch.

| 1 | 2 | 3 | 4 | 5 | 6 | 7 | 8 | 9 | 10 | 11 | 12

Take two 3-minute timings on lines 7–15.

```
                  1                  2                  3                  4
 7     Streets are as old as cities or towns, and some of the    12
              5              6              7            8
 8   oldest, like the Appian Way in Rome, are still in use.  The  24
            9             10            11            12
 9   whole growth of most towns followed the path where the road  36
         13            14            15            16
10   was first made; so while the buildings in town changed, the  48
           17            18            19            20
11   road remained just about the same.  Quite often one can get  60
          21            22            23            24
12   a history of a city by exploring the names of some streets,  72
           25            26            27            28
13   which were often named after local events or amazing people  84
         29            30            31            32
14   of great deeds.  Are there any such streets in your city or  96
            33            34            35
15   your community that refer to famous citizens?               105
     |  1  |  2  |  3  |  4  |  5  |  6  |  7  |  8  |  9  | 10 | 11 | 12    SI 1.30
```

FORMATTING A TABLE OF CONTENTS

A table of contents is an outline of the headings in a report and the page references to them.

To format a table of contents:

1. Center the title CONTENTS on line 13. (You may spread-center the title if you wish.)

2. Use the same margins as those used in the report.

3. Follow standard format for vertical spacing of outlines. (See p. 61.)

4. Use leaders (rows of periods) to connect the headings with the numbers. Leave 1 space between the words and the start of the leaders and 1 space between the end of the leaders and the *longest* page number. (Leaders should all end at the same spot.)

```
                      ↓13
                  C O N T E N T S
                                 ↓3
         I.  Introduction ............................. 1

        II.  The Machine (Hardware) ................... 1
             A.  The Microprocessor .................. 1
```

FORMATTING A COVER PAGE

A cover page contains the title of the report, the name of the writer, the name of the person for whom the report was prepared, and the date. For academic reports, it also contains the name of the course.

To format a cover page:

1. Center the report title and the writer's name in the upper 33 lines of the page.

2. Center the name of the person for whom the report was prepared (teacher), the person's title or company or the course name, and the date in the lower 33 lines of the page.

```
            THE HISTORY OF THE OLYMPICS
                   By Susan Lam




                 Ms. Sue Champion

                    TYPEWRITING

                January 15, 19--
```

JOB 73 A. TABLE OF CONTENTS

Prepare a contents page for your report. Begin with *I. Introduction;* use the side and paragraph headings in the report for the remainder of the contents. Standard format.

JOB 73 B. COVER PAGE

Prepare a cover page for your report. Use your name, your typing teacher's name, and today's date.

12-SECOND TIMINGS

Type each line three times, or take three 12-second timings on each line. For each timing, type with no more than 1 error.

23 It seemed to me that the birds got silent long before dark.
24 She put a stamp on it before she dropped it in the mailbox.
25 Six of us pitched in to give the car a push along the road.

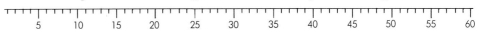

5   10   15   20   25   30   35   40   45   50   55   60

JOB 85/86 A. MULTIPAGE REPORT WITH ENDNOTES
Standard format.

HOW TO WRITE A GOOD LETTER

Organization Is the Key

By James R. Hoover

As is true with writing a report, a person who is well organized will write better letters than one who is not. As Reid and Wendlinger state in their book, "A well-planned business letter depends on the clear thinking you do before you compose your first sentence."[1] The need for clear, accurate thinking is also expressed by Fruehling and Bouchard when they state that "you must plan your letters before you write them."[2]

READ THE LETTER

If you write a letter in response to someone who has written to you, a good idea would be to read carefully the letter you have received. Some points will require a response, yet others need not be answered. As you read the letter, mark those points to which you must respond.

SEQUENCE THE ITEMS

Another helpful hint is for you to decide on the best sequence of items you wish to present.[3] This will help you to be sure you do not omit some important point and to present your information in a logical, direct order.

GET BACKGROUND

A third point to remember is that you should read any related letters or correspondence. Your task of writing a letter will become much easier if you know a little more about the subject or about the person who wrote you a letter.[4]

KNOW THE PURPOSE

"Your first step when planning your communication is to determine your main purpose."[5] Does your letter simply have to explain what you are going to do? Does it require a response? Is it trying to persuade? Does it ask someone to do a task for you? Or is it just trying to build goodwill? You have to know the purpose of your letter before these questions can be answered.

WRITE FOR THE READER

Above all else, make sure you write your letter from your reader's point of view.[6] Write your letter with words that your reader will understand. Try to think of how your reader is going to comprehend the words you have chosen for your letter. If you can accomplish this task, there is a very good chance that there will be no misunderstanding between the two of you.

NOTES

1. James M. Reid, Jr., and Robert M. Wendlinger, _Effective Letters_, 3d ed., McGraw-Hill Book Company, New York, 1978, p. 207.

(Continued on next page)

TEST

■ **GOALS**
To demonstrate competency by typing 35/3'/5e.
To demonstrate competency by formatting and correctly
typing a personal-business letter, business letters,
envelopes, a table, and a report with footnotes.

■ **FORMAT**
Double spacing   60-space line   5-space tab

PREVIEW PRACTICE

Type each line twice as a preview to the 3-minute timings below.

Accuracy   1   art are barns signs noted cheap their native living rotting
Speed   2   examples antiques products through country symbol today era

3-MINUTE TIMINGS

Take two 3-minute timings on lines 3–11.

```
              1                 2                 3                 4
3       Have you ever driven through the country and noted the   12
              5                 6                 7                 8
4     number of barns painted with the same sign, all selling the  24
              9                10                11                12
5     same product?  At the time farmers found it a cheap way for  36
             13                14                15                16
6     them to have their barns painted.  Makers of products found  48
             17                18                19                20
7     this to be an amazing idea to push their goods.  Today many  60
             21                22                23                24
8     of the barn signs are thought to be good examples of living  72
             25                26                27                28
9     native art.  They are a symbol of an era, and like antiques  84
             29                30                31                32
10    and old things, some are being preserved; but most of these  96
             33                34                35
11    barns are just rotting away or falling down.               105
      |  1  |  2  |  3  |  4  |  5  |  6  |  7  |  8  |  9  | 10  | 11  | 12    SI 1.30
```

JOB 74/75 A. PERSONAL-BUSINESS LETTER

Standard format. Use your own return address and to-day's date; use your own name as the writer. Workbook 75.

B & B Agency / 2800 Keystone Road / Sand Springs, OK 74063 / Ladies and Gentlemen: / In our class in office practice, our teacher showed your new film, You CAN Succeed. I thought the film was really good for young people who are trying to decide whether they want a career in business. ¶ Our Business Club will host the state meeting next year. As I am planning the program, I would like to use this film for one of our sessions. Will you please let me know how much it would cost to rent the film. / Yours truly,

JOB 74/75 B. BUSINESS LETTER WITH ENCLOSURE

Standard format. Workbook 77–78.

[Today's date] / Mrs. J. F. Rodriguez / 500 West Brady Street / Tulsa, OK 74103 / Dear Mrs. Rodri-guez: / Here is your ComputerWorld charge card. It allows you to charge your purchases at any of our 63 shopping centers in the Tulsa area. We know you will find your card a convenience. ¶ Also enclosed is a list of introductory specials we are offering this month. Just bring the list to one of our stores and use your new charge card to take advantage of these spe-cials. ¶ If I can be of any further service to you, please call me at 555-6100. / Sincerely yours, / Brandon Fielding / Credit Manager / [Your initials] / 2 Enclosures

■ **GOALS**
To use commas correctly between adjectives while typing sentences.
To type 35/5'/5e.
To reinforce report typing.
To format and type a report in space-saving style.

■ **FORMAT**
Drills: Single spacing   60-space line
5-Minute Timings: Double spacing   5-space tab

LAB 8

Commas Between Adjectives

Type lines 1–4 once, providing the missing commas. Edit your copy as your teacher reads the answers. Then retype lines 1–4 from your edited copy.

1 It's dangerous to drive quickly on a wet slippery highway.
2 Soft soothing music plays in most restaurants and offices.
3 Six of us in Jan's building heard the loud strident voice.
4 A hazy summer morning often becomes a hot humid afternoon.

PREVIEW PRACTICE

Accuracy
Speed

Type each line twice as a preview to the 5-minute timings below.

5 length quickly powerful production backspacing horizontally
6 also each have just line long page that time want when your

5-MINUTE TIMINGS

Take two 5-minute timings on lines 7–22.

```
                      1                              2
7       Two special, unique jobs that a word processor can ac-    12
           3                            4
8  complish for you are that it can set the length of the line    24
     5                        6                       7
9  you want to use and it can center a table in a snap.  These    36
                 8                        9
10 production tasks will hinder your speed when typing a table    48
            10                      11                     12
11 or a difficult letter, but not when you're using a powerful   60
                   13
12 word processor to aid you.                                     65
                      14                         15
13      When a letter is placed on a word processor, you never    77
              16                        17
14 have to be concerned about how long your line length should    89
       18                       19                      20
15 be because just one short command will assign an exact num-   101
             21                        22
16 ber of characters in each line.  A line length of 50 spaces   113
            23                       24
17 can be revised quickly to 60 spaces.                          120
                       25                            26
18      The word processor also saves the typist a lot of time   132
               27                        28
19 when typing tables.  One single command will center a group   144
       29                       30                      31
20 of words horizontally on a page.  You never have to be con-   156
                 32                        33
21 cerned about backspacing or counting the exact total number   168
            34                       35
22 of spaces in the words you center.                            175
   |  1  |  2  |  3  |  4  |  5  |  6  |  7  |  8  |  9  |  10  |  11  |  12   SI 1.37
```

JOB 74/75 C. TABLE (ENCLOSURE)
Standard format.

INTRODUCTORY SPECIALS

Title	Number	Sale Price
Graphics Cookbook	6278	$ 9.95
Secrets of BASIC	5254	14.95
Pascal With Style	5124	9.50
Robotics Age	6235	16.95
Computer Parade	6356	9.95
Match-Boxes	9108	29.95
Computers for Kids	7280	5.95
Word Wizard	9261	29.95
Story Machine	9434	39.95

JOB 74/75 D. BUSINESS LETTER
Standard format. Workbook 79–80.

(Today's date) / Mr. Scott L. Ulene / 2600 Lyle Street / Boise, ID 83075 / Dear Mr. Ulene: / Standing room only is the description of a typical meeting of the Compucats computer club. Each month we draw large crowds with our dynamic programs and demonstrations. At each meeting there are as many as 10 machines up and running for trying software out. This group meets at our store near the Reed Air Base, which makes it possible for us to attract members from many parts of the world and always leads to an interesting exchange of ideas. Why not become a member of this active group? Just return the enclosed card or come to the next meeting at 2 p.m. this Saturday / Yours very truly, /

Joe Farina, Manager / (Your initials) / Enclosure

JOB 74/75 E. REPORT WITH FOOTNOTES
Standard format.

COMPUTERS AND THE DISABLED
By Jose Moralles

The day is coming when personal computers will be as important to handicapped people as their wheelchairs, hearing aids, and seeing-eye dogs are today. Applications of hardware and software can actually become the eyes, ears, voices, and hands of those who cannot use their own.[1]

The concept may seem a bit strange to most home computer users, who depend on keying in programs, viewing monitor displays, and reading hard copy from a printer. How can a person with cerebral palsy who can't type, or a blind person who can't respond to screen prompts, use a computer?

Light pens can be held in the mouth, for example. They can be used to select menu options and draw on the screen. The Optacon, a device that translates output from a monitor into braille, is used by blind programmers. The "mouse" can be used as a screen pointer to make standard software accessible to people who can't type on the keyboard.

Communication networks and electronic bulletin boards are great for deaf people, who can work or socialize via the keyboard. Programs such as PC Speaks let a blind user scroll through the program while a speech synthesizer reads each screen aloud.[2] Other trends, such as electronic mail, at-home shopping, and data banks, will provide a new way of life for people who are unable to go out or communicate by telephone.

---

1. Joan Killough-Miller, "Computers Enable the Disabled," Home Computer Digest, Vol. 1, No. 2, September 1985, pp. 12–13.

2. David Carey, The Computer, Ladybird Books, Loughborough, 1986, p. 50.

In the chart below find the number of errors you made on the Pretest. Then type each of the designated drill lines four times.

Pretest errors	0–1	2–3	4–5	6+
Drill lines	24–28	23–27	22–26	21–25

Accuracy

21 placed conduct complex because creation processor therefore
22 needed clients without section business necessary deletions
23 insert require granted phrases approval prepared repeatedly
24 section helpful because without inserts document processing

Speed

25 papers before would legal take look that copy most made you
26 client breeze close might very well near with last have the
27 error; change today firms list both word used into when use
28 system button their quite that work top and for law all can

POSTTEST

Take another 5-minute timing on lines 5–20 on page 143 to see how much your skill has improved.

JOB 84 A. MULTIPAGE REPORT
Standard format.

WRITING A REPORT   10

How to Gather Data   23

By Ruth E. Riley   35

5] The purpose of a report is to ~~preserve~~ *save*   45
data so that it can be used on some   52
future date for some specific reason.   60
If you have ever given much thought to   67
how that data is collected, you know   75

that there are two basic methods of ~~ob~~   82
~~taining~~ *getting* it: (1) secondary research or   90
(2) primary research.   94

SECONDARY RESEARCH   100

"Research through published mate-   108
rial is secondary research."[1] This   117
would include all data that is obtained   125
~~through~~ *from* such sources as books, reports,   132
news papers, or pamphlets. This data   140
has been ~~written~~ *gathered* by ~~many~~ other people,   147
and you are using it for your report.   154
If you use any of the data from such a   162

source, you must give credit to the   169
person who first ~~wrote~~ *presented* it. The *most* comon   179
~~method~~ *way* of doing this is through a foot-   186
note or an endnote.   190

PRIMARY RESEARCH   196
~~Primary~~ *This kind of* research pertains usually   204
to research that has *not* been done by other   213
people. If you do your own research   221
and come up with *original, accurate* data that you want to   232
use *in* ~~for~~ your report, this "first hand"   240
data is known as primary ~~research~~ data.   246
Primary research ~~very~~ *may* often consist of   255
getting data from such sources as rec-   262
ords, interviews, ~~observations, experi-~~[2]   266
~~ments,~~ or questionnaires.[2]   272

---

1. Herta A. Murphy and Herbert   +17
W. Hildebrandt, Effective Business   +34
Communications, *4th ed.* McGraw-Hill Book Com-   +47
pany, New York, 1984, p. 466.   +52

2. Ibid.   +107

LEVEL 4

GOALS

1. Demonstrate keyboarding speed and accuracy on straight copy with a goal of 36 words a minute for 5 minutes with 5 or fewer errors.

2. Correctly proofread copy for errors and edit copy for revision.

3. Apply basic production skills in keyboarding and formatting copy for reports, correspondence, and forms from a variety of input modes— arranged, unarranged, rough draft, handwritten, incomplete and/or unedited.

4. Apply rules for correct use of the comma in written communications.

LESSON 84

■ **GOALS**
To identify how commas are used between adjectives while typing sentences.
To type 35/5'/4e.
To reinforce report typing.

■ **FORMAT**
Drills: Single spacing   60-space line
5-Minute Timings: Double spacing   5-space tab

LAB 8

Commas Between Adjectives

Type lines 1–4 once. Then repeat lines 1–4 or take a series of 1-minute timings.

1 A dozen anxious, excited scouts began their overnight trip.   12
2 Last night four neighbors bought Joan a healthy, happy pup.   12
3 The scarecrow is wearing a long, loose coat and a silk hat.   12
4 The salesperson who waits on me is the quiet, helpful type.   12

| 1 | 2 | 3 | 4 | 5 | 6 | 7 | 8 | 9 | 10 | 11 | 12

PRETEST

Take a 5-minute timing on lines 5–20. Circle and count your errors.

5   If you would take a close look at the firms that today   12
6 use a word processor to conduct their business, legal firms   24
7 might very well be near the top of the list.   33
8   Both small and large law firms use word processing for   45
9 the creation of legal forms or papers for their clients. A   57
10 legal firm might often require that all typed work is to be   69
11 done without error; therefore, the use of a word processing   81
12 system is quite helpful to legal firms.   89
13   Legal papers may require major, complex changes before   101
14 approval is granted. It is a breeze to change copy that is   113
15 prepared on a word processor because most inserts and dele-   125
16 tions can be made with the press of a button.   134
17   And last of all, legal work may have large sections of   146
18 words and phrases that are used repeatedly. These sections   158
19 can be placed into the document as often as necessary, when   170
20 and where they are needed.   175

| 1 | 2 | 3 | 4 | 5 | 6 | 7 | 8 | 9 | 10 | 11 | 12   SI 1.37

For Extra Speed

Tab-indent quickly, smoothly.

Return carriage or carrier quickly.

Release shift key instantly.

Get off space bar in a flash.

Keep eyes on copy so that you never lose your place.

UNIT 13 Keyboarding Skills Review
UNIT GOAL 35/5'/5e

■ GOALS
To identify and practice the alphabetic keys on which more
   drill is needed.
To build skill on the alphabetic keyboard.
To type 35/5'/5e.

■ FORMAT
Drills: Single spacing   60-space line   Tabs every 7
   spaces
5-Minute Timings: Double spacing   5-space tab

KEYBOARDING SKILLS

Type lines 1–4 once. In line 5 use your tabulator key to advance from one number to the next through the entire line. Repeat lines 1–4, or take a series of 1-minute timings.

Speed	1	She may go to town for a pen, but she must come right back.	12
Accuracy	2	Five or six big jet planes zoomed quickly by the new tower.	12
Numbers	3	If 56 days are left, then 47, 29, 38, and 10 will not work.	12
Symbols	4	With our 4% raise we bought 17 lb of #38 & #29--what a buy!	12
Technique	5	102 293 384 475 561 102 293 384 475

| 1 | 2 | 3 | 4 | 5 | 6 | 7 | 8 | 9 | 10 | 11 | 12 |

PRETEST 1

Take a 2-minute timing on lines 6–9 or type lines 6–9 twice to find out which alphabetic keys are the most difficult for you. Force yourself to type rapidly—push yourself to your fastest rate. Circle each letter typed incorrectly.

6 We amazed six judges by quietly giving back the four pages. 12
7 The expert quickly noted five bad zircons among the jewels. 24
8 Jack will exhibit very quaint games for Buzz's fall parade. 36
9 The exits were quickly filled by dozens of jumpy villagers. 48

| 1 | 2 | 3 | 4 | 5 | 6 | 7 | 8 | 9 | 10 | 11 | 12 |

PRACTICE 1

Type lines 10–22 once. Then repeat any of the lines that stress the letter errors you circled in Pretest 1.

AB	10	A air age aft ache arch autos B bat big bed bomb born bribe
CD	11	C cup car cow coke chip crack D den dot dog disk damp drive
EF	12	E elk eat elm east else eaves F for far fit fort folk frame
GH	13	G gym gas get gone grab given H how hop hip home horn haste
IJ	14	I ill icy ink iron into inlet J jar jet joy jump jinx joist
KL	15	K kid kit key kiss knit knock L lid law leg lace lean ledge
MN	16	M mud mix mop mine must march N nip net not news nice nerve
OP	17	O oar old out odds once ounce P pan pad paw pane part pound
QR	18	Q que qui quo quid quiz quilt R rag ran run rest rent reach
ST	19	S sly sum set scar sack skate T tan toe tap tact task their
UV	20	U use ups urn ugly uses union V vat vex vow vote vent value
WX	21	W wag wet was were when windy X mix fox axe text lynx exert
YZ	22	Y you yet yap year your yards Z zoo zig zip zinc zone zesty

POSTTEST 1

Take another 2-minute timing on lines 6–9 to see how much your skill has improved.

PRETEST 2

Take a 5-minute timing on lines 23–34 on page 132. Circle and count your errors. Use the chart on page 132 to determine which lines to type for practice.

Adjectives describe or modify nouns. Note the adjectives in italics:

brief speeches   *interesting* speeches   *brief, interesting* speeches
effective ideas   *unique* ideas   *effective, unique* ideas

When two or more adjectives describe the same noun, place a comma between the adjectives. In all other cases, use no comma. To determine whether the adjectives do describe the same noun, use the following test:

Janice gave a *factual, detailed* account. (Say "An account that was factual AND detailed." Does it make sense? Yes, proving that each adjective describes *account* and that the comma is needed.)

She distributed a *new summer* schedule. (Say "A schedule that is new AND summer." Does it make sense? No, proving that each adjective does not describe the noun *schedule*. No comma is needed.)

30-SECOND "OK" TIMINGS

Type as many 30-second "OK" (errorless) timings as possible out of three attempts on lines 5–7.

```
5  Holly acquired a prize for jumping over five feet backward,   12
6  but she very well won't receive any prizes for jumping for-   24
7  ward unless she can jump at least fourteen or fifteen feet.   36
   |  1  |  2  |  3  |  4  |  5  |  6  |  7  |  8  |  9  | 10  | 11  | 12
```

JOB 83 A. BOUND REPORT WITH ENDNOTES

Standard format (page 140), endnotes (page 121). 5-space and center tabs.

THE JOB INTERVIEW 10
By David L. Raintry 24

One of the most important meetings you ever 36 attend may very well be your job interview. 45 When you have been called by an employer and 54 are asked to come in for an interview, you can 63 take some positive steps to ensure that the ses- 73 sion is a positive one for you. 79

BEFORE THE INTERVIEW 85

You should try to get as much information as 95 possible on the company before the interview. 105 Do some research on the company, ask ques- 113 tions, talk to people, and gather as much data as 123 you can about the history and current status of 133 the company. Be sure to wear appropriate cloth- 142 ing for the interview, and be careful of your ap- 152 pearance. Lastly, be sure to check for the right 162 time and place of the interview.[1] 171

DURING THE INTERVIEW 177

During the interview, "be honest and sincere 187 at all times."[2] Be enthusiastic, be honest, be 198 yourself, and be courteous. It is just as important 209 that you be a good listener during the interview 219 as it is that you be a good speaker. 226

AFTER THE INTERVIEW 230

Evaluate your performance in the interview by 241 reading any notes you made during the session. 250 Send a follow-up letter to give thanks for the 260 interview and also to express any continued in- 269 terest in the company. "The type of letter you 278 write will depend on how things went at the in- 288 terview."[3] The follow-up letter should be sent 299 within two to five days after you have had your 309 interview.[4] It should be a short, well-organized 321 letter not more than one page in length. 329

NOTES 3

1. Herta A. Murphy and Herbert W. Hildebrandt, <u>Effective Business Communications</u>, 4th ed., McGraw-Hill Book Company, New York, 1984, pp. 378–380. 13 / 36 / 44 / 49

2. Ibid., p. 380. 55

3. Roy W. Poe and Rosemary T. Fruehling, <u>Business Communication, A Problem-Solving Approach</u>, 3d ed., McGraw-Hill Book Company, New York, 1984, p. 274. 65 / 90 / 99 / 108

4. Murphy and Hildebrandt, p. 386. 117

23   We realize today that a small computer may be required to prepare and   15

24 store the letters and memos that we produce. In some cases, a microcom-   29

25 puter and printer might be used to prepare all documents in final form. If   44

26 you work in an office that uses such a system to produce its paperwork,   59

27 what kind of equipment can you expect to use to store data?   71

28   The major piece of equipment, of course, is a computer system that   85

29 often includes a keyboard as well as the memory in which the data can be   100

30 stored until you choose to have it printed. But, if you wish, your data can   115

31 also be stored on a disk. A computer disk is quite a lot like the phonograph   131

32 record you use in your home in that it contains a series of grooves on which   146

33 the data can be stored. When all the data has been stored either in the   161

34 computer or on a disk, it can then be transferred to a printing device.   175

| 1 | 2 | 3 | 4 | 5 | 6 | 7 | 8 | 9 | 10 | 11 | 12 | 13 | 14 | 15 | SI 1.35

PRACTICE 2

In the chart below find the number of errors you made on Pretest 2. Then type each of the designated drill lines four times.

Pretest errors	0–1	2–3	4–5	6+
Drill lines	38–42	37–41	36–40	35–39

Accuracy

35 may today small realize letters computer keyboard equipment

36 all kind memos produce prepare required transfer phonograph

37 use cases piece expect include printed document transferred

38 lot been often quite grooves devices printing microcomputer

Speed

39 might final some used form disk like home and the lot we be

40 major which uses such what your home its but to in if an is

41 store until today have wish also when form disk you can all

42 homes disks often kind that work data then well may lot and

POSTTEST 2

Take another 5-minute timing on lines 23–34 to see how much your skill has improved.

LESSON 77

■ **GOALS**
To identify and practice the number keys on which more drill
  is needed.
To build skill in typing numbers.
To type a personal-business letter and a table.

■ **FORMAT**
Single spacing   60-space line

KEYBOARDING SKILLS

Type lines 1–4 (pages 132–133) once. In line 5 (page 133) use the shift lock for each word in all-capital letters. Repeat lines 1–4, or take a series of 1-minute timings.

Speed   1 All of them might work now to make the new year a good one.   12
Accuracy   2 Vi kept it blazing sixty minutes with a quart jug of cider.   12

| 1 | 2 | 3 | 4 | 5 | 6 | 7 | 8 | 9 | 10 | 11 | 12 |

(Continued on next page)

PROCESSOR 194

The processor is the part of the system that sends messages from the 209 keyboard to the other parts in the system, and it is the brain of your system. 225

STORAGE 229

If you want to save what you have typed, it is placed into storage. Some 244 word processors have their own storage; others have a disk or cartridge that 260 is used to store what you have typed. 268

PRINTERS 271

Impact Printers. "Impact printers print by striking the type against a 293 ribbon and the paper to produce a copy."[2] The most common kinds of 308 impact printers are daisy wheel, thimble, dot matrix, and line printers. 323

Nonimpact Printers. These printers are the newest on the market and 345 provide high quality for the printing process. One type, the ink-jet printer, 361 sprays ink on the paper to form the letters. Laser printers are very fast, but 377 their cost puts them out of the market for many users. With this method, 392 letters are formed by a narrow beam of light. Laser printers can produce 407 more than 100 pages a minute, with one or two type styles per page, in a 423 variety of type sizes.[3] 429

Watching for bottom margin? Remember that a footnote must go on the same page as the reference to it.

Separation line is 2 inches long. Single-space before and double-space after typing it.

1. Marilyn K. Popyk, Word Processing and Information Systems, 2d +38 ed., McGraw-Hill Book Company, New York, 1986, p. 74. +49

2. Ibid., p. 145. +70

3. Ibid., p. 148. +75

LESSON 83

■ **GOALS**
To recognize how commas are used between adjectives while typing sentences.
To type a bound report with endnotes.

■ **FORMAT**
Single spacing   60-space line

LAB 8

Commas Between Adjectives

Type lines 1–4 once. Then repeat lines 1–4 or take a series of 1-minute timings.

```
1  A sleek, colorful automobile was the highlight of the show.    12
2  Members of the strong, silent majority seldom speak loudly.    12
3  Diaz is a member of our unbeatable, hard-working judo team.    12
4  The bulky, noisy machine is obstructing everyone's advance.    12
   | 1 | 2 | 3 | 4 | 5 | 6 | 7 | 8 | 9 | 10 | 11 | 12
```

(Continued on next page)

Numbers	3	We saw 10 fish, 29 rabbits, 38 birds, 47 dogs, and 56 cats. 12
Symbols	4	We paid 12% on a loan of $900; they (Ann and Joe) paid 13%. 12
Technique	5	The metals are COPPER and GOLD and IRON and NICKEL and TIN.

```
| 1 | 2 | 3 | 4 | 5 | 6 | 7 | 8 | 9 | 10 | 11 | 12
```

PRETEST

Take a 2-minute timing on lines 6–8 or type lines 6–8 twice to find out which number keys are the most difficult for you. Keep your eyes on the copy as you type. Circle each digit typed incorrectly.

```
6   7364 6302 4951 2638 6504 9853 0298 2905 1174 4675 3701 1892   12
7   2506 9468 3277 1905 7688 7146 4904 2956 7331 2308 5251 7645   24
8   8405 7139 6672 5318 2604 5399 0842 7308 4296 7511 9405 8236   36
```

```
| 1 | 2 | 3 | 4 | 5 | 6 | 7 | 8 | 9 | 10 | 11 | 12
```

PRACTICE

Type lines 9–18 once. Then repeat any of the lines that stress the digit errors you circled in the Pretest.

```
1   9   We need 1 desk, 1 chair, 11 staplers, 11 pens, and 11 pins.
2   10  Player No. 22 ran 22 yards; then the score became 22 to 12.
3   11  Mel's ticket stub is for Seat 3, 13, 31, or 33--not for 43.
4   12  Through Gate No. 4 came Nos. 4, 14, 41, 44, 54, 48, and 43.
5   13  The scores were 54 to 45, 55 to 54, 52 to 25, and 53 to 51.
6   14  State highways 16, 26, 66, 126, 166, and 176 are now paved.
7   15  On May 17 send $77 to reserve 17 seats for the July 7 game.
8   16  On 6/8, 7/8, and 8/8 we sold 8 quarts and 8 pints of pears.
9   17  They have 9 pennies, 19 nickels, 29 dimes, and 39 quarters.
0   18  We led by 10 points at 20 to 30 and by 10 more at 20 to 40.
```

POSTTEST

Take another 2-minute timing on lines 6–8 to see how much your skill has improved.

JOB 77 A. PERSONAL-BUSINESS LETTER
Standard format (page 100). Workbook 101–102.

430 Mitchell Drive / Tempe, AZ 85281 / July 3, 19— / Mr. Ralph W. Fulton / Customer Relations Department / Interstate Bus Line / 5681 Lakeshore Drive / Tempe, AZ 85283 / Dear Mr. Fulton:

I would like your assistance in getting a refund for my bus ticket from Tempe to Santa Fe last week. The date of my trip was June 26.

Your agent said it would not be possible to refund my money because I did not cancel my trip at least 12 hours prior to the time of departure. However, on the way to the bus depot I was involved in an accident, and the car in which I was riding was unable to continue the trip to the bus depot. When I arrived in Tempe, the bus had already left for Santa Fe.

Any help you can give me in obtaining my refund would be greatly appreciated. / Sincerely yours, / Karen D. Stone / [*Your initials*]

JOB 77 B. TWO-COLUMN TABLE
Standard format (pages 110 and 112). Half sheet of paper. Workbook 103.

GENERAL DELIVERY ZIP CODES

Major Cities in Colorado

Boulder	80302
Colorado Springs	80901
Denver	80201
Fort Collins	80521
Grand Junction	81501
Greeley	80631

UNIT 14 Formatting Reports
UNIT GOAL 35/5'/5e

■ GOALS
To use commas correctly while typing compound sentences.
To format and type a bound report.

■ FORMAT
Single spacing   60-space line

LAB 7

Commas in Compound Sentences

Workbook 109–110.

Type lines 1–4 once, providing the missing commas. Edit your copy as your teacher reads the answers. Then retype lines 1–4 from your edited copy.

1 Spelling is very important but proofreading is needed too.
2 Sam's computer isn't working but no one is quite sure why.
3 Continuous paper was used but it was not the correct size.
4 The enter key will work and the return key will work also.

PRODUCTION WORD COUNT

The production word count (PWC) is used in production work to give you words-a-minute credit for operations such as using the tabulator, underscoring. In Job 82 A the PWC allows you credit for centering the title and subtitle lines, using the tabulator to indent paragraphs, and underscoring the paragraph headings and book titles.

The production word count assumes that you have set all necessary margins and tab stops and that your typewriter is in position to perform the first operation. In Job 82 A your carriage or carrier would be positioned at the centering point, ready to backspace for the title.

FORMATTING BOUND REPORTS

If a report is so thick or important that it needs a protective binder, the margins and tab stops should be moved 3 spaces to the right to provide space at the left for three-hole punching and/or for notebook binding.

JOB 82 A. BOUND MULTIPAGE REPORT
Standard format (pages 90, 92, 96, and 120). Workbook 108, 111–112.

WORD PROCESSOR COMPONENTS   15
Four Basic Features   29
Prepared by Diane E. Brooks   47

Although word processors can vary on many points such as cost, profile,   65
and features, all of them have four basic components: a keyboard, a   78
processor, a place for storage, and a printer. This report will briefly pre- 94
sent each of these features.   100

KEYBOARD   103
The keyboard of a word processor is very much like that which you have   119
been using on a typewriter. The real difference between the two is that a 134
word processor has some special function keys that allow you to do such   148
things as delete words, add words, change margins, and so forth. "The   162
function keys help you to perform automatically many tasks that would be   177
tedious and time-consuming on an ordinary typewriter."[1]   190

(Continued on next page)

LESSON 78

■ GOALS
To recognize how commas are used in compound sentences
while typing.
To identify and practice the symbol keys on which more drill
is needed.
To build skill in typing symbols.
To type a report with a table.

■ FORMAT
Single spacing   60-space line

LAB 7

**Commas in
Compound
Sentences**

Type lines 1–4 once. Then repeat lines 1–4 or take a series of 1-minute timings.

1   You must use a typewriter, and it might help you very much.   12
2   The word processor is very fast, and it is easy to use too.   12
3   You must edit the copy, or you will have to retype the job.   12
4   You cannot double-space the text, nor can you photocopy it.   12

     | 1 | 2 | 3 | 4 | 5 | 6 | 7 | 8 | 9 | 10 | 11 | 12

An "independent" clause is one that can stand alone as a sentence. Here are two examples of independent clauses: *Sandra bought a terminal. Eric chose a printer.* When two independent clauses are joined by the conjunction *and, but, or,* or *nor* into one compound sentence, place a comma before the conjunction:

Sandra bought a terminal, *but* Eric chose a printer.
They have two disk drives, *and* soon they will add another.

PRETEST

Take a 2-minute timing on lines 5–9 or type lines 5–9 twice to find out which symbol keys are the most difficult for you. Force yourself to type rapidly—push yourself to your fastest rate. Circle each symbol typed incorrectly.

5   We sold 16 quarts @ $4, 17 quarts @ $3, and 19 quarts @ $2.   12
6   Our #8365 makes 7% profit; #1083 makes 8%; #9274 makes 10%.   24
7   Ames & Day and Poe & Clay predicted a 60¢ and an 82¢ climb.   36
8   Computers use asterisks to multiply: 2 * 2 (4); 3 * 3 (9).   48
9   In math, 9 − 4 = 5 and 6 − 2 = 4; 9 + 4 = 13 and 6 + 1 = 7.   60

     | 1 | 2 | 3 | 4 | 5 | 6 | 7 | 8 | 9 | 10 | 11 | 12

PRACTICE

Type lines 10–19 once. Then repeat any of the lines that stress the symbol errors you circled in the Pretest.

@   10   They found 10 @ 56, 56 @ 47, 47 @ 38, 38 @ 29, and 29 @ 10.
¢   11   Soda is 56¢, candy is 47¢, gum is 29¢, and peanuts are 10¢.
*   12   Gray,* Moletti,* Young,* Hernandez,* and Jones* won prizes.
#   13   Our new scale shows #10 at 29#, #38 at 47#, and #29 at 56#.
$ 14   Our show tickets should cost us $10, $29, $38, $47, or $56.
%   15   Your sales increased 10%, 29%, 38%, 47%, and 56% last year.
&   16   Lee & Madera, Yung & Poe, and Day & Cole are all attorneys.
( ) 17   Lund (Utah), Leon (Iowa), and Troy (Ohio) were represented.
−   18   Label the square cartons as 47-10, 56-38, 38-47, and 10-29.
+ = 19   We know that 38 + 58 = 96, 29 + 10 = 39, and 56 + 47 = 103.

Take a 2-minute timing on lines 6–11; then take a 2-minute timing on lines 12–17. Circle and count your errors on each.

6	Working with plants could be an alluring and fun hobby	12
7	for you. You have missed a joyous time if you have not had	24
8	the chance to see a tiny sprig grow to an adult plant.	35
9	Plants can make a good pet for people living in apart-	47
10	ment house units. Plants do not annoy people, and all your	59
11	friends don't complain about the loud sound and noise.	70

12	Most plants require at least moderate light and warmth	12
13	to thrive. In addition, plants need to be misted, fed, and	24
14	watered on a regular basis so they can grow and live.	35
15	If you are like the many others who like their plants,	47
16	your zeal for growing them can increase rapidly. You might	59
17	undoubtedly be urging your friends to grow plants also.	70

```
| 1 | 2 | 3 | 4 | 5 | 6 | 7 | 8 | 9 | 10 | 11 | 12
```

In which timing did you make more errors? If in the first one (lines 6–11), type lines 18–21 four times and lines 22–25 two times. If most of your errors were in the second timing (lines 12–17), reverse the procedure.

18	bulk clip fill hold jump like mild plow ship till unit whip
19	bull coil hole hope hunt lime lips polo shop soil will yoke
20	alike apple blood chips cooks fills hills hopes loose poise
21	allow bills build clips folks ships smile thumb upper wills

22	acre drew feet last matt odds pass safe seen uses wave yard
23	away even hard less meet over past sash user very were west
24	apart awake bless chase creek event every fires glass haven
25	jewel level march offer phase refer satin sewer threw where

Repeat the Pretest to see how much your skill has improved.

CORRECTIONS REVIEW: ERASER, SPREADING, AND SQUEEZING

Review pages 57 and 59. Then use the following procedures to complete the correction review. *Error Correction:* Type line 26, then correct line 26 so that it looks like line 27. *Spreading Correction* and *Squeezing Correction:* Type lines 28 through 31, leaving the exact number of blank spaces shown in lines 29 and 31. Then type the words listed into the blank spaces.

	26	The teacher said their are four exercises do type by seven.
	27	The teacher said there are four exercises to type by seven.
	28	We will go too the fair. Four children went too the movie.
Insert *to*	29	We will go the fair. Four children went the movie.
	30	The to of them may drive. Would you to want to ride along?
Insert *two*	31	The of them may drive. Would you want to ride along?

POSTTEST   Take another 2-minute timing on lines 5–9 on page 134 to see how much your skill has improved.

JOB 78 A. REPORT WITH TABLE
Standard format (pages 87 and 122). Double spacing, 5-space tab. Workbook 104–107.

NEW PLANT LOCATIONS

Railroad Terminal

The findings in this report are the results of a six-month study on site locations. After investigation, it is the conclusion of this research team that the site location for our new railroad terminal should be in one of three cities: Nashville, Pittsburgh, or Salt Lake City.

We plan to hire 500 to 1000 employees when we are at full strength. Each of these cities is a major population center, and each should provide ample personnel resources.

One of the main concerns of site location is weather patterns, because much of the yard work will be done outside the main terminal. Average high temperatures and average days of rain or snow for each of the cities are given in the table below.

WEATHER INFORMATION

City	Temperature	Precipitation
Nashville	71 degrees	120 days/year
Pittsburgh	60 degrees	149 days/year
Salt Lake City	64 degrees	87 days/year

Transportation is available by rail, auto, bus, and air for each of the cities. This is a key factor in our final choice of site, because the bulk of our business will come from a number of carriers. The dollar amount that each of these carriers represents will be placed in the May report.

The final selection of this site will be made on June 30 at the district meeting to be held in Denver. Be prepared to commence work on this new site during the month of August.

LESSON 79

■ **GOALS**
To identify how commas are used in compound sentences while typing.
To review the use of and gain proficiency in operating the tab, the space bar, and the backspace key.
To practice two formatting techniques.

■ **FORMAT**
Single spacing   60-space line   Tabs every 9 spaces

LAB 7

Commas in Compound Sentences

Type lines 1–4 once. Then repeat lines 1–4 or take a series of 1-minute timings.

```
1  Keyboarding is popular today, and its demand will increase.    12
2  Please change the print wheel, but don't damage the ribbon.    12
3  We will go to the meeting, or we will send our new manager.    12
4  You should not remove the disk, nor should you stop typing.    12
   |  1  |  2  |  3  |  4  |  5  |  6  |  7  |  8  |  9  |  10  |  11  |  12
```

12-SECOND TIMINGS

Type each line three times, or take three 12-second timings on each line. For each timing, type with no more than 1 error.

```
5  They may not go up there if they have not taken the course.
6  If that order is a big one, we can make a very nice profit.
7  I know that we can do the job if we work at it for an hour.
```

PREVIEW PRACTICE

Type each line twice as a preview to the 5-minute timings below.

Accuracy
Speed

23 quite symbol squeeze quickly expanded processor corrections
24 keyboard document entire change right digit the and may for

5-MINUTE TIMINGS

Take two 5-minute timings on lines 25–39.

25   The add and delete functions of the word processor are   12
26 quite possibly the best features a system may have to offer   24
27 its users. If a letter, word, or entire line has to be in-   36
28 serted into a document, it is easy to squeeze it in at just   48
29 the right place. Nothing has to be erased or typed over in   60
30 order for the correction to be made. When the insertion is   72
31 made, the data that has already been typed on the screen is   84
32 "expanded" to allow a letter, digit, or symbol to be added.   96
33   With this feature, an operator can easily make changes 108
34 to the copy. Changes are made quickly; and a report, memo, 120
35 or letter can be typed in much less time than it would take 132
36 a person to do the same job on a typewriter keyboard. It's 144
37 a known fact that the add and delete features that are com- 156
38 mon to a word processor have made simple a task that in the 168
39 past was thought to be difficult. 175

| 1 | 2 | 3 | 4 | 5 | 6 | 7 | 8 | 9 | 10 | 11 | 12 | SI 1.37

LESSON 81

CLINIC

■ GOALS
To improve your typing skills using the Selective Practice routine.
To review the techniques of correcting errors.

■ FORMAT
Drills: Single spacing   60-space line
2-Minute Timings: Double spacing   5-space tab

KEYBOARDING SKILLS

Type lines 1–4 once. Then, as you type line 5, do what line 5 tells you to do as you type it. Repeat lines 1–4, or take a series of 1-minute timings.

Speed 1 It is the right time for us to go to the fair and have fun. 12
Accuracy 2 Even Jacques may gaze up to find six crows in the blue sky. 12
Numbers 3 Lee waited 10 days, 29 days, 38 days, 47 days, and 56 days. 12
Symbols 4 Joyce* and David* invested $6.80 for 2 boards @ $3.40 each. 12
Technique 5 Your margin will lock before you finish this line; use the release.

| 1 | 2 | 3 | 4 | 5 | 6 | 7 | 8 | 9 | 10 | 11 | 12

TECHNIQUE REVIEW

Tabulator Review

Type lines 8–19 once to determine which two groups (out of the three) gave you the most difficulty. Then repeat each difficult group once.

```
8    an        at        be        if        or        to        up
9    but       for       let       nor       one       six       two
10   five      four      last      nine      plus      sums      zero
11   fewer     first     joker     minor     ninth     sixth     tenth
```

Space Bar Review

```
12   The sun was high in the sky, but it was not hot in the car.
13   All of us must see it now if it is to be fun for all of us.
14   A big dog and a tiny cat ran down the road at a rapid pace.
15   If it is to be, then we will not have much to say about it.
```

Backspace Key Review

Backspace and underscore each underlined word immediately after typing it.

```
16   ah am an as at be by do go ha he ho if in is it me no so to
17   was one the you our for per off put how but not rib kit day
18   last week what plan that told good more seem sort like this
19   audit signs blame slept tithe shame visit gowns title burns
```

ALIGNING

A formatting technique.

To align inserts after guide words:

1. Locate exactly the printing point between the aligning scales.

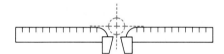

2. Insert the paper. Adjust it so that the guide word is just above the scale and the last character of the guide word is exactly in the center of the printing point. Use the paper release and/or the variable line spacer in the platen knob to make the adjustment.

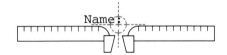

3. Leave 2 spaces between the end of the guide word and the insert. (Space three times—once for the last character of the guide word and twice for the spaces.)

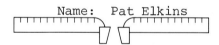

Practice: At four different places on a sheet of paper, type the printed guide words illustrated below. Use double spacing. Remove the paper, insert it, and then fill in the requested data—yours, not the data used in the illustration.

```
 Date:  February 3, 19--
 Name:  Pat Elkins
 City:  Topeka
State:  Kansas
```

TYPING ON RULED LINES

A formatting technique.

1. Preliminary step: On a blank sheet, type your name and underscore it. Note (*a*) exactly where the underscore touches or almost touches the aligning scale and (*b*) exactly how much room is between the letters and line.

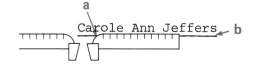

2. Then insert the paper with the ruled lines, and adjust it so that one of the ruled lines is in the position of an underscore. The ruled line should look like this:

(Continued on next page)

3. Type what is to be on the line.

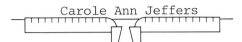

Carole Ann Jeffers

Practice: At various places and angles on a page, type underscore lines 30 spaces long. Remove the paper. Reinsert it. Type your name on each line.

LESSON 80

■ **GOALS**
To use commas correctly while typing compound sentences.
To review the use of and gain proficiency in operating the shift key, the shift lock, and the carriage/carrier return.
To type 35/5'/5e.

■ **FORMAT**
Drills: Single spacing   60-space line
5-Minute Timings: Double spacing   5-space tab

LAB 7

Commas in Compound Sentences

Type lines 1–4 once, providing the missing commas. Edit your copy as your teacher reads the answers. Then retype lines 1–4 from your edited copy.

1 We will study all the ads and then we will buy a computer.
2 You can view the screen but you can't find all the errors.
3 You may print your report now or you may wait until later.
4 Two errors are not acceptable nor is one error acceptable.

30-SECOND SPEED TIMINGS

Take two 30-second speed timings on lines 5 and 6. Then take two 30-second speed timings on lines 7 and 8. Or type each sentence twice.

5 One thing we must be sure to do at all times is not to type   12
6 so rapidly that we lose all control of the letters we type.   24
7 To be certain that the paper does not have too many errors,   12
8 we should not read too far ahead of the copy we are typing.   24

| 1 | 2 | 3 | 4 | 5 | 6 | 7 | 8 | 9 | 10 | 11 | 12

TECHNIQUE REVIEW

Type lines 9–22 once to determine which two groups (out of the three) gave you the most difficulty. Then repeat each difficult group once.

Shift-Key Review

9 a B c D e F g H i J k L m N o P q R s T u V w X y Z a B c D
10 Am An As At Be Do Go Ha Ho If In Is It Ma Me No Of Oh On Or
11 Ann Ben Cal Dee Fay Gus Hal Jan Ken Lyn Mel Nan Pat Ron Sal
12 Alma Clio Enid Erie Hope Hugo Kent Reno Vail Waco Yale Yuma
13 Chile China Egypt Ghana Haiti India Italy Japan Kenya Nepal

Shift-Lock Review

14 On MONDAY JANET was in YUMA; last TUESDAY she was in FARGO.
15 We drove to HARBOR-DELANEY, INC., to visit PHIL and ELAINE.
16 Is KELLY going to read EXODUS or TOPAZ or QB VII on FRIDAY?
17 Drive the HARBOR, the PASADENA, and the SAN DIEGO freeways.
18 We saw ANOKA on the 4th, AUSTIN yesterday, and TOWER today.

Return Review
(Return after each word.)

19 acorn camel churn cramp weigh hairy ivory laugh learn prowl
20 adorn blink cameo clamp repel lapel mourn panel usual yearn
21 blank charm drain flank grasp reach sharp train marsh pearl
22 champ dream frank grain ranch snarl trail harsh march plant

---